LEGAL INFORMATION ONLINE ANYTIME

24 hours a day

www.nolo.com

AT THE NOLO.COM SELF-HELP LAW CENTER, YOU'LL FIND

- **Nolo's comprehensive Legal Encyclopedia filled with plain-English information on a variety of legal topics**
- **Nolo's Law Dictionary—legal terms <u>without</u> the legalese**
- **Auntie Nolo—if you've got questions, Auntie's got answers**
- **The Law Store—over 250 self-help legal products including Downloadable Software, Books, Form Kits and eGuides**
- **Legal and product updates**
- **Frequently Asked Questions**
- **NoloBriefs, our free monthly email newsletter**
- **Legal Research Center, for access to state and federal statutes**
- **Our ever-popular lawyer jokes**

Quality LAW BOOKS & SOFTWARE FOR EVERYONE

Nolo's user-friendly products are consistently first-rate. Here's why:

- A dozen in-house legal editors, working with highly skilled authors, ensure that our products are accurate, up-to-date and easy to use
- We continually update every book and software program to keep up with changes in the law
- Our commitment to a more democratic legal system informs all of our work
- We appreciate & listen to your feedback. Please fill out and return the card at the back of this book.

An Important Message to Our Readers

1st edition

The Small Business Start-up Kit

By Peri Pakroo

NOLO

Keep Up to Date

To keep its books up-to-date, Nolo issues new printings and new editions periodically. New printings reflect minor legal changes and technical corrections. New editions contain major legal changes, major text additions or major reorganizations. To find out if a later printing or edition of any Nolo book is available, call Nolo at 510-549-1976 or check our website at www.nolo.com.

To stay current, follow the "Update" service at our website at www.nolo.com. In another effort to help you use Nolo's latest materials, we offer a 35% discount off the purchase of the new edition of your Nolo book when you turn in the cover of an earlier edition. (See the "Special Upgrade Offer" in the back of the book.) This book was last revised in November 2000.

First Edition	NOVEMBER 2000
Editor	BETHANY LAURENCE
Cover Design	TONI IHARA
Illustrations	ALEXIS MOLLOMO
Book Design	TERRI HEARSH
Proofreading	ROBERT WELLS
Indexer	THÉRÈSE SHERE
Printing	CONSOLIDATED PRINTERS, INC.

The small business start-up kit
p. cm
ISBN 0-87337-592

00-038001
CIP

For information on bulk purchases or corporate premium sales, please contact the Special Sales Department. For academic sales or textbook adoptions, ask for Academic Sales. Call 800-955-4775 or write to Nolo at 950 Parker Street, Berkeley, CA 94710.

Acknowledgments

Many thanks to Beth Laurence, for her sharp editing as well as her encouragement and understanding as I finished this book in the middle of a cross-country move. Thanks also to Jake Warner for his helpful input and suggestions, and his unwaverable sparkling energy. Thanks are also due to Janet Portman for her review of the material on commercial leases; Patti Gima and Steve Elias for lending their expertise in domain names and trademark law; and James Judd for assistance with the information on Internet sales taxes. As always, I was helped immensely by the support of all the Nolo editors, and I will miss all of you.

Alexis Mollomo provided the lovely illustrations within these pages, for which I'm happy and grateful—thanks, Ali. Thanks to Terri Hearsh for making the information in this book clear and attractive, as well as to Ely Newman and Andre Zivkovich for creating the forms CD-ROM. And a big thank you goes to the Nolo marketing folks for their smart and creative style in getting the word out about this book.

Without my partner in crime this last year might have squashed me. Showers of thanks and love to Turtle.

Dedication

I dedicate this book to my grandmother Eunice Michaelson Jones—a spitfire if ever there was one.

About the Author

Peri Pakroo is a writer, editor and owner of p-brain media™ (www.pbrainmedia.com), a content consulting and development firm. She began editing and writing for Nolo in 1996, specializing in small business and intellectual property issues, and edited such Nolo titles as *Starting & Running a Successful Newsletter or Magazine; Getting Permission: How to License & Clear Copyrighted Materials Online & Off; Music Law;* and *How to Write a Business Plan*. Besides working with legal and business issues, Peri has also edited two arts and entertainment weeklies, *The Stranger* and *The Weekly Alibi,* as well as a monthly food and lifestyle magazine, *la cocinita*. She lives with Juno, Kitty B and Turtle in New Mexico.

Table of Contents

1 Working for Yourself Is Easier Than You Think

A. Get Started—And Get On With Your Business 1/3

B. Making the Decision to Go Official 1/4

C. Get Ready for the Ride 1/5

2 Choosing a Legal Structure

A. Sole Proprietorships 2/2

B. Partnerships 2/5

C. Limited Liability Companies (LLCs) 2/11

D. Corporations 2/14

E. So, Which One to Choose? 2/19

3 Picking Winning Business Names That Won't Land You in Court

A. An Overview of Trademark Law 3/5

B. Trademark Issues Online 3/11

C. Name Searches 3/16

D. Choosing and Registering a Domain Name 3/21

E. Trademark Registration 3/23

F. Winning Names for Your Business, Products and Services 3/24

4 Choosing a Legal and Lucrative Business Location

A. Picking the Right Spot 4/2

B. Complying With Zoning Laws 4/6

C. Commercial Leases 4/9

D. When Your Home Is Your Office 4/10

5 Drafting an Effective Business Plan

A. Different Purposes Require Different Plans 5/2

B. Describing the Business, and Yourself 5/3

C. Making Financial Projections 5/8

D. Break-Even Analysis 5/10

E. Profit/Loss Forecast 5/19

F. Start-Up Cost Estimate 5/22

G. Cash Flow Projection 5/23

H. Putting It All Together 5/26

6 Federal, State and Local Start-Up Requirements

A. Step 1: File Organizational Documents With Your State
(Corporations, LLCs and Limited Partnerships Only) 6/4

B. Step 2: Obtain a Federal Employer Identification Number 6/5

C. Step 3: Register Your Fictitious Business Name With Your
County or State 6/8

D. Step 4: Obtain a Local Tax Registration Certificate
(a.k.a. "Business License") 6/11

E. Step 5: Obtain a State Seller's Permit 6/13

F. Step 6: Obtain Specialized Licenses or Permits 6/13

7 Insuring Your Business

A. Property Insurance 7/2

B. Liability Insurance... 7/3

C. The Wide World of Specialized Insurance Policies................................ 7/4

D. Investigating and Purchasing a Policy 7/5

8 Getting to Know Your Taxes

A. Tax Basics 8/2

B. Income Taxes for Sole Proprietors 8/9

C. Income Taxes for Partnerships 8/11

D. Income Taxes for LLCs 8/13

E. Estimating and Paying Your Taxes Quarterly 8/15

F. City and County Taxes 8/18

G. Sales Taxes 8/20

9 Entering Into Contracts and Agreements

A. Contract Basics 9/2

B. Using Standard Contracts... 9/7

C. How to Draft a Contract 9/8

D. Reading and Revising a Contract 9/14

E. Special Issues for Electronic Contracts 9/14

10 Bookkeeping, Accounting and Financial Management

A. Accounting Basics 10/4

B. Cash vs. Accrual Accounting 10/5

C. Step One: Keeping Your Receipts 10/7

D. Step Two: Setting Up and Posting to Ledgers 10/10

E. Step Three: Creating Basic Financial Reports 10/15

11 Growing Your Business and Hiring Workers

A. Employees vs. Independent Contractors 11/2

B. Special Hurdles for Employers 11/5

12 Getting Professional Help

A. Working With Lawyers 12/2

B. Working With Accountants and Other Professionals 12/5

C. Internet Legal Research 12/7

Appendixes

A State Contact Information

Small Business Start-Up Issues A/3

State Tax Agencies A/8

State Sales Tax/Seller's Permit Agencies A/13

LLC Offices A/18

State Unemployment Compensation Agencies A/24

Patent and Trademark Depository Libraries by State A/29

B How to Use the Forms CD-ROM

A. Installing the Form Files Onto Your Computer B/2

B. Using the Word Processing Files B/3

C. Using IRS Form Files B/4

D. Using the Charts B/6

E. List of Files Included on the Forms CD-ROM B/6

C Tear-Out Forms

Partnership Agreement

Application for Employer Identification Number (Form SS-4)

Determination of Employee Work Status for Purposes of Federal Employment
    Taxes and Income Tax Withholding (Form SS-8)

Election to Have a Tax Year Other Than a Required Tax Year (Form 8716)

Entity Classification Election (Form 8832)

Working for Yourself Is Easier Than You Think

A. Get Started—And Get On With Your Business 1/3

B. Making the Decision to Go Official 1/4

C. Get Ready for the Ride 1/5

You don't have an MBA. Hell, you've never taken a business class. You spent your college years studying literature and art history, and periodically dropping out to travel the world. And now you find yourself thinking about going into business for yourself—maybe restoring antiques, or illustrating books, or running a café, or selling software. "Me, a businessperson?" you skeptically wonder. You keep trudging to work each morning, but as the hours tick by you find yourself fantasizing more and more about kissing your 9-to-5 job goodbye. You jot down some notes, work out some kinks in your plan and continue to wonder whether it just might fly....

Unfortunately, most people who have toyed with business ideas this way never get to find out whether they would have worked or not. For a variety of practical, financial and psychological reasons, most folks just don't take the leap from idea to reality. This is really a shame, since there's nothing that complex or difficult about turning a business idea into an actual working business. Most prospective entrepreneurs would be surprised —and encouraged—to know that the line between "I'm thinking about starting my own business" and "I own and run my own business!" can be crossed in large part by completing a short list of bureau-cratic tasks. This book will explain what those tasks are and how to complete them.

Stephen Parr, owner and director of Oddball Film and Video, a stock film and video footage company in San Francisco, California:

I started making video art in the 1970s. After a while I started collecting all these weird bits of film because it was cheaper than shooting it myself. I gathered all kinds of old, found footage like military training films, educational films, home movies and all kinds of other images and put them together into montages, which I screened in nightclubs as background visuals. I was showing them all over—nightclubs in New York, Chicago, San Francisco—and I made some money by selling the tapes to the clubs.

Then I started getting calls from these companies in Silicon Valley who produce industrial videos, like training films and promotional programs for corporate trade shows. Video game companies were calling, too. Companies like Sega, Sun Microsystems and Silicon Graphics wanted to pay me for my footage. The guy I lived with at the time thought I should go into business selling the stock footage I had collected, but at the time, I didn't know if I could make a living doing it. I didn't know anything about the stock footage business. There were a few companies doing it, but they were in New York or L.A., and they seemed really huge.

But since I liked working with images and since the business had already started to take off on its own, I finally decided to formalize it. I started by picking a company name. I wanted something interesting that conveyed what I did. We came up with Oddball. It's a word that people don't really use anymore, more of a '40s or '50s expression—an oddball is someone kind of weird, unbalanced, or unusual, you know? Well, from there, I just kept compiling more footage, and over the years I started logging it, and buying more.

At the most basic level, my business involves finding, organizing and preserving historical footage. And then distributing it. Our clients include ad agencies; news organizations; docu-mentary and feature film makers; industrial, corporate and music video producers; educa-tional filmmakers; and anyone who needs off-beat and unusual images. In one way we're like a library. We archive and license historical visual information.

These days, I spend most of my time trying to organize and publicize my business. We just launched our website, and that takes time to maintain. And I spend a lot more time trying to obtain films than actually looking at them. Still, what I do at Oddball is an extension of the work I've been doing since the 1970s. I guess it became a business the day I decided I wasn't going to do anything else.

A. Get Started—And Get On With Your Business

You undoubtedly already know that getting a business off the ground isn't easy. You've got a million different details to work out—how you'll produce your product or service, how much you'll charge, what marketing strategies to use, how to manage your cash flow—and you need to nail all of this down before you stand to make a dime. You'll likely find that very few, if any, other businesspeople have done exactly what you're setting out to do, so you'll have to answer a lot of questions on your own (or with your partners). It can be scary and lonely—and while exhilarating, it's almost always stressful.

But as compared to working out the details of how your business will run and become successful, clearing the bureaucratic hurdles isn't a big deal at all. Dealing with governmental start-up requirements has been done millions of times before by all types of different businesses. While the bureaucracy governing small business often seems like a convoluted maze, you can take comfort in the fact that the procedures are standard, they apply more or less the same to everybody, and that the answers *are* out there. Unlike your unique business strategy that you'll need your best creative wits to devise, conquering the bureaucracy is essentially a no-brainer. Yes, it requires some patience and fortitude, but by no means do you need any special skill, education or experience. As long as you do a bit of homework and arm yourself with an overview of the process (as you're doing by reading this book), you'll be able to meet all the small business registration requirements without breaking a sweat.

You can usually start a sole proprietorship (the legal term for a one-owner business) or a partnership (a business with more than owner) by registering with just one government office. And for business owners who want protection from personal liability for business debts—often referred to by the legal jargon "limited liability"—the simplest corporations or limited liability companies (LLCs)

have only a couple more registration tasks to complete. In other words, once you've got your business idea developed to a certain degree, all you need to do is visit a few government offices, fill out some forms and pay some fees—and suddenly your idea will have become an actual, legitimate business.

Keep in mind that there's certainly a lot more to starting a successful small business than dealing with bureaucratic requirements. For starters, you'll need to have a sound business idea, and you'll need to be able to develop good management skills to guide it to success. This book, however, largely leaves these issues for other resources to cover. Unlike many other small business guides, we're not going to spend your precious time quizzing you on whether you have the right personality to be your own boss, or evaluating your business idea, or helping you to identify the personal goals that you hope to achieve by starting a business. If you need more help deciding whether or not you want to start a business or what kind of business you should start, you should probably buy a different book. If, on the other hand, you want a book that cuts to the chase and explains systematically what you need to do to launch a business officially and legally, this book is for you.

 Nolo offers free resources online for small business start-ups. If you do need more guidance on other aspects of starting a small business, consult the Small Business section of Nolo.com's Legal Encyclopedia. You'll find several articles on business start-up issues, such as starting the right kind of business and how to raise start-up money. Go to www.nolo.com/category/sb_home.html.

But this book is also for those of you who are somewhere in between: fairly certain you want to give your idea a try but not quite ready to march down to city hall to register your business. In addition to explaining the start-up requirements that apply to most small businesses, this book also outlines the preliminary work you should do before heading out to file all your official forms. In Chapters 2 through 5, we discuss fundamental tasks such as choosing the right legal structure for your business (sole proprietorship, partnership, LLC or corporation), coming up with a catchy and legally sound business name, and choosing a location that's good for business. We also explain how to draft a business plan that will help you define your business, plan for profitability and attract lenders and investors. If you've already taken care of some or all these tasks, you can either skip these chapters or use them as a guide to evaluate what you've already done.

Finally, to help you all the way through your start-up days, in later chapters we introduce you to a number of basic issues that every ongoing business needs to deal with. These include insurance, taxes, contracts and agreements, and bookkeeping and accounting. Though they're not exactly start-up requirements, they're important to understand in the dawning days of your business so that you'll be able to handle them later when business is fast and furious.

Valerie Hoecke, owner of Fire Engine Red, a Web development firm in San Francisco, California:

The legal steps of starting my business weren't really that bad. The hardest thing seemed to be figuring out in which order to do all the steps. My advice to people just starting would be to keep your wits about you; laugh at the fact that maybe you have been standing in the wrong line or made a trip to the wrong office on any particular day. Business owners need to have a sense of humor about their mistakes and be prepared to make errors and backtrack once in a while. Looking back, the start-up process seemed a bit trying at the time, but now I wish that all my business problems were so simple!

Finally, keep in mind that businesses with employees have significant additional responsibilities. In Chapter 11, we offer a general overview of the laws and regulations that govern businesses with employees. If you're thinking about hiring employees, that chapter will help you figure out if you're ready to tackle the many requirements that come with your first hire. Chapter 11 also explains the difference between employees and independent contractors—an important distinction, because using independent contractors does not subject you to most of the laws that apply when you hire employees. If you do decide that you need to hire any employees, you'll probably need to do further reading. An excellent and exhaustive resource is Nolo's *The Employer's Legal Handbook,* by attorney Fred S. Steingold.

B. Making the Decision to Go Official

Some of you may be facing a different question. Instead of wondering whether or not to start a business, you may be trying to decide whether or not to formalize your business—to go the official route and register your business with the appropriate agencies in your state. For instance, maybe you've been doing freelance graphics work on the side for a number of years, but now you're thinking of quitting your 9-to-5 job to take on graphics work full-time. If you're not sure whether you want to register your business and open it up to the world of government regulations, the information about registration requirements in this book will put you in a better position to make a decision. Chapter 6 walks you through the many governmental requirements that apply to all new businesses, and explains how to go about finding and satisfying any additional requirements that may apply to your specific business.

Stephen Parr, owner and director of Oddball Film and Video, a stock footage company in San Francisco, California:

What a business really is, is you deciding you have a business. It's really nothing more than that.

Generally speaking, anyone with a good-sized or otherwise visible business should bite the bullet and complete all of the necessary registration tasks to become official. Operating under the table can all too easily be exposed, and the government can come after you for fines and penalties, and might even padlock your business, simply for operating without the necessary paperwork. And if you're making a profit, ignoring the IRS is definitely a bad idea. Besides fines and back taxes, you could even face criminal charges and jail time.

On the other hand, tiny, home-based, hobby-type businesses can often operate for quite some time without meeting registration requirements. If you're braiding hair or holding an occasional junk sale out of your garage, for instance, you can probably get by without formal business registration—at least for a while. Keep in mind, however, that just because it may be possible doesn't mean it's the best option. Often, formally registering your business can benefit you, the owner, as well, since you can then write off business expenses and reduce your personal taxes. In Chapter 8, Section A3, we discuss hobby businesses in more depth, including how tax laws deal with businesses that continually lose money.

C. Get Ready for the Ride

One of the main ideas we want you to take away from this book is that there's nothing mysterious or even terribly complex about the process of starting your own business. Whether you've drafted a highly specific business plan with the help of accountants and consultants or you've scratched it out on a cocktail napkin, the process of turning that idea into a legitimate business is the same. That process is covered in this book.

How you build and run your business, on the other hand, is where the real challenge comes in. You'll need confidence to get your business rolling—and you'll need guts, too. Lots of times you may well find that the questions burning in your mind have no defined answer, because no one has asked that question or tried that idea before. You probably wanted to start a business in the first place so that you could make your own decisions—but you'll likely find that this can often be quite a heavy burden. You may not believe it now, but some days you'll probably find yourself wishing you had a boss.

You'll need to learn to trust yourself, both when you feel optimistic and when you suspect that one of your ideas is less than brilliant. You'll also have to develop a sense for when you need help, and to be judicious in taking the advice of people around you. Part of the art of controlling your own destiny is accepting the wisdom of others, while maintaining your own focus and direction. It's not always an easy balance to maintain, but you'll undoubtedly get better at it as you gain experience in running your own show. The bottom line: Think hard, keep your mind open—and fight like hell to make your ideas a reality.

Take the leap.

Michele Harrell, owner of Acceptances.com, a secure transaction processing service for the Internet, in Oakland California:

I think it's important to remember that by starting a business you are not only creating a way to make money, you are also designing a way in which you will spend a huge portion of your time. Many people starting businesses today are redefining the workplace, creating environments that enhance the lives of themselves and their employees. Unfortunately, others are creating their own personal versions of hell. In starting your own company, you have the opportunity to create a way of working that can make you immensely happy. I believe the real work lies in creating a great life for yourself. And it takes just as much work to build a business that makes you unhappy as it does to start one that enriches your life on a daily basis.

More Small Business Products From Nolo

Small Business Pro 4.0

This CD-ROM contains more than 125 legal forms and the complete text of six of Nolo's best-selling business titles, including *Legal Guide for Starting & Running a Small Business, Tax Savvy for Small Business, The Employer's Legal Handbook, Marketing Without Advertising,* and *How to Write a Business Plan.*

How to Create a Buy-Sell Agreement & Control the Destiny of Your Small Business

by attorneys Anthony Mancuso & Bethany K. Laurence

This book explains how to protect your business interests by drawing up a "pre-marital" agreement between you and your business owners that sets out a plan for what happens if you or a co-owner leaves the company. A must for any new business with more than one owner.

Legal Guide for Starting & Running a Small Business

by attorney Fred S. Steingold

This Nolo title covers all the legal info you need to get your business off the ground and running, including how to raise start-up money, attract the best help, buy or sell a business or franchise, negotiate a favorable lease, insure your business and resolve legal disputes.

How to Write a Business Plan

by Mike McKeever

This guide explains how to write a business plan, whether for your own purposes or to attract money from lenders or investors, including how to evaluate the profitability of your business idea, estimate operating expenses, determine assets, liabilities and net worth and find potential sources of financing.

The Trademark Registration Kit (Quick & Legal)

by attorneys Patricia Gima & Stephen Elias

This guidebook walks you step-by-step through the nuts and bolts of registering a trademark with the U.S. Patent and Trademark Office.

Tax Savvy for Small Business

by attorney Frederick W. Daily

This title offers plain-English tax laws and rules on business deductions, plus tax info on LLCs, partnerships, corporations and more.

Marketing Without Advertising: Inspire Customers to Rave About Your Business to Create Lasting Success

by Michael Phillips & Salli Rasberry

This guide explains the secret of attracting customers without pricey ads, including how to build trust with potential customers, encourage customer recommendations, improve customer service, list products and services widely and inexpensively and use the Internet to market services and products.

Nolo's Quick LLC: All You Need to Know About Limited Liability Companies (Quick & Legal)

by attorney Anthony Mancuso

This book explains the basics of limited liability companies, and helps you figure out whether structuring your business as an LLC is the right way to go.

LLC Maker™

by attorney Anthony Mancuso

Windows software that assembles LLC articles of organization according to each state's legal requirements, plus an operating agreement and other LLC formation paperwork.

More Small Business Products From Nolo

Form Your Own Limited Liability Company
by attorney Anthony Mancuso
    This book offers instructions and forms to
    create an LLC in your state, as well as a full
    explanation of LLCs and how they work.

The Employer's Legal Handbook
by attorney Fred S. Steingold
    Here's a comprehensive resource that
    compiles all the basics of employment law in
    one place. It covers safe hiring and firing
    practices, wages, hours, employee benefits,
    taxes and liability, discrimination and sexual
    harassment.

Hiring Independent Contractors:
The Employer's Legal Guide
by attorney Stephen Fishman
    This book explains all the tricky IRS rules
    and provides forms and instructions for
    hiring ICs.

Domain Names: How to Choose & Protect a
Great Name for Your Website (Quick & Legal)
by attorneys Stephen Elias & Patricia Gima
    This plain-English how-to book teaches you
    how to select, register and protect a great
    domain name.

Nondisclosure Agreements: Protect Your
Great Ideas When You Share Them With Others
by attorney Stephen Fishman
    This eFormKit, available at Nolo.com,
    explains how to protect your trade secrets
    with a nondisclosure agreement (or "confi-
    dentiality agreement") before sharing them
    with potential partners, and includes eight
    different nondisclosure agreements.

Throughout the text, we have included the
following icons to help organize the material and
underscore particular points:

 Tip. A commonsense tip to help you understand or comply with legal requirements.

 Warning. A caution to slow down and
consider potential problems.

 See an Expert. A suggestion to seek the
advice of an attorney or tax expert.

 Fast Track. An indication that you may be
able to skip some material that may not be
relevant to your situation.

 Other Resources. A suggestion to consult
another legal or tax resource.

Checklist. A quick summary of the start-up
steps included in each chapter.

Chapter 1 Checklist

☐ Decide whether to formalize your business.

☐ Research business start-up steps.

☐ Brace yourself for start-up mayhem.

Choosing a Legal Structure

A. Sole Proprietorships 2/2

   1. Pass-Through Taxation 2/4

   2. Personal Liability for Business Debts 2/4

   3. Creating a Sole Proprietorship 2/5

B. Partnerships 2/5

   1. General vs. Limited Partnerships 2/5

   2. Pass-Through Taxation 2/6

   3. Personal Liability for Business Debts 2/6

   4. Partnership Agreements 2/7

C. Limited Liability Companies (LLCs) 2/11

   1. Limited Personal Liability 2/11

   2. LLC Taxation 2/12

   3. LLCs vs. S Corporations.. 2/13

   4. Forming an LLC.. 2/14

D. Corporations 2/14

   1. Limited Personal Liability 2/15

   2. Corporate Taxation 2/16

   3. Forming and Running a Corporation 2/18

E. So, Which One to Choose? 2/19

Chances are you already have a rough idea of the type of legal structure your business will take, whether you know it or not. That's because in large part, the ownership structure that's right for your business—a sole proprietorship, partnership, LLC or corporation—depends on how many people will own the business and what type of services or products it will provide, things you've undoubtedly given lots of thought. For instance, if you know that you will be the only owner, then a partnership is obviously not your thing. (A partnership by definition has more than one owner.) And if your business will engage in risky activities (for example, trading stocks or repairing roofs), in addition to buying insurance you'll almost surely want to form an entity that provides personal liability protection (a corporation or a limited liability company), which can shield your personal assets from business debts and claims. Lastly, if you already plan on enticing new employees with stock options in the hopes of "going public" some day, then forming a corporation will be the route to take.

If you've considered these questions, then you'll be ahead of the game in choosing a legal structure that's right for your business. Still, you'll need to consider the benefits and drawbacks of each type of business structure before you make your final decision.

In all states, the basic types of business structures are:

- sole proprietorships
- partnerships
- limited liability companies (LLCs), and
- corporations.

To help you pick the best structure for your business, in this chapter we explain the basic attributes of each type. And yes, we will help you answer the most common question new entrepreneurs ask about choosing a business form: Should I choose a business structure that offers protection from personal liability (a corporation or an LLC)? As a hint as to what our advice will be, consider that if you focus your energy and money into getting your business off the ground as a sole proprietorship or a partnership, you can always incorporate or form an LLC later.

Limited Liability

One basic distinction that you'll probably hear mentioned lots of times is the difference between businesses that provide their owners with "limited liability" and those that don't. Corporations and LLCs both provide their owners with limited personal liability. Sole proprietorships and general partnerships do not.

So what does limited liability mean? Basically, that the creditors of the business cannot normally go after the owners' personal assets to pay for business debts and claims arising from lawsuits. (We discuss liability for business debts in detail in the sections that follow.)

As you read about specific business types in this chapter, you'll see how a decision to form a limited liability entity (a corporation or an LLC, mainly) would dramatically affect how you run your business. On the other hand, while sole proprietorships and partnerships are somewhat simpler to run than corporations and LLCs, they may leave an owner personally vulnerable to business lawsuits and debts.

A. Sole Proprietorships

Sole proprietorships are one-owner businesses. Any business with two or more owners cannot, by definition, be a sole proprietorship. If you know that there will be two or more owners of your business, you can skip ahead to Section B, below.

Technically, a sole proprietorship is simply a business that is owned by one person and that hasn't filed papers to become a corporation or an LLC. Sole proprietorships are easy to set up and to maintain—so easy that many people own sole proprietorships and don't even know it! For instance, if you are a freelance photographer or writer, a craftsperson who takes jobs on a contract basis, a salesperson who receives only commissions or an independent contractor who isn't on an employer's regular payroll, you are automatically a sole proprietor. This is true whether or not you've registered your business with your city or obtained any licenses or permits. And it makes no difference whether you also have a regular day job. As long as you do for-profit work on your own (or sometimes with your spouse—see "Running a Business With Your Spouse,") and have not filed papers to become a corporation or a limited liability company, you are a sole proprietor.

Kimberly Torgerson, owner of Your Word's Worth, a freelance editing and writing service in Northern California:

I like the variety and flexibility of freelancing. Until a short while ago, I tended to take on projects that would enable me to work intensely, then take lots of time off to write, travel or just putter. Recently, though, I bought property—which means I'm not taking much time off these days. I just say YES to new projects. The challenge is setting my course as people's deadlines shift. So far, so good.

⚠ Ignoring local registration requirements may get you in trouble. If you've started a business without quite realizing it—for example, you do a little freelance computer programming, which classifies you as a sole proprietor by default—don't let the fact that you're technically already a sole proprietor fool you into thinking that you've satisfied the governmental requirements for starting a business. Most cities and many counties require businesses—even tiny home-based sole proprietorships—to register with them and pay at least a minimum tax. And if you do business under a name different from your own, such as Custom Coding, you usually must register that name—known as a fictitious business name—with your county. In practice, lots of businesses are small enough to get away with ignoring these requirements. But if you are caught, you may be subject to back taxes and other penalties. I explain how to make the necessary filings with the appropriate government offices in Chapter 6.

Running a Business With Your Spouse

If your spouse will participate in your business, consider creating what's sometimes called a "husband-wife sole proprietorship." You can create a sole proprietorship and have your spouse do "volunteer" work (without pay) for your business. Technically, there will only be one owner—you. But this set-up allows your spouse to provide services for the business without being classified as an employee, freeing the business from having to pay payroll tax. That not only saves you money but, if you have no other employees, also allows you to avoid the time-consuming recordkeeping involved in being an employer. Similarly, by choosing not to classify your spouse as a partner or an independent contractor, the spouse won't have to pay self-employment taxes and your business won't have to file a partnership tax return. Of course, your spouse will not be a legal owner of the business—although in many states, marital property laws will give your spouse a share in your business anyway.

However, if you and your spouse each want to be active partners in a co-owned business, each with an official say in management, you should create a partnership (or an LLC or corporation), even though this will mean filing more complicated tax returns and other business paperwork. If your spouse tries to squeak by as a volunteer in a husband-wife sole proprietorship when you're really working together as a partnership, you run the risk of the IRS auditing you and deciding that you're a partnership—and socking your spouse with back self-employment taxes.

1. Pass-Through Taxation

In the eyes of the law, a sole proprietorship is not legally separate from the person who owns it. This is one of the fundamental differences between a sole proprietorship and a corporation or LLC. The fact that a sole proprietorship and its owner are one and the same has two major effects: one related to taxation (explained in this section), and the other to personal liability (explained in the next).

One key feature of being a sole proprietor is that at income tax time, you simply report all business income or losses on your individual income tax return. The business itself is not taxed. The IRS calls this "pass-through" taxation, because business profits pass through the business to be taxed on the business owner's tax return. The only difference between reporting income from a business and reporting wages from a job is that along with Form 1040, you'll need to include Schedule C, on which you'll provide your business's profit and loss information. One helpful aspect of this arrangement is that if your business loses money—and, of course, many start-ups do in the first year or two—the business losses can be used to offset any taxable income you have earned from other sources.

> **EXAMPLE:** Rob has a day job at a coffee shop at a modest salary. His hobby is collecting obscure records at thrift stores and rummage sales. Contemplating the sad fact that he has no extra money to spend at the flea market on Saturday morning, he decides to start selling some of the vinyl gems he's found. Still working his day job, he starts a small business that he calls Rob's Revolving Records.
>
> During his first full year in business, he sees that a key to consistently selling his records is developing connections and trust among record collectors. Unfortunately, while he is concentrating on getting to know potential buyers and others in the business, sales are slow. At year-end he closes out his books and sees that

his website, marketing items like business cards, and other incidental supplies have cost him nearly $9,000, while he made only $3,000 in sales. But there is some good news: Rob's loss of $6,000 can be counted against his income from his day job, which will reduce his taxes and translate into a nice refund check, which he'll put right back into his record business.

! Keep in mind that your business can't lose money forever, at least not if you want to avoid trouble with the IRS. See our discussion of tax rules for money-losing businesses in Chapter 8, Section A3, "Hobby Businesses: Possible Source of Tax Deductions."

Be ready for the day you'll owe taxes. Once your business is underway and turning a profit, you'll undoubtedly be more concerned with taxes than in the early days of your business, when you're probably losing money. We provide an overview of the taxes faced by small businesses in Chapter 8. Taxes can get fairly complicated however, and you may need more in-depth guidance. For detailed information on taxes for the various types of small businesses, be sure to read *Tax Savvy for Small Business*, by attorney Frederick W. Daily (Nolo). This book gives exhaustive information on deductions, recordkeeping and audits, which will help you minimize your tax bill and stay out of trouble with the IRS.

2. Personal Liability for Business Debts

Another crucial thing to know about operating your business as a sole proprietor is that you, as the owner of the business, can be held personally liable for business-related obligations. This means that if your business doesn't pay a supplier, defaults on a debt, loses a lawsuit or otherwise finds itself in financial hot water, you, personally, can be forced to pay up. No question, this can be a sobering possibility, especially if you own (or soon hope to own) a cool house, car or other treasures. Personal liability for business obligations stems from the fundamental legal attribute of being a sole proprietor: you and your business are one and inseparable.

As explained in more detail in Sections C and D of this chapter, the law provides owners of corporations and LLCs with what the law calls "limited personal liability" for business obligations. This means that, unlike sole proprietors and general partners, owners of corporations and LLCs can normally keep their house, investments and other personal property, even if their business fails. In short, if you are engaged in a risky business, you may want to consider forming a corporation or an LLC (although a thorough insurance policy can often cover your butt when it comes to lawsuits and claims against the business).

Commercial insurance doesn't cover business debts. While commercial insurance can protect a business and its owners from some types of liability (for instance, slip-and-fall lawsuits), insurance never covers business debts. The only way to limit your personal liability for business debts is to use a limited liability business structure such as an LLC or a corporation (or a limited partnership or limited liability partnership).

3. Creating a Sole Proprietorship

Setting up a sole proprietorship is incredibly easy. Unlike an LLC or a corporation, you generally don't have to file any special forms or pay any special fees to start working as a sole proprietor. All that's required is that you declare your business to be a sole proprietorship when completing the general registration requirements that apply to all new businesses, such as getting a business license from your county or city, or a seller's permit from your state.

For example, when filing for a business tax registration certificate with your city, you'll often be asked to declare what kind of business you're starting. In some cities this involves checking a "sole proprietorship" box on a form, while other cities have separate tax registration forms for sole proprietorships. Similarly, other forms you'll file, such as those to register a fictitious business name and to obtain a seller's permit, will also ask for this information. (These and other start-up requirements are discussed in detail in Chapter 6.)

B. Partnerships

Bring two or more entrepreneurs together into a business venture, stir gently and—poof!—you've got a partnership. By definition, a partnership is a business that has more than one owner and that has not filed papers with the state to become a corporation or an LLC (or a limited partnership or limited liability partnership).

Partnerships still have to fulfill local registration requirements. If you're going into business with others, don't let the fact that you're automatically a partnership fool you into thinking that you've satisfied the governmental requirements for starting a business. Most cities and many counties require all businesses to register with them and pay at least a minimum tax. And if you do business under a name other than the partners' names, you usually must register that name—known as a fictitious business name—with your county. We explain how to make the necessary filings with the appropriate government offices in Chapter 6.

1. General vs. Limited Partnerships

Usually, when you hear the term "partnership," it means a general partnership. As we discuss in more detail below, general partners are personally liable for all business debts, including court judgments. In addition, each individual partner can be sued for the full amount of any business debt (though that partner can in turn sue the other partners for their share of the debt).

Another very important aspect of general partnerships is that any individual partner can bind the whole business to a contract or business deal—in other words, each partner has "agency authority" for the partnership. And remember, each of the partners is fully personally liable for a business deal gone sour, no matter which partner signed the contract. This combination of personal liability and the agency authority of each partner is important to understand before getting into a general partnership (we'll discuss more details about general partnerships below).

There are also a couple of special kinds of partnerships, called limited partnerships and limited liability partnerships. They operate under very different rules and are relatively uncommon, so we'll touch on them only briefly.

A limited partnership requires at least one general partner and at least one limited partner. The general partner has the same role as in a general partnership: he controls the company's day-to-day operations and is personally liable for business debts. The limited partner contributes financially to the business (for example, invests $100,000 in a real estate partnership) but has minimal control over business decisions or operations, and normally cannot bind the partnership to business deals. In return for giving up management power, a limited partner gets the benefit of protection from personal liability. This means that a limited partner can't be forced to pay off business debts or claims with her personal assets, but she can lose her investment in the business. But beware: A limited partner who tires of being passive and starts tinkering under the hood of the business should understand that her liability can quickly become unlimited that way. If a creditor can prove that the limited partner took acts that led the creditor to believe that she was a general partner, she can be held fully and personally liable for the creditor's claims.

Another kind of partnership, called a limited liability partnership (LLP) or sometimes a registered limited liability partnership (RLLP), provides all of its owners with limited personal liability. In some states, these partnerships are only available to professionals, such as lawyers and accountants, and are particularly well suited to them. Most professionals aren't keen on general partnerships because they don't want to be personally liable for another partner's problems—particularly those involving malpractice claims. And forming a corporation to protect personal assets may be too much trouble, and some states won't allow these professionals to form an LLC. The solution is often a limited liability partnership. This business structure protects each partner from debts against the partnership arising from professional malpractice lawsuits against another partner. (A partner who loses a malpractice suit for his own mistakes, however, doesn't escape liability.)

2. Pass-Through Taxation

Like a sole proprietorship, a partnership (general or limited) is not a separate tax entity from its owners; instead it's what the IRS calls a "pass-through entity." This means the partnership itself does not pay any income taxes; rather, income passes through the business to each partner, who pays taxes on his share of profit (or deducts his share of losses) on his individual income tax return (Form 1040, with Schedule E attached). A partnership, however, must also file what the IRS calls an "informational return"—Form 1065—to let the government know how much the business earned or lost that year. No tax is paid with this return—just think of it as the feds' way of letting you know they're watching.

3. Personal Liability for Business Debts

Since a partnership is legally inseparable from its owners, just like a sole proprietorship, you'd be right in guessing that general partners are personally liable for business-related obligations. What's also crucial to understand is that in a general partnership, the business actions of any one partner bind the other partners, who can be held personally liable for those actions. So if your business partner takes out an ill-advised high-interest loan on behalf of the partnership, makes a terrible business deal or gets in some other business mischief without your knowledge, you could be held personally responsible for any debts that result.

EXAMPLE: Jamie and Kent are partners in a profitable landscape gardening company. They've been in business for five years and have earned healthy profits, allowing them each to buy a house, decent wheels and even a few luxuries, including Jamie's collection of garden sculptures and Kent's roomful of vintage musical instruments. One day Jamie, without telling Kent, orders a shipment of exotic poppy plants that he is sure will be a big hit with customers. But when the shipment arrives, so do agents of the federal drug enforcement agency who confiscate the plants, claiming they could be turned into narcotics. Soon thereafter criminal charges are filed against Jamie and Kent, resulting in several newspaper stories. Though the partners are ultimately cleared, their attorney fees come to $50,000 and they lose several key accounts, with the result that the business runs up hefty debts. As a general partner, Kent is personally liable for these debts even though he had nothing to do with the ill-fated poppy purchase.

Before you get too worried about personal liability, keep in mind that many small businesses don't face much of a risk of racking up large debts, making potential personal liability less of an issue. For instance, if you're engaged in a low-risk enterprise such as freelance editing, landscaping or running a small band that plays weddings and other social events, chances are that your risk of facing massive debt or a huge lawsuit is pretty small. For these types of small, low-risk businesses, a good business insurance policy that covers most liability risks is almost always enough to protect their

owners from a catastrophe like a lawsuit or fire. Insurance won't cover regular business debts, however, so if you have significant personal assets like fat bank accounts or real estate and plan to rack up some business debt, you may want to limit your personal liability with a different business structure, such as an LLC or a corporation.

4. Partnership Agreements

By drafting a partnership agreement, you can structure your relationship with your partners pretty much however you want. You and your partners can establish the respective shares of profits (or losses) each partner will receive, what the responsibilities of each partner are, what should happen to the partnership if a partner leaves, and take care of any of a number of other issues. It is not legally necessary for a partnership to have a written agreement—the simple act of two or more people doing business together creates a partnership. But only with a clear written agreement will all partners be sure of the important—and sometimes touchy—details of their business arrangement.

In the absence of a partnership agreement, your state's version of the Uniform Partnership Act (UPA) or Revised Uniform Partnership Act (RUPA) kicks in as a standard, bottom-line guide to the rights and responsibilities of each partner. Most states have adopted the UPA or RUPA in some form. In California, for example, if you don't have a partnership agreement, then California's RUPA states that each partner has an equal share in the business's profits, losses and management power. Similarly, unless you provide otherwise in a written agreement, a California partnership won't be able to add a new partner without the unanimous consent of all partners. (California Corporations Code § 16401.) In short, it's important to understand that many of the legal provisions contained in the UPA or RUPA can be overridden if you and your partners have your own written agreement.

What a Partnership Agreement Can't Do

Although a general partnership agreement is an incredibly flexible tool in defining the ownership interests, work responsibilities and other rights of partners, there are some things it can't do. These include:

- freeing the partners from personal liability for business debts
- restricting any partner's right to inspect the business books and records
- affecting the rights of third parties in relation to the partnership—for example, a partnership agreement that says a partner has no right to sign contracts won't affect the rights of an outsider who signs a contract with that partner
- eliminating or weakening the duty of trust (the fiduciary duty) owed by each partner to the other partners.

There's nothing terribly complex about drafting a partnership agreement. They're usually only a few pages long, and cover basic issues that you've probably thought over to some degree already. Partnership agreements typically cover at least the following issues:

- name of partnership and partnership business
- date of partnership creation
- purpose of partnership
- contributions (cash, property and work) of each partner to the partnership
- each partner's share of profits and losses
- provisions for taking profits out of the company (often called partners' draws)
- each partner's management power and duties
- how the partnership will handle departure of a partner, including buy-out terms
- provisions for adding or expelling a partner, and
- dispute resolution procedures.

These and any other terms you include in a partnership agreement can be dealt with in more or less detail. Some partnership agreements cover each topic with a sentence or two; others spend up to a few pages on each provision. Of course, you need an agreement that's appropriate for the size and formality of your business, but it's not a good idea to skimp on your partnership agreement.

Recommended reading on partnerships. *The Partnership Book,* by attorneys Denis Clifford and Ralph Warner (Nolo), is an excellent step-by-step guide to putting together a solid, comprehensive partnership agreement. Also, *How to Create a Buy/Sell Agreement and Control the Destiny of Your Small Business,* by attorneys Bethany Laurence and Anthony Mancuso (Nolo), explains how to draft terms that will enable you to deal with business ownership transitions.

Take a look at the short sample partnership agreements on the following pages to see how a very basic partnership agreement can be put together. You'll also find a blank partnership agreement in Appendix C and on the CD-ROM that comes with this book. These samples are about as basic as it gets—the bare minimum—and you'll almost surely want to use something more detailed for your business.

Partnership Agreement #1

Alison Shanley and Peder Johnson make the following partnership agreement.

Name and Purpose of Partnership

As of September 22, Alison and Peder are the sole owners and partners of the Vermont Fly-Fishing Company. The Vermont Fly-Fishing Company shall be headquartered in Rutland, Vermont, and will sell fly-fishing equipment by mail order.

Contributions to the Partnership

Alison and Peder will make the following contributions to the partnership:

Alison Shanley	cash	$10,000
	desk, miscellaneous office furniture	1,000
	Total contribution	$11,000
Peder Johnson	cash	$7,000
	computer system	$2,000
	Total contribution:	$9,000

Profit and Loss Allocation

Alison and Peder will share business profits and losses in the same proportions as their contributions to the business.

Management of Partnership Business

Alison and Peder will have equal management powers and responsibilities.

Departure of a Partner

If either Alison or Peder leaves the partnership for any reason, including voluntary withdrawal, expulsion or death, the remaining partner shall become the sole owner of the Vermont Fly-Fishing Company, which shall become a sole proprietorship. The remaining owner shall pay the departing partner, or the deceased departing partner's estate, the fair market value of the departing partner's share of the business as of the date of his or her departure. The partnership's accountant shall determine the fair market value of the departing partner's share of the business according to the partnership's book value.

Mediation of Disputes

Alison and Peder agree to mediate any dispute arising under this agreement with a mutually acceptable mediator.

Amendment of Agreement

This agreement may not be amended without the written consent of both partners.

Alison Shanley	Peder Johnson
Signature _____	Signature _____
Date _____	Date _____
Address _____	Address _____
_____	_____
Social Security # _____	Social Security # _____

Partnership Agreement #2

Christine Wenc, Simon Romero and Brendan Doherty agree to the terms of the following agreement.

1. **Name of Partnership.** Christine, Simon and Brendan are partners in the Wenc & Romero Partnership. They created the partnership on July 12, 1999.

2. **Partnership Purpose.** The Wenc & Romero Partnership will provide newspaper clipping services to clients.

3. **Contributions to the Partnership.** Christine, Simon and Brendan will contribute the following to the partnership:

    Christine: $1,000 cash; one Macintosh computer (value $1,500) and one monitor (value $500).

    Simon: $1,000 cash; one fax machine (value $400); one laser printer (value $1,200).

    Brendan: $500 cash; various office equipment (value $500).

4. **Profits and Losses.** Christine, Simon and Brendan shall share profits and losses as follows:

Christine	40%
Simon	40%
Brendan	20%

5. **Partnership Decisions.** Christine, Simon and Brendan will have the following management authority:

Christine	2 votes
Simon	2 votes
Brendan	1 vote

    No partner may accept a new client without the agreement of the others.

6. **Additional Terms to Be Drafted.** Christine, Simon and Brendan agree that in six months they will sign a formal partnership agreement which covers the items in this agreement in more detail, and the additional following items:
    - each partner's work contributions
    - provisions for adding a partner
    - provisions for the departure of a partner
    - provisions for selling the business.

7. **Amendments.** This agreement may not be amended without the written consent of all partners.

Christine Wenc

Signature_____ Date _____

Simon Romero

Signature_____ Date _____

Brendan Doherty

Signature_____ Date _____

C. Limited Liability Companies (LLCs)

Like many business owners just starting out, you might find yourself in this common quandary: On one hand, the thought of having to cope with the risk of personal liability for business misfortunes scares you; on the other, you would rather not deal with the red tape of starting and operating a corporation. Fortunately for you and many other entrepreneurs, you can avoid these problems by taking advantage of a relatively new form of business called the limited liability company, commonly known as an LLC. LLCs combine the pass-through taxation of a sole proprietorship or partnership (business taxes are paid on each owner's individual income tax returns) with the same protection against personal liability that corporations offer.

⚠ **If you're going into business on your own, find out up-front whether or not your state allows one-person LLCs.** While 49 states do, Massachusetts and the District of Columbia do not (they require at least two owners). It's widely expected that Massachusetts and D.C. will eventually join the majority and allow one-person LLCs, so if you live in Massachusetts or D.C. double-check with the LLC filing office (the Secretary of State or Department of Consumer & Regulatory Affairs, respectively) before you rule out the possibility of forming a one-person LLC.

1. Limited Personal Liability

Generally speaking, owners of an LLC are not personally liable for the LLC's debts. (There are some exceptions to this rule, discussed below.) This protects the owners from legal and financial liability in case their business fails, or loses a lawsuit, and can't pay its debts. In those situations, creditors can take all of the LLC's assets, but they generally can't get at the personal assets of the LLC's owners. Losing your business is no picnic, but it's a lot better to lose only what you put into the business than to say goodbye to everything you own.

EXAMPLE: Callie forms her own one-person mail-order business, using most of her $25,000 in savings to establish a cool website and buy mailing lists. Callie realizes that she'll have to buy a significant portion of her sales inventory up front to be able to ship goods to her customers on a timely basis, so she plans to buy those items on credit. While she is willing to risk her $25,000 investment to pursue her dream, she is worried that if her mail-order business fails, she will be buried under a pile of debt. Callie decides to form an LLC so that if her business should fail, she'll only lose the $25,000; no one will be able to sue her personally for the business debt that she owes. She feels more secure going into business knowing that even if her business fails, she can walk away without the risk of losing her house or her car.

Keep in mind that, like a general partner in a partnership, any member of a member-managed LLC can legally bind the entire LLC to a contract or business transaction. In other words, each member can act as an agent of the LLC. (Some LLCs are managed by managers, instead of by members. In manager-managed LLCs, any *manager* can bind the LLC to a business contract or deal.)

While LLC owners enjoy limited personal liability for many of their business debts, it's important to realize that this protection is not absolute. There are several situations where an LLC owner may become personally liable for business debts or claims. Understand, however, that this drawback is not unique to LLCs—the limited liability protection given to LLC members is just as strong as if not stronger than that enjoyed by the corporate shareholders of small corporations. Here are the main situations where LLC owners can still be held personally liable for debts:

- **Personal guarantees.** If you give a personal guarantee on a loan to the LLC, then you are personally liable for the repayment of that loan. Since personal guarantees are often required by banks and other lenders, this is a good reason to be a conservative borrower. Of course, if no personal guarantee is made, then only the LLC—not the members—are liable for the debt.

- **Taxes.** The IRS or the state tax agency may go after the personal assets of LLC owners for overdue corporate federal and state tax debts, particularly overdue payroll taxes. This is most likely to happen to members of small LLCs who have an active hand in managing the business, rather than to passive members.

- **Negligent or intentional acts.** An LLC owner who does something carelessly, or even intentionally, that ends up hurting someone will usually face personal liability. For example, if an LLC owner takes a client to lunch, has a few martinis and injures the client in a car accident on the way home, the LLC owner can be held personally liable for the client's injuries.

- **Breach of fiduciary duty.** LLC owners have a legal duty to act in the best interest of their company and its members. This legal obligation is known as a "fiduciary duty," or is sometimes simply called a "duty of care." If an LLC owner violates this duty, she can be held personally liable for any damages that result from her actions (or inactions). Fortunately for LLC owners, they normally will not be held personally responsible for any honest mistakes or acts of poor judgment they commit in doing their job. Most often, breach of duty is found only for serious indiscretions such as fraud or other illegal behavior.

- **Blurring the boundaries between the LLC and its owners.** When owners fail to respect the separate legal existence of their LLC, but instead treat it as an extension of their personal affairs, a court may ignore the existence of the LLC and rule that the owners are personally liable for business debts and liabilities. Generally this is more likely to occur in one-member LLCs; in reality it only happens in extreme cases. It can easily be avoided by opening a separate LLC checking account, getting a federal employer identification number, keeping separate accounting books for your LLC and funding your LLC adequately enough to be able to meet foreseeable expenses.

2. LLC Taxation

Like a partnership, an LLC is not a separate tax entity from its owners; instead it's what the IRS calls a "pass-through entity." This means the LLC itself does not pay any income taxes; instead, income passes through the business to each LLC owner, who pays taxes on his share of profit (or deducts his share of losses) on his individual income tax return (for the feds, Form 1040 with Schedule E attached). But an LLC, like a partnership, does have to file Form 1065—an "informational return"—to let the government know how much the business earned or lost that year. No tax is paid with this return.

One flexibility of LLCs is that members can choose to have the company taxed like a corporation rather than as a pass-through entity. (In fact, partnerships now have this option as well.) True, for many LLC owners one of the most popular features of the LLC is pass-through taxation, so you may wonder why any of them would choose to be taxed as a corporation. The answer is that, because of the income-splitting strategy of corporations discussed in Section D2a, below, in some instances LLC members can come out ahead by having their business taxed as a separate entity at corporate tax rates. For example, if the owners of an LLC become successful enough to keep some profits in the business at the end of the year (or regularly need to keep significant profits in the business for upcoming expenses), corporate tax rates can save them money. That's because federal income tax rates for corporations start at a lower rate than the rates for individuals. For this reason, many LLCs start out being taxed as partnerships, and when they make enough profits to justify keeping some in the business (rather than doling them out as salaries and bonuses), they opt for corporate-style taxation.

3. LLCs vs. S Corporations

Before LLCs came along, the only way all owners of a business could get limited personal liability was to form a corporation. Problem was, many entrepreneurs didn't want the hassle and expense of incorporating, not to mention the headache of dealing with corporate taxation. One option was to form a special type of corporation known as an S corporation, which is like a normal corporation in most respects, except that business profits pass through to the owner (as in a sole proprietorship or partnership), rather than being taxed to the corporation at corporate tax rates. In other words, S corporations offered the limited liability of a corporation with the pass-through taxation of a sole proprietorship or partnership. For a long time, this was an okay compromise for small-to-medium-sized businesses, though they still had to deal with many of the corporate aspects that S corporations retained (we'll talk more about these below).

Now, however, there is a better option: the limited liability company. Like S corporations, LLCs combine limited personal liability with pass-through tax status. But a significant difference between these two types of businesses is that LLCs are not bound by the many regulations that govern S corporations.

Here's a quick run-down of the major areas of difference between S corporations and LLCs. Keep in mind that we'll discuss corporations, including S corporations, in more detail in the next section.

- **Ownership restrictions.** An S corporation may not have more than 75 shareholders, all of who must be U.S. citizens or residents. This means that some of the C corporation's main benefits—namely, the ability to set up stock option and bonus plans and to bring in public capital with an IPO—are pretty much out of the question for S corporations. And even if an S corporation initially meets the U.S. citizen or resident requirement, its shareholders can't sell shares to another company (like a corporation or an LLC) or a foreign citizen, on pain of losing S corporation tax status. In an LLC, any type of person or entity can become a member—a U.S. citizen, a citizen of a foreign country, another LLC or a corporation or limited partnership.

- **Allocation of profits and losses.** Shareholders of an S corporation must allocate profits according to what percentage of stock each owner has. For example, a 25% owner has to receive 25% of the profits (or losses) even if the other owners want a different division. Owners of an LLC, on the other hand, may distribute profits (and the tax burden that goes with them) however they see fit, without regard to each member's ownership share in the company. For instance, a member of an LLC who owns 25% of the business can receive 50% of the profits if the other members agree (subject to a few IRS rules).

- **Corporate meeting and recordkeeping rules.** For S corporation shareholders to keep their limited liability protection, they have to follow the corporate rules—issuing stock, electing officers, holding regular board of directors' and shareholders' meetings, keeping corporate minutes of all meetings, and following the mandatory rules found in their state's corporation code. By contrast, LLC owners don't need to jump through most of these legal hoops—they just make sure their management team is in agreement on major decisions and go about their business.

- **Tax treatment of losses.** S corporation shareholders are at a disadvantage if their company goes into substantial debt—for instance, if it borrows money to open the business or buy real estate. That's because an S corporation's business debt cannot be passed along to its shareholders unless they have personally co-signed and guaranteed the debt. LLC owners, on the other hand, normally can reap the tax benefits of any business debt, co-signed or not. This can translate into a nice tax break for owners of LLCs that carry debt.

4. Forming an LLC

Before you decide the LLC is the best thing since easy cheese, you should be aware that an LLC might not be as cheap to start as a partnership or sole proprietorship. To form an LLC, you must file Articles of Organization with your Secretary of State or other LLC filing office. A few states charge significant filing fees, plus annual dues (alternately called minimum taxes, annual fees or renewal fees). These fees can push the costs of starting an LLC into the several-hundred-dollar range. Illinois, for instance, charges a $500 filing fee, and California requires that you pay a minimum annual LLC tax of $800 when you start your LLC—on top of its $70 filing fee.

Many brand-new business owners aren't in the position to pay this kind of money right out of the starting block, so they start out as partnerships until they bring in enough income to cover these costs. And if you're thinking of forming a corporation instead, keep in mind that most states charge at least as much in fees for corporations. This plus the added expenses of running a corporation (legal and accounting fees, for example) will almost always make a corporation more expensive to run than an LLC.

Some LLCs must comply with securities laws. LLCs that have owners who do not actively participate in the business may have to register their membership interests as securities or, more likely, qualify for an exemption to the registration requirements. For a brief overview of securities law, read the "LLC FAQ" in Nolo's Small Business Center at www.nolo.com/category/sb_home.html.

And for information about exemptions to the federal securities laws, visit the Securities and Exchange Commission's website at www.sec.gov/smbus/qasbsec.htm#eod6.

Recommended reading on LLCs. *Form Your Own Limited Liability Company*, by attorney Anthony Mancuso (Nolo), gives detailed information on LLCs, including step-by-step instructions and forms for creating one. For a briefer treatment, consult *Nolo's Quick LLC: Limiting Your Liability*, also by Anthony Mancuso. It offers an overview of LLCs as well as comparisons to other business structures, but does not include any start-up forms.

D. Corporations

For many, the term "corporation" conjures up the image of a massive business empire more akin to a nation-state than a small business. In fact, a corporation doesn't have to be huge, and most aren't. Stripped to its essentials, a corporation is simply a specific legal structure that imposes certain legal and tax rules on its owners (also called shareholders). A corporation can be as large as IBM or, in many cases, as small as one person.

One fundamental legal characteristic of a corporation is that it's a separate legal entity from its owners. If you've already read this chapter's sections on sole proprietorships and partnerships, you'll recognize that this is a major difference between those unincorporated business types and corporations. Another important corporate feature is that shareholders are normally protected from personal liability for business debts. Finally, a significant aspect of corporations is that the corporation itself—not just the shareholders—is subject to income tax.

Publicly traded corporations are a different ball game. This section discusses privately held corporations owned by a small group of people who are actively involved in running the business. These corporations are much easier to manage than public corporations, whose shares are sold to the public at large. Any corporation that sells its stock to the general public is heavily regulated by state and federal securities laws, while corporations that sell shares without advertising and only to a select group of people who meet specific state requirements are often exempt from many of these laws. If you plan to sell shares of a corporation to the general public, you should consult a lawyer.

1. Limited Personal Liability

Generally speaking, owners of a corporation are not personally liable for the corporation's debts. (There are some exceptions to this rule, discussed below.) Limited personal liability is a major reason why owners have traditionally chosen to incorporate their businesses: to protect themselves from legal and financial liability in case their business flounders or loses an expensive lawsuit and can't pay its debts. In those situations, creditors can take all of the corporation's assets (including the shareholders' investments), but they generally can't get at the personal assets of the shareholders.

> **EXAMPLE:** Tim and Chris publish *Tropics Tripping,* a monthly travel magazine with a focus on Latin America. Because they both have significant personal assets, and because they will have to borrow a lot of capital to start up their magazine, they form their business as a corporation to protect their personal assets in case their magazine fails. They do great for a few years, but suddenly their subscription and advertising revenue starts to suffer when a recession plus political unrest in several Latin American countries reduces interest in travel to that area. Hoping the situation will turn itself around, Tim and Chris forge ahead—and go deeper into debt as it proves impossible to pay printing and other bills on time. Finally, when their printer won't do any more print runs on

credit, Tim and Chris are forced to call it quits. *Tropics Tripping*'s debts total $250,000, while business assets are valued at only $90,000—leaving a $160,000 debt to creditors. Thankfully for Tim and Chris, they won't have to use their personal assets to pay the $160,000, because as owners of a corporation, they're shielded from personal liability.

 Forming a corporation is no longer the only option for owners who want to limit their personal liability. With the advent of limited liability companies, corporations aren't the only business entities that provide limited liability status for all owners. See Section C on LLCs, above.

Forming a corporation to shield yourself from personal liability for business obligations provides good, but not total, protection for your personal assets. Here are the principal areas where corporation owners still face personal liability.

- **Personal guarantees.** If you give a personal guarantee on a loan to the corporation, then you are personally liable for the repayment of that loan. Since such a personal guarantee is often required by banks and other lenders, this is a good reason to be a conservative borrower. Of course, if no personal guarantee is made, then only the corporation—not the shareholders—is liable for the debt.
- **Taxes.** The IRS or the state tax agency may go after the personal assets of corporate owners for overdue corporate federal and state tax debts, particularly overdue payroll taxes. This is most likely to happen to owners of small corporations who have an active hand in managing the business, rather than to passive shareholders.
- **Negligent or intentional acts.** A corporate owner who does something negligently (that is, carelessly), or perhaps even intentionally, that ends up hurting someone can't hide behind the corporate barrier to escape personal liability. Shareholders are subject to personal liability for wrongs they commit—such as

attacking a customer or leaving a wet floor in a store—that result in injury.

- **Breach of fiduciary duty.** Corporate owners have a legal duty to act in the best interest of the company and its shareholders. This legal obligation is known as a "fiduciary duty," or is sometimes simply called a "duty of care." If an owner violates this duty, she can be held personally liable for any damages that result from her actions (or inactions). Fortunately for corporate owners, run-of-the-mill mistakes or lapses in judgment aren't usually considered breaches of the duty of care. Most often, breach of duty is found only for serious indiscretions such as fraud or other illegal behavior. For example, if a corporate officer falsified some financial data in order to seal a deal with a client, that officer may be held personally liable for any damages that result from his breach of duty to the company.

- **Blurring the boundaries between the corporation and its owners.** When corporate owners ignore corporate formalities and treat the corporation like an unincorporated business, a court may ignore the existence of the corporation (in legal slang, they may "pierce the corporate veil") and rule that the owners are personally liable for business debts and liabilities. To avoid this, it's important for corporate owners not to allow the legal boundary between the corporation and its owners to grow fuzzy. Owners need to scrupulously respect corporate formalities such as holding shareholders' and directors' meetings, keeping attentive minutes, issuing stock certificates and maintaining corporate accounts strictly separate from personal funds.

Don't be fooled into thinking that incorporating will solve all your liability problems. Limited personal liability can prevent you from losing your home, car, bank account and other assets—but it won't protect you from losing your investment in your business. A business can quickly get wiped out if a customer, employee or supplier wins a big lawsuit against it and the business has to be liquidated to cover the debt. In short, even if you incorporate to protect your personal assets, you'll want to purchase appropriate insurance to protect your business assets. (Insurance is discussed in Chapter 7, "Insuring Your Business.") But remember, insurance won't help if you simply can't pay your normal business debts.

2. Corporate Taxation

The words "corporate taxes" raise a lot of fear and loathing in the business world. Fortunately, the reality of corporate taxation is usually less depressing than the hype. Here are the basics—think of it as Corporate Tax Lite. If you decide to incorporate, you'll likely want to consult an accountant or small business lawyer who can fill you in on the fine print. (See Chapter 12 for information on finding and hiring a lawyer.)

The first thing you need to know is that for tax purposes, you'll be treated differently depending on whether you operate as a regular corporation (also called a C corporation) or you elect S corporation status for tax purposes. An S corporation is the same as a C corporation in most respects, but when it comes to taxes, C and S corporations are very different animals. A regular, or C, corporation is itself subject to taxes, while an S corporation is treated like a partnership for tax purposes and doesn't pay any income taxes itself. Like partnership profits, S corporation profits (and losses) pass through to the shareholders, who report them on their individual returns. (In this respect, S corporations are very similar to LLCs, which also offer limited liability along with partnership-style tax treatment.) These two types of corporations are explained in more detail just below.

a. C Corporations

As a separate tax entity, a regular corporation must file and pay income taxes on its own tax return, much like an individual does. After deductions such as employee compensation, fringe benefits and all other reasonable and necessary business expenses have been subtracted from its earnings, a corporation pays tax on whatever profit remains. Often in small corporations where all of the owners of the business are also employees, all of the corporation's profits are paid out in tax-deductible salaries and fringe benefits—leaving no corporate profit and thus no corporate taxes due. (The owner/employees must, of course, pay tax on their salaries on their individual returns.)

Fringes and Perks

Like employee salaries, corporations can deduct many fringe benefits as business expenses. If a corporation pays for benefits such as health and disability insurance for its employees and owner/employees, the cost can usually be deducted from the corporate income, reducing a possible tax bill. (There's one main exception: benefits given to an owner/employee of an S corporation who owns 2% or more of the stock can't be taken as deductible business expenses.)

As a general rule, owners of sole proprietorships, partnerships and LLCs can deduct the cost of providing these benefits for employees, but not for themselves. (These owners can, however, deduct a portion of their medical insurance premiums, though it's technically a deduction for the individuals, not a business expense.)

The fact that fringe benefits for owners are deductible for corporations may make incorporating a wise choice. But it's less likely to be a winning strategy for a capital-poor start-up that can't afford to underwrite a benefits package.

Initial rates of corporate taxation are comparatively low (see "Marginal Tax Rates for Corporations," below). Corporations that keep some profits in the business from one year to the next rather than paying out all profits as salaries and bonuses can take advantage of 15%–25% tax brackets. This practice, sometimes called income-splitting, basically involves strategically setting salaries at a level so that money left in the business is taxable only at the 15% or 25% corporate tax rate (for income up to $50,000 or $75,000). Since any amount of "reasonable" compensation to employees is deductible, corporate owners have lots of leeway in setting salaries to accomplish this.

Marginal Tax Rates for Corporations

The following chart shows tax rates for corporations. For example, if a corporation's taxable income was $75,100, it would pay 15% of its first $50,000 of income, 25% of the next $25,000, and 34% on its remaining $100 in income. The corporation's marginal tax rate—the tax rate a corporation would pay on the last dollar of its income—would be 34%.

Taxable Income	Marginal Tax Rate
0 to $50,000	15%
$50,001 to $75,000	25%
$75,001 to $100,000	34%
$100,001 to $335,000	39%
$335,001 to $10,000,000	34%
$10,000,001 to $15,000,000	35%
$15,000,001 to $18,333,333	38%
Over $18,333,333	35%

Keep in mind that these corporate rates don't apply to professional corporations, which are subject to a flat tax of 35% regardless of the level of corporate income.

EXAMPLE: Alexis and Matt run Window to the Past, Inc., a glass manufacturing business that specializes in custom work for architectural renovations. Toward the end of the year, they calculate that year's profit to be approximately

$145,000. They decide to give themselves each a $50,000 bonus out of the profit (on top of their $40,000 salaries). Because both salaries and bonuses are tax-deductible business expenses, this reduces Window to the Past's taxable income to $45,000. The result is the corporate profit of $45,000 will be taxed at only 15%, the lowest rate. (If Alexis and Matt had left all the profits in the business, the profits over $75,000 would have been taxed at 34%, and profits over $100,000 would have been taxed at a whopping 39%.) Of course, the bonuses Alexis and Matt give themselves increases their personal income. They'll each be taxed on the bonuses on their individual returns at 31%, rather than 28% (but it still beats the higher corporate tax rates of 34% and 39%).

This income-splitting strategy is available only to shareholders who also work for the corporation. If they're not at least part-time employees, then shareholders won't be in a position to earn salaries or bonuses, and will be able only to take money from the corporation as dividends. This brings us to the vexing problem of double taxation, routinely faced by larger corporations with shareholders who aren't active employees. Unlike salaries and bonuses, dividends paid to shareholders cannot be deducted as business expenses from corporate earnings. Since they're not deducted, any amounts paid as dividends are included in the total corporate profit and taxed. And when the shareholder receives the dividend, it is taxed at the shareholder's individual tax rate as part of his personal income. As you can see, any money paid out as a dividend gets taxed twice: once at the corporate level, and once at the individual level.

You can avoid double taxation simply by not paying dividends. This is usually easy if all shareholders are employees, but probably more difficult if some shareholders are passive investors anxious for a reasonable return on their investment.

b. The Un-Corporation: S Corporations

Unlike a regular corporation, an S corporation does not pay taxes itself. Any profits pass through to the owners, who pay taxes on income as if the business were a sole proprietorship, a partnership or an LLC. Yet the business is still a corporation. This means, of course, that its owners are protected from personal liability for business debts, just as shareholders of C corporations and members (owners) of LLCs are.

Until the relatively recent arrival of the LLC (discussed in Section C), the S corporation was the business form of choice for those who wanted limited liability protection but not the two-tiered tax structure of a C corporation. Today, relatively few businesses are organized as S corporations, since S corporations are subject to many regulations that do not apply to LLCs. (See Section C above for an outline of the differences between S corporations and LLCs.)

3. Forming and Running a Corporation

Besides tax complexity, a major drawback to forming a corporation—either a C or an S type—is time and expense. Unlike sole proprietorships and partnerships, you can't clap your hands twice and conjure up a corporation. To incorporate, you must file Articles of Incorporation with your Secretary of State or other corporate filing office, along with often hefty filing fees and minimum annual taxes. And if you decide to sell shares of the corporation to the public—as opposed to keeping them in the hands of a relatively small number of owners—you'll have to comply with lots of complex federal and state securities laws. Finally, to protect your limited personal liability, you need to act like a corporation, which means adopting bylaws, issuing stock to shareholders, maintaining records of various meetings of directors and shareholders and keeping records and transactions of the business separate from those of the owners.

⚠ **Corporations must comply with securities laws.** Corporations must either register their shares with the Securities and Exchange Commission or qualify for an exemption to securities registration requirements. For a brief overview of securities law, read the "Corporations FAQ" in Nolo's Small Business Center at www.nolo.com/category/sb_home.html. And for information about small business exemptions to the federal securities laws, visit the Securities and Exchange Commission's website at www.sec.gov/smbus/qasbsec.htm#eod6.

To sum up, the protection afforded by incorporating comes at a price. Figure in the likelihood that you'll have to hire lawyers, accountants and other professionals to keep your corporation in compliance, and it's easy to see how expensive running a corporation can be.

📖 **Recommended reading on corporations.** For more information on the many complexities of running a corporation, be sure to read *The Corporate Minutes Book,* by attorney Anthony Mancuso, published by Nolo.

E. So, Which One to Choose?

The differences between the various types of business organizations basically boil down to one legal issue: the personal liability of owners for business debts. While the issue of personal liability can have a huge impact on successful small businesses a few years down the road, business owners who are just starting out on a shoestring often care most about spending as little money as possible on the legal structure of their business. This is certainly an understandable approach; far more new businesses die painful deaths because they don't control costs than because they lose costly lawsuits. In short, for many new small businesses, incorporating or organizing as an LLC is as unnecessary an expense as a swank downtown office or a gleaming chrome espresso machine in the lunchroom.

That said, owners of any business that will engage in a high-risk activity; that might rack up large business debts; or that will have a number of investors, should always insist on limited personal liability, either with an LLC or a corporation. This is even more true if the business can't find or afford appropriate insurance.

If you've decided limiting your personal liability is worth the extra cost, you still need to decide between a corporation and an LLC. With the LLC's arrival, many business owners who want limited liability protection realize that incorporation normally only makes sense if a business needs to take advantage of the corporate stock structure to attract key employees and investment capital. No question, corporations may have an easier time attracting capital investment by issuing stock privately or publicly. And businesses in the Internet and other hot technology industries may find it easier to attract and retain key employees by issuing employee stock options. But for businesses that never go public, choosing to operate as an LLC rather than a corporation normally makes the most sense if limited liability is your main concern. If the corporate stock structure isn't something you want or need for your business, the simplicity and flexibility offered by LLCs offer a clear advantage over corporations.

Analyzing Your Risks

Starting a business is always risky. In some businesses, however, the risks are particularly extreme. If you're planning to launch an investment firm or start a hazardous waste management company, there is little doubt that you'll need all the protection you can get, including limited personal liability as well as adequate insurance. Other businesses are not so obviously risk-laden, but still could land you in trouble if fate strikes you a blow. Here are a few red flags to watch for when analyzing how risky your business is:

- using hazardous materials, such as dry cleaning solvents or photographic chemicals, or hazardous processes, such as welding or operating heavy machinery
- manufacturing or selling edible goods
- driving as part of the job
- building or repairing structures or vehicles
- caring for children or animals
- providing or allowing access to alcohol
- allowing activities that may result in injury, such as weightlifting or skateboarding, and
- repairing or working on items of value, such as cars or antiques.

If you've identified one or more serious risks your business is likely to face, figure out whether business insurance might give enough protection. Some risky activities, such as job-related driving, are good candidates for insurance and don't necessarily warrant incorporating. But if insurance can't cover all of the risks involved in your business, it may be time to form an LLC or a corporation.

Keep in mind that insurance will never insulate you from regular business debts, so if you foresee your business going into serious debt, an LLC or corporation may be the best business structure for you.

☑ Chapter 2 Checklist

☐ Identify the number of owners of your business.

☐ Analyze your business's risks and decide how much protection from personal liability you'll need.

☐ Determine how you'd like the business to be taxed (as a pass-through entity or as a corporation).

☐ Decide if your business would benefit from the stock structure of a corporation (by being able to distribute stock options and sell stock).

☐ Choose a business structure.

☐ If you will structure your business as a partnership, draft and sign a partnership agreement.

☐ If you will structure your business as an LLC or corporation, file articles with your state and draft bylaws (corporations) or an operating agreement (LLCs).

■

Picking Winning Business Names That Won't Land You in Court

A. An Overview of Trademark Law 3/5

    1. What Is a Trademark? 3/5

    2. When Do Trademarks Conflict? 3/8

    3. The Dilution Exception 3/11

B. Trademark Issues Online 3/11

    1. The Web Has Changed the Rules 3/11

    2. Domain Name Conflicts and Cybersquatting 3/12

    3. Using Meta Tags That Conflict With Trademarks 3/15

C. Name Searches 3/16

    1. Sources of Name Information... 3/16

    2. Searching the Federal Trademark Database 3/18

    3. Analyzing Your Search Results 3/20

D. Choosing and Registering a Domain Name 3/21

    1. Picking a Great Domain Name 3/21

    2. Registering Your Domain Name 3/22

E. Trademark Registration 3/23

F. Winning Names for Your Business, Products and Services 3/24

There's a lot of room for personal and professional creativity when picking a business name, but there are also legal requirements and pitfalls that you absolutely need to understand. In particular, it's important for all business owners to understand the basics of trademark law, which establishes and protects legal rights to names of businesses, products and services.

If you choose a business or product name that's too similar to a competitor's name, for instance, you could find yourself accused of violating the competitor's trademark (called "infringing" or "unfairly competing") and you could be forced to change your business name and possibly pay money damages. No question, changing a business name can be a serious blow to a business that has worked hard to build name recognition among its customers—not to mention the cost of changing signs, stationery, pre-printed invoices and the like.

But suppose you plan to open a local business so small that you don't even expect to compete with businesses in the next county, much less in another state or country. You probably wonder if the arcane world of trademark law really affects you. Just 20 years ago the answer would have clearly been no—you didn't really have to worry too much about national or global name conflicts back then. As long as a quick search of your phone book didn't reveal any obvious local conflicts and you didn't call your business "Ford," "IBM" or some other famous name, you were fine. But in today's world of the Internet, mail order and rapidly growing national chains, the idea of "local" obviously isn't what it used to be. Even if you're opening just a tiny bookstore in a small town, if you inadvertently choose the same name as an Internet store that sells books, you may very well find yourself being accused of infringing the online store's trademark—even if the online store's headquarters are on a different continent.

One good way to figure out how educated and concerned you need to be about trademark law is to consider what the consequences will be if you are forced to change your business name. If a name change would be cheap and easy and wouldn't seriously confuse your customers, then don't lie awake nights worrying about picking a name that's absolutely bulletproof. However, if changing your name would be messy or expensive (changing signs, Yellow Pages ads and business directory listings, to mention a few possibilities), you'll want to take the time and trouble to be sure the name you plan to use doesn't already belong to someone else.

Have we convinced you that paying attention to the law of business names is important? Good. Now we'll explain how to go about choosing a name that won't land you in legal hot water and, once chosen, how to secure the maximum legal protection for it. We'll also cover some non-legal aspects of naming your business, including tips and advice on how to approach the naming process in the best way for your particular business.

⚠ Trademark isn't the only legal issue related to business names. Besides watching out for trademark conflicts, business owners also need to comply with other legal rules. Many businesses must comply with their county's fictitious business name requirements (see Chapter 6, Step 3). Typically this means you'll need to register a fictitious business name statement (or similar document) with your county clerk and possibly publish it in a local newspaper. And for corporations, LLCs and limited partnerships, the name of the business must be approved by the state filing office (usually the Secretary or Department of State) before it will accept Articles of Incorporation, Articles of Organization or a Statement of Limited Partnership.

Getting the Terms Straight

One reason the law of business names often seems confusing is that it is riddled with lots of arcane and often overlapping legal jargon. For example, local, state and federal agencies often use different terms to describe the same or very similar legal concepts. Here's a brief rundown of the terms you should understand, all of which are discussed in greater detail in the rest of this chapter.

- The term **"legal name"** means the official name of the entity that owns a business. The legal name of a sole proprietorship is simply the full name of the owner—for example, John Potter. If a general partnership has a written partnership agreement that gives a name to the partnership, then that name is the legal name. Otherwise, the legal name of the general partnership is simply the last names of the owners. (Many sole proprietorships and partnerships present their business to the public under a name that's different from their legal name—see fictitious business names, below.) And for corporations, LLCs and limited partnerships, the legal name is the name registered with the state filing office (usually the Department or Secretary of State).

- A **"trade name"** is simply the name that a business holds out to the public, which may or may not be the same as the name of the business owner or the business's legal name. John O'Toole's Classic Cars, Amoeba Records and Nolo are examples of trade names. You see trade names on business signs, in the telephone book and on invoices. In many transactions, such as opening a bank account or applying for a loan, you'll need to provide both the owners' names, the legal name of the business (if different), and the trade name of the business (if different).

- The term **"fictitious business name"** is used when the trade name of a business is different from its legal name. For instance, if John O'Toole named his sole proprietorship Turtle's Classic Cars, the name "Turtle's Classic Cars" would be a fictitious business name because it does not

contain the owner's last name, "O'Toole." A fictitious business name is sometimes called a **"DBA"** name; DBA stands for "doing business as," as in: "John O'Toole, doing business as Turtle's Classic Cars." Corporations and LLCs may also have to file fictitious name statements if the name they hold out to the public differs from the legal name they registered with the state. For example, if the owners of Southern Colusa County Auto Mechanics Ltd. Liability Co. decide to operate repair shop under the fictitious name "Grease Monkeys," they'll have to file a fictitious name statement.

- The legal name of a business that must register with the state to be legally created is called a **"corporate name,"** an **"LLC name,"** or a **"limited partnership name."** If a corporation, LLC or limited partnership operates under the same name that's registered with the Department or Secretary of State, then its corporate, LLC or limited partnership name will be both its legal name and its trade name.

- A **"trademark"** (sometimes called simply a mark) is any word, phrase, design or symbol used to market a product or service. Technically, a mark used to market a service, rather than a product, is called a service mark, though the term "trademark" is commonly used for both types of marks since they essentially refer to the same basket of legal protections. Owners of trademarks have legal rights under both federal and state law, which give them the power in some cases to prevent others from using their trademark to market goods or services.

- **"Business name"** tends to be a catch-all term that can refer to any of the names used by a business—the name of a business itself, a corporate name, a fictitious business name and the names of a business's products and services. When we use it—or when you see it someplace else—be sure you keep in mind the difference between the various types of business names.

Business Names and Trademarks Often Overlap

Many trade names double as trademarks and service marks for products and services of the business. For instance, when McDonald's (trade name) advertises McDonald's French fries, the trade name "McDonald's" also becomes a trademark because it is used to identify the maker (or brand) of French fries. And when the company puts up a sign in front of its restaurant, the term "McDonald's" becomes a service mark, identifying who's providing the fast food service of that restaurant. In other words, any time you use your trade name to identify a product, service or business location, you're using the trade name as a mark—either a trademark or a service mark. As you can see, a name can wear a bunch of different hats: it can be a trade name, a legal name and a trademark (or service mark) all in one. Keep this in mind as we discuss the legal and practical issues involved with business names—understanding that name issues sometimes overlap is helpful in this often complex area of law.

Legal Name	Trade Name	Trademarks/Service Marks
McDonald's Corporation	McDonald's	McDonald's French fries Big Mac Mayor McCheese Golden arches symbol
Microsoft Corporation	Microsoft	Microsoft Word Windows 95 Internet Explorer "Where do you want to go today?" slogan
Trader Joe's Company	Trader Joe's	Trader Joe's Baked Tortilla Chips Trader Giotto's Italian Roast coffee beans Trader Darwin's vitamins
Ronco, Inc.	Ronco	Popeil Pocket Fisherman Dial-O-Matic Food Slicer
Kraft Foods, Inc.	Kraft	JELL-O Gelatin Cheez Whiz Tang Instant Breakfast Drink "It's the cheesiest" slogan for Kraft Macaroni & Cheese "Good to the last drop" slogan for Kraft Maxwell House Coffee

A. An Overview of Trademark Law

In a nutshell, trademark law—which is really a catchall term referring to a large body of statutes, regulations and court decisions—prevents a business from using a name or logo that is likely to be confused with one that a competing business already uses. This general rule applies both to the name of a business as well as to the names of any of its products or services.

Trademark Protects More Than Names

In this chapter, we talk mostly about how trademark applies to business names. But the rules we discuss apply to a lot more—logos, designs, slogans and packaging features can also be protected by trademark. For example, Nike's slogan, "Just Do It," and American Express's mantra, "Don't leave home without it," are protected by the law of trademark. For more information on using trademarks in other aspects of your small business, be sure to read *Trademark: Legal Care for Your Business and Product Name*, by Kate McGrath and Stephen Elias (Nolo).

Allowing businesses to have exclusive use of certain names helps consumers to identify and recognize goods in the marketplace. When you buy Racafrax brand of wood glue, for instance, you'll know that it will be similar in quality to the Racafrax glue you bought last time. By contrast, if any company was allowed to call their glue "Racafrax Glue," customers would never know what they were getting. And because customers would never know when they were using the Racafrax company's glue, the Racafrax company wouldn't be able to build customer trust or goodwill, even if its glue was the best available. In this way, consumers and businesses alike benefit from trademark protection.

This section will give you a rundown of what's protected by trademark law and how to determine and protect your rights to the names you use. A basic knowledge of this area will help you understand what steps you should take as part of forming your business to avoid infringing others' rights (and opening yourself up to lawsuits). And it will also give you the legal basics you'll need to protect your business name and to understand whether your rights are being infringed by others down the road.

⚠️ **Pick a name with an eye toward avoiding legal trouble—you can't afford a court fight.** The main reason to learn the basics of trademark law is not so you can successfully defend your name in court against another business that claims a superior right to use it. Even if you were to win a complex and expensive court fight, you'd be a huge loser when it comes to time, worry and legal fees. Far better to avoid disputes in the first place by choosing a safe name that has a very low likelihood of leading to customer confusion and, therefore, an infringement lawsuit.

1. What Is a Trademark?

The definition of "trademark" is essentially this simple: any word, phrase, logo or other device used to identify products or services in the marketplace is a trademark. This includes the names of products or services themselves and often the name of the business that's selling them. Using a name in public commerce to identify goods or services for sale—not just on internal documents or on product samples that aren't available to the public—is enough to make it a trademark; there is no registration requirement. However, registration with the U.S. Patent and Trademark Office will greatly strengthen your power to enforce your rights to the trademark. For example, if you federally register your trademark, you can stop any subsequent user in your field from using the same or a confusingly similar mark anywhere in the United States. (Trademark registration is covered in Section E.)

Keep in mind, however, that a key part of the definition of a trademark is that it must be used to identify goods or services for sale. So if you don't use the name of your business or product or service in public in conjunction with something you're trying to sell, it isn't considered a trademark. For example, if a software company called ZZP Web Masters markets bookmarking software for the Internet called "WebWorm," then the name WebWorm is a trademark. If the only marketing done for WebWorm is an ad that reads, "Manage your bookmarks with WebWorm," then the business name ZZP Web Masters will not be a trademark because it's not used in public to sell WebWorm. But an ad that reads, "WebWorm: The best bookmarking software on Earth, by ZZP Web Masters," includes two trademarks: the product name WebWorm and the trade name ZZP Web Masters. For practical purposes, however, many if not most business names are also considered trademarks, since most businesses do use their names to promote or sell their product or service.

Trademarks vs. Service Marks

You've probably heard the term "trademark," which applies to names, logos and slogans that identify products (such as Chia Pet), a whole lot more than the term "service mark," which is used when a name identifies a service (such as H&R Block Tax Preparation Services). One reason for this is that, since the legal rules for trademarks and service marks are virtually identical, the term "trademark," or sometimes just "mark," is commonly used for both types of marks. But since technically the two terms do refer to different things, you should be aware of the distinction, especially if your businesses will primarily provide services.

---

a. Trademark Rights

The power of a trademark comes from the fact that you may be entitled to exclude others from using the same mark. If you were the first to use the trademark, then you own certain rights to it and can take legal action against others who use it illegally. In legal terms, if someone "infringes your trademark" by using it in a way that's likely to confuse your customers or that has "diluted" your trademark, you can take them to court and force them to stop using it, and maybe even to pay damages. For example, if ZZP Web Masters had been selling WebWorm for two years and then another company started selling a similar product called "WebWorm," ZZP Web Masters could sue the other company and force it to stop using the product name "WebWorm." If ZZP Web Masters could prove that their business suffered because of the infringement, they might also be entitled to some financial compensation (damages) from the other company. We'll discuss when use of a similar trademark can cause customer confusion or trademark dilution in Sections 2 and 3, below.

So far, so good—you're probably even wondering why everyone says trademark issues are such a bear to deal with. Here's why: Just because you own a trademark doesn't mean you can always prevent someone else from using it (and likewise, another owner of a trademark can't always prevent you from using his mark). Unlike a copyright, which generally gives the same level of protection to all owners, a trademark gives widely varying degrees of protection to the owner, depending on a variety of circumstances. So, as we explain below, the key legal point isn't so much whether you own a trademark as whether it qualifies for trademark protection—and if so, how much.

b. Strong vs. Weak Marks

The general rule is that distinctive business names such as Yahoo! and Mountain Dew receive the strongest legal trademark protection. Below we define "distinctive" in more detail, but for the moment, it's important that you understand why distinctive names get more protection. The theory is that distinctive names like Pepsi or Cisco make strong connections in the minds of consumers, and play a big role in consumers' buying choices. The opposite is considered to be true for names that aren't very distinctive, such as Quality Vitamins or Brite Paint. Since distinctive names are considered to play such a big role in helping consumers choose among brands, it follows that the more distinctive a name is, the more likely it is that customers will be confused (in legal theory at least) by more than one business using the name. To avoid this confusion, the law gives more protection to distinctive names, and less or none to names that are merely ordinary and descriptive. After we define the meanings of distinctive and ordinary and descriptive, we'll talk more about when two similar trademarks are likely to cause customer confusion, in Section 2 below.

A truly distinctive trademark (also called a "strong trademark") is one that clearly distinguishes the product or service it represents from others. Memorable, unusual names like Xerox or 3M are additional good examples of distinctive marks. While there's no magic formula for what makes a trademark distinctive, strong marks tend to be surprising or fanciful names that often have nothing to do with the business, product or service. Still more examples of distinctive marks include Chia Pet, Velcro and Comet (cleanser).

On the flip side, a weak trademark consists of ordinary, descriptive words that merely describe aspects of the product or business, such as durability ("Sturdy Knapsacks"), location ("The Edge of Town Tavern") or other qualities ("Speedy Dry Cleaners," "Tasty Vegetables"). Also, trademarks that include personal names are usually considered to be ordinary marks and therefore weak. (But, as we explain below, weak trademarks can become stronger with use.)

An additional reason why ordinary, descriptive trademarks aren't strongly protected, at least at first, is to make sure that competitors aren't unfairly prevented from using common words to describe their own products. For example, a food delivery service company called "Galloping Gourmet" wouldn't be able to monopolize the word "gourmet" and stop a deli from using the name "Tom's Gourmet Sandwiches."

c. How Trademarks Can Grow Stronger

A weak trademark can eventually offer good protection if it becomes distinctive and therefore stronger through use. Called "acquiring a secondary meaning" in legalese, this is particularly likely to occur when a product or service with a weak mark becomes a lasting success, making it likely that the public will associate the mark with the product or service being sold. For example, as the designer clothing brand Tommy Hilfiger has become popular nationwide, its previously weak trademark grows stronger as customers come to associate the ordinary name with a particular company. Examples of the weak-to-strong phenomenon include Burger King, Tom's Natural Toothpaste, Ben & Jerry's Ice Cream, and The Yellow Pages.

d. Unfair Competition Laws

What if your weak trademark never becomes strong? Just because you have a weak trademark doesn't mean that your business name will be totally free for others to use. Because of a legal doctrine called unfair competition, being the first to use a descriptive name may offer all the protection you need. While unfair competition law is a separate body of law from trademark law, it can have the same effect. It's based on the idea that it's not fair for another business to rip off your business's good reputation.

For example, if you've been selling dry cleaning services in Bakersfield under the name Jean's Quick Cleaners, and someone else in the same city opens Jeanne's Quick Cleaners, you could claim unfair competition and likely have them prevented from using that name. As you can see, unfair competition law can have the same result as trademark law: it can prevent another business from using a name identical or confusingly similar to yours if you used the name first. Keep in mind, however, that your right to stop trademark infringement is stronger than your right to stop unfair competition, so it will be easier to prevent someone from using your business name if it's trademarked.

2. When Do Trademarks Conflict?

As you surely know, plenty of businesses share the same name, or at least part of the same name, without violating each other's trademark rights. Examples include United Airlines and United Van Lines; Ford Motor Company and Ford Modeling Agency; and Scott Paper Products and Scott Sunglasses. Legally, that's because trademark infringement occurs only when the use of a mark by two different businesses is likely to cause customer confusion. (An exception to this rule, called the "dilution" doctrine, is explained in Section 3, below.) If customers aren't likely to be confused, then both businesses may legally use the same mark. But if customer confusion is likely, then the rightful owner of the mark can prohibit the other businesses from using it, and can sue for damages (financial compensation) for any unauthorized use.

Dual uses of the same or similar mark can cause customer confusion by making it unclear what company actually makes a product or service or by misleading customers as to the source of the product. Customer confusion can happen in a number of different ways. Sometimes dual uses of a mark lead customers to believe that a certain company made a product when it actually did not. Or a customer may see trademarks being used in two different places and think that the companies are jointly owned or somehow affiliated, which may not be true.

Determining whether two marks legally conflict (in other words, whether customer confusion is

likely) is one of the trickiest bits of trademark law. It's important to understand that whether or not customer confusion is likely is a legal determination—not a commonsense one. In making this determination, courts deem the following factors to be particularly important:

- how strong (distinctive or well known) the original trademark is
- how much the products or services really compete against one another, and
- how similar the trademarks are in appearance, sound or meaning.

We'll look at each of these in more depth in the next few sections.

a. How "Strong" Is the Mark?

As we discussed above, distinctive marks receive the most protection (are the "strongest") because, in legal theory, they are more likely to stick in consumers' minds and play a role in their buying choices. Since strong trademarks tend to stick in customers' minds, so the theory goes, it's likely that customer confusion will happen if more than one company uses a strong trademark. To protect consumers from such confusion, courts will typically prohibit more than one company from using a strong trademark. Besides protecting consumers, prohibiting multiple uses of a strong trademark prevents businesses from stealing customers or getting a free ride off another business's good reputation by using their trademark.

For example, the very strong and well-known trademark Microsoft is firmly implanted in millions of people's minds. If a company called itself Microsoft Consulting, chances are that plenty of people would be confused about whether Bill Gates had anything to do with that consulting company. If Bill Gates sued Microsoft Consulting for trademark infringement, he would have a very good chance of winning.

Trademark law doesn't give much, if any, protection to weak trademarks because they don't trigger a strong association in customers' minds between the mark and a particular product or service (or so the legal thinking goes)—since they are merely descriptive of the product or service. For that reason, courts are less inclined to find that customer confusion is likely when dual use of a weak trademark is involved. Note that this is true even if customer confusion does in fact exist. For example, if Smith Jewelry and Smith Hardware exist in the same town, customers may wonder if they're owned by the same family, but trademark law still won't protect the name of either business, since the name Smith is so common. (However, unfair competition law may protect the hardware-store Smiths if the jewelry-store Smiths started getting into the hardware business, making the businesses direct competitors.)

b. Do the Products or Services Actually Compete?

If the products or services that share the same trademarks are in completely unrelated fields or industries, or if they're sold in non-overlapping geographical regions (and not on the Internet), there's obviously far less chance that customers will be confused by the other company's trademarks. In other words, the less products or services actually compete, the less likely it is that there will be a trademark violation. For example, a pizza joint named Rocket Pizza probably won't be confused with a record store named Rocket Records, even if they exist in the same city. And an auto shop named Armadillo Repairs in Portland, Maine, most likely won't run into any trademark conflicts with Armadillo Auto Repairs in San Diego. Being so far apart and serving purely local customers, chances are slim that customers would confuse the two companies.

> **EXAMPLE:** You open a coffee shop in Austin, Texas and name it Pam's Coffee Stop. A year into your business, you're driving through Albuquerque, New Mexico, and notice a small café also named Pam's Coffee Stop. After

thinking about it, you decide that there's little chance of a trademark violation by either business. The trademark is ordinary and descriptive and therefore weak, plus the shops are so far away from each other that they're not competitors. But this gets you thinking about trademark laws and you wonder what you'd do if a big national chain started using the name and moved into your area. The answer is, you would retain the right to use the name because you were the first to use it in your area (as long as the national chain hadn't registered the name with the U.S. Patent and Trademark Office before you first used it). But the chain could prevent you from expanding into other areas of the country if this ever became your goal.

 The World Wide Web and other long-distance marketing techniques are creating millions of new competitors. As we mentioned at the beginning of this chapter, with the arrival and widespread use of the Web, the fast expansion of mail-order catalog businesses, and ever more frequent travel, the old rule that small, local businesses don't have to worry about trademarks from other geographical regions has largely gone out the window. Today even small, local businesses commonly establish websites, hundreds of thousands of businesses send out catalogs, and even some local restaurants and hotels seek to reach a national (or even world-wide) pool of tourists. The upshot is that many formerly local businesses that just a few years ago never would have been confused with each other are now competitors, which of course increases the likelihood of customer confusion and trademark infringement if their names are the same. Be sure to read Section B below on new trademark issues and considerations in today's ever smaller world.

Of course, there are plenty of gray areas where two businesses aren't in head-to-head competition, but use the same marks for products that are similar enough to make a customer stop and think, for example, "Is a Parker calendar made by the same company as Parker pens?" Even though a company with the same name may not be stealing business from a competitor, it may be unintentionally taking advantage of that company's goodwill and getting a free ride from its advertising. Again, the answer as to whether infringement exists in these gray areas often depends on how strong the original trademark is (as we discussed above). If the original trademark is weak, there's probably not much goodwill or reputation to rip off (few customers would be confused by the similar name), so a court wouldn't be likely to say there was infringement. But if the original trademark is strong, there's a greater likelihood that the newer trademark will rip off the older one's reputation, making it likely for the court to agree that there's been an infringement.

> **EXAMPLE:** Your pet products company begins selling a toy that looks like a cross between a dog and a weasel, which you name the Garden Weasel. Soon after your toy hits the market, the makers of the nationally marketed Garden Weasel 5-in-1 garden tool contact you, claiming that you are infringing their trademark. Since you feel that the products are unrelated enough to minimize the chance of customer confusion (the products don't compete with one another), your first thought is to stick with the Garden Weasel name. Think again. The Garden Weasel trademark is distinctive (memorable and unusual) and therefore strong. If you are sued—and you may well be—defending the lawsuit is likely to cost you tens or possibly even hundreds of thousands of dollars that you almost surely can't afford. And if the Garden Weasel mark is strong enough, you may lose the suit, even though the products don't compete. A better approach would probably be to tweak your name a bit, to something like the Lawn Weasel or the Garden Ferret, for instance.

c. Sight, Sound and Meaning Test

Obviously, dual use of identical trademarks can cause customer confusion, as we discussed above. But what about merely similar trademarks? If two marks look alike, sound alike or have the same meaning, the courts could decide that they conflict with each other, just as if they were identical. It is essential to understand that small or superficial differences between two trademarks may not be enough to prevent customer confusion. The difference in spelling, for example, does not make the name "Ekzon" sufficiently different from "Exxon" to avoid trademark problems. And even though they're expressed in two different languages, the names "Le Petit Fleur" and "The Little Flower" have the same meaning, which increases the likelihood that some customers could confuse the two.

> **EXAMPLE:** You open an auto lubrication business and name it Jiffy Oil. A few weeks later, you receive a stern letter from the attorneys of Jiffy Lube, a national chain of auto lubrication businesses. The letter informs you that the name "Jiffy Oil" infringes on their rights to the trademark "Jiffy Lube," since customers are likely to confuse the two names because the names are very similar, are used to describe an almost identical service, and mean pretty much the same thing. They demand that you change your business's name or be

taken to court. You'd be wise to comply with their demand. Their "Jiffy Lube" trademark, though a descriptive term (for fast lubrication), has become a very strong mark over time since customers have come to recognize it as a specific brand of service. And because your shop is a direct competitor of Jiffy Lube, the chance of customer confusion is high.

Christopher Johnson, Publisher of the *Weekly Alibi* (formerly *NuCity*), a free weekly newspaper in Albuquerque, New Mexico

When you are starting a small business there are so many things to think about—important things, like financing, initial marketing, etc. For many people (myself included), the last thing to cross your mind is whether the use of your business name is legal. About three years after I started my weekly newspaper, NuCity, *right when the company was finally stable, a weekly newspaper with a similar name (*New City*) in a different state took note of us and threatened litigation for trademark infringement. So, just at the time that my newspaper was really taking off, I had to decide between fighting a weak lawsuit or changing the name of the paper altogether. Of course, we came up with a much better name, and though it was an expensive process to change all our printed and marketing materials, in the end it was well worth it. Rest assured that the first thing that we did prior to making a final decision on our new name was to verify that no one else had a trademark on that name. I now own the national and international trademark rights to "Weekly Alibi," and can't wait to act like a moron and threaten other newspapers with lawsuits.*

In the future, I will check to see if a name is available before I start any business. If you are starting a business where your name has significant marketing value, it is well worth your time to check to see if your chosen name is available to use and then to complete the process to secure your trademark rights to it.

3. The Dilution Exception

As we've mentioned several times, there is a big exception to the rule that says one trademark infringes another only where there is the likelihood of customer confusion. Even when customer confusion is improbable, courts will stop a business from using a trademark that's the same as or similar to someone else's if the use has diminished—or "diluted"—its distinctiveness. This legal protection kicks in only when a mark is so well known that even if you were to use it in a different context than the original trademark, lots of people would think of the original trademark. For example, a court might stop an athletic shoe manufacturer from using the trademark Exxon or a gas station from calling itself Nike. Even though customers would not be likely to confuse an oil company with a shoe maker, this sort of copying is a legal no-no, since allowing others to use the very famous trademark can chip away at its distinctiveness and slowly reduce its legal strength.

B. Trademark Issues Online

As in many other legal areas, the traditional principles of trademark law are scrambling to keep up with the fast clip of technological change. The Internet has changed many of the rules regarding trademark issues, just as it has created some entirely new ones. This section outlines a number of Net-related concerns regarding trademarks and business names.

1. The Web Has Changed the Rules

As described in the previous section, one of the touchstones of trademark infringement cases is whether or not the two trademarks in question are likely to cause customer confusion. In the pre-Internet world, small, locally oriented businesses didn't have to worry too much about name conflicts as long as no one in their area had a similar name. Today, however, physical distance is often made irrelevant by the omnipresence of the Web.

Particularly if you plan to put your business online, you'll have to worry not only about trademarks of businesses already on the Web, but also those of businesses located anywhere the Web reaches—which, of course, is just about everywhere. Another way of saying this is that if you create a Web page for a small home-based business, your business is no longer local in character—you're essentially launching a national or worldwide business that can compete with businesses everywhere, whether or not those businesses are online.

For example, if you create a website for your antique restoration business, Dalliance Designs, you could be competing with every antique restoration business in the country. If one of these owns the trademark "Dalliance Designs," the fact that you now share the market with that business opens a potentially ugly can of legal worms.

Again, pay attention to the fact that the Web has changed trademark rules for everybody—even businesses that don't go digital. As more and more small businesses launch websites introducing themselves in a keystroke to consumers all over the globe, your purely local, offline business might find itself in competition with businesses several time zones or even continents away. Although courts are still chewing over many trademark issues raised by online commerce, it is already clear that, in some circumstances at least, a Web business with the same name as yours poses just as much a threat of a trademark lawsuit as does a real-life, bricks-and-steel business across the street.

EXAMPLE: Jarrod is a mechanic who opens a small machine shop in a rural area of California. He's lived in the area for 30 years, and knows every business for miles around. Nevertheless, as part of choosing a name for his business, Jarrod carefully checks the phone book and the county register for fictitious business names and ultimately settles on his first choice, Checkers Tool and Die.

All goes smoothly for a few months, until a customer compliments Jarrod on his slick-looking website. This leaves Jarrod totally confused since he hates computers and has only a vague notion of what the Web is. But in talking with his customer about this mysterious website, Jarrod realizes that a machine shop in Florida is also using the name "Checkers Tool and Die," and sells a number of specialized parts via an online catalogue. This doesn't particularly worry Jarrod until his customer (a lawyer with a new Beamer, naturally) goes on to explain that if the distant business can prove it owns the trademark to "Checkers Tool and Die" and convinces a court that it shares the same market as Jarrod, it might be able to force Jarrod to stop using the name.

Although at least one customer has been confused, Jarrod doesn't really expect the Florida outfit to go after him—after all, his business is small, local, provides primarily repair services (with parts as a sideline) and doesn't sell on the Web. Nevertheless, even the possibility of legal trouble worries him—especially because he'd like to open a retail machine parts shop next to his repair shop. After learning that the Florida outfit has been using the name Checkers Tool and Die for years and seems to be putting lots of energy into expanding their website, Jarrod decides to be safe and spend the time and money necessary to change the name of his business to White Mountain Tool & Die before he expands.

2. Domain Name Conflicts and Cybersquatting

Besides making sure that your business name won't create trademark trouble, if you plan to create a website for your business you'll also need to choose a domain name that's legally safe. A domain name (such as nolo.com) is part of a website's URL (such as http://www.nolo.com/index.html), which functions as its Internet "address" online. Later in this chapter we discuss the process of choosing and registering a domain name; for now, we'll focus on the trademark issues to beware of regarding domain names.

The first thing you should understand is that, generally speaking, your domain name will function as a trademark if you conduct business at your site—if you offer products or services for sale. This is true whether or not you register it with the U.S. Patent and Trademark Office (PTO). (As discussed elsewhere in this chapter, registering your domain name with the PTO will strengthen your power to enforce your trademark rights to it, but using it for a commercial purpose is all that's technically necessary to establish your trademark rights to it.) For instance, amazon.com is the domain name for a huge website that sells books and videos—and the name amazon.com also serves as a trademark. This means that trademark law prohibits anyone else from using the name amazon.com for their business.

Keep in mind, however, that if your domain name is generic such as software.com or books.com, it won't qualify for much trademark protection. This rule is the same as for generic business or product names such as lawyer, building supplies or pet food—the law will generally not allow you to establish any trademark rights to these generic terms. But as we discussed earlier (in talking about weak trademarks), even generic domain names can grow stronger with use. Consider etrade.com, which has become almost synonymous with online stock trading. Originally, the name wouldn't have deserved much trademark protection since it wasn't distinctive at all—anyone can slap an "e" on the beginning of a word; now, however, the mark has acquired "secondary meaning" and is entitled to trademark protection.

For most business owners, the best way to make sure their customers will find them online is to simply tack ".com" onto their regular business names. However, while trademark law will allow two or more companies to use the same name as long as it won't confuse customers, the technical limitations of the Web won't allow for two identical domain names. In other words, Ford Trucks and the Ford Modeling Agency won't be able to both use ford.com as their domain name. Since each website must have its own unique address, you may be out of luck if someone is already using your business name plus .com as their domain name. As you can imagine, this is where things can get sticky.

a. Dealing With Domain Name Conflicts

First, keep in mind that if you're starting a brand-new business that you haven't named yet, you might want to make an effort to choose a name that also can be used as a domain name. That way, you can register it as a domain name right away and sidestep the whole issue of what to do if your domain name is already taken. You'll need to decide for yourself how important it is to you to have a domain name that's the same as your business name. If it's really important, then you may have to work hard to come up with a business name that's good for business, available as a domain name and available as a trademark. If it's not that important, then your naming process will be somewhat easier—but you may regret it down the road when your business name can't be registered as a domain name.

There are a few possible scenarios when someone is using your business name as their domain name. One is that you may simply have missed your chance to get that domain name yourself—even though you have trademark rights to it—and will either have to choose a different name or buy it from whoever registered it first. These are likely to be your only options if your mark isn't nationally famous and if it's not likely that customers will be confused by another business using your name.

EXAMPLE: Gene and Beth run a bookstore in New Orleans called Lexicon. After about a year of planning, they decide to launch a website—but are disappointed to find out that the domain name lexicon.com was already taken. By doing a "WhoIs" search on the Web (at www.networksolutions.com), and by going to the lexicon.com website Gene and Beth discover that the owner of lexicon.com is a freelance editor in Chicago. Since Gene and Beth's bookstore doesn't have any national exposure, it would be unlikely that they would be able to force the editor in Chicago to give up the name since the editor's site probably would not confuse customers into thinking there was some association with their bookstore.

On the other hand, asserting trademark rights against someone using your trademark as a domain name may be possible if:

- their use of the trademark is likely to cause customer confusion, or
- your trademark is distinctive and nationally known—even if the other party's use of it is not likely to cause customer confusion. (Recall from Section A above that laws against trademark dilution protect famous marks from use by others, even if customer confusion is not likely.)

EXAMPLE: Let's go back to Gene and Beth's bookstore, Lexicon, but this time assume that the bookstore already had a well-established national mail-order catalog business and the name Lexicon was familiar to a national audience. In this situation, they might be able to assert their trademark rights in court and force the Chicago editor to give up the lexicon.com domain name.

Keep in mind that you will have to weigh carefully the pros and cons of attempting to force someone to give up a domain name based on a potential trademark infringement. On the one hand, the possibility of prevailing and getting the domain name you want may make this course worth it, depending on your business model. On the other hand, remember that lawsuits are costly in time and money, and can easily exceed $10,000 in legal and court fees (and can sometimes cost ten times that amount). If your case is a marginal one, you may be better off simply choosing a different domain name or even buying the name from the other party.

⚠ If you don't defend your trademark from known infringers, you could lose your trademark rights. While this chapter doesn't cover the issues involved in trademark infringement in any depth, you should know that your trademark rights can become weakened if you fail to defend your trademark when you know or should know that it's being infringed. For this reason, it's probably a good idea to pursue a website or any other business or individual that infringes your trademark. For more in-depth information on defending your trademark and dealing with infringers, see *Trademark: Legal Care for Your Business and Product Name*, by Stephen Elias and Kate McGrath (Nolo).

b. Dealing With Cybersquatters

Finally, another possibility you may face is that the domain name you want has already been registered by someone who wants to sell it back to you at a profit. For instance, say you owned a well-known car racing magazine called *Auto Racing Today*. When you were ready to launch a website, you discovered that the domain name autoracingtoday.com was already registered by another business, who offered to sell the name back to you for $250,000 (actually a modest amount compared to similar sales). This practice, known as "cybersquatting," became a real problem in the late nineties before businesses realized the importance of reserving domain names as soon as possible.

A recent federal law known as the Anti-Cybersquatting Consumer Protection Act makes cybersquatting illegal and provides remedies for victims, including getting the domain name back and possibly receiving money damages. To win a cybersquatting lawsuit, you'll have to sue the cybersquatter in federal court and prove a number of things (lawyers call these "elements"):

- the domain name registrant (the cybersquatter) acted in bad faith by registering the name solely to make a profit by selling it back to you
- your mark was distinctive at the time the domain name was registered
- the domain name is identical or confusingly similar to your trademark, and
- you were the first to use the trademark in commerce.

An alternative to a lawsuit is to use a procedure set forth by ICANN (short for International Corporation for Assigned Names and Numbers), the international group now in charge of Internet domain name policy. ICANN's process for resolving cybersquatting disputes is known as the Uniform Domain Name Dispute Resolution Policy (UDRP), and typically will cost far less and take less time than a lawsuit. The case you'll have to prove is similar to what would be involved in a federal lawsuit, that:

- the domain name is identical or confusingly similar to your trademark
- the registrant has no legitimate interests in or rights to the domain name, and
- the domain name was registered and/or is being used in bad faith.

Another advantage of the ICANN procedure is that it can be used in international domain name disputes, while a lawsuit based on the Anti-Cybersquatting Act can only be brought against domain name registrants in the United States. For more information, visit ICANN's website at www.icann.org.

3. Using Meta Tags That Conflict With Trademarks

Meta tags are keywords embedded in the HTML source code of Web pages that search engines like Yahoo! or Excite look for when conducting a

search. For instance, if you did a Yahoo! search for the term "digital video," the search engine would check the meta tags of all the pages on the Web, and return to you the ones that contained "digital video" in their source code. Assuming that sites such as *DV Magazine* and Sony Electronics would have included the term "digital video" in their meta tags, your search would bring up those sites and those of whoever else used that meta tag.

When using meta tags for your site, be careful not to use someone else's trademark without their permission—doing so may subject you to a trademark infringement lawsuit. It's becoming common for trademark owners to sue others who use their trademarks as meta tags to deceptively lure browsers to their sites. For example, a site called Calvin Designer Label used the words "Playboy" and "Playmate" as meta tags so that anyone searching for those words would be directed to the Calvin page. *Playboy* magazine sued, and a federal court found Calvin Designer Label liable for infringement and ordered it to stop using *Playboy's* trademarks as meta tags.

On the other hand, there may be instances in which using someone else's trademark in your meta tags may be legally okay—even without their permission. Generally speaking, this is more likely if the use is for a legitimate descriptive purpose. In another *Playboy* case, the famous magazine sued Terri Welles, a former Playmate, for using the terms "Playmate of the Year" and its abbreviation "PMOY" at her website, www.terriwelles.com, and within its meta tags. Ms. Welles had won the title Playmate of the Year in 1981, and was using her site to promote herself for her modeling career. A court found that her use of "Playmate of the Year" and "PMOY" was permissible, since she had earned the title and was using it legitimately to describe herself. Her case was also strengthened by the fact that her site offered numerous disclaimers that her site was not endorsed by or affiliated with *Playboy* magazine.

Remember also that owners of weak, descriptive trademarks don't have much, if any power to stop you from using part or all of their trademark. For instance, you could safely include the words "house" and "garden" in the meta tags of your home design website without being afraid that *House & Garden* magazine would sue you. The same goes for using the word "news" for your hiking site, without fear of a lawsuit from *U.S. News & World Report* magazine. Of course, using actual trademarked phrases like "U.S. News & World Report" or "House & Garden" as meta tags would probably get you into trouble.

Unfortunately, there's no clear test for determining whether a use of someone else's trademark is permissible as a meta tag. The only way to get a definitive answer may be through a lawsuit, something you probably don't want to risk. Proceed with caution when using any trademarks owned by others in your website or in its meta tags, and definitely avoid any deceptive use of trademarks in an effort to lure browsers to your site.

C. Name Searches

By now you get the picture that a dispute over business names is no walk in the park. To avoid potential trademark hassles later on, you need to do some digging before you finally settle on a name for your business. The main way to accomplish this is to conduct a name search to find out whether another business is already using a name that's identical or similar to the one you want to use. As you'll see in the next few pages, the main practical question here is how extensive that search should be in your particular case. The information in this section will help you figure out how to go about researching your chosen name, and what to do once you've found one that you'll be able to use—and protect—as a trademark.

⚠️ **This section on doing a name search covers how to find out if someone is already using a name as a trademark, not as a domain name.** The techniques to find out whether a name is being used as a trademark are different and more complex than finding out whether a name is available as a domain name. To find out if a domain name is available, simply go to the Network Solutions site at www.networksolutions.com and enter the name you want. Their interactive database will tell you whether it's available and if not, who has registered it. Doing a name search for trademark purposes, on the other hand, requires consulting more sources, as described in this section.

As you should now understand, how thoroughly you should search will depend largely on the size and geographical scope of your business and your plans for its future. If you plan from day one to sell a product nationally—whether via catalog, through retailers or online—you'll obviously need to worry about trademarks across the country. If, on the other hand, you're starting a small home-based service business, don't plan to advertise and are relatively certain you won't expand geographically, a search of names in your county, and perhaps state, could be enough from a practical point of view (though we recommend that you always search widely so that you at least know what's out there).

Also keep in mind that the extent of your search isn't only how widely you search geographically, but also how deeply you search—in terms of looking not only for identical names, but also for those that are merely similar or have a slight resemblance to yours. Searching for the exact name (also called a "direct hit" search) is quick and cheap, but risks missing look- and sound-alikes. A more in-depth search, such as one that looks for names with slight variations in spelling, is safer, but can get quite complicated and expensive.

1. Sources of Name Information

Before you start researching your chosen name, it's important to realize that there is no one place to look. In large part, this is because a business can—and millions do—establish a trademark simply by using it. Since millions of marks aren't registered with the government, in addition to checking federal and state trademark databases you'll want to check many other sources of information, such as business directories and phone books, for unregistered trademarks. You should check some or preferably all of the following resources for name conflicts, depending on how extensive a search you need; methods for searching these databases are discussed below in Section 2.

a. The World Wide Web

We recommend this one first because it is huge, fast and free. By using several of the Web's search engines, such as Yahoo!, AltaVista or Excite, you can quickly see whether someone else on the Web is using a specific term and how they are using it. Search engines are easy to use; simply enter the terms you're looking for (often called a "query") and the engine will scan the Web and retrieve any sites that contain the terms in your query. Consult the "help" area of the particular search engine you're using for more detailed instructions on how to construct your queries.

Another easy way to check trademarks online is to go to the Network Solutions website at www.networksolutions.com and put in variations of the name you want to use. If another company has reserved a domain name that contains your trademark, chances are you won't be able to use it. If the domain name qualifies as a trademark—which essentially means that they're using it to sell a product or service online—then, as described earlier in this chapter, you may not be able to use it as a trademark if your use would be likely to confuse customers.

b. Phone Directories

Don't overlook the phone book as a valuable collection of local name information. If you find someone who's using the name you want in your local area and your businesses are similar, there's no reason to waste money searching the federal trademark register or other government databases.

Keep in mind that if your businesses are different enough, you might be able to use the name. If the name you want isn't in your phone book, make sure you use other sources, such as the Thomas Register, discussed just below.

c. Industry Sources

Trade publications and business directories can be great sources of business name information (and they can also give you good ideas for names). You can also call trade associations and chambers of commerce to ask if they can provide lists or directories of businesses in the area.

 A particularly useful (and free) resource for finding unregistered trademarks is the Thomas Register website (www.thomasregister.com). It's a cross-industry database that includes hundreds of thousands of trademarks and service marks. But always keep in mind that any particular list you use to search for unregistered marks, such as the Thomas Register, may be incomplete.

d. Federal Trademark Database

Everyone starting a business, no matter how tiny and local, should search the federal trademark database to determine whether the name they want to use has already been registered by a similar business in the United States. The most important reason to do this is to avoid being sued for "willful infringement." That's because if you use a trademark already registered at the federal level (even if yours is a tiny, local business), you can be sued for knowingly violating someone else's trademark—even if you didn't actually check the federal database and know it was there. Searching the federal database can be complicated, and there are a few different ways to go about it (including hiring a trademark search firm to do the work for you). Search options for the federal trademark database are discussed below in Section 2.

e. State Databases

Many state corporation and LLC filing offices (usually the Secretary of State) maintain databases of registered names of corporations, limited partnerships and LLCs. To check to see if a name appears in your state's corporate, LLC or limited partnership database, contact your state corporate filing office to determine its process for name searches. You may be able to search for names by phone, by mail or online.

In addition, check your state's trademark registry. This registry is often part of the Secretary of State's department, though sometimes it's its own department. Find out the trademark office's rules for searching, or you can hire a trademark search firm to do the work for you. Search firms are discussed below, in Section 2.

f. County Fictitious Business Name Databases

Many counties maintain a database of fictitious business names (FBNs) that have been registered in that county. Even if you won't be using a fictitious business name—because you'll use your own name or your corporate, limited partnership or LLC name—it's a good idea to check the FBNs used by other businesses in your county or state. Depending on how widely you're planning to search, you may want to search nearby counties or every county in the state.

Keep in mind that the free or relatively cheap searches offered by state and county agencies usually check only for exact matches—and won't tell you whether a similar name is included in that database. If, for example, the county clerk's office tells you that "The Dog House" does not appear in its fictitious name database, you might be surprised later to find that "The Dawg Haus" has been in business for years. In short, you may have to do a more extensive search than the one provided by the state or county office.

⚠ Lots of trademarks can't be found in any county or state databases. It's important to remember that, just because a name doesn't appear in any county or state name databases, doesn't mean another business doesn't already own that trademark. Use of the name, not registration, is what creates trademark ownership. Plenty of businesses own trademarks that they have never registered, so it's important to check for unregistered trademarks using the resources we discussed in subsections a, b and c, above. And many businesses won't bother registering at the state level, but will register a federal trademark. That's one reason why, if you plan to invest time and money in establishing your trademark, it's essential that you do a federal trademark search, too.

> **EXAMPLE:** Tom and Jen, both veterinarians in California, search their county's fictitious business name database for the name "Critter Care," which they want to use for the animal hospital they're planning to open. They don't find anyone else using the name in their area, so they believe they can use it. But just to be safe, Jen decides to check the California state trademark directory for the name. She finds out that a California corporation has already obtained state trademark protection for the name "Critter Care." Since that corporation was doing business under its own name and not a fictitious one, it didn't have to register with any county fictitious name databases, so even if Tom and Jen had checked fictitious names statewide they wouldn't have found it. (Tom and Jen also would have found the name by checking the Secretary of State's corporate name database.)

2. Searching the Federal Trademark Database

As discussed above, to avoid a charge of willful infringement it's a very good idea to check the federal trademark registry, maintained by the U.S. Patent and Trademark Office. Only the tiniest of microbusinesses should consider not checking this registry, and only after careful thought and consideration. Most businesses should accept the fact that the Internet and other communication technologies have simply created too many potential trademark conflicts and rightly conclude that they need to search the PTO's database of federally registered trademarks.

If possible, begin your search with the free trademark database on the PTO's website. The PTO's database consists of all federally registered marks and all marks for which registration is pending. To start, go to the PTO's Trademark Electronic Business Center at http://www.uspto.gov/web/menu/tmebc/index.html and choose "Search." Then follow the instructions you see on the screen.

If using the Internet isn't feasible for you, visit your local Patent and Trademark Depository Library (PTDL)—there's at least one in every state —and use their research materials. (For a list of PDTLs, see Appendix A.) If a PTDL isn't convenient, a large public library or special business and government library near you should carry the federal trademark register, which contains all federal trademarks and service marks arranged by categories of goods and services.

Another option is to hire a professional search firm to do the work for you. You can order a complete search of registered and unregistered marks through Trademark Express, Thompson and Thompson, CCH Trademark Research Corporation or one of the PTDLs that offer electronic search services for very reasonable fees (for example, see the Sc[i]3 website at www.sci3.com).

If you decide to hire a search firm, the cheapest and easiest type of national search is a direct-hit search, which will reveal whether another business has registered an identical name with the federal Patent and Trademark Office (PTO). You can often hire one of the companies mentioned above to do a direct-hit search for you for less than $50. But while direct-hit searches are quick and cheap, they

usually won't turn up trademarks that are similar, but not identical, to the name you're considering. For example, if you want to name your softball training center "The Strike Zone," a direct-hit search may not turn up a trademark for "The S. Zone." And as discussed above, any mark that looks like, sounds like or means the same as your name could present a trademark conflict.

More extensive national searches take a lot more time and money, but may be necessary if you plan for your business to reach a wide audience and want to eliminate any risk of infringing someone else's existing trademark. For an in-depth search, it may make the most sense to hire a search firm; expect a fee of roughly $200 to $350 for a professional, comprehensive search. If you do decide to hire search services, you're likely to save money if you do some quick, preliminary searches on the Internet yourself—to rule out some of your choices. For more information on national trademark searches, see *Trademark: Legal Care for Your Business and Product Name,* by Stephen Elias and Kate McGrath (Nolo).

3. Analyzing Your Search Results

If, after your search, you determine that the name you've chosen does not already belong to someone else (or that someone else isn't using a similar name), you can go ahead and use it. Assuming you really are the first user of the name, you'll own the trademark, which will give you the right to stop others from using it in certain situations. But since registering a trademark conveys important additional rights and protections, you may want to register your name with the federal and state governments. The basics of trademark registration are discussed in Section E.

But what if your search (or a search done by a professional firm) turned up an identical or similar name to the one you want to use? If the name is a famous trademark, it's probably time to pick a new name. Remember that if using your business name diminishes a famous trademark's distinctiveness or disparages its reputation for quality, the owner of the famous trademark may stop you from using your name even if its customers aren't likely to be confused between its products and yours.

 If your business will have a website, check to see if a similar domain name is free too. As mentioned above in Section B2, if your Internet business will be important to you it may be worth it to pick a name that can also be used as a domain name. You can check whether a domain name is available at the Network Solutions site at www.networksolutions.com.

If the name has been registered for official trademark protection, especially at the federal level, you should take that as a huge "No Trespassing" sign that should be taken seriously. Owners of federally registered trademarks have the right to use their trademarks anywhere in the country, and it is easy for them to sue and recover damages. If your search shows that the name is being used but isn't registered at the federal or state level, then you might have a bit more leeway—but not much more. Since use, not registration, conveys trademark

rights, you still need to be very careful not to infringe that owner's rights.

That being said, there are a few instances when taking a name that is already being used by someone else is okay. As we just mentioned, if the name is being used for a company that provides a very different product or service than the one you plan to sell, then you may have good reason to move forward with your plans to use the name. This is especially true if the two businesses serve only local markets and are hundreds of miles apart.

For example, just because a tiny clothing store in Boston calls itself Nature's Calling doesn't mean that you, in Aspen, Colorado, can't use Nature's Calling for your plumbing business. But if you wanted to start a clothing store in your town called Nature's Calling, and one already exists in Boston, then you should at the very least do more research before using it. If a federal trademark register search indicates that the Boston store has registered the mark "Nature's Calling," your subsequent use is a clear legal no-no. But even if the name is not registered and the Boston store seems like a local outfit, it could have plans to expand its territory—or, as is even more likely—to create a website. Neither of these actions would necessarily forbid your use of the name on your original store, but could prevent you from using it more widely. The bottom line is that even if you feel certain that your business is different enough from that of the trademark owner to allow you to use the name, you should proceed only with lots and lots of caution.

 How Would You Feel? If you are uncertain as to whether your proposed trademark would infringe an existing trademark, use a variant of the Golden Rule: How would you feel if you owned the existing trademark and someone started to use it? Ask a few friends the same question. If any of the answers are "Pissed off," consider choosing a different name or at least invest a few hundred dollars in a consultation with an experienced trademark lawyer.

Nolo offers several other resources on name and trademark issues. For more help with understanding the nuances of different types of trademarks, picking a bulletproof one, and searching trademarks and registering one, by far the best source of sophisticated information is *Trademark: Legal Care for Your Business and Product Name,* by Stephen Elias and Kate McGrath (Nolo). For specific information on the registration process, including step-by-step instructions, read *The Trademark Registration Kit,* by attorneys Patricia Gima and Stephen Elias. And you'll find lots of free information on trademarks and business names in the Patent, Trademark and Copyright area of Nolo.com's Legal Encyclopedia, which you'll find online at www.nolo.com/category/pct_home.html.

D. Choosing and Registering a Domain Name

If you plan to have a website for your business, you'll probably need to create and choose a domain name for it. We say "probably" because it is possible to have a website that uses someone else's domain name, such as that of your Internet Service Provider (ISP). It's fairly common for ISPs to allow their users to maintain Web pages using the domain name of the ISP, with the user's name as the suffix. The standard format for the URL is www.ispname.com/~username. For instance, if someone used Netcom as their ISP and their user name was ted2000, their personal Web page address would be www.netcom.com/~ted2000.

Since many ISPs offer a limited-size Web page as part of their service, this is likely the cheapest way to create a presence online. But since you'll likely only be allowed a tiny website (if any) as part of your ISP service, any decent-sized business will almost certainly need a larger site. Factor in how simple and inexpensive it is to register your own domain name, and it hardly makes sense not to do so.

Registering a domain name is separate from setting up a website. When you register a domain name, all that you're doing is securing the right to use that address for your website. You'll still need to find a company to host your site, which means keeping your website files on their servers. Depending on the size of your site, you may have to pay upwards of $100 per month. (If you or one of your associates is computer savvy, you can set up your own server for considerably less money over the long haul.) To find a local Internet Service Provider, look in your phone book under categories such as "Internet Access Provider," "Web Hosting" or "Computers—Internet Services." Or, to find one online, go to www.score.org, Business Resources, and enter your zip code. The site will give you a list of Web hosting companies in your area, along with how much they charge, what kind of hosting they do, and a link to their site.

1. Picking a Great Domain Name

Choosing a domain name should be simple—a great domain name should be memorable, clever and easily spelled. But keep in mind that names that aren't ordinary and descriptive won't qualify for much trademark protection. Many good domain names—for instance, coffee.com, drugs.com and business.com—are not eligible for trademark protection because they are the names of whole categories of products or services. Likewise, domain names that use surnames or geographic names are likewise unlikely to get trademark protection. (Of course, it's possible for a generic name, such as etrade, to become famous and develop "secondary meaning," as we discussed in Section A2, above.)

Many of these generic names, however, are potentially powerful because of the way people find information on the Internet, so consider carefully whether it will benefit you to choose a domain name that's distinctive and protectable or easy to find and not protectable. One good strategy may be to choose to use one of each, such as peets.com and coffee.com. But even if you come up with a domain name or names that are brilliant from a marketing standpoint, remember that one of the key points of this chapter is that your domain name is at risk if it legally conflicts with any one of the millions of commercial trademarks that already exist.

A huge downside in picking a domain name is that millions of names are already taken. For example, if your business name is Flaky Cakes, you may find that FlakyCakes.com already belongs to someone else, so you'll have to use a different domain name (or change your business name). Assuming you are willing to choose a different domain name (this could be an advantage if your business name is a bore), you'll need to get to work. You can use "MyNameFinder" at the Network Solutions site (www.networksolutions.com) to come up with some creative combinations. Enter a keyword or two that are relevant to your business, and MyNameFinder will return a list of domain names that are still available.

For instance, say you are starting a fly-fishing website, but you know that flyfishing.com and flyfish.com are taken. You go to MyNameFinder and put in the keywords "fly," "fish" and "sport." MyNameFinder returns the following list of available domain names:

fishfly.org	flyfishsport.com
fishflysport.com	flyfishsport.net
fishflysport.net	flyfishsport.org
fishflysport.org	flysport.net
fishsport.net	flysport.org
fishsport.org	sportfly.com
fishsportfly.com	sportfly.org

Again, even if you find a domain name that's available, it's important to make sure the domain name you pick doesn't conflict with someone else's trademark. At the risk of being a little repetitive, let's step back for a moment and make sure you understand this crucial point. Remember, your domain name will probably function as a trademark just as your regular business name will—assuming you conduct business at your site. (This is true whether or not you register it with the U.S. Patent and Trademark Office—registering your domain

name with the PTO will strengthen your power to enforce your rights to it, but using it for a commercial purpose is all that's technically necessary to establish your rights to it.) It follows that you are not allowed to use a domain name that's likely to cause customer confusion between your company and another, whether that company is online or off.

2. Registering Your Domain Name

Once you've found a domain name that's legally safe, go online to a domain name registrar—we suggest Network Solutions (NSI) at www.networksolutions.com. But if you'd like to do some comparison shopping, a list of approved registries is offered at www.internic.net/alpha.html. At NSI's site, you'll first be prompted to enter your proposed domain name in order to see if it's already been registered. If it has been, you'll need to choose a different name (or pursue other options; see Section B2 above). If the domain name is not already included in NSI's database, then you'll be allowed to proceed and register the name. Fees will vary depending on what options you choose, but all are quite affordable. Once you've chosen your options, simply enter information about your business and provide credit card information (or if you prefer, call NSI and do it by phone).

That's pretty much it. All it takes is about five minutes to go from You to You.com. Other than remembering to renew (how often depends on the renewal period that you choose), there's not much else to it.

You may want to register several domain names. In addition to your business name, you may want to register the names of your products or services, or other related names. Remember that names of your products or services may be as or more important from a marketing perspective than your business name. It's also a good idea to register common misspellings of your primary domain name and names that reflect the nature of your products or services. For example, if you design and sell gourmet aprons, and your primary domain name is countrystyle.com, you might also want to register aprons.com so that customers who are looking for aprons and enter "aprons.com" into their browser will land at your site.

Apply for federal trademark registration with the PTO. In addition to applying for protection for your business name, you should also try to register your domain name with the PTO. While you don't need to register to establish your rights to your domain name, registering it will strengthen your power to enforce your rights to it against infringers, and will prevent someone else from registering the same name, which could save a lot of headache in the future.

For far more information on choosing and registering domain names, as well as avoiding domain name conflicts, check out Nolo's free Internet Law Center at http://nolo.com/category/ ilaw_home.html. Also read *Domain Names: How to Choose & Protect a Great Name for Your Website,* by attorneys Stephen Elias & Patricia Gima (Nolo), an excellent book that goes into far more detail in this area than is possible here.

E. Trademark Registration

By now you understand that registering your trade-mark with the federal and/or state government will strengthen your rights to it and make it easier to protect the name in case of a dispute. Registration is simply the process of notifying the state or, more commonly, the U.S. government that you're using a particular trademark. When registration is complete, the trademark gets placed on an official list of registered names commonly called a trade-mark register. The U.S. Patent and Trademark Office (PTO) maintains two registers, the Principal Register and the Supplemental Register. State trademark offices have their own systems.

When people refer to a federally registered trademark, they're generally talking about marks on the Principal Register. Trademarks that appear on the Principal Register get the most protection, and the penalties can be harsh for those who improperly use a name that appears on it. The Supplemental Register, on the other hand, is reserved for weaker, less distinctive trademarks that don't qualify for the Principal Register. The main function of the Supplemental Register is to provide notice of a mark's current use to anyone who does a trademark search. After five years on the Supplemental Register, a mark may qualify to be moved to the Principal Register if it's been in continuous use during that period.

Most states maintain just one register for all trademarks. State registration doesn't give as many benefits as federal registration, so it generally makes most sense to register federally for the widest scope of protection. Some trademarks, however, don't qualify for federal registration because they aren't used in national, international or territorial commerce—in other words, they're only used within the state. These marks can only be registered at the state level. Although use of a trademark on the Internet almost guarantees the right to apply for federal registration, if you truly are only using the mark within your state, state registration may be the only option.

The Patent and Trademark Office (PTO)—the office that administers federal trademarks—provides registration forms and instructions, which are available from a number of sources, including the PTO's website at http://www.uspto.gov. For simple trademarks such as business names (as opposed to trademarks for special packaging or product design —called "trade dress" in the biz), the instructions will probably be easy enough to follow. (You can also fill in and submit the form online at the PTO's Trademark Electronic Business Center—for detailed instructions on filing online see "Registering a Trademark Online," below.) But as with any legal system, there are tricks and traps. So for more information on federally registering your trademark, we recommend *The Trademark Registration Kit,* by Patricia Gima and Stephen Elias (Nolo).

State registration processes are generally similar to the federal system's procedure. Contact your state's trademark office for more information.

Registering a Trademark Online

If You Haven't Yet Used Your Trademark:
Go to the PTO's Trademark Electronic Business Center at http://www.uspto.gov/web/menu/ tmebc/index.html and choose "Filing." To file electronically (you'll need to pay with a credit card), click eTEAS. Or, to complete the application online, print it out and send it in, click printTEAS (you'll need to print out your completed application and mail it to the PTO with a check). Then follow the instructions provided. Choose the "intent-to-use" (ITU) option, since you haven't yet used your trademark in commerce, and provide a drawing or image of the mark. Be prepared to respond to the trademark examiner's questions and concerns within the deadlines assigned to you.

If You Have Already Used Your Trademark Commercially:
Go to the PTO's Trademark Electronic Business Center at http://www.uspto.gov/web/menu/ tmebc/index.html and choose "Filing." To file electronically (you'll need to pay with a credit card), click eTEAS. Or, to complete the application online, print it out and send it in, click printTEAS (you'll need to print out your completed application and mail it to the PTO with a check). Then follow the instructions provided. Choose the "actual use" option, since you are already commercially using the mark. Provide the information as requested: a drawing or image of the trademark, samples of how the trademark is actually being used, the first date the trademark was commercially used anywhere and the first date the trademark was used outside your state. Be prepared to respond to the trademark examiner's questions and concerns within the deadlines assigned to you.

F. Winning Names for Your Business, Products and Services

Now that you have a general idea of the legal hurdles you need to clear and the snags and traps to watch out for, let the naming begin! Despite the hassles involved in learning a little trademark law, choosing names for your business and its products or services remains one of the more fun parts of starting your business. It gives you a chance to use your creative juices to come up with a name that is both marketable and infused with your individual personality (or the collective personalities of your business partners). A business name can help you establish the overall vibe of your business, from strictly professional to downright funky to a dozen things in between.

Besides legal restrictions and personal preferences, the traditions and realities of your particular industry or business will probably have a lot to do with what kind of business name you choose. Good, memorable business and product names range from the clever (SuperFantastic Bubble Plastic, Netscape Navigator, Liquid Paper) to the straightforward (24-Hour Fitness, Fruit Roll-Ups, Jenny Craig Weight Loss Centres) to sometimes even the cryptic (Yahoo!, Chia Pet, Floam). In part because there really are so many different kinds of businesses and so many approaches to choosing a distinctive name, it's impossible to give any kind of specific advice on choosing a great name. There are, however, a few things that are helpful to keep in mind when choosing your business names.

- Especially for small local businesses, sometimes straightforward, informative names work better than fancy ones. For example, if you plan to open a shop selling aquarium supplies and tropical fish in Seattle, "Seattle Aquariums & Fish" may be a far more effective name than "The Lure of the Ocean." Also, since humble, descriptive names qualify for less trademark protection (unless they are already famous; see Section A2, above), choosing an ordinary name—especially one with a geographic identifier—will make you less likely to infringe on someone else's trademark, since ordinary, descriptive names don't qualify for much protection (assuming you make sure no one else is already using it in your immediate area).

- Think about how your customers will locate your business and your products. If you don't expect customers to seek out or remember your company as a whole, but only its products, it's silly to focus much attention on the business name (which you may never use as a trademark). For instance, while millions of people know the product The Clapper and its commercial jingle ("Clap on! Clap off! The Clapper!"), few know or care who its makers are.

- Before you finally commit to a name, get some feedback from potential customers, suppliers and others in your support network. They may come up with a downside to a potential name or suggest an improvement you haven't thought of. Doing this type of homework is especially important if you will market your goods or services to customers who are members of several different ethnic groups. You obviously don't want to choose a name or symbol and learn later that it offends or turns off a key group of customers. For example, one organization we know couldn't figure out why it got such a cold shoulder from Mexican-Americans. The answer turned out to be that the shape, size and type used on their signs were similar to a "No Trespassers—Keep Out" sign widely used in Mexico. And virtually everyone with email has by now seen a widely circulated humor piece on a number of advertising translation blunders—such as Kentucky Fried Chicken's "finger lickin' good" slogan reading in China as "eat your fingers off."

- Niche businesses are often identified by their trade name, even when the focus is on the products, meaning that it is wise to pay particular attention to picking a memorable name if you will try to capture a particular,

small field. The publisher of this book, Nolo, is a good example. Even though book buyers in other fields usually identify books they want by title or author, since Nolo books occupy a specific niche, many customers have come to recognize its name, often going into a bookstore and asking where the Nolo books are. In other words, Nolo has come to mean "self-help law" to many customers familiar with it, in contrast to the name HarperCollins —a large publisher of books on many topics —which might not evoke anything particular in most book customers' minds.

- In certain service businesses where an owner's (or small group of owners') personal attention and savvy is important (for example, architecture or accounting), it is common to use the owner's name, as in Charles Schwab. In other service and retail businesses, it is more common to use creative names— Kinko's and Fuddrucker's come to mind— and not only for the business itself, but sometimes for its products, too.

EXAMPLE: David and Donna operate a car wash named Storm, which develops a good deal of name recognition in the city. Besides relying on the reputation of their trade name, they come up with clever names for various service packages (such as Sunday Shower, Typhoon Tuesday and the Everyday Squall Special) in hopes that those names will catch on as well.

- Be sure your trade or business name will still be appropriate if and when your business grows. For example, if you open Miami Surf Shop, will it be a problem (or an advantage) if you want to open a second store in Orlando? Especially if you plan to sell products on the Internet, you should think twice about giving your business a geographical identifier. Similarly, if you start a business selling and installing canvas awnings using the name Sturdy Canvas Awnings, your name might be a burden if you decide to also start making other products such as canvas signs. On the other hand, the name Sturdy Canvas would let you move into all sorts of canvas products, such as duffel bags, canvas signs and drop cloths.

Think national even if you act local. As discussed throughout this chapter, even though you may plan to open just one local office or store, it's a good idea to be sure your name is safe from trademark conflicts on a statewide or even national basis (and, if appropriate, from domain name conflicts). That way if your business takes off, you won't bump into someone else who already uses the name in another area or online.

☑ Chapter 3 Checklist

☐ Familiarize yourself with the basics of trademark law, including what types of trademarks qualify for maximum legal protection.

☐ Draft lists of business, product and domain names that could work.

☐ If you plan to do business online, check to see whether your proposed business names are available as domain names. (Ideally, your domain name(s) will be the same as your business and/or product names.)

☐ If the online aspect of your business will be important to you, narrow your list to those names which are available as domain names.

☐ Do a trademark search of the names on your list.

☐ If any names are already being used as trademarks, eliminate the ones which are either already famous trademarks or would lead to customer confusion if you also used the name.

☐ Choose between the names that are still on your list.

☐ Register your business and product names as domain names whenever possible.

☐ Register your business and product names as trademarks.

Choosing a Legal and Lucrative Business Location

A. Picking the Right Spot 4/2

    1. Planting Yourself in Rich Soil 4/2

    2. Keeping Rent Within Your Budget 4/3

    3. Getting the Right Physical Features 4/4

B. Complying With Zoning Laws 4/6

    1. Making Sure That You Comply With Zoning Laws 4/7

    2. Finding Out What Laws Apply to Your Business 4/7

    3. Dealing With Snags in Zoning Approval 4/8

C. Commercial Leases 4/9

D. When Your Home Is Your Office 4/10

    1. Zoning Restrictions on Home Offices 4/11

    2. The Home-Office Tax Deduction 4/13

    3. Insurance and the Home Business 4/16

For many types of businesses, location can mean the difference between feast or famine. Other enterprises will do more or less the same whether they're located in downtown Manhattan or in a deep crevasse on Mars. Not only does the importance of location vary greatly from business to business, but what makes a location desirable for one business might not work for another. Since there's no universal definition of what makes a location good for business, it's important for every business owner to figure out how location will (or will not) contribute to the success of her business—and to choose a spot accordingly.

That being said, there are some basic issues to consider when choosing a business location. For one, you'll want to make sure the location makes economic sense. You won't want to spend a fortune for a spot on an exclusive commercial strip unless it's really going to pay off. It's obviously important that the rent for your business space fits into your overall budget. But don't be too frugal in this area—even the best-run business will fail if its customers can't find it or don't want to go to an unsafe neighborhood. And, of course, the location that you choose needs to be legally acceptable for whatever you plan to do there. Especially if you are planning to work from home or in a non-business area, you'll need to check zoning laws to see if they prohibit your type of business. This chapter will help you figure out how to find a suitable place that meets all the needs of your business and complies with your local laws.

Planning to work from home? If you plan to use your home as your office, you can skip directly to Section D, which discusses special issues for home businesses. Working from home can be a much simpler arrangement than renting a separate space, but it could put you in violation of zoning and other laws that regulate residential and business spaces. In Section D, we'll alert you to what laws you may need to comply with and discuss other legal issues such as the home-office tax deduction.

A. Picking the Right Spot

Number one on your list should be to figure out how important location is to your business. For some businesses, the classic "location, location, location" advice definitely applies. But for others, location may be a lot less important than getting affordable rental space. And for plenty of businesses, location is practically irrelevant: wholesalers, service businesses that do all their work at the customer's location (like roofers or plumbers), mail-order companies and Internet-based businesses are just a few examples. Especially if you can pass on your rent savings to your customers, picking a spot in an out-of-the-way area might be to your advantage. In other words, if location isn't that crucial to your business, don't blow all your start-up money on an expensive space in a thriving location.

If, on the other hand, you determine that location will be important to your business success, you'll need to figure out the best place to locate so that lots of customers can find you. It's one thing to know that you need a good location, but it can be harder to figure out what makes a location good. Ask yourself questions like these:

- Will customers come on foot?
- Will customers drive and, if so, where will they park?
- Will more customers come if you locate near other similar businesses?
- Will the reputation of the neighborhood or even of a particular building help draw customers?

Often there is no one answer. As you struggle to answer these and similar questions, here are a few things you'll want to consider.

1. Planting Yourself in Rich Soil

The key to picking a profitable location is to figure out what factors will increase customer volume for your unique business, and then to concentrate on finding a location that achieves as many of them as possible. For example, if you're opening a coffee shop, you may assume your customer volume will be highest if there's lots of pedestrian traffic nearby during the hours you plan to be open. Furthermore, if you envision your cafe to be a mellow place to sit and read, you'd probably prefer a university area or shopping district full of people with time to kill, rather than an area buzzing with busy business-people. If, on the other hand, you plan to open a small coffee shop with no tables—just fast, high-volume service—a busy downtown office district might be the right spot.

Audrey Wackerley, owner of RetroFit, a vintage clothing store in San Francisco, California:

When we first opened we got a space in the perfect neighborhood, with lots of thrift stores, coffee shops and other walk-in type businesses on a strip with lots of foot traffic (plus, it was only a few blocks from my apartment). But we were on a cross street a few doors around the corner from Valencia Street, the main strip. We did okay, but nothing like the shops on Valencia itself. Finally we got a good deal on a storefront on Valencia Street, and we moved. Our business practically tripled! We do pay a bit more for the better space, but our boost in sales more than makes up for it.

Keep in mind that different types of businesses attract customers in different ways. One key distinction is foot traffic versus automobile traffic. An auto repair shop, for example, will obviously draw customers in radically different ways than the coffee shop. For the auto shop, the choicest locale is a well-traveled street, where it will be seen by many drivers who will easily be able to pull into the lot. For an urban coffee shop, on the other hand, a popular location might be in an area where there are lots of people passing on foot. But of course no rule is absolute, and even some coffee shops thrive because commuters stop for "to go" coffee and baked goods every morning.

Also think about whether it would benefit your business to be around similar businesses that are already drawing the type of customers that you want. A women's clothing store, for example, would no doubt profit from being near other clothing shops, since many women shopping for clothes tend to spend at least a few hours in a particular area. The point is, the perfect location for any business is a very individual matter. Spend some time figuring out the habits of the customers you want to attract, and then choose a location that fits.

2. Keeping Rent Within Your Budget

One obvious and important issue in finding a business space is finding a space that you can afford. Chances are that you have found or will find a fabulous spot that you can only dream about because the monthly rent is so high. While it's okay to dream, don't be foolish enough to overpay for a space that you can't afford. As part of your business planning (discussed in detail in Chapter 5), determine how much rent you can afford each month and stick to it.

One good way to research how much rent is reasonable for an area is to call a commercial broker or agent in your area and have a chat about how much space generally goes for in the areas you're considering. Brokers and agents are great sources of information on the going rates for rent in various neighborhoods. They'll generally give you an average figure for what commercial space costs per square foot per year in a given area; once you have this figure, you can compare it to the costs of any potential spaces you're considering. Keep in mind that agents and brokers are self-interested professionals, and may benefit from higher rents. In other words, don't necessarily accept the figures you're told are the going rate as written in stone.

Remember that square footage rates are generally given in cost per year, so once you multiply the rate by the square footage of a space, you'll need to divide it by 12 to determine the monthly rent.

EXAMPLE: Jennifer and Oliver are planning to open a theater in a certain neighborhood of their city. The call a few real estate brokers out of the phone book whose ads indicated they handle commercial space leasing. All the brokers say that commercial space in area they're interested in generally goes for $10 per square foot (Jennifer and Oliver know that this is an annual figure, which works out to about 83 cents per square foot per month). A few weeks later, Jennifer and Oliver notice a building for rent, and call the agent to find out more information about it. The agent tells them that the monthly rent is $1,800, and that the space is 2,400 square feet. Jennifer and Oliver do the math and see that this place is going for slightly less than the going rate for the area:

$1,800 per month
x 12 months per year = $21,600 per year

$21,600 per year
÷ 2,400 square feet = $9 per year per square foot

They figure that if the space rented out for the going rate, $10 per square foot, they'd have to pay $2,000 per month for the space.

$10 per square foot per year
x 2,400 square feet = $24,000 per year

$24,000 per year
÷ 12 months per year = $2,000 per month

They're not quite ready to enter a lease, but the fact that this space is somewhat of a bargain ($9 per square foot) puts it near the top of their list.

While being realistic with your rent is important, don't sabotage your business by picking a cheap, but bad, location. This may seem obvious, but sometimes new business owners become blind to common wisdom when presented with an opportunity to rent a super-cheap space. Even if they've already determined that location will play a key role in their success, they either believe that the savings in rent will make up for slow sales or they convince themselves that they'll be the pioneers in a new area that is sure to swell into a hot business district by the middle of next week. While this does occasionally happen (god bless those brave pioneers), it's generally a poor idea to move into a dead section of town, since it almost certainly won't bloom fast enough to support your business in its financially vulnerable start-up days. Unless you have a sound reason to believe that you'll get enough customers in your oddball location, don't let the lure of low rent tempt you into a bad business decision. Remember that, at least in popular urban areas, rent can be the highest overhead expense for many new businesses.

3. Getting the Right Physical Features

When picking your space, the biggest consideration is sometimes not where it is but what it is. Ask yourself: Are the building facilities appropriate or adaptable for my business? For example, if you're planning to open a coffeehouse, you might fall in love with a beautiful brick warehouse space in a funky shopping district, but if the place doesn't have at least minimal kitchen facilities, you should probably forget it. Unless you can convince your landlord to put in the needed equipment—plumbing, electrical work and the rest (which is discussed below)—it's highly unlikely that laying out the cash to do it yourself will be worth it. Sure, some improvements might be relatively cheap, such as putting up a wall or two or adding new light fixtures. But if the building lacks something major that is essential to your business operation, you should take it as a sign that the place isn't right for you—even if it has loads of other great qualities. You'll have to decide for yourself which features your business absolutely can't live with, or live without.

EXAMPLE: Charlotte and Sandra plan to open an alternative health store that will offer products such as medicinal herbs, aromatherapy products and yoga supplies. They also plan to offer services such as aromatherapy sessions and consultations with nutritionists and herbalists. Since they have high hopes for the service side of their business, Charlotte and Sandra know that their physical space needs to be comfortable and appealing to customers. After looking at a number of storefront spaces in their chosen neighborhood (near the university, of course), they find one that seems just perfect—until they notice the lack of windows. Except for the glass front door, the place has almost no natural light. Even though not having windows doesn't absolutely prevent them from doing business, Charlotte and Sandra decide that given their expected customer base (and their own feelings), they need a brighter space.

Another consideration that's important for many businesses these days is having modern phone and other data lines into the business. Anyone who spends much time on the Web these days knows that old, slow lines can seriously impact your productivity (and drive you crazy to boot). Slow lines can also slow down your faxes and can even result in dropped telephone connections—not exactly a good thing for business. When you're considering a specific space, ask the agent or the landlord for any information on the phone and data lines into the space, such as whether it's connected to a fiber optic network or is wired for DSL or a T1 line (high-volume Internet connections). Also, find out if the landlord has sold the rights to the risers (wire conduits) in the building to a single telecommunications provider such as MCI or AT&T—if so, you could be stuck with that provider.

Besides high-tech communications wiring, don't overlook plain-old electrical power as an important consideration in choosing a business space. Make sure that any space you're looking at has enough power for your needs, both in terms of number of outlets in your space and the capacity of the circuits. If you'll mostly be running computer equipment, a copier, a coffee machine and the like, chances are that any reasonably equipped commercial space will have enough power for you. But if you'll be running machinery or other electricity-hungry equipment, make sure to find out from the landlord how much juice the circuits can handle and whether a generator is available during power outages. Also, if you'll keep sensitive computer equipment at your office, ask the landlord how many hours of air-conditioning are included in the terms of your lease, and negotiate longer hours if necessary.

Another common need for many businesses is adequate parking. If a significant percentage of your customers will come by car and there isn't enough parking at your chosen spot, it's probably best to look elsewhere. In fact, the city might not allow you to operate there if parking isn't adequate. (See Section B on zoning laws regarding parking.)

Before you spend lots of time searching for a space, you should find out if your type of business is subject to local planning or health department requirements. For instance, if you're starting a small food manufacturing business to produce energy bars, you may need to rent a space with a certain number of vents, a fire-resistant roof and walls of proper material and adequate thickness. Contact your city or county departments of planning, health, fire or other appropriate agency to find out.

B. Complying With Zoning Laws

A certain spot may be good for your business, but if it's not properly zoned for what you plan to do, forget it. Local zoning laws (often called "ordinances," or "land use regulations") prohibit certain activities from being conducted in particular areas. To use an obvious example, a nightclub wouldn't be allowed to operate in a district zoned for residential use. Sure, only a fool would try to open a disco on a quiet residential street—but there are less obvious zoning no-nos that you must observe.

Zoning ordinances typically allow certain categories of businesses to occupy different districts of a city or county. For example, mixed commercial and residential uses might be allowed in one district while another district allows heavy industry and warehouses. So if you open your small jewelry-making business in a space zoned for commercial use, you could be in for a real headache if zoning officials decide you're a light-industrial business that's not allowed to operate in a commercial district. Similarly, you may not be allowed to run a commercial business—particularly one that's open to the public—in an industrial zone.

Besides regulating the types of businesses allowed in certain areas, zoning laws also regulate specific activities. Depending on your area, you might be subject to laws regulating parking, signs, water and air quality, waste management, noise and the visual appearance of the business (especially in historic districts). And in addition to these regulations, some cities restrict the number of a particular type of business in a certain area, such as allowing only three bookstores or two pet shops in a certain neighborhood. Finally, some zoning laws specifically regulate home businesses. Home-office regulations are discussed separately in Section D, below.

Expect Zoning Laws on Parking Spaces and Business Signs

Local zoning laws commonly require a business to provide parking, and they also may regulate the size and type of business signs. Be prepared for your city or county to look into both these issues. If there's already a parking problem in your proposed area, you may have to come up with a plan for how to deal with the increased traffic your business will attract.

Also be ready for zoning officials to get really nitpicky about your business sign. Many local laws limit the size of business signs (no signs over five feet by three feet, for instance), their appearance (such as whether they're illuminated, flashing, colorful or made of neon), and their placement (flat against the building, hanging over the sidewalk or mounted on a pole). There are even some regulations attempting to limit the use of foreign language on signs. Be sure to find out what your local regulations are before spending money on having signs made.

One of the key things to understand about zoning laws is that more often than not, they're enforced for the sake of the other people and companies in the neighborhood (this is particularly true of home-based businesses). While some areas are strict about their zoning laws, most of the time you won't have a zoning official knocking unannounced on your door unless neighbors have complained or you're in flagrant violation of the laws. Since enforcement is often triggered by complaints, it's a good idea to get to know your neighbors and develop good relationships with them.

1. Making Sure That You Comply With Zoning Laws

The first thing to remember is that you should never sign a lease for a business space without first knowing that you'll legally be able to do business there. (One exception to this is that it's okay to sign a contingent lease, with a clause stating that the lease won't be binding if you don't get zoning approval.) Being forced to move your business is a headache enough, but not nearly as catastrophic as being held liable for payment on a lease for a space that you can't use.

When trying to find out if you'll be able to do business at a potential location, never assume that you'll be allowed to do a certain activity simply because the previous tenants of the space did it. For all kinds of reasons, some businesses get away with zoning violations, even for long periods of time. Typically, however, new occupants are scrutinized more carefully than already existing businesses. It may not be fair, but it's common for a new business to be told it can't do what an old one had long been doing.

It's also possible that the previous tenants were operating outside the zoning restrictions—but with an official OK. For example, the previous occupants might have had a zoning variance (an exception to zoning laws) for their particular business—one that won't necessarily be extended to you. And lots of times when zoning laws change, businesses that are already in place are allowed to keep doing what they were doing, even if the activity violates the new zoning law (a system referred to as "grandfathering"). When a tenant with a grandfathered exception leaves and new occupants come in, however, the new business will normally have to abide by the new zoning law.

2. Finding Out What Laws Apply to Your Business

How do you find out whether a given location is properly zoned for your business and whether you need to get any approvals? The answer varies from area to area. In some cities and counties, zoning approval is part of the tax registration process (discussed in Chapter 6). In San Diego, for instance, when you apply for your business tax certificate you must also pay a $12 Zoning Use Clearance fee to have your business approved for the location listed on your application. The city of Albuquerque also requires businesses to get zoning approval before allowing them to obtain a tax registration certificate, though there is no fee for the zoning clearance. Other cities, such as Boston, don't require proof of zoning approval before issuing a tax registration certificate—but that doesn't mean you should take the zoning laws any less seriously. Whether or not you're required to deal with your local zoning depart-ment before starting your business, you'll still be subject to their monitoring and enforcement on an ongoing basis.

If your city doesn't include zoning approval as part of its start-up requirements for new businesses, you'll need to do some detective work. Generally this involves talking with your local zoning officials. Most zoning agencies are part of city or county planning departments. Look under "Planning" or "Zoning" in the government section (blue pages) of your white-pages phone book. If your business will be located in a city, you probably only need to worry about city zoning ordinances. Businesses in rural areas should contact the county zoning/planning offices.

Getting zoning approval typically begins with filling out a form issued by the city planning department in which you provide information about your proposed location and what you plan to do there. In some cities, you may be required to submit detailed building plans to show exactly how you intend to use the space in question. Your application may be evaluated simply upon the information you provide in the form, or the zoning department may send out an inspector to more closely examine the potential business space. Once the zoning department has all the information it requires to make a decision, it will either approve your application without limitations, approve it with certain conditions or deny it altogether.

How Vigilant Are Zoning Officials?

There's a world of difference in how strict zoning officials are from area to area. Many zoning departments aren't terribly rigid about enforcement, mostly responding to complaints from neighbors or other citizens about businesses that create a nuisance or other trouble. In a few areas, however, zoning agents relish sniffing out minor infractions and enforcing their zoning ordinances to the letter.

If you're considering going ahead with your business despite what you consider to be a minor zoning problem, you should do your best to find out how strict the zoning police are in your area. Start by asking other local business-people about their experiences. If they tell you that there's little enforcement other than responding to complaints, you can breathe a little easier about what might be a minor infraction, such as including tennis-racket stringing (which officials might consider a light-industrial activity) at your sports shop in an area zoned only for commercial use. Even so, it never pays to engage in a prohibited activity that is fundamental to your business—while tennis rackets could be strung elsewhere, a health club wouldn't want to have to locate its juice bar two blocks away.

But no matter how mellow your zoning department, at the very least you need to know what the rules are for your proposed location. Paying scant attention to the rules while counting on lax enforcement is just plain dumb.

---

3. Dealing With Snags in Zoning Approval

If your zoning board has a problem with any of the activities you plan to conduct at your chosen location, you have a few options, usually ranging from making appropriate changes to your business to giving up on that location and finding a new one. Obviously, some zoning conflicts are simply not fixable, such as opening a nightclub on a quiet cul-de-sac. But the good news is that a creative (and, when necessary, assertive) business owner can often persuade zoning officials or the zoning appeals board to work out an acceptable accommodation that will allow the business to use the desired location.

For borderline situations, one approach is simply to advocate an interpretation of the zoning law that's favorable to you *before* you get an official "No." Communicate with zoning officials and try to persuade them to give you their seal of approval.

If the zoning officials have already denied your application, it's usually possible to appeal their decision, usually to a higher authority within the zoning agency, such as a board of appeals. If you're successful, the zoning board may grant you a "variance," which is basically a one-time exception to the local zoning laws. Or the board may give you a "conditional use permit," which essentially gives you approval to operate your business as long as certain conditions are met, such as restricting the maximum occupancy to a certain number or providing additional parking spaces.

When lobbying for an exemption from a zoning requirement, remember that you're asking for special treatment, so make your case as persuasive as possible. If your business will be valuable to the community, present evidence of that fact. Proof can include demographic data about the area, testimony from community leaders or statements from other local business people. Your goal is to show that the value of allowing your business in the area is greater than the trivial zoning conflicts that may exist. If you can compromise in some other area, offer to do so.

EXAMPLE: Carolyn wants to open a small printing shop, Nelson's Press, on a commercial strip where storefront space is cheap and plentiful. Before signing a lease, she applies for zoning approval. The local zoning board rejects her application because Carolyn's proposed location is zoned commercial, while her print shop would technically be a light-industrial business. Carolyn decides to try to get an exception, because her printing operation will be small (only one small offset printing press) and would be an asset to the neighborhood, which needs new businesses.

She submits detailed plans of her business to the zoning board, showing the business's small scope and including specific protocols for dealing with toxics such as ink. (At the same time she files a Certificate of Disclosure of Hazardous Substances with her city's Office of Emergency Services.) She also submits letters from other business owners in the neighborhood, documenting how commerce in the area has languished for years and arguing that new businesses would help revitalize the strip. Many of the business owners also note that a local printer would be convenient for the existing area businesses, who currently have to go across town for their print jobs. A few weeks later, Carolyn gets a conditional use permit allowing her to proceed with her printing business, as long as she doesn't expand her business with additional presses and follows a number of standard rules governing the chemicals she'll use in printing.

C. Commercial Leases

Chances are that you'll rent rather than buy a space for your business. After all, most small start-ups don't have the funds to purchase real estate, and it's usually not a good idea to saddle your business with high interest payments anyway. But just because you've rented plenty of apartments or flats over the years, don't assume that you know the score when it comes to leasing business space.

It's crucial to understand from the get-go that, practically and legally speaking, there are oceans of differences between commercial leases and residential leases. Commercial leases are not subject to most consumer protection laws that govern residential leases—for example, there are no caps on deposits or rules protecting a tenant's privacy. Also, commercial leases are generally subject to much more negotiation between the business and the landlord, since businesses often need special features in their spaces, and landlords are often eager for tenants and willing to extend special offers. While a residential tenant will usually just take an apartment or flat more or less as-is, a business will often need to modify the existing space—for example, by adding cubicles, raising a loading dock or rewiring for telephones and computers.

Since every company must negotiate modifications that are suitable for its own operations, commercial leases are relatively flexible creatures. Of course, your bargaining power will vary a great deal from situation to situation. For example, getting a landlord to accept your demands would probably be a lot easier for a long-term lease in a largely vacant office building than for a six-month lease in a hot commercial area. Likewise, local landlords are often more willing to make concessions than huge property management companies or real estate investment trusts.

When negotiating a commercial lease, keep in mind that the success or failure of your business may ride on certain terms of the lease. The amount of the rent is an obvious concern, as is the length of the lease. (You probably don't want to tie yourself to a five- or ten-year lease if you can help it, in case your business grows faster than you expect or the location doesn't work out for you.) But other, less conspicuous items spelled out in the lease may be just as crucial to your business's success. For instance, if you expect your shoe-repair business to depend largely on walk-in customers, be sure that your lease establishes your right to put up a sign that's visible from the street. Or, if you are counting on being the only sandwich shop inside a new commercial complex, make sure your lease prevents the landlord from leasing space to a competitor. If you are starting a new Web company that you expect to grow quickly, make sure there's room for expansion.

The following checklist includes many items that are often addressed in commercial leases. Pay attention to terms regarding:

- rent, including allowable increases and method of computation
- whether the rent you pay includes insurance, property taxes and maintenance costs (called a gross lease) or whether you will be charged for these items separately (called a net lease)
- the security deposit and conditions for its return
- the length of lease (also called the lease term) and when it begins
- whether there's an option to renew the lease or expand the space
- if and how the lease may be terminated, including notice requirements, and whether there are penalties for early termination
- exactly what space is being rented, including common areas such as hallways, rest rooms and elevators, and how the landlord measures the space (some measurement practices include the thickness of the walls)
- specifications for signs, including where they may be placed
- whether there will be improvements, modifications (called buildouts when new space is being finished to your specifications) or fixtures added to the space, who will pay for them and who will own them after the lease ends (generally, the landlord)
- who will maintain the premises
- whether the lease may be assigned or subleased to another party, and
- whether disputes must be mediated or arbitrated as an alternative to court.

Many businesses must comply with the Americans with Disabilities Act. The Americans with Disabilities Act (ADA) requires all businesses that are open to the public or that employ more than 15 people to have premises that are accessible to disabled people. Make sure that you and your landlord are in agreement about who will pay for any needed modifications, such as adding a ramp or widening doorways to accommodate wheelchairs.

D. When Your Home Is Your Office

No question about it, home is where the office is these days. Now that personal computers and networking software are both powerful and affordable, it's easy for anyone to set up an inexpensive home office that can take care of virtually all of the business tasks that used to be done in high-tech commercial offices.

And besides the fact that new communications technology has largely conquered the problem of physical distance, many modern home businesses don't take up much physical space. In plenty of situations, space for a bookcase, a file cabinet, a phone and your computer may be all you need. Factor in the money saved by not paying commercial rent or commuting costs, and it may be foolish not to at least start your business from home.

But before you get too euphoric about opening a machine shop in the den, it's important to realize a home business isn't immune from a number of the requirements that affect businesses in general. Like a business operated from a commercial office space, a business run from your home needs to comply with zoning requirements in your area. Before setting up shop you should check your local zoning restrictions, and you should also be aware of several key insurance and tax rules, which we discuss below.

Is your business right for a home office? While many types of businesses lend themselves to being run out of a residence, others don't. Make sure you've considered whether using your home as your office is a good idea. Ask your-self questions like the following:

- How will you deal with customers and suppliers? Will they be able to easily park and pick up or unload material if necessary?
- Will customers take you and your company seriously if you work out of your house?
- Will your business require a lot of space for performing services or storing supplies?
- Can you work productively in your home, considering distractions like kids, the couch, the refrigerator and the TV?
- If you rent, will your landlord give your business the OK?

Businesses that require nothing but a small office and don't generate much coming and going—such as graphic design, accounting and Web development businesses—and businesses where most of the dirty work is routinely done off-site—such as construction and plumbing—are particularly well-suited for home offices.

Kimberly Torgerson, owner of Your Word's Worth, a freelance editing and writing service in Berkeley, California:

Setting up my home office was much harder than navigating the licensing agencies to start up my business. Where to put the fax? How to get the monitor set up just right? How to organize a spaghetti tangle of cables? Someday I'd like to get a sleeker setup, with everything in a tailored niche, but for now I put money into upgrading equipment, not furniture.

1. Zoning Restrictions on Home Offices

As with leased office spaces, you need to make sure that the business activities you plan to do in your home are acceptable to your local zoning officials. You may also have to apply for a special "home occupation permit" before you begin. (Zoning laws typically refer to home offices as "home occupations.")

Since your home is most likely in an area zoned for residential use only (some loft-type or urban apartments might be zoned for mixed use), the types of businesses allowed by your neighborhood ordinances will likely be pretty limited. A few areas actually forbid home businesses altogether. But most cities and counties allow home offices that have little likelihood of causing noise or pollution, creating traffic or otherwise disturbing the neighbors. Writers, artists, attorneys, accountants, insurance brokers and piano teachers are examples of businesspeople commonly allowed to work from home. Typically not allowed are retailers, automotive repair shops, cafes or bars, animal hospitals or breeders, or any type of adult-oriented businesses.

Watch out for special private land-use restrictions. If you live in a condo, a co-op, a planned subdivision or a rental property, you are likely subject to land use restrictions in addition to your local laws. Condo regulations, for instance, often contain language restricting or sometimes even prohibiting business use of the premises. Or your apartment lease might forbid business from being conducted on the property. Be sure to check the documents governing your property to see if there are any such rules.

To find out how your city or county deals with home offices, call the planning department and ask them for any information they have on home occupations. Some areas have special pamphlets with information explaining home office restrictions and how to obtain any necessary permits. In other places, all that's available might be a grainy photocopy of the municipal code, which you'll have to decipher yourself. If there's no approval or permit process for home businesses in your area, it's generally up to you to comply with your area's zoning code.

Keep in mind that the best way to avoid trouble with zoning officials is to do your best to minimize your business's impact on the neighborhood. As long as you're not in flagrant violation of the zoning laws regarding home businesses, you'll probably be fine as long as your neighbors are happy (see Tip below).

Assuming that your local zoning laws do allow your type of home business, they are likely to impose some restrictions, such as allowing only residents of your home to be employees, restricting the number of customers that may come to your house, limiting the percentage of your home's floor space that can be used for business and prohibiting signs outside of your house that advertise the business. In Milwaukee, Wisconsin, for example, home businesses may not employ anyone who doesn't live at the residence, and the business may not use more than 20% of the usable floor area of the home (including the basement). In Austin, Texas, it's illegal for any equipment or materials associated with the home business to be visible from the street. And in Sacramento, California, home businesses are not allowed to use any trucks larger than one-half ton—which rules out many full-size pick-up trucks.

Besides these general limitations, cities often impose additional restrictions upon specific types of home businesses. For instance, while a city might forbid any type of home business from having a neon sign, it might also have a special rule for landscapers that doesn't allow landscaping supplies to be kept at the home office. Be sure to find out if there are special rules for your type of business in your city.

If you find out that your city will allow your type of home business in your area, your contact with the zoning office may be done. Many cities do not require any special permit, as long as the home business complies with all of the rules and restrictions contained in its planning code (such as the rules discussed above). Some cities, however, require all home business owners to get a "home occupation permit," a bit of red tape that may involve a fee. Obtaining such a permit is usually a simple matter of filling out a form provided by the planning department and paying whatever fee may be required. If your business meets the restrictions your city imposes, your permit will be issued.

If you don't meet all of your city's rules for having a home occupation, or your area just isn't zoned for your type of home business, in some cities you may be out of luck and simply won't be allowed to run your business from home. In other cities, however, a home business that meets most but not all of the city's restrictions may be allowed to operate, but only after obtaining a home occupation permit. In San Diego, for instance, no permit is required from home businesses that meet all of the city's criteria (no business signs, no employees on premises, etc.). But if the home business deviates from the criteria, the city may allow the business to proceed, but only with a home occupation permit. Acceptable deviations in San Diego include having one employee or having one client who visits your home office by appointment or using more than one vehicle for business.

Keep in mind that the zoning agency is probably not the only land-use regulatory agency in your area. While your activity might be okay with zoning officials, operating out of your home may not pass other departments' requirements. For example, if you're starting a catering business, chances are your county health department won't let you work out of your home kitchen. You may be allowed to convert your garage or another separate structure into a professional kitchen, but of course that requires building permits as well as county health inspections and, of course, zoning compliance or permission.

Let your neighbors in on your business plans. As mentioned earlier, getting to know your neighbors can be a huge help in avoiding problems with zoning officials. For instance, if your business requires people to be coming and going from your house or packages to be delivered daily, your neighbors might jump to the nutty conclusion that you're a drug dealer and report you to the city. Even though you can show your drug of choice is vitamin C, the city might discover technical zoning violations that never would have otherwise turned up. In short, communicating with your neighbors and dealing with any of their concerns about issues such as parking and noise will greatly reduce the likelihood that the zoning police will come knocking on your door.

2. The Home-Office Tax Deduction

If your office is located in your home, you may be able to claim a portion of your home expenses—such as rent, depreciation, property taxes, utilities and insurance—as a special deduction when reporting federal taxes. The IRS's general rule is that if your home office qualifies (we discuss the rules just below), you can deduct a pro rata share of home-office expenses—which simply means a share that's proportional to the percentage of home space that you use for your business.

To qualify for the home-office deduction, your home-office space must be used exclusively and regularly as a principal place of business. No question, the words "exclusively," "regularly" and "principal place of business" are IRS-speak, and have specific, nit-picky meanings. First, we'll explain these terms so that you'll know whether you can deduct your home-office expenses, and then we'll tell you how to figure out just how much is actually deductible. (For information on how businesses in general are taxed, refer to Chapter 8, "Getting to Know Your Taxes.")

 Many business expenses for home businesses are fully deductible without the home-office deduction. A common misconception is that you need to qualify for the home-office deduction before you can claim any expenses associated with your home-based business. Not true. You can deduct business expenses necessary for your business whether they're incurred in your home or anyplace else, even if you don't qualify for the home-office deduction. For instance, you can always deduct the portion of your home long-distance phone bill that you spend on business-related calls. Other deductible business expenses might include office supplies, furniture and equipment that you use in your home office, and the cost of bringing a second telephone line into your home for business use. For the rest of this chapter, when we mean expenses that can only be claimed with the home-office deduction, we'll say "home-office expenses."

a. Using Your Home Office Exclusively and Regularly for Business

The IRS will allow you to deduct home-office expenses only for office space in your home that is 100% dedicated to business use. For example, a graphic designer who sometimes sits at the kitchen table to do illustrations can't claim business deductions for using the kitchen (assuming the kitchen is also sometimes used for nonbusiness uses like cooking and eating). A spare room, however, that's set up as an office space and used only for business would probably meet the "exclusive use" test. But if the room contains a bed for the occasional overnight guest or doubles as storage space for clothing, technically, it wouldn't qualify.

The "regular use" test is generally pretty easy to pass. As long as you use your home-office space for business on a frequent, continuing basis, rather than for a once-in-a-while garage sale or lemonade stand, the "regular use" test will probably be satisfied.

EXAMPLE 1: Stacey runs a hat-making business. She makes the hats in an extra room of her house where she has a sewing machine and all her supplies, as well as a computer and a file cabinet containing her sales and other financial information. Since the only use of that room is for the hat-making business, it will meet the IRS's criteria of exclusive use. And since Stacey has made and sold hats for a couple years, with consistent monthly sales, she'll have no trouble proving that she uses the space regularly for business.

EXAMPLE 2: Parisha has a full-time job at a plant nursery, but also does occasional freelance work in photography. She has a darkroom in her basement that she uses to develop photos for her assignments. Her darkroom is dedicated to her photography business, but she spends most of her time working at the plant nursery and has only done one photo shoot in the last six months. Parisha would be ill-advised to claim her darkroom expenses as a home-office deduction, since she doesn't regularly use it for business.

b. Using Your Home Office as Your Principal Place of Business

Besides fulfilling the exclusive and regular use requirements, your home-office space must also be the main place where you do business—with two exceptions explained below. Thankfully, since 1999, the principal place of business rule has been fairly easy to satisfy. Before that year, business owners often had to use an imprecise formula to balance how "primary" their various places of business were. Now, however, the rule is simple. Your home office will qualify as the principal place of business if:

- you use the office to conduct administrative or management activities for your business, and
- you do not have an office or other business location outside your home set up to conduct these activities.

This rule is just as straightforward as it sounds. As long as you use your home office to keep track of your business files, do your bookkeeping and accounting, maintain your client databases or conduct whatever other type of administration your business involves, it will be considered your principal place of business.

If your home office doesn't qualify as your principal place of business under the test described above, there are two other ways you may be able to qualify for the home-office deduction:

- you regularly meet clients or customers at home, or
- you use a separate structure on your property for your home office.

In these two cases, it doesn't matter whether your home office or separate structure is your principal work space. But remember—the rule still applies that your home office space must be exclusively and regularly for business.

c. Figuring Your Deductible Home-Office Expenses

Once you've determined that your home-office expenses are, in fact, deductible, you'll need to figure out exactly how much you can deduct. Obviously you can't deduct all of your housing costs—only the expenses that are attributable to business purposes.

The general rule is that expenses that are unrelated to your business space are not deductible at all, such as the cost of repainting your bedroom or replacing your dining room window. Expenses that affect the specific business space (called direct expenses) are fully deductible, such as installing new carpeting for your office space, replacing a broken window in the office space and repairing the heating vent in your office space. Expenses that affect the whole house (called indirect expenses) are deductible, but only to the extent that they are business-related. For instance, you can deduct a percentage of the cost of a new foundation, a new water heater, real estate taxes and the gas and electric bill.

To calculate the portion of indirect costs attributable to your business, you should first figure out what percentage of your home you use for business purposes. Then you'll use that percentage to calculate how much of your regular home expenses can be deducted as home-office expenses.

You can calculate the percentage of your home being used for business in one of two ways: the "square footage" method or the "number of rooms" method. Either approach is acceptable to the IRS.

The square footage method simply divides the square footage of the business space by the square footage of the whole house. For instance, if you use 250 square feet for business, and your whole house takes up 1,000 square feet, then your business space uses 25% (250/1,000) of your home. The number-of-rooms method is just as simple: if your house has five similarly sized rooms, and you use one of them for business, then the business uses 20% (1/5) of your home. Once you have calculated a space percentage for your business, you'll use it to calculate how much of your home expenses are deductible home-office expenses. Rent is an easy expense to prorate. For instance, if your business uses 25% of your home, and your rent is $800 per month, then $200 per month is a deductible home-office expense (25% x $800).

Homeowners, however, need to calculate a "depreciation deduction," which is somewhat more complicated than simply deducting a percentage of their monthly mortgage payments. If you own your home, first you'll need to break down the value of your home into the value of the building itself

versus the value of the land. Then calculate yearly depreciation for the building only—not the land. The depreciation rate for the building will depend on when it was purchased, so you'll have to do some research as to the tax rules in effect at that time. Finally, divide the yearly depreciation figure by the percentage of space your business takes up in your home. That figure—the depreciation deduction—can be claimed as a business expense.

Get information from the horse's mouth. The IRS offers examples and detailed instructions in two publications: Publication 587, *Business Use of Your Home,* and Publication 946, *How to Depreciate Property.* These publications are available online at http://www.irs.treas.gov/forms_pubs/pubs/index.htm.

Claiming a depreciation deduction may subject you to capital gains taxes when you sell your home. Under current federal tax laws, when you sell your home you're exempted from capital gains taxes on gains up to $250,000 as long as you've owned and lived in the home for at least two of five years. However, if you claim depreciation deductions for a home office, the total of those deductions will be subject to capital gains tax when you sell your house. In other words, if you sell your house at a gain of $200,000, you'd normally be exempt from capital gains taxes. But if over the years you'd claimed $10,000 in depreciation deductions for an office you ran from home, that $10,000 would be subject to capital gains tax. A way to avoid this is to stop using your home office for two years before selling your home.

Other indirect expenses such as homeowners' insurance, utilities, repairs and taxes can be partially deducted, depending on how much they're used for the business. Generally speaking, you can use the percentage of space your business uses in the home to prorate these expenses. It's important to note, however, that the IRS has specific rules as to which indirect expenses may be deducted for a home office. For instance, if your business space takes up 25% of your home, you may not be able to simply deduct 25% of your water bill, since your business probably doesn't use 25% of your home's water—most of the water goes for home uses such as washing clothes and dishes, bathing and watering the garden.

Recommended reading on the home-office deduction. For more detailed information on tax deductions for home offices, read *Tax Savvy for Small Business,* by attorney Frederick W. Daily (Nolo).

3. Insurance and the Home Business

While lots of home-based businesses might not have to worry too much about insurance in their very early days, there are a few special issues to watch out for if you plan to run a business from home. In a nutshell, don't expect your homeowner's or renter's policy to automatically cover you for business-related losses, including theft or damage of business property, as well as personal injury claims related to your business. Not having additional coverage can be a real catastrophe if your computer system is stolen or destroyed in an earthquake, or if a client trips and falls over your garden hose on the way up your front walk.

Potentially even worse, your regular homeowner's or renter's policy might be voided entirely—even for home-related claims—if the insurance company finds out you are running a business in the home without their knowledge. Some companies require you to tell them about any home business (and may bill you for added coverage) or they'll invalidate your policy. Compared to the risks of having the whole policy yanked from under you, paying some extra premium dollars will probably be well worth it.

For more information on small business insurance, see Chapter 7.

Chapter 4 Checklist

- [ ] Determine how much rent you can afford.

- [ ] Decide what neighborhood would be best for your business.

- [ ] Find out what the average rents are in the neighborhoods you're considering.

- [ ] Identify the features and fixtures your business space will need.

- [ ] Make sure any spaces you're considering are or can be properly zoned for your business.

- [ ] Examine any commercial lease carefully before signing and negotiate the best deal you can.

- [ ] If working from home, make sure your business activities won't violate any zoning restrictions on home offices.

- [ ] Familiarize yourself with the rules on home-office deductions before claiming them on your tax return.

- [ ] Be sure your home office is adequately insured (insurance is further discussed in Chapter 7).

Drafting an Effective Business Plan

A. Different Purposes Require Different Plans 5/2

B. Describing the Business, and Yourself 5/3

    1. State Your Business's Purpose 5/3

    2. Describe Your Business 5/4

    3. Define Your Market 5/4

    4. Analyze Your Competition 5/5

    5. Describe Your Marketing Strategy 5/7

    6. Describe Your Business Accomplishments 5/8

C. Making Financial Projections 5/8

D. Break-Even Analysis 5/10

    1. Making Estimates 5/11

    2. Categorizing Your Expenses 5/11

    3. Estimate Your Sales Revenue 5/12

    4. Calculate Your Average Gross Profit Percentage 5/13

    5. Estimate Your Fixed Costs 5/16

    6. Calculate Your Break-Even Point 5/17

    7. Analyze Your Result 5/18

E. Profit/Loss Forecast 5/19

F. Start-Up Cost Estimate 5/22

G. Cash Flow Projection 5/23

H. Putting It All Together 5/26

If you think only Type A personalities compose business plans, you're wrong. Talk to a random sample of successful business owners—even the most laid-back—and you'll be amazed at how many took the time to put their business plans into writing. If you're truly determined to succeed, you'll follow their example. Why? Because without a plan, you're leaving far too many things to chance. Just as a blueprint is used to ensure that a building will be structurally sound, a business plan will help you see whether your business will be financially able to stay afloat.

The idea of a business plan is simple: to bring together in one document the key elements of your business. These include what products or services you'll sell, what they'll cost to produce and how much sales revenue you expect during your first months and years of operation. Most important, your plan will help you see how all the disparate elements of your business relate to one another, which will allow you to make any necessary alterations in order to maximize your business's potential to turn a profit.

Business plans are often written by business owners who want to borrow money or attract investment. This is good as far as it goes—lenders and investors do want to understand as much as possible about how a business will work before deciding whether to back it financially. Unless you're prepared to show them a well-thought-out plan for how you expect your business to become profitable, you won't have much chance of convincing them to finance your project.

But creating a business plan is just as good an idea if you don't need to raise start-up money. The process of creating one often brings up issues and potential problems that you hadn't thought of before. And the discipline involved in developing financial projections such as a break-even analysis and a profit and loss forecast will help you decide if your business is really worth starting, or if you need to rethink some of your key assumptions. As any experienced businessperson will tell you, the business you decide not to start (often because its business plan doesn't pencil out) can be more important to your long-term success than the one you bet your economic future on. This chapter will explain how to create a thorough business plan. If you've already written one, you may want to skip this chapter—or you might find the information here useful in double-checking your plan. Yes, of course we remember you have zero time to waste, so we will keep our focus on the essential elements and spare you the fluff.

 For the full treatment, read Mike McKeever's _How to Write a Business Plan_ (Nolo). This book describes the many different items of financial information you can include in your plan in far more detail than we have space for here, and explains how to put them together into a plan that fits your needs.

A. Different Purposes Require Different Plans

All good business plans have two basic goals: to describe the fundamentals of your business idea, and to provide financial calculations to show that it will make good money. But, depending on how you intend to use it, a business plan can take somewhat different forms.

- If you will use your plan to borrow money or interest investors, it should be carefully written and edited to sell your vision to skeptical people. Normally this means that it should include a persuasive introduction and a request for funds, in-depth market research information, an evaluation of your main competitors, your key marketing strategies and a management plan. In addition, it should contain detailed financial information, including your best estimates of start-up costs, revenues and expenses. Finally, since your plan will be submitted to people you don't know well, the writing should be polished and the format clean and professional.

- If your plan will primarily be for your own use—that is, if you don't need to raise money—don't worry so much about making a sales pitch or slick presentation (although you'll probably want to do a quick market and competitive analysis). But don't skimp when it comes to doing your numbers. You'll need to include estimates of start-up costs, revenues and expenses. The last thing you want is to experience the very real misery of starting a business that never had a chance to make a solid profit.

Plan to get the help you need. Not all business-people are great writers. But excellent writing skills can be a big help in creating a compelling business plan. Consider paying a freelance writer with small business savvy to help you polish your plan. Similarly, if you are challenged by numbers, find a bookkeeper or accountant to provide the needed help.

B. Describing the Business, and Yourself

The first several sections of your plan should describe the beauty of your business idea. If you will show your plan to potential lenders, investors or people you want to work with, you'll want to show them right up front that you've hit upon a product or service that customers really want. In addition, you'll want to show that you are exactly the right person to make your fine idea a roaring success. Your goal is to have them say, "Wow! What a great business idea! And yes, I see exactly why Carlos Burns is the ideal person to make it a big success."

To accomplish these goals, you should include the following:

- a statement of the purpose of your business
- a detailed description of how the business will work
- an analysis of your market
- an analysis of your competitors
- a description of your marketing strategy, and
- a resumé setting forth your business accomplishments.

Again, depending on how you intend to use your business plan, you may be able to skip some of these elements. For example, if you don't need to raise start-up money and are writing a plan mostly for your own use, you may decide to skip the resumé of your own business accomplishments. But think twice before you leave out too much. Any new business will need to introduce itself to loads of people—suppliers, contractors, employees and key customers, to name a few—and showing them part or all of your business plan can be a great way to do it.

1. State Your Business's Purpose

What will your product or service be? And why does the great big world—or your small town or narrow niche market—need the product or service you want to offer? The first paragraph of your plan should address this question as directly and compellingly as possible. For example, if you're planning to open a pet-grooming salon, you might start with the proposition that in today's increasingly busy world, pet owners need and want to keep their pets clean and groomed, but often don't have time to do it themselves. Similarly, if you want to start a sea kayaking guide service, you might start with the proposition that more and more people are participating in this exciting sport, but need equipment, planning, training and logistics to do it in other parts of the world.

A statement of business purpose doesn't generally need to be complicated or lengthy. In fact, some of the best state the obvious. No problem—if the need for your business will be clear to lenders or investors (for example, a sandwich shop in a fast-growing office area), one paragraph may be all you need. But if the value of your business idea isn't so readily apparent (for example, an innovative software company), you will want to say more.

Show how your business will solve a real problem or fill an actual need. And, just as important, explain why customers will pay you to accomplish the task.

2. Describe Your Business

Once you've stated the need that your business will fill, describe exactly how you'll accomplish it. In this section, don't write a bunch of fluffy text about how brilliant your entrepreneurial idea is. Instead, outline in detail exactly how your business will operate. While the degree of detail may vary depending on what kind of business you're starting and who will be reading your business plan, your description should include specifics such as:

- how you will go about providing your product or service
- where you will buy key supplies
- how customers will pay you
- how many employees you will have and what they will do
- what hours you will operate, and
- where you will be located (if possible, include details about how your customers will find you).

Keep in mind that even the smallest, simplest business involves a swarm of pesky details. While you're writing your business description, don't assume there's anything obvious about your business, even if it's a tiny one-person operation. For example, if you plan to start a pet-grooming business, how many different types of services will you offer—shampooing? flea bathing? nail cutting? hair trimming? teeth cleaning? Will you charge separately for each individual service, sell them in packages, or both? How will you attract customers and regularly stay in touch with the best ones? How will you accommodate animals with special needs such as allergies or with behavioral problems such as aggressiveness? How will people drop off and pick up their pets? Will your business need insurance in case an animal is injured or dies while in your care?

A little repetition is okay. The description of how your business will operate is likely to be the longest section of your plan and will probably discuss one or more topics that are also covered elsewhere. No problem. For example, a key issue like how you will establish and keep a competitive edge is appropriate to mention as part of your big-picture business description as well as in the marketing strategy section (see Section 5, below).

Never hesitate to take advantage of your business description as a tool to change or refine your business idea. Almost always, when you write and rewrite this section you'll come up with ideas and questions you haven't yet thought through. If so, great—this gives you an opportunity to fill in the gaps cheaply and easily before you actually open for business. And again, even if you discover a flaw so big that you decide not to start the business after all, your business plan has done its job. While undoubtedly disappointing, it's far better for your business to fail on paper than in real life.

3. Define Your Market

Who will buy your product or service? Even the most innovative business will fail if it doesn't quickly find enough customers to make a profit. In this section, your task is to demonstrate to a potential investor or lender (or convince yourself) that there are indeed customers out there, ready and willing to buy your product or service. Use whatever data you can get your hands on to demonstrate this. And don't neglect your imagination—unconventional arguments are fine as long as they are convincing. Here is a brief list of points you may wish to make:

- Similar businesses have been successful. For example, if several fitness clubs with Internet access are all the rage in L.A., you might explain why this is a good indication that your similar business would succeed in Chicago, where the market is currently dominated by less cutting-edge gyms.

- Marketing surveys or demographic reports point to a growing need for your product or service. For instance, to buttress your contention that there will be a need for your new line of paralegal training materials, point to U.S. government reports listing paralegals as being one of the fastest-growing occupations.
- Media reports confirm the popularity of and demand for your business. For example, include newspaper clips or transcripts of television news reports on the surge of demand for antibacterial air fresheners as evidence that your germ-killing Sani-Scent™ will sell.
- Your conversations with potential customers show a need for your business. It's often a good idea to carry out an informal survey of your most likely customers and include the results. For example, if you will run a business repairing and reconditioning acoustic guitars and similar stringed instruments, you might include results of a survey of guitarists and other musicians on what kind of repair services they need, as well as quotes from them saying that they'd use your services.

Besides claiming that there is a solid market for your business, do your best to define and describe exactly who makes it up. If you're opening a bar with live entertainment, for instance, you might identify your market as primarily childless, urban 21- to 35-year-olds who tend to have more disposable income and leisure time than others. Similarly, if you're planning an antique restoration service, you might identify your target market as professionals and others in the 40–70 age range with household incomes of $100,000 or more. The better you can show that you know exactly who your market is, the more confident lenders and investors will be that you can actually find these people and sell to them.

 Include a prototypical profile of your target customer. Explain what this fictional person's needs are and why and how she uses your product or service. Do your best to flesh out a believable person, right down to the color of her socks. Creating a typical customer gives a face to an otherwise abstract market definition, and can give your market analysis more impact.

4. Analyze Your Competition

Just because you have a great business idea doesn't mean you'll be successful—other businesses may have already cornered the market or be poised to do so. For example, lots of small-business owners who ran successful movie-rental businesses were wiped out when chains like Blockbuster rolled out thousands of megastores. It's often all too easy for a bigger, better-capitalized outfit to copy your best features and pull the rug out from under your business. Use this section to explain why your business really will have few direct competitors—or, if competitors will abound (as is far more likely), to show how your business will develop and keep an edge. Don't be shy about detailing competitors' strengths as well as weaknesses as part of showing why your business will better meet customers' needs.

In discussing the competition, it's important to put yourself in the shoes of a customer who is comparing your business to a competitor's. From the customer's perspective, what factors are most important in choosing which business to patronize? Some obvious considerations are quality of products or services, convenience (access), reliability and price. Your competitors will probably excel in some of these areas and be weaker in others. The same will probably be true of your business. The trick is for you to find a spot, or niche, among the competition, and offer a combination of elements —such as price and convenience—that no one else offers.

! Think twice before you attempt to compete on price. No matter how efficient your business is and how little you charge, someone will always charge less. Given the purchasing power and other efficiencies of big business, few little operators can successfully compete on pricing alone. Far better to look for another edge—quality, uniqueness and customer convenience, to mention a few.

EXAMPLE: John wants to open a business to sell and service classic cars. In developing his business idea, he discovers that there are about a dozen existing companies within a 20-mile radius of his proposed location who already provide some or all of the services he envisions. Before finally committing to opening the business, he needs to identify and create a convincing competitive edge. One day, talking to a friend, he realizes that his edge could be the development of a better system for finding parts. If he could locate new and used classic car parts nationwide, rather than just in his region, he would have a huge advantage over other shops. John begins by developing a database of websites that specialize in classic and reproduction car parts, organized by make and model. By using these online dealers— plus the other dealers nationwide who aren't online, but whom John will become familiar with as he attends regional trade shows and does more national business—John will be able to get parts faster than any of his competitors. Putting some extra energy into the parts aspect of his business gives John a key marketing hook to convince his knowledgeable (and often finicky) customers that his business really is a step ahead.

Businesses With Specialized Knowledge Are Hard to Copy

The business with the most knowledge about how to beat out its competitors usually wins. But what is business knowledge, and how can you exploit it? In the broad sense, it's anything a business knows how to do that can give it a meaningful edge over competitors. Common examples include:

- the ability to buy products for resale cheaper than competitors can
- having a great location
- having a unique, hard-to-duplicate product
- knowing how to implement excellent customer service, and
- having superior customer accessibility— longer hours, better parking, etc.

Consider the example of Laura and Brad's import business. They were importing clothing from Guatemala, but with competition from hundreds of other small importers, it was hard to make a dime. Then, leaving Brad to manage the business for a few weeks, Laura spent some time working with a dozen weavers in a small Guatemalan town. They focused on creating specially woven and dyed Guatemalan fabric suitable for luxury window coverings. Realizing that the high end of the import business was an underexploited niche, Laura quickly created a product with a hard-to-copy look and a solid profit margin. In short, she transformed a not particularly savvy, barely profitable import business into a highly intelligent, highly profitable one.

5. Describe Your Marketing Strategy

By now you've shown that there are people out there who will buy your product or service from you instead of from your competitors. Great, but your job isn't done. Investors and others interested in supporting your business will want to know how you'll reach your customers in a cost-effective way. Explaining how you'll go about this is essentially outlining your marketing strategy.

Any marketing strategy worthy of the name should be based on the particular characteristics of the market you're trying to reach, with the goal being to reach as many customers as possible for the least expense. For instance, if you're trying to reach a very tiny group of people, such as left-handed ophthalmologists, or even a slightly larger audience, such as digital video editors, it makes no sense to spend the big bucks required for television advertising. On the other hand, if your market consists of all children between the ages of six and ten, TV advertising might be an efficient way to reach them.

In describing your plan for reaching your customers, explain what methods you will use, such as radio or newspaper advertising, Web marketing or directory listings such as trade directories or the Yellow Pages. If you plan to use non-traditional guerrilla marketing tactics such as putting up posters all around town or staging publicity stunts, explain exactly what you plan to do. And no matter what kind of marketing strategy you outline, be sure to explain why you think it will work.

Small businesses that don't have much of a marketing budget shouldn't be shy about their smaller-scale plans. Even if you don't plan to spend much (if any) money on marketing or advertising, you should have a plan for how you'll reach your first customers. In your business plan, simply explain what this strategy is. The following example shows how a small business with a minimal advertising and marketing budget might explain their strategy.

EXAMPLE: Turtlevision's Marketing Strategy. We plan to keep our marketing costs very low, at least for the first year or two. Rather than spending money on traditional advertising, our strategy will be to list our services in local video-related directories and utilize various online communities to promote ourselves. In addition, our plan for the early days of Turtlevision is to offer our services at a discount to various nonprofit organizations to develop our portfolio and to generate good word of mouth about our work. For example, Turtlevision is currently working with the nonprofit Film Foundation to stream a monthly short film and video series on the Web. Our hope is that recommendations from our satisfied customers will give Turtlevision a start in the right direction.

Spam is bad. No matter how delectable you find the potted meat product, do not fool yourself into believing that sending out masses of unsolicited emails (a practice known as "spamming") will be good for your business. Most Web-savvy entrepreneurs already know what nutritionists have told us for years—spam is bad for you. At the very least, it's bad for any goodwill that may exist for your business. No one likes getting junk email, no matter what fabulous deal it may offer. Be a good net citizen and use more savory marketing tactics than spam.

Marketing without advertising can be successful. Especially in niche or local markets, people often make purchasing decisions based on the recommendations of people they respect, not on ads. If you doubt this, think about how you chose your dentist, plumber or the company that recently fixed your roof. Chances are good that you got a recommendation from someone you trusted. To be the beneficiary of positive word of mouth, you need to run an excellent business. Assuming you do, there are loads of cost-effective ways to let potential customers know about your great service. For a book full of great ideas, read *Marketing Without Advertising,* by Michael Phillips and Salli Rasberry (Nolo). Its subtitle, "Inspire Customers to Rave About Your Business to Create Lasting Success," explains exactly why every small businessperson should read it.

6. Describe Your Business Accomplishments

Above and beyond demonstrating the beauty of your business idea, you'll want to show that you're the right person to run it. Do this by creating a resumé showing your business accomplishments. Here you have the chance to highlight all of your relevant experience and training, as well as any other personal information likely to inspire confidence in you as a businessperson.

Prospective lenders and investors will want to know the following things about you:

- **Do you understand the business?** Emphasize that you understand the basic tasks of the business inside and out. Surprisingly, lots of people start small businesses in areas where they are amateurs. (For example, a person who isn't mechanically inclined but who loves German cars may want to open a VW repair shop.) Lack of hands-on experience will likely be a red flag to investors, who know a non-expert boss can't roll up her sleeves and help out in emergencies. Do your best to show them otherwise.
- **Can you manage people?** All sorts of organizations, including small businesses, fail because their leaders—no matter how technically competent—can't work well with others. Bad people management is one of the surest ways to create a poor workplace atmosphere, one with low morale, mediocre productivity and high turnover. If you have successfully worked with, and preferably led, people, you should emphasize this experience.
- **Do you understand money?** A surprising number of people who open small businesses don't know how to make money. Even though

their business idea is a good, competitive one and their employees are energetic, they manage to make such poor financial decisions that their businesses don't prosper. Knowing this, people who will consider funding your business will want to see if you or another key person in your business has money-making skills. If you do—even if your experience was in a very different business—emphasize it.

C. Making Financial Projections

Besides describing how your business will work, including how it will reach plenty of customers and fend off competitors, you'll also need to do some number-crunching to show that your business will in fact turn a profit. All the rosy descriptions in the world won't make your business a success if the numbers turn up red.

Projecting the finances of your business may seem intimidating or difficult, but in reality it's really not terribly complex. Basically, it consists of making educated guesses as to how much money you'll need to spend and how much you'll take in, and then using these estimates to calculate whether your business will be sufficiently profitable.

Predicting and planning the finances of your business is not just important to attract investors, but to demonstrate to you and your family whether or not your business idea will fly. If your first projections show your business losing money, you'll have an opportunity while still in the planning stage to make sensible adjustments, such as raising your prices or cutting costs. If you neglect to make tight financial projections, you won't realize your plan is a money-loser until you actually start losing money. At that point, it may be too late to turn things around.

Nonetheless, many new entrepreneurs avoid crunching their numbers, often due to fear that their estimates will be wildly off-base and yield useless results. This is a poor reason to avoid forecasting your finances. If you do your best to make realistic predictions of expenses and revenues and accept that your guestimates will not be absolutely correct, you can learn a great deal about what the financial side of your business is likely to look like in its early months and even years of operation. Even a somewhat inaccurate picture of your business's likely finances will be much more helpful than having no picture at all.

For a basic understanding of your business's projected financial situation, you'll need to make the following estimates and calculations, all of which are discussed in detail in the rest of this chapter:

- **a break-even analysis.** Here you use income and expense estimates for a year or more to see whether, in theory at least, your business will be able to turn a profit. If you have trouble projecting a solid profit, you might need to consider abandoning your idea altogether.

- **a profit/loss forecast.** Here you'll refine the sales and expense estimates that you used for your break-even analysis into a formal, month-by-month projection of your business's net profit for at least the first year of operations.

- **a start-up cost estimate.** As the name suggests, this is simply the total of all the expenses you'll incur before your business opens. These costs should be included in your business plan to give a true picture of how much money you'll need to get your business off the ground.

- **a cash flow projection.** Even if your profit/loss forecast tells you that your business will have higher revenues than expenses, that doesn't mean that you'll always have enough cash available on key dates such as when rent is due or when you need to buy more inventory. A cash flow projection lays out how much cash you'll have—or how much you'll be short—month by month. This lets you know if you'll need to get a credit line or set up other arrangements to make sure funds are available.

Get to Know Your Numbers

The calculations involved in accounting aren't terribly complex. The main reason people get confused is not that they're bad at math—it's that they don't understand what the numbers mean. It's important that you take a little time early on to learn what your key financial numbers are, and how they relate to one another. To help you keep the numbers straight, keep in mind this formula:

$$
\begin{array}{rl}
 & \text{sales revenue} \\
- & \text{costs of sale (variable costs)} \\
\hline
= & \text{gross profit} \\
- & \text{overhead (fixed costs)} \\
\hline
= & \text{net profit} \\
- & \text{taxes} \\
\hline
= & \text{after-tax profit} \\
\hline
\end{array}
$$

You'll have a much easier time understanding all the various financial calculations involved in accounting—including break-even, profit/loss and cash flow analysis—once you're familiar and comfortable with this basic formula.

All you really need to make these financial forecasts are a calculator and some simple ledger sheets, though if you have a computer and accounting software your job will be even easier. Blank ledger sheets, which are nothing more than blank rows and columns for you to fill in with your numbers, are available at any office supply store. If you use accounting software, most of your calculations can be done automatically, with the click of a button, which can be very helpful when you're in the planning stages and trying out lots of different numbers. If you plan to use software for bookkeeping and accounting once your business is started, you might as well also use it for preparing your financial projections. Accounting software is relatively easy to figure out and will definitely save you lots of time in the long run. Quicken and Quickbooks, both by Intuit, are very popular and priced within reach of just about any budget. Magazines such as *Home Office Computing, MacWorld* and *PC World* are good sources of information on other programs.

Once you start shopping for accounting and bookkeeping software, you'll probably also find special business plan software. These programs, however, usually provide you with only a word processing function and some empty spreadsheets to fill in. Most real accounting software allows you to do the same kinds of spreadsheets, and usually a lot more. Chances are the word processing program you already have is a lot more powerful than whatever is offered with a business plan program.

The rest of this chapter will walk you step by step through each of these financial forecasts, which, when completed, will tell you whether your business will actually make enough money to pay the bills and turn a profit. Assuming the answer is yes, you'll also see whether you need to obtain start-up money from investors or lenders and, if so, how much. Finally, once your business is up and running you can refer back to your forecasts to see how your performance is measuring up.

D. Break-Even Analysis

Your break-even point is the amount of income you'll need to cover your expenses before you make a dime of profit. In other words, it's the point at which the income you'll bring in will cover your expenses. Expenses include the costs of your product or service to you (also known as variable costs, since they change depending on how much product or service you provide), plus your overhead, like rent, salaries and utility bills (commonly called fixed costs).

Since break-even analysis offers a glimpse of your ultimate profitability, it's a great tool for weeding out losing business ideas. For example, if you see that you'll need to achieve a highly optimistic sales number just to cover your costs, you'll

probably want to rethink your entire business plan. Maybe there will be a way you can adjust parts of your business so that a more reachable sales volume will result in a profit. If not, it might be best to ditch your less-than-brilliant business idea.

To find your break-even point, first make a best-guess estimate of your sales revenue for the products or services you plan to sell. Then predict how much profit you'll make on each sale (by subtracting the costs of a sale from the revenue from a sale), and figure out a "gross profit percentage," which tells you how much of each sales dollar exceeds the cost of the product or service itself. Finally, you'll estimate what your fixed costs such as rent and insurance will be. After a few calculations, you'll see whether the profit you'll make on each individual sale (also called gross profit) adds up to enough to cover your fixed costs.

Before we go into the details of calculating your break-even point, let's look at a very oversimplified example to illustrate the overall process. All the calculations are explained in more detail below; for now, just focus on the process as a whole.

EXAMPLE: Michele is starting a business selling her own handmade jewelry. To calculate her break-even point, she would make her very best estimate of how much jewelry she thinks she could sell in a year. She figures she could sell an average of 20 pieces a month at $20 apiece, making her yearly income $4,800. Then she'd figure out how much she'd make on each sale, above the cost of materials. (For this super-simplified example, let's leave the cost of her time out of the equation.) Since the materials for each piece cost Michele $5, she'd be making $15 on each sale. In other words, her gross profit would be $15 per piece. Next she would calculate her gross profit percentage, which is her gross profit ($15) divided by her selling price ($20). This puts her gross profit percentage at 75%, which means that .75 of each sales dollar exceeds of the cost of the piece of jewelry itself. Next Michele would figure out what her fixed costs would be—say the cost of her tools, and the monthly cost of her booth at a local arts and crafts mall. She figures that these fixed costs total $50 per month, or $600 per year.

To calculate her break-even point, Michele will divide her annual fixed costs ($600) by her gross profit percentage (.75) to arrive at a break-even point of $800. This means that just to cover the costs of the materials, and her tools and booth, Michele must bring in $800 per year, and anything above that amount will be her pre-tax profit. Since she earlier estimated that she could sell $4,800 worth of jewelry per year, Michele figures that she'll easily reach her break-even point—and make a healthy profit as well.

Before we explain exactly how to do the calculations, we'll quickly discuss two items that you need to understand before actually crunching your numbers: making financial estimates and categorizing your expenses.

1. Making Estimates

When you estimate your income and expenses, your estimates should extend over enough time to catch up with seasonal fluctuations. Depending on your type of business, your revenue and expenses may vary wildly from month to month. For example, if you plan to manufacture custom snowboards, most of your sales will be in late fall and early winter months, while the opposite would be true if you made surfboards. A good way to account for this is to make estimates for each month of the year, then add them up to get a yearly figure. We recommend covering at least a one year period, which is enough time to account for normal ups and downs, but not so long as to be overly speculative.

2. Categorizing Your Expenses

Your business expenses need to be divided into two categories: fixed expenses (fixed costs) and variable expenses (variable costs). This division is not only important for your break-even analysis, it's a standard method of categorizing expenses for accounting and tax reporting. It's key that you understand the difference.

- **Fixed costs.** Commonly referred to as "overhead," these include all regular expenses not directly tied to the product or service you provide. Rent, utility bills, phone bills, payments for outside help like bookkeeping services, postage and most salaries (except in service businesses) are common fixed costs.
- **Variable costs.** These costs—sometimes also called product costs, costs of goods or costs of sale—are directly related to the products or services you provide and include inventory, packaging, supplies, materials and sometimes labor used in providing your product or service. They're called "variable" precisely because they go up or down depending on the volume of products or services you produce or sell. (In the case of services, one of the biggest variable expenses is almost always the wages or salary of the service provider—see "Salaries and Labor Costs—Fixed or Variable?" below.)

Salaries and Labor Costs—Fixed or Variable?

Whether you'll categorize labor expenses as fixed or variable costs often depends on the type of workers you pay and the kinds of products or services you're selling. Salaries or wages of managers and employees who are necessary to keep your business going (you, or your bookkeeper, for example) are usually best seen as fixed costs. But salaries or wages for employees who create the products or provide the services you sell may be more appropriately treated as variable costs. For example, an ad agency that pays six freelance copywriters to service clients' accounts should treat their paychecks as variable costs.

A good test of whether a labor cost should be designated as fixed or variable is to ask yourself: If I sell one, ten or 100 more products or services this week, will my labor costs go up? If not, you're probably looking at a fixed cost. For instance, suppose you're trying to decide whether your receptionist's salary should be categorized as a variable cost or a fixed cost. If you produce and sell 100 more Mr. Hankey dolls, will your reception costs go up? Probably not. So your receptionist's salary should be part of your overhead. But if you have to hire five temporary employees to handle the phones at Christmastime to handle the spiking demand for Mr. Hankeys, their wages should be classified as variable costs. (Hint: money paid to workers who are temps or independent contractors are usually categorized as variable costs, because it's usually tied to providing a product or service.) Of course, at some point selling more products or services at a permanently increased level will probably lead to expansion of your business and increased overhead, because you'll have to hire more support staff, managers and other necessary employees just to get along. At that point, you might revisit your allocation of fixed and variable costs.

3. Estimate Your Sales Revenue

Start your break-even analysis by making your best estimate of annual sales revenues. Your estimate will obviously depend on several different variables, such as your type of business, what you plan to charge for each product or service you'll offer and how successful you'll be at selling products and services. Though at first it may seem overwhelming to project revenues based upon so many untested variables, it is essential that you take the plunge and try out some numbers. Even though your estimates won't be anywhere near 100% accurate, they'll force you to focus and refine key elements of your business idea and may even help you spot big potholes in your plan. And besides, you need these estimates in order to move ahead with your break-even calculations, so get over it and start estimating.

One good way to estimate how much money you'll be bringing in is to compare your business with similar ones. Retail businesses, for example, often measure annual sales revenue per square foot of retail space. Thus, if you plan to open a pet supply store, you'll want to find out the annual sales revenue per square foot of other pet supply shops. While direct competitors probably won't share this information, industry trade publications almost always provide it. Attending industry trade shows where you can meet and talk to people who own similar businesses in other parts of the country is also a good way to gather valuable information.

EXAMPLE: Inga is planning to open a used bookstore in Milwaukee called Inga's Book Haus. She plans to sell mostly used books, which generally have a high profit margin, but she'll also stock a limited selection of new books at the front of the store to attract more customers. She'll also sell some miscellaneous trinkets like postcards and magnets.

As part of trying to figure out how much sales revenue she can realistically expect for Inga's Book Haus, Inga calls up a couple friends who happen to be in the book business. One who works at a nearby used bookstore confides to Inga that the store sells approximately $450 worth of books per square foot per year. Another friend owns a new-and-used bookstore in Madison; she tells Inga that they bring in about $400 annually per square foot. Neither of these stores is exactly like the one Inga envisions; the one in Milwaukee doesn't sell any new books, and the one in Madison does a healthy trade in textbooks, which Inga doesn't expect at her store. To round out her information, Inga also looks into some trade publications and does a bit of sleuthing at local new-and-used bookstores, examining their prices and how busy they seem to be. Ultimately she decides that an annual income of $350 per square foot is realistic. She has her eye on a few storefronts, all around 1,200 square feet, so she estimates her annual revenues to be $420,000.

Basing your projected revenue on the numbers of other similar companies' is also a good estimation method for nonretail businesses such as wholesaling or manufacturing companies. However, it can be somewhat tricky finding a solid basis for comparison for nonretail businesses. Unlike retail businesses, sales per square foot wouldn't really apply. If you're not already well-acquainted with your field, you'll have to do some research. Study similar businesses with an eye for how many employees they have, how wide their distribution is and how much annual income they earn. Base your income projections on similarly sized businesses with a comparable range of distribution.

If yours is a service business, your estimate of sales revenue will depend on how many billable sales you'll be able to make each month. A big part of doing this is to estimate how many hours you and any employees will work and how much you'll be paid per hour by your clients. But don't overlook the fact that all of your time won't be billable—you won't be providing services every

hour you're at work. For example, if you run a landscaping business, a sizable portion of your time will not be performing landscaping work but managing your accounts, maintaining your equipment and soliciting new clients. You'll need to make a realistic assessment of how much of your time is taken up by these non-billable activities and how much time is spent on providing actual services to clients to get an accurate picture of how much money will be flowing in.

4. Calculate Your Average Gross Profit Percentage

Your next task is to figure your average gross profit percentage. It may sound complex, but basically it's just a figure that represents how much of each sales dollar will be left over after paying for the costs of the products or services themselves. There are a number of steps involved in calculating this figure, but none involve anything more than simple math (addition, subtraction, multiplication and division). It's definitely a number you want to figure out, as it's a crucial piece of your break-even puzzle. Once you know your average gross profit percentage, you'll easily be able to figure out how much money you'll need to bring in to cover all the costs of your business.

In a nutshell, to figure your average gross profit percentage you'll need to:

1. Figure out your gross profit for each major category of your products or services.
2. Determine an average gross profit for your business overall, including all your products and services, and
3. Divide your average gross profit by your average selling price.

In case you're wondering what the difference is between "gross profit" and "average gross profit," here's a quick explanation (the details will be covered as we go through the calculations below). When you sell an individual product, the money that you earn above the cost of the item itself (called your variable cost, or sometimes cost of goods) is called gross profit. For instance, if your pet store sells a doghouse for $200, and you bought the doghouse for $110, then what's left over for you after the sale is $90—your gross profit. If your business sells more than one kind of product (like most), you'll need to figure an *average* gross profit for your total product line in order to get a realistic picture of how much of your income will be left over after paying for all your products. For instance, the average gross profit for your pet store would include all of your products in the calculation—cat scratching posts, pet food, play toys, etc.—including their sales price, and what they cost you.

The next few subsections take you through the process of calculating your business's average gross profit.

a. Figure Your Gross Profit by Category

As described above, your gross profit is the amount of money you make on each sale, above the cost of the product or service itself (aka the variable cost, or cost of sale). Gross profit is determined simply by subtracting the variable cost of your product or service from its sales price.

Variable costs are generally fairly easy to estimate. If you're selling products bought from a wholesaler, your variable costs may be as simple as what you pay for the products themselves. If you'll assemble the products, then include your costs for the parts and labor needed to put them together. Also remember to include items like packaging or freebies in your variable costs. If you only sell services, variable costs basically include the pay of whoever provides the services (you or perhaps an employee), not including time spent on administrative tasks and managing accounts, which is generally considered to be a fixed, not variable, cost. It can sometimes be tricky to figure out the variable costs of a service business. Do your best to separate out the costs that are not associated with individual projects—those are your fixed costs.

> **EXAMPLE:** Turtlevision, a digital video editing service, pays its staff editor $50 per hour for 80 hours per month of editing work. In addition, Turtlevision pays an office assistant $15 per hour for 100 hours per month of administrative work. Turtlevision's monthly variable costs would include the editor's salary of $4,000, but not the salary paid to the office assistant, which is not tied to any particular client or project.

One kink in figuring out your business's gross profit is that your selling prices and variable costs may vary a great deal from product to product (or service to service). For instance, say you buy cat collars for an average of $4, and sell them for an average price of $10 (your gross profit per cat collar would be $6). Doghouses, on the other hand, cost you an average of $110, and you sell them for an average price of $200 (your gross profit per dog house would be $90).

To account for these differences you should categorize your products or services and figure an average gross profit for each category. There are a few steps to follow, but hang in there—each one is pretty simple.

First, estimate the average selling price and average variable cost for products or services with roughly similar selling prices and variable costs. For instance, you might group all your animal collars together—for cats, dogs and ferrets—since their selling prices ($9 to $13) and variable costs ($3 to $5) aren't too different. Don't lump together products or services with considerably different selling prices or variable costs. As a general rule, the more tightly you define your categories, the more accurate your estimates will be.

After you've estimated the average selling price and average variable cost for each category, subtract the average variable cost from the average selling price for each category, and you'll have an average gross profit dollar figure for each category.

	Animal collars	Bird houses	Dog houses
Average selling price	$11	$60	$200
− Average variable cost	$4	$30	$110
= Average gross profit	$7	$30	$90

The next step is to figure out a gross profit percentage for each category. A gross profit percentage tells you how much of each dollar of sales income is gross profit. To calculate each category's gross profit percentage, divide the average gross profit figure by the average selling price.

Animal collars category:

	Average gross profit	$ 7.00
÷	Average selling price	$11.00
=	Gross profit percentage	63.6%

Using the above example, it follows that if you sold $1,500 in cat collars, 63.6% of that—$954— would be gross profit, or the amount left over after paying costs of sale. As you can see, converting your gross profit into a percentage allows you to quickly figure out how much of your income will be left over after variable costs have been covered.

b. Calculate Your Average Gross Profit

After you've found the gross profit percentage for each category, you'll be able to determine your average gross profit for your business as a whole.

First, estimate your annual sales revenue per category. Earlier you estimated your total annual sales revenues; now divide that figure as best you can into your estimates for each category. For example, if you estimated total annual revenues of $100,000 for your pet supply business, divide that among your categories, such as collars, birdhouses and doghouses—say $25,000 in collar sales, $40,000 in birdhouses and $35,000 in doghouses. Base your division on your best sense of which categories and products will make up a big part of your business, and which will have a smaller share. Then, for each product category, multiply the esti-

mated sales revenue by the category's gross profit percentage (arrived at above) to arrive at your total gross profit dollars per category.

Animal collars category:

	Estimate sales revenue	$25,000
x	Gross profit percentage	63.6%
=	Total gross dollars	$15,900

Finally, add together the gross profit dollar amounts for each category to arrive at a total annual gross profit for your business. Divide the total annual gross profit figure by the total annual sales that you estimated for all products or services. The result will be an average gross profit percentage for your business.

Let's look at how this process works with Inga's Book Haus.

EXAMPLE: As you may recall, Inga plans to sell new and used books, plus some peripheral items such as postcards and refrigerator magnets. Since the profit margins for new books, used books and trinkets are different, Inga figures a gross profit percentage for each of these categories. (Inga might want to establish separate categories for hardback, paperback and coffee-table books, but we'll keep things simple.)

To accomplish this, first Inga estimates an average variable cost for each category. In addition to the cost of the merchandise, she includes the cost of free bags, bookmarks and wrapping paper for gifts. For instance, used books cost her an average of $3, and she figures the bookmarks and bags that go with each sale will cost her an average of 10¢. So her total average variable cost in the used book category is $3.10. She doesn't include fixed costs, like rent or salaries, here.

Next, Inga fills in an average selling price for each product category. Her average selling price for used books, for example, is $7. She then subtracts the average variable cost (arrived at above) from the average selling price to get an average gross profit figure for each product category. Subtracting her average variable cost for used books ($3.10) from her average selling price for used books ($7.00) leaves her with an average gross profit for used books of $3.90.

Used book category:

	Average sales price	$ 7.00
−	Average variable cost	3.10
=	Average gross profit	$ 3.90

To determine the gross profit percentage, she'll simply divide the gross profit by the selling price in each category to get a gross profit percentage for each category. Dividing her average gross profit for used books ($3.90) by her average selling price ($7.00) gives Inga a gross profit percentage of 56% for used books, a good percentage. That means that for every dollar she'll bring in from used books, 44 cents per dollar will be eaten up on Inga's costs, leaving 56 cents per dollar to cover fixed costs and go towards a net profit. Her gross profit percentage for new books is 33%, and for trinkets it's an impressive 70%.

New book category:

	Average gross profit	$ 3.90
÷	Average selling price	12.00
=	Gross profit percentage	33%

Trinkets category:

	Average gross profit	$ 1.40
÷	Average selling price	2.00
=	Gross profit percentage	70%

Using the gross profit percentages and estimated sales revenues for each category, Inga can calculate the gross profit dollar figure for each category. For example, her estimated annual sales of used books is $300,000. (Remember from Section 3 that Inga estimated her total annual sales revenue to be $420,000. She thinks used books will account for a little over 2/3 of her sales.) By multiplying $300,000 by the used book category's gross profit percentage (56%), she estimates an annual gross profit of $168,000. Adding up the gross

profit figures for each category, Inga figures that her total gross profit will be $215,000. Finally, by dividing this amount by her annual estimated revenues of $420,000, she easily determines her total gross profit percentage, which is 51.2%.

	New books	Used books	Trinkets
Average variable cost per product	$ 8.00	$ 3.00	$ .50
+ bookmarks, bags	.10	.10	.10
= Average total cost	$ 8.10	$ 3.10	$ .60
Average selling price	$12.00	$ 7.00	$2.00
+ Average total variable cost	8.10	3.10	.60
= Average gross profit	$ 3.90	$ 3.90	$1.40
Average gross profit	$ 3.90	$ 3.90	$1.40
÷ Average selling price	12.00	7.00	2.00
= Gross profit percentage	33%	56%	70%
Average sales	$100,000	$300,000	$20,000
x Gross profit percentage	33%	56%	70%
= Annual gross profit	$ 33,000	$168,000	$14,000

Annual gross profit	
New Book	$ 33,000
+ Used Books	168,000
+ Trinkets	14,000
= Total annual gross profit	$ 215,000
÷ Total annual sales	42,000
= Average gross profit percentage	51.2%

5. Estimate Your Fixed Costs

You're done with the hard part—compared to calculating your gross profit percentage, fixed costs are a breeze. Simply estimate your monthly fixed expenses, including items like rent, utility bills, office supplies, uncollectable debts—basically, any costs you expect to have independent of the product or service you sell. Since many of these costs recur monthly, it's usually easiest to estimate them per month and total them for one year. It's also a good idea to throw in a little extra, say 10% or so, to cover miscellaneous expenses that you can't predict. Once you've arrived at a total, you'll know that you'll need to make at least this much gross profit (and probably a healthy chunk more) to keep your business afloat.

EXAMPLE: Here is a list of Inga's monthly estimates for fixed costs:

Rent	$ 3,500
Wages for part-time clerks	2,500
Utilities	800
Telephone	700
Office equipment	700
Insurance	500
Advertising	700
Accounting	300
Electronic payment system fees	300
Misc.	1,000
Total fixed expenses per month	11,000
Annual total fixed expenses (monthly expenses x 12)	$132,000

Don't forget you have to eat. Notice that Inga has chosen not to list a salary here as an expense. She, like many sole proprietors, figures that her savings, help from friends and family, and some extra crumbs the business may produce should be enough to live on for the short term. Once she figures out how much profit the business will bring in regularly, she'll decide how much profit she can expect to take out of the business and add it to her fixed costs. Not including payments for your own living expenses in your break-even analysis, however, can be dangerous, at least if you're planning to live off your business's profits from the get-go. If this is your plan, you should add to your fixed costs the minimum amount you'll need to take out of the business to cover your living expenses. Then, if you can't project your

income to be higher than your fixed costs when the amount you'll need for living expenses is included, you'll know you can't plan on living off the company. This may be a clue that your business is not a good bet.

Keep fixed costs as low as reasonably possible. If your business is slow to get started—and lots of businesses take months or even years to become solidly profitable—high fixed costs can quickly eat up your savings. Rather than committing yourself to high overhead, it's usually better to keep expenses low, allowing increases only when your income justifies spending more. For example, few businesses really depend on a pricey physical location. If your business won't depend on a big casual walk-in trade, don't overpay for a trendy zip code. Operating from a low-cost warehouse district, an older office building or even your garage may work just fine.

6. Calculate Your Break-Even Point

Once you have estimated your fixed costs (from Section 5, above) and your average gross profit percentage (from Section 4, above), it's easy to figure out how much revenue you'll need to break even. Remember, your gross profit percentage represents how much of each dollar of revenue is actual profit, left over after paying for the product or service itself. To figure out your break-even point, you'll divide your estimated annual fixed costs by your gross profit percentage. The result will be your break-even point—the amount of sales revenue you'll need to bring in just to cover your costs.

EXAMPLE: The break-even point for Inga's Book Haus will equal her annual fixed expenses divided by her average gross profit percentage.

Annual fixed expenses	$132,000
÷ Average gross profit percentage	(51.2%)
= Break-even point	$257,813

If you're having trouble understanding how this equation works, you're not alone. Conceptually, it's a little tricky to see how dividing your fixed costs by your gross profit percentage yields your break-even point. Think of it this way: However much money your business brings in, some of it will be eaten up by the cost of the product or service itself (your variable costs), leaving you a reduced amount left over to pay your bills. How much is left over is determined by your gross profit percentage—this number tells you just how much will be left over, on average, from each dollar, after paying for your product or service itself (your variable costs). When you divide your estimated annual fixed costs by your gross profit percentage, the resulting number (the break-even point) is the exact amount that's enough to cover your fixed costs.

Let's look at another extra-simplified example to illustrate this concept. Remember Michele from earlier in the chapter, who was going into business selling jewelry? Her gross profit percentage was .75, meaning that for every dollar she brought in, .25 would be eaten up by the cost of the jewelry materials, leaving Michele .75 to cover her fixed costs. Michele's fixed costs were $600 per year. So, you're wondering, why isn't Michele's break-even point $600? Because if Michele earned exactly $600 in a year, only 75% of that would be available to cover her fixed costs—the other 25% would have already been eaten up by the costs of her jewelry, and she wouldn't be able to pay all of the $600 worth of fixed costs. To account for this, Michele needs to divide her fixed costs ($600) by her gross profit percentage (.75) to arrive at the higher amount that she'll need to bring in that will cover her fixed costs, *understanding that 25% of the revenue that will cover her fixed costs is eaten up by the cost of the jewelry*. Dividing $600 by .75 results in $800, her break-even point; if Michele brings in $800, .25 of it will go towards the cost of the product, and the rest ($600) is just enough to cover her fixed costs.

7. Analyze Your Result

If your estimated revenue exceeds your break-even point, great—but that's not the same thing as saying you are free to put the excess money in your pocket. Again, remember that every dollar you bring in doesn't come for free; the cost of your product or service also has to be covered. The portion of excess sales revenue that's really yours (ignoring taxes for the moment) is equivalent to (you guessed it) your gross profit percentage of that excess revenue. In order to determine how much of the excess revenue is pre-tax profit, multiply the excess by your gross profit percentage. The result is your estimated net profit.

> **EXAMPLE:** Earlier, Inga estimated her annual sales revenue to be $420,000—over $160,000 more than she needs to break even.

Estimated revenue	$420,000
– Break-even point	$257,813
= Excess revenues	$162,187

To figure out how much of her excess revenue will be actual pre-tax profit, Inga multiplies it by her gross profit percentage.

Excess revenues	$162,187
x Gross profit percentage	51.2%
= Net profit	$83,040

Inga is happy to see her projections show a profit. But she needs to remember that none of her estimates included any payments to herself, meaning she'll probably need to take some of that net profit just to meet her living expenses.

If, on the other hand, your break-even point is higher than your expected revenues, you'll have some decisions to make. You'll have to decide whether certain aspects of your plan can be amended in order to come up with an achievable break-even point. For instance, perhaps you could find a less expensive source of supplies, do without an employee or save rent by working out of your home.

But don't change your numbers without a very good reason. When confronted by a break-even point that exceeds your estimated revenues, you may be tempted to tweak and squish your numbers into a profitable forecast, even if those numbers aren't realistic. Unless you really do have a good reason to think you can break even at a lower point, this is a temptation to guard against. For example, to have your plan pencil out in the black, you might boost your sales estimates in hopes that you'll somehow be able to pull it off. But can you really sell 500,000 Sausage Shooters™, 3,000 books on medieval dentistry or 2,000 Tori Spelling™ mini-tees per month?

Generally speaking, when trying to pencil out a more profitable break-even point, it's best to focus on your costs. The most reliable way to tilt a business from the red to the black is to reduce what you will pay out, not to make a more optimistic projection of what you'll take in.

E. Profit/Loss Forecast

If your break-even analysis shows that, based on realistic estimates of revenue and expenses, your business will turn a profit, your next job is to use these figures to create the profit/loss forecast component of your business plan. Similar to a break-even analysis, a profit/loss forecast (sometimes called a P & L forecast) uses your estimates for sales revenue and variable costs to calculate your gross profit, then subtracts your fixed expenses from gross profit to arrive at net profit. If you use accounting software, it will generate a P & L statement automatically once you enter monthly sales and expense estimates.

The main difference between a P & L and the break-even analysis just discussed has to do with timing. A break-even analysis looks at profit and loss on a yearly basis, while your P & L forecast calculates monthly net profit. A P& L also differs from a cash flow forecast, which we discuss in the next section, in the kinds of income and expenses that it includes. A cash flow forecast looks at all sources of income and expenses, including loans, transfers of personal money into the business, start-up costs, and all other types of cash inflows and outflows. A P & L, on the other hand, is only concerned with money earned from normal business operations. For this reason, a P & L forecast will tell you whether your business operations are generating enough income to cover your expenses, something you can't glean from a cash flow forecast.

Here's how to translate your break-even figures into a profit/loss forecast. Start by breaking down your annual sales estimate into monthly amounts. If you expect significant seasonal fluctuations in sales, account for them here.

Next, figure your gross profit for each month. The easiest way to do this is to multiply each month's sales revenue by the gross profit percentage for your business as a whole, which you calculated earlier. (If you rounded off your gross profit percentage, you'll get a slightly different gross profit figure here than you did in your break-even analysis.)

Then enter your monthly fixed expenses by category, and add them together to get monthly totals. Then, for each month, subtract your total fixed expenses from your gross profit and enter the result in the net profit row. If the result is a negative number, it means your expenses are more than your gross profit. Put parentheses around the result; in accounting symbols, a number in parentheses is a negative number.

Your profit/loss statement doesn't include all your income or expenses. Other income and costs such as loans and start-up expenses aren't included in your P & L statement, which reflects only money earned and spent as part of providing your products or services. For the full picture of all money that comes into and goes out from your business—including start-up costs, loans, taxes and other money that isn't earned or spent as part of your core business operation—you'll need to do a cash flow analysis. (Predicting your cash flow is covered in Section G, below.)

EXAMPLE: Inga's one-year profit/loss forecast for her bookstore is shown below:

Inga's Book Haus Profit/Loss Forecast: Year One Total

	Jan	Feb	Mar	April	May
Sales Revenues	$30,000	$35,000	$35,000	$35,000	$35,000
Gross Profit (51.2%)	**15,360**	**17,920**	**17,920**	**17,920**	**17,920**
Fixed Expenses					
Rent	3,500	3,500	3,500	3,500	3,500
Salaries	2,500	2,500	2,500	2,500	2,500
Utilities	800	800	800	800	800
Telephone	700	700	700	700	700
Office Equipment	700	700	700	700	700
Insurance	500	500	500	500	500
Advertising	700	700	700	700	700
Accounting	300	300	300	300	300
Fees for electronic payment system (EPS)	300	300	300	300	300
Miscellaneous	1,000	1,000	1,000	1,000	1,000
Total Fixed Expenses	**11,000**	**11,000**	**11,000**	**11,000**	**11,000**
Net Profit (Loss)	**$4,360**	**$6,920**	**$6,920**	**$6,920**	**$6,920**

June	July	Aug	Sept	Oct	Nov	Dec	Year Total
$35,000	$35,000	$35,000	$35,000	$35,000	$35,000	$40,000	$420,000
17,920	**17,920**	**17,920**	**17,920**	**17,920**	**17,920**	**20,480**	**215,040**
3,500	3,500	3,500	3,500	3,500	3,500	3,500	42,000
2,500	2,500	2,500	2,500	2,500	2,500	2,500	30,000
800	800	800	800	800	800	800	9,600
700	700	700	700	700	700	700	8,400
700	700	700	700	700	700	700	8,400
500	500	500	500	500	500	500	6,000
700	700	700	700	700	700	700	8,400
300	300	300	300	300	300	300	3,600
300	300	300	300	300	300	300	3,600
1,000	1,000	1,000	1,000	1,000	1,000	1,000	12,000
11,000	**11,000**	**11,000**	**11,000**	**11,000**	**11,000**	**11,000**	**132,000**
$6,920	**$6,920**	**$6,920**	**$6,920**	**$6,920**	**$6,920**	**$9,480**	**$83,040**

A completed P & L will outline your business's profitability month-by-month. If some months show that your expenses are higher than revenues, don't panic—most start-up businesses lose money for at least a few months—but you will need to figure out how to make it through these lean months (such as by getting a start-up loan). More important in the big picture is whether you can see a trend toward stable profitability. If not, you may need to revisit parts of your plan (or possibly scrap your idea all together). But as mentioned earlier, resist the temptation to inflate your sales estimates; a more realistic approach is to lower your costs. Once you have a P & L that shows consistent profits each month, based on realistic estimates, you're ready to move forward.

F. Start-Up Cost Estimate

If your profit/loss forecast shows your projected income will be higher than expenses each month, great—but you haven't yet accounted for an important category of expenses: business start-up costs. The worst part about start-up costs is that you need to pay them before your business is actually making any money. That's why you should have a firm grasp on what you really need

to spend to successfully start your business and a plan for where that money will come from. Of course, potential lenders or investors will want to see that you've accounted for these costs in your planning. But it's also important that you understand for yourself how high this initial financial hurdle will be so that you can figure out how to clear it. Obviously, you don't want to start a business with high start-up costs but low projected profits, since it will take you far too long to recover your initial investment.

⚠ **Buy only what your business really needs.** Too many new small business owners weigh down their new enterprises with unneeded start-up costs. Unless a particular item is absolutely necessary to generate revenue, don't buy it—or, if you do, spend as little as possible on it. Sure you need a desk, but unless customers will see it (and sometimes even if they will), repainting a door and laying it across a couple of secondhand filing cabinets at a net cost of $40 makes a lot more sense than laying out $800 for a new one.

Compared to the projections we just went through, estimating your start-up costs is a breeze —just list them and add them up. Include items like business registration fees and tax deposits you need to pay up front, rent and security deposits you'll have to pay before business starts, costs of any initial inventory, office supplies, equipment and anything else you'll have to cover before your business starts bringing in money.

EXAMPLE: Inga makes a list of the start-up expenses she expects to pay before she'll start selling books.

Initial inventory	$20,000
Rent deposit (security deposit and last month's rent)	7,000
Office supplies, stationery	500
Fax machine	500
Business registration fees	200
TOTAL	28,200

If you don't have enough cash to pay all of your start-up costs out of pocket, you'll either need to come up with the money or figure out a way to spread the costs over the first few months of business when you'll have at least some cash flowing in. For instance, maybe you could lease, rather than buy, needed equipment.

The next (and final) financial projection we'll do as part of your business plan—a cash flow projection—will help you plan and manage your incoming and outgoing cash so that you can cover needed expenses when they come due.

G. Cash Flow Projection

To round out the collection of financial information in your business plan, you should include a cash flow projection. While your profit/loss forecast may have shown that your business should make enough sales at a high enough price to cover your estimated expenses, a cash flow projection analyzes whether the cash from those sales, as well as from other sources such as loans or investments, will come in fast enough to pay your bills on time. Cash flow management is important once your business is up and running, especially if you plan to stock a good-sized inventory or extend credit to customers. A high sales volume won't be enough to cover your expenses if your customers are slow to pay you and your checking account is empty.

Cash flow projection is also important in your planning stages in order to show how you plan to survive the first few lean months of business— particularly after you figure in your start-up expenses. If you'll have more than enough cash to cover your expenses for the first months of business, then you're one of the lucky few. More likely you'll be pressed to figure out how to cover a cash deficit for at least the first few months, and maybe longer. One way to do this is to put off or cut some expenses. Another is to get a loan or sell part of your business to investors, or to hit up your family or friends for a loan. The important thing is

to do your best to predict your cash needs in advance, both to give yourself ample time to come up with a plan for getting the cash, and to inspire more confidence in lenders or investors.

Your cash flow projection will use many of the same figures you developed for your profit/loss forecast. The main difference is that you'll include all cash inflows and outflows, not just sales revenues and business expenses. Also, you'll record costs in the month that you expect to incur them, rather than simply spreading annual amounts equally over 12 months. Inflows and outflows of cash that belong in your cash flow analysis include loans, loan payments and start-up costs. Once you're turning a profit, you'll also include tax payments in your cash flow analysis, but for now let's assume that you'll be free from taxes for your first year.

For each month, simply start your projection with the actual amount of cash your business will have on hand. Next, fill in your projected cash-ins for the month, which should include sales revenues, loans, transfers of personal money— basically any money that goes into your business checking account. Add these together along with the cash you have at the beginning of the month to get your total cash-ins for the month.

Next enter all your projected cash-outs for the month, such as your fixed expenses and any loan payments. Remember also to include costs of your products and materials you use in your products or services—your variable costs. Add together all your cash-outs to obtain a total for the month. Subtract total monthly cash-outs from total monthly cash-ins and the result will be your cash left at the end of the month. That figure is also your beginning cash balance at the start of the next month; transfer it to the top of the next month's column, and do the whole process over again.

EXAMPLE: Inga completes her cash flow projection for her first year in business as shown on the next two pages. She starts her projection one month early to account for the

Inga's Book Haus Cash Flow Projection: Year One

	Dec	Jan	Feb	Mar	Apr	May
Cash at Beginning of Month	$0	($17,200)	($16,540)	($8,920)	($3,400)	$4,220
Cash-ins						
Sales Paid	0	30,000	35,000	35,000	35,000	35,000
Loans and Transfers	15,000	0	0	0	0	0
Total Cash-ins	**15,000**	**12,800**	**18,460**	**26,080**	**31,600**	**39,220**
Cash-outs						
Start-up Costs	28,200	0	0	0	0	0
Books & Other Products	0	14,640	17,080	17,080	17,080	17,080
Rent	3,500	3,500	3,500	3,500	3,500	3,500
Salaries	0	2,500	2,500	2,500	2,500	2,500
Utilities	0	800	800	800	800	800
Telephone	0	700	700	700	700	700
Office Equipment	0	1,400	0	2,100	0	0
Insurance	0	3,000	0	0	0	0
Advertising	0	700	700	700	700	700
Accounting	0	300	300	300	300	300
EPS Fees	0	300	300	300	300	300
Loan Payments	0	500	500	500	500	500
Misc.	500	1,000	1,000	1,000	1,000	1,000
Total Cash-outs	**32,200**	**29,340**	**27,380**	**29,480**	**27,380**	**27,380**
Cash at End of Month	**($17,200)**	**($16,540)**	**($8,920)**	**($3,400)**	**$4,220**	**$11,840**

June	July	Aug	Sept	Oct	Nov	Dec	
$11,840	$17,360	$21,980	$29,600	$34,420	$42,040	$49,660	$165,060
35,000	35,000	35,000	35,000	35,000	35,000	40,000	420,000
0	0	0	0	0	0	0	15,000
46,840	52,360	56,980	64,600	69,420	77,040	89,660	600,060
0	0	0	0	0	0	0	28,200
17,080	17,080	17,080	17,080	17,080	17,080	19,520	204,960
3,500	3,500	3,500	3,500	3,500	3,500	3,500	45,500
2,500	2,500	2,500	2,500	2,500	2,500	2,500	30,000
800	800	800	800	800	800	800	9,600
700	700	700	700	700	700	700	8,400
2,100	0	0	2,800	0	0	0	8,400
0	3,000	0	0	0	0	0	6,000
700	700	700	700	700	700	700	8,400
300	300	300	300	300	300	300	3,600
300	300	300	300	300	300	300	3,600
500	500	500	500	500	500	500	6,000
1,000	1,000	1,000	1,000	1,000	1,000	1,000	12,500
29,480	30,380	27,380	30,180	27,380	27,380	29,820	375,160
$17,360	$21,980	$29,600	$34,420	$42,040	$49,660	$59,840	$224,900

money she must spend before she opens her bookstore. In her cash-in section, she figures in $15,000 that she will put into the business: $10,000 of her own savings and an interest-free loan from her sister of $5,000. In her cash-out section, she includes what she'll pay for the initial set-up of the business, as well as that month's rent and a $500 allowance for unexpected expenses. Inga also includes in her cash-out section a $500 payment each month to her sister for the loan.

Notice that Inga's cash-outs look a bit different than her expenses in her profit/loss forecast, even though they add up to the same totals. The reason is that Inga's cash-out section of her cash flow projection reflects that some expenses are paid in lump sums, rather than monthly, such as her insurance, which is paid twice a year. She also breaks up her estimates for office expenses into lump payments, as she doesn't expect to spend equal amounts each month.

Also notice that Inga's estimated paid sales (as opposed to sales on credit) for the year come to the same total as her estimated annual sales revenue. That's because for her first year at least, Inga doesn't plan to take credit cards or checks, only cash and ATM purchases. That way all her sales will be paid immediately.

Inga's happy to see that by the end of April she should have cash left in the bank after all her expenses are paid (though she hasn't yet provided for money for her living expenses). Still, she needs to close the cash deficits that she predicts for her first three months in business. Based on her cash flow projection, an extra $17,200 up front would keep her cash flow (barely) in the black. She decides to apply for a loan of $15,000 and try to juggle expenses to cover the remaining $2,200 shortfall.

Once you've completed a year's worth (or more, if you want) of a cash flow projection, you'll have a blueprint for your business's financial situation from month to month. If any months are projected

to have a cash deficit, you'll need to tweak your plan to make sure you can cover all of your important expenses. As usual, this means you'll have to juggle, reduce or cut costs. A cash flow projection that shows difficulty in paying all your bills won't only scare investors away, it may mean that your plan needs serious revision. On the other hand, if your cash flow projection shows that you'll be in the black every month, then you'll be in a good position to show your numbers to potential sources of money—and to get your business under way.

! Your cash flow projection will be more complicated if you do any credit transactions. Since cash flow analysis is concerned with when your business receives or spends money, not when sales or purchases are made, you'll need to account for delayed payments if you do any sales or purchases on credit.

 Recommended reading on business plans. Mike McKeever's *How to Write a Business Plan* (Nolo) offers more detail on how to complete your cash flow analysis, including how to deal with credit transactions.

H. Putting It All Together

Congratulations! You've finished the descriptive and financial aspects of your business plan. While you kick back and enjoy a cold one, think about how you want to put all the information together. If you put the plan together for your own information, then you might want to simply review it, edit anything that needs fixing, print it out and put it into a binder for your reference. If you plan to present the information as part of a loan request or as a package for investors to review, you might want to do some extra polishing. As mentioned earlier, consider hiring a writer to help you develop the information into a well-written, persuasive document. The bottom line is to package the information as needed for different purposes.

☑ Chapter 5 Checklist

☐ Decide how you will use your business plan: to attract investors or for your own use as a blueprint for your business.

☐ Draft sections of your business plan that describe your business in detail.

☐ Put together financial projections for your business, including a break-even analysis, a profit/loss forecast and a cash flow analysis.

☐ Have a friend or business associate look over your plan—both the descriptive elements and the financial analysis—and make edits or suggestions.

☐ Edit your plan and prepare a final draft. Assemble the various sections of the plan into a final document, and package it as necessary for however you intend to use the plan.

■

Federal, State and Local Start-Up Requirements

A. Step 1: File Organizational Documents With Your State
   (Corporations, LLCs and Limited Partnerships Only) 6/4

B. Step 2: Obtain a Federal Employer Identification Number 6/5

   1. What an FEIN Is and Who Needs One 6/5

   2. Applying for an FEIN 6/5

C. Step 3: Register Your Fictitious Business Name With Your
   County or State 6/8

   1. The Importance of Filing an FBN Statement 6/8

   2. Who Needs to Register 6/8

   3. Filing With Your County 6/9

   4. After You've Filed 6/11

D. Step 4: Obtain a Local Tax Registration Certificate
   (a.k.a. "Business License") 6/11

E. Step 5: Obtain a State Seller's Permit 6/13

F. Step 6: Obtain Specialized Licenses or Permits....................................... 6/13

   1. Zoning and Local Permits 6/14

   2. State and Federal Regulations 6/15

   3. License and Permit Information Resources 6/15

By now you've finished hammering out the details of how you plan to operate your business. In a perfect world, you could hang up your "open" sign and start selling your products or services at a nice profit. Sorry! In the real world of small business, things are not quite that easy. Before a business can legally begin, it needs to complete a number of pesky requirements with governmental agencies from the city to the federal level. Although none of these requirements are difficult or even terribly time-consuming, lots of entrepreneurs get stymied at this point because it's so hard to find one centralized source of information that explains what they need to do. They're left to ferret out each bureaucratic requirement one by one and hope they've found all of them by the time they start doing business.

For example, your city tax office can tell you what forms you must file there, but won't tell you how to obtain a permit in order to sell retail goods. And while your state sales tax agency may be able to tell you everything you need to know about the process of getting a seller's permit, they'll be of no help in explaining the process of obtaining a federal employer identification number, which is required for most businesses (even those without employees). The process of finding out what you need to do and how to go about doing it can feel like putting together a jigsaw puzzle without knowing how many pieces it should have or how it should look when completed.

To help you figure out what you need to do and where you need to do it to officially launch your business, we've pulled all the basic start-up requirements together into one chapter for you. We will guide you through the bureaucratic maze and explain the typical registration requirements that apply to most businesses. (There are a few extra requirements for businesses with employees, which are outlined in Chapter 11.) While there are indeed far more specific regulations for small businesses, such as those relating to toxic waste disposal, than we could cover here—particularly at the state and city level—this chapter explains the basic regulatory structure that every businessperson will have to deal with, and points out which agencies typically deal with certain types of requirements. By the time you finish reading this chapter, you'll know a number of registration requirements that you will have to complete, plus you'll have a good idea of where to check for other requirements that may apply to you, depending on what type of business you're starting and where you'll be conducting it.

Sure, dealing with city and state bureaucrats can be a mind-numbing endurance of pain. But once the mystery is taken out of the registration process and you have a clear idea of which requirements apply to you or are likely to, you'll be able to tackle the bureaucracy with a minimum of time and stress.

Jennifer Mahoney, owner of an illustration service in Northern California:

I'm lucky enough to have a technical skill to combine with a regular drawing skill that puts me in a market niche among illustrators. Lacking any entrepreneurial "uncles," it took me a while to get a clue about the business world, like finding untapped markets, understanding agreements, getting paid, handling copyright issues, and finding out how many regulatory bodies need a portion of my modest income. It all felt like groping in the dark: where are all the rules written down? I'm doing well for myself now, supporting my family, but I wish it hadn't taken me so long to figure out.

⚠ It may take more time to start a corporation, LLC or limited partnership. Although the process of starting a company that offers limited liability—a corporation, LLC or limited partnership—isn't rocket science, the process is more complex than starting a sole proprietorship or general partnership. While this chapter outlines the basic start-up requirements for businesses that offer limited liability, you will need to understand the additional formalities and requirements that come with starting one. For example, if you plan to create one of these types of businesses, you may need to comply with federal and state securities laws. In Section A, below, we give you a brief overview of the extra formation step (Step 1) you'll have to take to set up a business with limited liability. Once you have formed your corporation, LLC or limited partnership, you'll be ready to use the information in this chapter on permits, licenses and tax-filing requirements. As we mention in Section A, Nolo offers several self-help products that give in-depth, detailed information about starting and running these business types. If you're planning to start a corporation, LLC or limited partnership, be sure you take advantage of one of these excellent guides.

Here is a list of the general start-up steps we walk you through below:

Step 1: File organizational documents with the Secretary of State or similar filing office (corporations, LLCs and limited partnerships only).

Step 2: Obtain a federal employer identification number (FEIN).

Step 3: Register your fictitious business name with your county or state.

Step 4: Obtain a local tax registration certificate (a.k.a. business license).

Step 5: Obtain a permit to sell retail goods and collect state sales tax.

Step 6: Obtain specialized vocation-related licenses or environmental permits if necessary.

"Why Am I Filling Out All These Forms?"

Understanding why such a tangled bureaucracy governs small businesses can go a long way in helping you conquer it with a minimum of time and frustration. At the most basic level, there are three purposes to the various permit and license requirements that businesses must complete.

- **To identify you.** No matter what kind of business you run, society has an interest in seeing to it that you are accountable for your actions. That's why businesses that don't use their owners' names as part of their business names must often register a fictitious business name statement with their state or county. That way, if a member of the public has a problem with Racafrax Designs or Acme Sandblasting, she can easily find out who the owners are and complain to them and, if necessary, sue them.

- **To protect the public.** Government agencies issue permits and licenses in an attempt to ensure that your business offers safe products or services that won't harm people or the environment. For example, if you open a food service business, your city's department of health understandably wants to make sure that your kitchen is sanitary, and will likely require that you obtain a permit, license or other official approval before you can start serving snacks.

- **To keep track of your finances for tax purposes.** Several of the registration requirements are based on the government's nasty habit of taxing everything that moves (and lots of things that don't). To be sure that they collect every possible tax and fee, local, state and federal governments use various registration requirements in order to keep tabs on your business.

A. Step 1: File Organizational Documents With Your State (Corporations, LLCs and Limited Partnerships Only)

Unlike sole proprietorships or partnerships, businesses that offer limited liability don't just pop into existence as soon as their owners start selling products or services. If you want to create one of these types of businesses, you'll need to take the step of filing registration papers with your state filing office, which typically is the Secretary or Department of State. (Contact info for each state's Secretary of State is included in Appendix A.) Since these business structures are regulated at the state level, each state has different rules for creating and managing them. For the most part, however, these laws are fairly similar. For corporations, the organizational document is usually called the articles of incorporation; for LLCs it's generally called the articles of organization (although some states call it a certificate of organization or formation). Limited partnerships also have to file registration documents with the state. To create any of these business structures you'll need to do additional reading or consult other resources (see Nolo's other resources, below).

When you file your organizational documents with your state, you will usually be registering your corporate, LLC or limited partnership name at the same time. Typically, the agency in charge (most often the Secretary of State) must approve all names before they can be registered, otherwise your organizational papers will be rejected. One of the main factors for approval is whether or not another business of the same legal structure (corporation, LLC or limited partnership) in your state has already taken the name business name you want to use. In other words, a California corporation may not use a name that's used by an existing California corporation; a New Mexico LLC may not use a name that is used by another New Mexico LLC, and so on. Some states check all of their name databases—LLC, corporate and limited

partnership—regardless of whether you're creating an LLC, corporation or limited partnership. To save time and headaches, do some research before you file your papers to make sure your proposed name is available. You can usually call or write to the state filing office, and they'll tell you whether it is. Quite a few states now also allow you to check for name availability online. Ask your state's filing office for its procedure.

 When you find an available name, reserve it if you can. Many states allow you to reserve a corporate, LLC or limited partnership name once you've learned it's available. Doing so is a good idea, as it can't then be taken by someone else before you have a chance to file your papers.

It's also very important to remember that just because your name is accepted by your state filing office doesn't mean it's free and clear for you to use. As discussed in detail in Chapter 3, trademark and unfair competition laws may prevent you from using a name used by another business, including businesses that aren't included in your state's corporate, LLC or limited partnership name databases. For instance, the name of a general partnership in your state wouldn't be registered in your state's corporate name database, but may for years have been using the name you want. Or the name you've chosen may have been taken by a corporation in another state, so it similarly would not appear in your state's database. To avoid running afoul of trademark and unfair competition laws, doing a trademark search is a good idea before choosing any name for your business, or for its products or services. Be sure to read Chapter 3 for a full discussion of the legal issues surrounding business names.

Nolo publishes a wide range of information on corporations, LLCs and limited partnerships. *Quick and Legal LLC: Limiting Your Liability* and *Form Your Own Limited Liability Company* (includes forms on disk), by attorney Anthony Mancuso, offer guidance on creating an LLC and legal and tax information about this form of business. In addition, Nolo's website provides interactive WebForms, which will create LLC articles for you after you answer a few questions online (not all states). Finally, *Your Limited Liability Company: An Operating Manual,* also by attorney Anthony Mancuso, offers detailed information on how to manage LLCs in compliance with various state and federal laws.

On the corporate side, *The Corporate Minutes Book: The Legal Guide to Taking Care of Corporate Business,* by attorney Anthony Mancuso, provides forms and instructions for running a corporation and handling corporate meetings and documentation. And at Nolo's website you'll find several downloadable eFormKits for handling various corporate tasks. Nolo also publishes state-specific books for starting and running corporations in California, New York and Texas. For more information on limited partnerships, see *The Partnership Book* by attorneys Denis Clifford and Ralph Warner.

B. Step 2: Obtain a Federal Employer Identification Number

Sole proprietors and partners don't need to explicitly "create" their business by registering with any state office; once they're engaged in business activity, their business more or less exists by default. (See Chapter 2 for more information about creating all types of businesses, including sole proprietorships and partnerships.) If you're starting a sole proprietorship or a partnership, getting a federal employer identification number (FEIN) from the Internal Revenue Service should be your first task in registering your business, mainly because you can get one without having to be registered with any other agency and before you've filled out any other forms.

Corporations and LLCs must also apply for an FEIN, but they must first file their organizational documents with the state (see Step 1, above).

1. What an FEIN Is and Who Needs One

A business's federal employer identification number (alternately called an FEIN, an EIN and an employer ID) is roughly equivalent to a Social Security number for an individual. It's a number used by the government to identify your business, which you'll use over and over again on most of your important business documents. To mention just a few places you'll use it, you'll typically need to enter it on your business's local tax registration forms, your federal tax return and any applications for business licenses.

Some of you are probably saying, "But I don't plan to have employees—why do I need an employer ID number?" Blame the IRS for the confusing terminology. Although it's called an "employer" ID number, FEINs are required for most businesses, even if they don't have employees. The one exception is that sole proprietors with no employees can use their own Social Security number instead of an FEIN. Partnerships, LLCs and corporations need FEINs whether they have employees or not.

2. Applying for an FEIN

There's no fee for an FEIN, and thanks to a mail-in and phone system, getting one is super easy. Simply fill out and submit IRS Form SS-4, according to the instructions just below. (This book contains two copies of Form SS-4: one in Appendix C, which you can tear out and use, and one on CD-ROM, along with the IRS's instructions for completing the form.) If you submit the form by mail you'll get your FEIN in about four weeks.

Better yet, by using the IRS's free Tele-TIN phone-in system you can file by phone and get your number the same day, and then send in Form SS-4. To get your FEIN the same day, simply call the appropriate Tele-TIN number for your location (listed on the SS-4 form) and relay the information from your completed SS-4 form to the IRS representative, who will then give you your FEIN over

the phone. Enter the FEIN in the upper right corner of the SS-4, sign and date the form, and mail
or fax it to the Tele-TIN service center within 24
hours of the phone call.

A sample of SS-4 appears below. Although most
of the information you'll have to put on the form is
pretty basic, we offer the following tips to help
you get the job done.

Line 1 asks for the legal name of the entity that
is applying for the FEIN. Sounds simple
enough, but depending on your business
it can get a little tricky.

Sole proprietors should enter their full
individual name—first, last and middle
initial. Do not enter any fictitious business
name (FBN) you use or plan to use. (A
fictitious business name is a name you
use for your business that doesn't contain
your legal name. FBNs are explained in
more detail in the next section.)

A partnership should use the legal
name of the partnership as it appears in
the partnership agreement. For example,
say Gene Cook and Beth Lynch own a
partnership that they name "Cook and
Lynch, Partners" in their partnership
agreement. This is the name they would
put for Item 1. If you own a partnership
but don't have a written partnership
agreement (and you definitely should; see
Chapter 2), insert the name you plan to
use for all official business and on all
government forms—either a business
name that contains each partner's last
name, or the trade name that you will
present to the public (also known as your
"fictitious business name" or your "DBA
name," discussed below). (See Chapter 3
for the full spiel on the various types of
business names.)

An LLC should enter the official company name as it appears in its articles of
organization (or certificate of organization
or formation). A corporation should use
its legal name as it appears in its articles

of incorporation (or certificate of organization).

Line 2 asks for the trade name of the business.
This is the same as asking for your
fictitious business name or your "doing
business as" (DBA) name. You can leave
this line blank if you plan to do business
under the same name you entered in line
1. For example, if Gene Cook and Beth
Lynch plan to do business under the
name Cook and Lynch, Partners, and they
entered that name in line 1, they can
leave line 2 blank. Similarly, if a sole
proprietor named Stacey Stickler will use
just her name to identify her landscape
design services, she too can leave line 2
blank.

But when your company's legal name
doesn't match its trade name, you should
enter the trade name on line 2. For
example, if Stacey Stickler uses a business
name that's different than her name—
even a business name that contains her
name, say Stickler's Landscape Design—
she should enter "Stickler's Landscape
Design" on line 2. And a partnership that
wants to do business under any name
other than its legal name would do the
same thing. For example, if "Cook and
Lynch, Partners" want to do business under
the trade name "CooLyn Enterprises,"
they will enter "Cook and Lynch, Partners"
on line 1 and "CooLyn Enterprises" on
line 2. (More on trade names and fictitious
business names just below.)

While it may seem like we're splitting hairs, this
is actually quite important. Think about it: the
FEIN form introduces you and your business to the
IRS, and identifies you in an official way. Not only
do you want to be sure to give the IRS the correct
names, but, more importantly you want to be
consistent with the names you give in order to
avoid snafus with the IRS and other government
agencies. For example, if the Cook and Lynch
partnership goes back and forth between calling

Form **SS-4**

(Rev. April 2000)

Department of the Treasury
Internal Revenue Service

Application for Employer Identification Number

(For use by employers, corporations, partnerships, trusts, estates, churches, government agencies, certain individuals, and others. See instructions.)

► Keep a copy for your records.

EIN

OMB No. 1545-0003

Please type or print clearly.

1 Name of applicant (legal name) (see instructions)

2 Trade name of business (if different from name on line 1)

3 Executor, trustee, "care of" name

4a Mailing address (street address) (room, apt., or suite no.)

5a Business address (if different from address on lines 4a and 4b)

4b City, state, and ZIP code

5b City, state, and ZIP code

6 County and state where principal business is located

7 Name of principal officer, general partner, grantor, owner, or trustor—SSN or ITIN may be required (see instructions) ►

8a Type of entity (Check only one box.) (see instructions)

Caution: If applicant is a limited liability company, see the instructions for line 8a.

☐ Sole proprietor (SSN) _____

☐ Partnership   ☐ Personal service corp.

☐ REMIC   ☐ National Guard

☐ State/local government ☐ Farmers' cooperative

☐ Church or church-controlled organization

☐ Other nonprofit organization (specify) ► _____

☐ Other (specify) ►

☐ Estate (SSN of decedent) _____

☐ Plan administrator (SSN) _____

☐ Other corporation (specify) ► _____

☐ Trust

☐ Federal government/military

(enter GEN if applicable) _____

8b If a corporation, name the state or foreign country (if applicable) where incorporated

State

Foreign country

9 Reason for applying (Check only one box.) (see instructions)

☐ Started new business (specify type) ► _____

☐ Hired employees (Check the box and see line 12.)

☐ Created a pension plan (specify type) ►

☐ Banking purpose (specify purpose) ► _____

☐ Changed type of organization (specify new type) ► _____

☐ Purchased going business

☐ Created a trust (specify type) ► _____

☐ Other (specify) ►

10 Date business started or acquired (month, day, year) (see instructions)

11 Closing month of accounting year (see instructions)

12 First date wages or annuities were paid or will be paid (month, day, year). **Note:** If applicant is a withholding agent, enter date income will first be paid to nonresident alien. (month, day, year) . . . . ►

13 Highest number of employees expected in the next 12 months. **Note:** If the applicant does not expect to have any employees during the period, enter -0-. (see instructions) . . . . ►

Nonagricultural	Agricultural	Household

14 Principal activity (see instructions) ►

15 Is the principal business activity manufacturing? . . . . ☐ Yes ☐ No

If "Yes," principal product and raw material used ►

16 To whom are most of the products or services sold? Please check one box. ☐ Business (wholesale)

☐ Public (retail)   ☐ Other (specify) ►   ☐ N/A

17a Has the applicant ever applied for an employer identification number for this or any other business? . . . . ☐ Yes ☐ No

Note: If "Yes," please complete lines 17b and 17c.

17b If you checked "Yes" on line 17a, give applicant's legal name and trade name shown on prior application, if different from line 1 or 2 above.

Legal name ►   Trade name ►

17c Approximate date when and city and state where the application was filed. Enter previous employer identification number if known.

Approximate date when filed (mo., day, year) | City and state where filed

Previous EIN

Under penalties of perjury, I declare that I have examined this application, and to the best of my knowledge and belief, it is true, correct, and complete.

Business telephone number (include area code)
(   )

Fax telephone number (include area code)
(   )

Name and title (Please type or print clearly.) ►

Signature ►

Date ►

Note: Do not write below this line. For official use only.

Please leave blank ►	Geo.	Ind.	Class	Size	Reason for applying

For Privacy Act and Paperwork Reduction Act Notice, see page 4.

Cat. No. 16055N

Form **SS-4** (Rev. 4-2000)

their business "Cook and Lynch" and "CooLyn Enterprises" on government documents, they will almost surely experience a raft of bureaucratic headaches.

C. Step 3: Register Your Fictitious Business Name With Your County or State

Recall from Chapter 3 that any trade name that doesn't contain the legal names of the owners (for sole proprietorships or general partnerships) or that doesn't match the company's corporate, limited partnership or LLC name on file with the state is called a fictitious business name (FBN). Fictitious business names are sometimes called assumed names or "DBAs" for "doing business as"—as in, "Spikey Andrews, doing business as Coffee Corner" or "Alibi Corporation, doing business as Ferryville Bait and Tackle." Some states simply use the term "trade name," though this can be confusing because it doesn't indicate whether the name is the same as or different from the legal name. In this chapter and the rest of the book, we'll use the term fictitious business name for any business name that doesn't contain the legal name(s) of the business owner(s).

Most states require a business that uses a fictitious business name to register that name, usually with the county clerk in the county where its primary business site is located. Depending on your state, this requirement goes by different names: fictitious name certification, DBA filing, trade name registration, or something similar. FBN registrations are typically done at the county level, although in some states, you register your FBN with the Secretary of State or other state agency. The registration process is covered in more detail below.

States like to keep track of business names and who uses them for a couple of reasons. One is to prevent customer confusion between two local businesses that use the same name. (That's why, before a business can register its fictitious business name, many states either search their business name registry or require that the business do so to make sure the name isn't already being used.) Another reason is to give customers a quick way to find out who the owner of a company is without having to hire a private investigator. This allows customers to easily contact the owners with a complaint or to take legal action against them. Requiring owners to register their business names makes it harder for fly-by-night businesses to operate anonymously and defraud customers.

1. The Importance of Filing an FBN Statement

Do not neglect or put off registering your fictitious business name. Without proof of registration, many banks will not open an account under your business name. Also, if you don't register your name, it won't appear in any fictitious name databases in your state, so it will be less likely that other businesses will find out you're using it, and as a result, another business may start using it. Even though you have other legal avenues to stop another business from using a name that you used first (see Chapter 3), the possibility of customer confusion between the two businesses and a name dispute with another business are definitely things you should try to avoid. If you lose a dispute over a name, at the very least you'll have to redo stationery, signs and anything else that contains the name, such as T-shirts or maybe even your company logo.

2. Who Needs to Register

Rules for registering fictitious business names are different depending on which business structure you use. Here are the general rules:

Sole proprietorships. Generally speaking, if a sole proprietor includes his last name in the business name—such as O'Toole's Classic Cars—he does not need to file an FBN statement. But it is not enough to include just initials or part of a name, such as a nickname. For example, a business called J.R.'s Classic Cars would likely have to file a fictitious name statement indicating that it really is John O'Toole's business.

In addition, in many states, if your business name falsely implies that more than one owner is involved, a fictitious business name statement must be filed. If Jason Todd were a sole proprietor, for example, and named his business Jason Todd and Sons, or Jason Todd & Associates, he would probably have to file an FBN statement, even though he included his last name in his business name. Check with your county clerk for your state's rules.

Partnerships. If a partnership includes the last names of all the partners—for example, Lawrence Anderson and Nancy Fawcett name their business "Anderson and Fawcett Metal Designs"—no statement usually needs to be filed. Otherwise, filing an FBN statement will be necessary. For example, if three partners, Lynch, Cook and Briggs, did business only under the name "Lynch & Cook," an FBN statement would likely be required. Check with your county clerk for your state's specific rules.

Corporations, LLCs and limited partnerships. A business whose name is registered with the state— generally corporations, LLCs and limited partnerships—does not need to file an FBN statement unless it operates under a name that's different from its official name as stated in its articles of incorporation, articles of organization or certificate of limited partnership. For example, an LLC that registered with the Secretary of State under the name "Landmark Lanes, LLC" wouldn't have to file an FBN statement as long as it conducted business under the name "Landmark Lanes, LLC." Any other trade name, "Landmark Bowl," for instance—or even "Landmark Lanes" without the "LLC" tacked onto the end—may be considered to be "fictitious" and would likely have to be registered. The same is often true for corporations: if "Inc." is included in the name in the articles of incorporation, but not in the company's trade name, an FBN statement usually must be filed. Check with your

county clerk or Secretary of State or other state filing office to determine your state's specific rules.

3. Filing With Your County

In some states FBN registration is done with the Secretary of State or other state agency; however in most states, you'll register your FBN at the county level. (This is generally true despite the fact that most laws governing fictitious business names are state laws.) The result is that each county in your state may have different forms and fees for registering an FBN. Your first step should be to call your county clerk's office to find out its requirements and fees. Many counties allow you to order the FBN registration form by phone; others require you to send a written request for it along with a self-addressed stamped envelope. Or, unless you live a good distance from the nearest county clerk, it may be easiest just to go to the office to complete the process in person.

Unfortunately, most states do not provide much, if any, online information about FBN requirements, and barely any states or counties offer an online filing system. (Florida is one exception.) With the rapid state of change in government websites, however, this may change in the very near future —maybe even by the time you read this book. So it's worth taking a look at your state's governmental websites to see if there are any FBN resources there. (The CD-ROM that comes with this book contains a file with links to state business-related websites. See Appendix B for information on how to use this file with your Web browser.) If you can't find any information online, you'll need to complete the process the old-fashioned way: by obtaining and filling out a paper form.

a. Searching the County (or State) Database

In many areas, you'll be instructed to search the county or state database of registered fictitious business names before submitting your statement, in order to see if anyone else has already registered the name you want to use. Typically, you can search a county's database (often an easy-to-search computerized system) for free if you go to the office in person, or you can sometimes pay a fee for a staff person to do the search for you. If you want the clerk's office to do the search, you must usually submit the request and fee by mail.

⚠ Searching a county database usually isn't enough. Oftentimes fictitious business names are registered at the county level, and you may be required to search your county database before registering your fictitious name to make sure it isn't already registered. Ironically, this requirement may well do more harm than good. Why? Because lots of people who find that no one in the county has registered a certain name are misled into believing that the name is free to use. The truth of the matter is that only the tiniest of businesses can feel safe by doing merely a county-wide search of a name they want to use. If someone else is using the name in a neighboring county, or even in a different state or country, you may well run into legal trouble, depending on your geographical scope and the products or services you sell. Particularly with the explosion of e-business, geographical distance is becoming irrelevant as the World Wide Web is making neighbors out of businesses on opposite sides of the globe.

To avoid being accused of unfair competition or trademark infringement, it is wise to check neighboring counties' FBN databases, look into state registries of corporate and LLC names, or even do a full international trademark search. Failing to do an appropriate search puts you at risk not only of lawsuits, but also of having to change your name down the line when you already have stationery, business signs and invoices printed up. Be sure to read Chapter 3 on trademark and business name issues for more information on choosing and researching a name that won't get you into legal trouble.

b. Completing and Submitting an FBN Statement

If you've determined that the name you've chosen is free to use (both at the county level and with regard to trademark issues), simply fill out the FBN statement and submit it to your county clerk (or other agency, depending on your state) along with the appropriate fees. You typically can submit the form in person or by mail. Depending on the county, fees range from $10 to $50 for registering one business name and one business owner. Sometimes you may be charged an additional fee, around $5 to $15, to register additional business names to be used at the same business location or to register additional owners.

c. Publishing Notice of Your FBN Statement

Once you've filed your name and paid the necessary fees, you may have one more task to complete, depending on your state's law. Many states require you to have your FBN statement published in an approved newspaper in the county where you filed it. The county clerk or state agency often will provide a list of acceptable publications for posting your FBN statement, though usually any newspaper of general circulation in the county will suffice. Publishing your statement is dead simple; just take a copy of your completed statement to your publication of choice, which will have a standard format to present the required information.

💡 Obscure publications often charge the lowest fees. As long as a newspaper is on the approved list or otherwise doesn't violate your county's rules (for instance, in some counties you can't publish an FBN statement in a free newspaper), there's nothing wrong with picking the cheapest one.

The published notice must run for a certain frequency and duration, usually once a week for a month or so. After the FBN has been published for the required period, you'll usually need to submit an affidavit (sometimes called Proof of Publication) with the county clerk or state agency to show that publication has been completed. Many newspapers that provide publication services will automatically send in the affidavit for you after your ad has completed its run. Make sure to find out whether the publication you use will do this or not (and it's not a bad idea to double check afterwards to see whether they've actually done it). If not, you'll have to get the affidavit from the publication yourself and submit it to the county clerk or state agency within the prescribed deadline. If the affidavit isn't filed in time, you may have to start the process all over again.

Check with your county clerk for the details of whether publishing the FBN notice is required, for how long, and if and when an affidavit must be filed after publication.

Save your ad receipt. For practical reasons, you may need to prove that you completed your fictitious business name filing requirements, specifically publication, before your ad has actually completed its publication run. Banks, for instance, want to see that you have met fictitious name rules before they allow you to open an account in that name. Fortunately, a receipt from the newspaper that's publishing your statement showing that you have paid for publication, along with a copy of the FBN statement certified by the county clerk or state agency, is generally sufficient to prove that you've met all the registration requirements even though the ad hasn't yet run for four weeks. So be sure to get a certified copy of your FBN statement back from the county clerk or state agency when you submit it, as well as a receipt from the newspaper when you pay for publication of the statement.

4. After You've Filed

Your FBN registration will be good for a certain period of time, usually for five years or so, after which it must be renewed. You (or someone at your business) should keep track of your expiration date, as your county clerk or state agency may not notify you when your expiration approaches. Also, if certain facts in your statement change, such as the number of owners or your business address, you may have to renew your FBN statement. Check with your county clerk or state agency to find out which types of changes trigger a renewal requirement. If you no longer want your FBN registered, you may file a form (often called a Statement of Abandonment) to cause the registration to expire.

D. Step 4: Obtain a Local Tax Registration Certificate (a.k.a. "Business License")

Most cities require all businesses (including home businesses) to register with that city's tax collector, regardless of business structure, size, name or type of business. Businesses located in rural, unincorporated areas must usually register with the county clerk rather than a city tax collector. (While we often refer to city tax collectors and city requirements for businesses in this section, just keep in mind that if you're operating outside of a city, the same types of requirements generally apply, but are often administered by county government instead.)

Depending on where you register, the locality may use different names for the process: tax registration, business tax application, business license application or tax certification, to name a few. We use the terms "tax registration" and "tax registration certificate" in this book—and we recommend that you don't use the term "business license" when you really mean "tax registration certificate" (or whatever term is used in your locality for tax registration). True licenses, which are discussed in Section F, below, are typically administered at the state level, and must be obtained by certain businesses if they engage in regulated activities, such as selling alcohol or cutting people's hair.

Getting such a license often involves taking a test or otherwise proving you're qualified to do a certain activity.

 Some businesses need additional licenses and permits. It's important to understand that your tax registration certificate (a.k.a. business license) is not the same as a specialized license your business might need—such as a permit from the local health department for handling food, or from the Federal Communications Commission for broadcasting over the radio waves, or from a regional air management district for emitting particles into the air. Section F, below, discusses these specialized licenses and permits. Whether or not you need one of these licenses or permits, you'll still need to get a tax registration certificate.

Why do you need to register with your local tax collector? Because just like the federal and state governments, your local government wants a cut of your business income. And the tax registration requirement is basically your local government's way of keeping track of your business so that it will be able to collect any taxes it owes. Cities and counties have been known to tax businesses with even more flair and creativity than the feds or the states do. Localities tax businesses based on criteria such as net profit, gross income, number of employees, total payroll, number of vehicles, number of machines and sometimes even seating capacity. In addition, most cities categorize businesses and use different tax structures for each category. In Charlottesville, Virginia, for instance, bakeries are charged a .2% (.002) tax on gross receipts, landscapers pay a rate of .36% and architects and other professionals pay a rate of .58%. Other types of businesses in Charlottesville pay flat fees, such as wineries ($500 per year), coin machine operators ($150) and fortunetellers ($1,000).

Besides being assigned a category and a tax rate, businesses may be subject to special taxes for particular activities. In Chicago, for instance, businesses that sell soft drink syrup or fountain soft drinks must pay an extra "Fountain Soft Drink" tax of 9% of the syrup price, and amusement operators must pay an extra "Amusement Tax" of 7% of the admission price.

For the privilege of registering to pay local taxes, you'll have to pay an annual fee, which varies a lot from city to city. To register in Philadelphia, for instance, you'll need to pay a fee of $200, while Seattle charges only $75. Sometimes the annual fee depends partly on how much tax your business is expected to owe the following year, based on city (or county) tax rates. If the fee is based on estimated taxes, at least part of the registration fee may be a nonrefundable administrative fee—in that case, the other part of the fee will go toward paying your estimated taxes or will be returned to you if your taxes turn out to be lower than expected. In Oakland, for instance, registering your business with the city costs $30, but you must also pay your estimated tax based on your business category and your estimated income for the next year. The estimated tax portion—but not the $30 fee—will be credited towards your tax bill for the next year.

For your city's requirements, call your city tax collector, whose office will probably be listed under "Tax Collector" in the city government section of your white pages. The tax collector's office will be able to provide you with the forms necessary to register in your city, as well as any breakdown of business categories and tax tables. If you're doing business outside city limits, call your county clerk, who'll usually be listed under "County Clerk" in the county government section of the phone book.

Kimberly Torgerson, owner of Your Word's Worth, a freelance editing and writing service in Berkeley, California:

It took me much less than 24 hours to get started as a freelance editor and writer; I wandered to the Berkeley business licensing office, talked with the helpful folks there, paid some fees, and bought a used computer. My biggest challenge starting out was convincing my mother that my business was real.

E. Step 5: Obtain a State Seller's Permit

In most states, any business—whether it's a sole proprietorship, LLC, corporation or any other type—must have a seller's permit if it sells any tangible goods to the public. Tangible goods are things you can touch, like furniture or food. Businesses that sell only services are often exempt from the seller's permit requirement. In the five states that do not impose general sales taxes (Alaska, Delaware, Montana, New Hampshire, and Oregon), you may not be required to get a permit for most sales transactions—though keep in mind that local governments in those states may charge sales taxes (as in Alaska) and that certain transactions in those states may be subject to something similar to a sales tax, though it may have a different name. If you live in one of those states, be sure to check with the sales tax agency to find out if your specific transactions will be subject to tax, and if you'll need a seller's permit. (Contact information is included in Appendix A.)

In states that do charge sales taxes, a seller's permit will allow your business to collect sales taxes from customers to cover the sales tax that you'll owe to the state (if any). You'll typically pay any taxes you owe at year-end, or sometimes quarterly if your sales volume is high enough.

It's important to understand that if you plan to sell tangible goods, you'll often need a seller's

permit whether or not those sales will be taxable. For instance, most states exempt certain sales from state sales tax, such as sales of food or sales to an out-of-state customer. But in most states, you'll need a seller's permit even to conduct these types of nontaxable sales. This means you'll need to get a sales permit before you begin to sell tangible goods; when the sales are made you'll distinguish the taxable ones from the nontaxable ones. When it comes time to report and pay sales taxes to the state, you'll be taxed only on the taxable sales. (We cover reporting and paying sales taxes in more depth in Chapter 8.)

Keep track of your service and product sales separately. Many businesses both perform services and sell products. A metalsmith, for instance, both repairs jewelry and sells his raw materials, such as precious metals and gemstones. If a business sells both labor and goods, it will need a seller's permit (assuming it's in a state that requires one). Plus, to assure proper tax reporting, that business will need to keep its labor sales separate from sales of goods, since sales of services aren't taxed. (Chapter 10 explains simple bookkeeping and how to account for taxable sales separately from tax-exempt sales.)

To obtain a seller's permit, contact the agency in your state that governs sales taxes. (Appendix A of this book provides contact information for sales tax/seller's permit agencies by state.) The process of obtaining a seller's permit typically consists of submitting a simple application form and sometimes paying a fee. Some states require businesses to post a deposit if they have a blemished history paying their sales taxes on time.

F. Step 6: Obtain Specialized Licenses or Permits

Depending on the nature of your business, you might be finished with your list of bureaucratic tasks. But before you run off to rev up your cash register, cool your jets—you may be surprised to find out that even your simple little business is subject to an extra regulation or two. Some business activities aren't allowed until you obtain a license or permit to do them, and some business locations require special approval from the local planning department for what you plan to do there. These extra requirements are especially likely to apply to your business if it has any potential for harming the environment or hurting the public, but they also apply in lots of seemingly risk-free situations.

Figuring out what additional permits or licenses you might need can be confusing, because there are literally hundreds of independent agencies from the local to the federal level that regulate various businesses. Obviously you don't want to waste your time calling each and every one of them to find out whether your business is subject to its rules. This section will put you on the right track by first outlining the basics on what types of activities are regulated and by whom. This should help you recognize when your business is likely to face a special regulation. Then we'll direct you to a few resources that help to make sense of the crazy patchwork of local, state and federal regulations on small businesses.

 Local regulations have a different focus than state or federal ones. Very generally speaking, local regulations tend to focus on the location of your business and whether it poses a nuisance or a threat to public safety. State and federal regulations typically focus more on the job you're doing and whether or not you're competent at it.

1. Zoning and Local Permits

Local business regulations usually have to do with the physical location of the business and the safety of the premises and equipment. City zoning laws, for instance, regulate which activities are allowed in particular locations. If a certain location is zoned exclusively for residential use, if there's not enough parking to support your business, or if there are too many similar businesses nearby, your business location might not be approved by the zoning board. Even if your business activities are acceptable for the time being, you might not be allowed to put up the sign you want or put in additional seating once your business takes off.

If your business doesn't comply with zoning laws, you'll either need to get a permit known as a conditional use permit, or be granted an exception to the law (sometimes called a variance). Your city or county planning department is generally in charge of zoning laws. Contact them to find out whether your business complies with local rules, and, if not, how to request a Conditional Use Permit or a zoning variance. (Chapter 4 discusses zoning laws and picking a business location.)

Audrey Wackerley, owner of RetroFit, a vintage clothing store in San Francisco:

Getting the right permits turned into a total hassle for our clothing store. After we'd been in business for a year and a half, a cop walked in our store and said we needed a "second-hand" permit. We had never even heard of one! It's not like we hadn't really made an effort to get all the permits we needed—before we opened we spent hours in all these different buildings downtown, waiting in endless lines (it's a lot like going to the DMV), asking a million questions to find out what permits we needed to open our store. We had a business license, a seller's permit, a sign permit...we thought we had everything we needed. But all of a sudden this cop said he'd shut us down if we didn't get the second-hand permit within five days. Five days! The permit cost $700, which was a real stretch for us right then. But what could we do? We had to scramble to get the money together and buy that stupid permit. The cop also let us know that we needed a separate jewelry permit in order to sell jewelry, but getting the second-hand permit was enough of an ordeal. We just decided to stop selling jewelry.

Assuming your business has met zoning requirements, it still might need to be approved by other city agencies, such as the fire or police departments, the building inspector or the department of public health. To ensure compliance with local laws, such as health and fire codes, noise laws and environmental regulations, you may need one or more permits from these agencies. When you register with your local tax collector, you'll often receive information on these agencies and which types of businesses need to contact them. Your county clerk might also be able to direct you to information about which regulatory agencies to contact in your particular area.

2. State and Federal Regulations

State-level regulations often focus on how you conduct your business. For instance, your state wants to make sure that your cosmetologists are competent and that your carpenters do safe work. Your state regulates these business activities through licensing. Businesses are more likely to need a state license or permit if they are highly specialized or if they affect the public welfare; in other words, if there's a risk that poor handling of the business activities might harm the public, chances are that a state license is required. Common examples of state-licensed businesses are bars, auto shops, healthcare services and waste management companies.

John Tilles, co-founder of Portland River Company, a river rafting outfit in Portland, Oregon:

I was impressed by Oregon's straightforward and simple process for starting a business. On the other hand, the absolute toughest and most frustrating aspect of our business is staying on top of the permit regulations in order to use state and federal land and rivers. This is a constantly changing scenario, and the politics involved are often nonsensical.

Don't assume that your business is so simple or straightforward that you don't need a special license. You'd be amazed at how many activities states regulate: to name a few, locksmiths may need a license from the Bureau of Security and Investigative Services; people who train guide dogs may need one from the State Board of Guide Dogs; and furniture makers may be subject to licensing from the Bureau of Home Furnishings. If you think some of these regulations sound far-fetched, take a look at a list of your state's regulatory agencies—you'll quickly see we're not making this stuff up.

Businesses aren't nearly as heavily regulated by the federal government as by local and state offices, but if your business engages in certain activities, you may need a federal permit or license. These activities include (with the relevant federal office indicated):

- operating a common carrier such as a trucking company (Interstate Commerce Commission)
- constructing or operating a radio or television station (Federal Communications Commission)
- manufacturing drugs or meat products (Food and Drug Administration)
- manufacturing alcohol or tobacco products, or making or selling firearms (Bureau of Alcohol, Tobacco and Firearms)
- providing investment advice or counseling (Securities and Exchange Commission).

3. License and Permit Information Resources

Fortunately, many states have special agencies that act as clearinghouses for information on permits and issuing agencies, and several of them have very helpful websites. If you aren't sure what regulations might apply to your business, contact one or all of them to help you figure out what you need to do to keep your business in full compliance with all license and permit regulations. The Appendix contains several state-by-state listings of agencies in charge of various license and permit requirements. We've also included state links to business-related websites on the accompanying CD-ROM. (Appendix B explains how to use these links with your Web browser.)

Keep in mind that while the Web is a potentially awesome resource for navigating the permit requirements in your area, many state and local governments are still lagging in posting this kind of practical information. Don't waste your precious time searching endlessly through a state website trying to find the information you need—if it's not readily available at the site, chances are it's either not there or is so hopelessly buried that it's not worth your time to ferret it out. In these situations, it may well be better to just get on the phone or even go to the state office in person.

☑ Chapter 6 Checklist

☐ File organizational documents with the Secretary of State or similar filing office (corporations, LLCs and limited partnerships only).

☐ Obtain a federal employer identification number (FEIN).

☐ Register your fictitious business name with your county or state.

☐ Obtain a local tax registration certificate.

☐ Obtain a permit to sell retail goods and collect state sales tax.

☐ Obtain specialized vocation-related licenses or environmental permits if necessary.

■

Insuring Your Business

A. Property Insurance 7/2

B. Liability Insurance 7/3

C. The Wide World of Specialized Insurance Policies 7/4

D. Investigating and Purchasing a Policy 7/5

Except for some specific types of insurance, such as liability insurance for a company vehicle if your state requires it or other types of insurance if you have employees, there's no legal requirement that you obtain property or liability insurance for your business. But just because you don't have to get insurance coverage doesn't mean it's not a good idea. Even if you form a corporation or an LLC, which shields your personal assets from business liabilities (see Chapter 2), it won't protect you from losing your business if disaster strikes. Careful as we may be, fate does sometimes deal us a blow, and you'll undoubtedly be thankful you've taken the steps to protect yourself if and when it does.

There is something of an art to insuring your business: you want to get the maximum protection from insurance without blowing your whole bankroll on policies for every conceivable risk. Once you start to look, you'll find every imaginable type of insurance policy out there, though your business will likely need only a few of them at most. The two most common and generally useful types of policies are property insurance and liability insurance. We'll explain the basics of these two types, and introduce you to the many other kinds of policies you can purchase to cover specific risks involved in your business. We'll also shine some light on the process of shopping for and buying the policies you need.

Employers are subject to special insurance rules. As discussed in Chapter 11, if you are an employer you will be subject to a number of additional insurance requirements—you must typically pay for workers' compensation insurance, unemployment insurance and state disability insurance. These insurance programs are specifically for employers and are largely regulated at the state level. Refer to that chapter for the special rules governing employers' and employees' contributions to these insurance programs.

A. Property Insurance

As the name implies, property insurance simply covers your business for damage or loss to your business property. There is, of course, a good deal of variation—on what property and what risks are covered, and to what extent—from policy to policy. Be sure you're absolutely clear on these issues when choosing a policy.

As far as what property is covered, you'll want to make sure that the premises themselves as well as the business assets that are kept there are covered, including:

- fixtures to the property, such as lighting systems or carpeting
- equipment and machinery
- office furniture
- computers and accessories (monitors, CD-ROM drives, modems, printers)
- inventory and supplies, and
- personal property that's kept at the business site.

Most basic policies will cover these items.

If you rent your business space, your lease may require that you obtain a specific amount or type of property coverage. Be sure to check your lease for any insurance requirements before you purchase a policy.

Besides establishing what property is covered under a property insurance policy, you'll need to understand which types of losses will be covered. Read a policy carefully to determine what causes of damage are insurable. Most small business property insurance policies you'll run across will provide either basic, broad or special form coverage, with "special" offering the broadest coverage and "basic" the narrowest. A basic form policy will commonly cover fire, explosions, storms, smoke, riots, vandalism and sprinkler leaks. A broad form policy typically covers damage from broken windows and other structural glass, falling objects and water damage. With both basic and broad form policies, certain risks may be listed as excluded (not covered). (Also note that theft isn't typically covered under either a basic or broad form policy, a fact that surprises many business owners.) Special form coverage offers the widest range of protection, as it typically covers all risks (including theft), unless specifically excluded. While premiums for special form policies will be more expensive, it may be worth it if your business faces several or unusual risks—or simply if you want to make sure you're covered against theft.

Keep in mind that a basic policy will likely not cover the property of others that you may have at your business premises. For instance, if you rented a laptop and it was destroyed in an office fire, chances are that the computer wouldn't be covered under a typical policy. If you expect to regularly have property that belongs to others at your business location, you should make sure to get a policy that covers such property.

If the policy you're considering excludes one or more items that you want covered, find out whether it can be included and at what cost. You may have to purchase what's commonly called a rider or an endorsement to add special coverage to the policy. For example, accounting records, cash and deeds are often excluded from standard property insurance policies, but can usually be covered with some extra paperwork—and an additional premium. There also may be other ways to bring the property you want covered under the scope of policy. For example, if you want the policy to cover your personal stereo that you keep at your office, but the policy only covers business property, one option is to transfer title of the stereo to the business.

⚠ If you have a home-based business, you may need to adjust your homeowner's policy. As discussed in Chapter 4, it's important for owners of home-based businesses to figure out whether their homeowner's policy forbids business use of the home or excludes coverage of business-related claims. You need to make sure that your homeowner's policy won't be limited or voided entirely by running a business out of your home. It's better to come clean with your insurance company about your home business and maybe spend some extra premium dollars than to find out after a catastrophe that your homeowner's coverage has been voided by your business activities. (See Chapter 4, Section D, for more on home businesses.)

Finally, be sure you clearly understand the dollar limits on your policy and any deductibles or co-payments you'll have to make. Also, make sure the policy covers the replacement cost of the property, not merely its current (depreciated) value. Computer equipment, for example, depreciates incredibly fast. If you lose your two-year-old computer to theft, you'd definitely want your insurance to pay for a new computer rather than the value of the stolen one, which may be barely enough to cover the shipping costs of the new one (a slight exaggeration, perhaps, but you get the point).

B. Liability Insurance

Liability coverage insures you against the notorious slip-and-fall situation: someone injures himself on your premises and sues you for the ranch. A general liability policy (versus a product liability or vehicle liability policy, discussed below) will cover damages that your business is ordered to pay to an individual (customer, supplier, business associate, whoever) who was injured on your property. Say, for instance, someone puts their foot through a floorboard weakened by dry rot, or trips on an electric cord, or is hit by a shelving unit that falls over. In this age of fast and furious personal injury lawsuits, one accident like this could result in a verdict against your business for thousands, tens of thousands or even millions of dollars, even if you were only marginally at fault. For this reason, liability insurance is advised for any business that has even minimal contact with the public.

A related, though technically different, type of insurance is product liability insurance, which protects you from lawsuits by customers claiming to be hurt by a product you provided. Remember the woman who sued McDonald's for millions after she was burned by their hot coffee? That's the type of thing product liability insurance is designed to protect against. If your business provides a product to the public that has a risk of harming anyone, you might consider this type of insurance—even if your risk seems as absurd as the scalding-coffee scenario. It can be expensive, but a lot less so than a multimillion dollar award to a victorious plaintiff.

Finally, be sure to obtain auto liability insurance (at the least) for any vehicles used for business, including employees' personal cars that are used for business purposes. Auto liability coverage will not be provided by a general liability policy (if you have one), and is legally required in all but four states (Mississippi, New Hampshire, Tennessee and Wisconsin). Even if it's not required in your state, it's foolish not to protect yourself against this very potentially devastating risk. In addition, some states require drivers to be covered by other types of auto insurance, including personal injury protection (PIP) coverage and uninsured/underinsured motorist (UM/UIM) coverage. If your state mandates certain types of coverage, it will generally also require that you purchase a certain minimum level of the insurance. Check with your state's department of motor vehicles to find out what insurance requirements exist for drivers in your state.

Coverage for employees' personal cars that are used for business is known as "non-owned auto liability insurance," and it protects your business if an employee hurts someone or damages property while driving for business. (Many non-owned auto liability insurance policies do not cover employees; they may need to get their own coverage.) It's important you get this type of coverage even if your state doesn't require it.

C. The Wide World of Specialized Insurance Policies

Property and liability insurance are the two most important types of coverage for small businesses, but there are loads of other kinds of policies as well. Below we list some of the more common ones. Keep in mind that a broad property or liability policy might already cover one or more risks listed here. For instance, if you have special form property insurance (discussed in Section A above), you'll likely be insured against theft.

- **Business interruption insurance:** This type of insurance will cover you if your business is forced to close for a period of time for a reason covered under the policy, such as damage from a fire or earthquake. In that case, your policy will pay approximately what you would have earned if you had been open as normal.
- **Malpractice insurance:** Often expensive, this type of insurance protects you from lawsuits arising from professional mistakes. Doctors and lawyers are typically covered by malpractice insurance, as well as other professionals such as real estate agents and accountants.
- **Theft insurance, including burglary, robbery and employee theft:** Since many basic policies do not cover losses due to theft, you may want to purchase specific insurance to cover you in case office equipment is stolen. Be sure to find out whether the policy covers employee theft as well; if not, you can usually purchase that type of coverage separately.

Other types of insurance include credit insurance for accounts receivable, intellectual property insurance, and disability insurance for owners of the business (not the same as state-mandated disability insurance for employees, discussed in Chapter 11). Check with your insurance agent or broker about whether your specific business might need one or more of these special types of coverage.

D. Investigating and Purchasing a Policy

The key to making an intelligent and cost-effective insurance purchase is to do your homework. Understanding the fine-print details is absolutely essential in order to compare policies and purchase the best one for your business. For example, when pricing out different insurance companies it's useless to compare two policies unless they cover the same types of property, the same risks, and up to the same dollar amounts. All these details need to be fully fleshed out and understood before you can make an informed decision.

Insurance brokers who gather information from different insurance companies can be of great help in deciphering policies and figuring out your best deal. Make sure your broker understands all the nooks and crannies of your specific business activities and the risks that are, or may be, involved. Preferably, use a broker who specializes in policies for your type of business. You may be surprised to learn that specially tailored policies may exist for your type of business. For instance, a "producer's package policy" for filmmakers covers several risks unique to the film business, such as the costs of a production—often in the tens or hundreds of thousands of dollars—in case your negatives are destroyed. An insurance broker who knows your type of business will be able to direct you to these specialized policies, while a run-of-the-mill broker may not.

You'll probably encounter insurance companies that offer package deals, which can often be cheaper than buying several individual policies separately. As long as all your needs are met, these package deals can be a good way to go. As always, be sure you understand the extent of coverage in each area rather than relying on any promises that the package covers "all your business needs."

☑ Chapter 7 Checklist

☐ Determine what business property you need covered.

☐ Contact an insurance agent or broker to answer questions for you and to price out various policies.

☐ Be sure to obtain a property insurance policy that covers against all the types of losses that your business may face (theft, fire, water damage, to name a few).

☐ Obtain liability insurance if your business will have contact with the general public, or if there's a substantial risk that someone will sue your business for injuries or damages.

☐ Obtain product liability insurance if there's a chance that your product will injure anyone.

☐ Obtain auto liability coverage for any vehicles used for business, including the personal cars of employees that are used for business.

☐ Obtain any specialized coverage that your business may need.

Getting to Know Your Taxes

A. Tax Basics 8/2

    1. The Agencies Behind the Taxes 8/4

    2. Understanding Deductions 8/5

    3. Hobby Businesses: A Possible Source of Tax Deductions 8/7

B. Income Taxes for Sole Proprietors 8/9

    1. Federal Income Taxes 8/9

    2. State Income Taxes 8/11

C. Income Taxes for Partnerships 8/11

    1. Federal Income Taxes 8/11

    2. State Income Taxes 8/13

D. Income Taxes for LLCs 8/13

    1. Federal Income Taxes 8/13

    2. State Taxes 8/14

E. Estimating and Paying Your Taxes Quarterly 8/15

    1. Who Must Pay Estimated Taxes? 8/16

    2. When to Make Estimated Tax Payments 8/17

    3. Calculating and Paying Your Estimated Taxes 8/18

F. City and County Taxes 8/18

    1. Business Taxes 8/19

    2. Property Taxes 8/20

G. Sales Taxes 8/20

    1. Taxable vs. Non-Taxable Sales 8/20

    2. The Nexus Requirement 8/21

    3. Sales Taxes Online 8/22

    4. Sales to Final Users vs. Sales to Resellers 8/23

    5. Using Resale Certificates 8/24

    6. Use Taxes 8/24

    7. Keeping Track of Your Sales 8/25

    8. Calculating, Paying and Filing Sales Taxes 8/25

It's no fun for any profitable business to share a big chunk of its hard-won earnings with the government. But like it or not, as soon as your business is in the black, everyone, from your city and county to your state and, of course, the IRS, will demand a piece of the action. Although it's not necessary to become a tax expert before going into business, it is important for you to know what taxes you'll be subject to and how to go about paying them. Understanding the taxes you'll face will help you in at least three ways:

- You'll be better able to plan your finances, which may even involve deciding whether you'll have enough cash to stay in business.
- You'll be able to avoid tax-reporting and deposit errors, which can result in hefty—sometimes even business-threatening—penalties.
- You'll be able to make good business decisions that will reduce your tax burden.

Even if your business won't make a fast profit, you may owe taxes. Lots of new businesspeople believe that if there is no profit, there is no tax. Sorry, but local taxes on gross receipts and taxes on sales of retail goods (sales taxes) are but two examples of taxes that need to be paid regardless of whether a business is turning a profit. So even if your business may not be profitable for a year or two, you need to prepare yourself for paying some taxes.

This chapter will give you simple, straightforward information on the taxes that owners of sole proprietorships, partnerships and LLCs will face. It will also provide basic instructions for filing and paying them correctly and on time. After covering the basics, we offer three sections that discuss the specific tax rules that vary according to business type—there's a separate section for sole proprietorships, partnerships and LLCs. Simply read the section that's appropriate for your business form. Then, in the last three sections, we cover paying estimated taxes, local taxes and sales taxes, all of which apply more or less evenly to all business types. If your business has employees, refer to Chapter 11, "Growing Your Business and Hiring Workers," for information on the special taxes faced by employers.

The details of corporate taxation are beyond the scope of this book. This chapter offers only some broad outlines of corporate taxation. The full maze of corporate tax rules is far too complicated for us to cover in detail. If you're thinking about incorporating, keep in mind that doing so will subject you to more complicated (and occasionally unpleasant) tax rules. We present an overview of the potential tax advantages and disadvantages of the corporation in Chapter 2, Section D. If you need detailed information beyond that, take a look at *Tax Savvy for Small Business,* by attorney Frederick Daily, or *How to Form Your Own Corporation* for California, New York and Texas, by attorney Anthony Mancuso, all published by Nolo.

You may need professional help to deal with your taxes. Tax rules and filing procedures can be quite complex, even for a relatively simple business. This chapter is meant to give you the big picture. Especially if your business is large, is incorporated or has a number of employees, you will likely need to do additional reading and possibly hire an experienced accountant or even a tax lawyer. Chapter 12 discusses other resources and publications for small businesspeople, as well as how to work with experts.

A. Tax Basics

One of the first things you should understand is that there's little rhyme or reason to the world of taxes. Don't drive yourself nuts by trying to figure out the logic of a system that has virtually none. The bottom line is that the federal, state and local governments tend to tax everything that breathes or moves (and lots of things that do neither). And this includes virtually every aspect of a business that can be quantified. For example, depending on the type of business and its location, a business might be taxed on its gross income, net profit, gross retail sales, how many employees it has, how much employees are paid, how much property the

Talking About Income—Key Terms Defined

A lot of different jargon is used to describe the money that comes into and flows out of your business. These financial terms are discussed in more detail elsewhere in the book where we discuss financial projections and accounting (Chapters 5 and 10). But since these concepts are also important in understanding your taxes, here are some brief definitions.

- **Gross vs. net.** It's crucial to understand this distinction. "Gross" generally refers to total revenue, before deducting expenses such as salaries, rent, product costs or office supplies. "Net" means what's left over after subtracting costs and expenses. (As you can see, a "gross" figure will be higher than a "net" figure, since deductions come out of the "gross" and result in the "net.") Thus "gross income" (sometimes called "gross receipts" or "gross sales") refers to the total money brought in by your business, before you've begun to cover any of your costs. "Net profit" refers to your income after deducting costs and expenses. In some contexts, "net" may refer to your after-tax profit—in other words, it may reflect not only your costs and expenses, but also any taxes you owe on your income. Be aware that the terms "gross" and "net" are often bandied about loosely, and it's important to understand what deductions are included when using these terms.

- **Fixed vs. variable expenses.** Fixed expenses are the ones that will be more or less the same regardless of how much business you're doing. They include rent, utility bills, insurance premiums and loan payments. Variable expenses are the costs of the products or services themselves and anything that goes along with your product, like packaging or shipping. Variable expenses increase or decrease depending on how much business you're doing.

- **Gross profit.** Gross profit is a specific term that refers to how much money you make on each sale above the cost of the item itself (its variable cost). Unlike the term "gross income," which refers to all the money your business brings in before expenses are accounted for, the term "gross profit" does take into account the cost of the product or service you're selling. For example, if you sell a widget for $5 that cost you $3, your gross profit is $2. The term "profit margin," or "gross margin" is also sometimes used to mean the same thing. The key thing to remember about gross profit is that fixed expenses such as rent or utility bills still haven't been deducted—only the cost of the product or service itself.

- **Net profit** is what's left over after subtracting fixed expenses from gross profit. Put another way, net profit means the amount of money you have left over after subtracting all expenses—fixed and variable—from your gross income. Sometimes the term "net income" is used to mean the same thing as "net profit."

- **Current vs. capital expenses.** Current expenses include ordinary, day-to-day business expenses such as office supplies or salaries. For tax purposes, you can deduct them from your business income in the year that you pay for them. Capital expenses, on the other hand, include payments for business assets (also called "capital," "fixed" or "depreciable" assets) that have a useful life of one year or more, such as computers or office furniture. Capital expenses generally can't be totally deducted in the year they occur, but need to be deducted over a number of years—a process known as depreciation, capitalization or amortization.

business owns or leases, the seating capacity of the business or how many vehicles the business owns —and the list goes on and on.

To complicate matters further, the many different taxes are administered by different government agencies, each with its own rules, forms and filing procedures. It's little wonder that the mere mention of taxes often induces nausea and sometimes even panic in otherwise well-adjusted businesspeople.

1. The Agencies Behind the Taxes

The first step in understanding small business taxes is to recognize who levies which taxes. Here's a quick breakdown.

- **Federal taxes.** The United States Internal Revenue Service, the top dog of tax agencies, collects the following taxes from small businesses and their owners: taxes on individual or corporate income; self-employment taxes (which go to the Social Security and Medicare systems); and payroll taxes. (See Chapter 11 for information on payroll taxes.)

- **State taxes.** While not all states are the same, states typically collect the following taxes from businesses: taxes on business income, sales taxes on sales of retail goods (after the business has collected the sales tax from its customers), and payroll taxes (see Chapter 11 for information on payroll taxes). States also often collect special taxes (called "excise taxes") on certain types of business activities such as distributing alcohol, cigarettes or gasoline. In addition, some states collect taxes on corporations, LLCs and limited partnerships.

- **County and city taxes.** Cities, counties, or sometimes both typically impose taxes on businesses based upon several factors. Most cities assign businesses to categories (for example, retail businesses, wholesalers, services, to name a few) and then tax each category based on certain criteria, such as gross receipts, gross payroll or number of

employees. In addition, counties often assess and collect property taxes on real and personal property owned by businesses within the county. Cities and counties also may impose a sales tax. This tax may be collected by the state along with the state sales tax.

Forms and Schedules and Returns, Oh My!

We talk a lot in this chapter about tax forms, tax schedules and tax returns. Basically, these are simply different names for the papers you fill out with your financial information and submit to your federal, state or local tax agency. Technically, a "tax form" is the principal document that businesses and their owners must complete with all the basic information about the business's or individual's income. For instance, every individual who earns income must fill out Form 1040, *Individual Income Tax Return*, and all partnerships and LLCs must file Form 1065, *Partnership Return of Income*. A "schedule" is an additional sheet of information required by the IRS that businesses and business owners must attach to their tax forms. For instance, sole proprietors must submit Schedule C with their Form 1040 to report their income from their business, and partners and LLC owners usually need to report their business income on Schedule E. Plus, partnerships and LLCs must include various schedules with their Form 1065s. Finally, a "tax return" is simply a general term for the whole package you send off to the IRS: your tax form and any schedules.

A tax by any other name is … a fee. In addition to the taxes listed above, your business may have to pay additional fees for business licenses and/or tax registration. For instance, many cities and counties require all businesses in the area to register with the local tax collector and pay a registration fee. And if your business requires a special license such as a permit to handle food, or a cosmetology license, you'll usually have to pay for it. While these fees arguably could be called taxes, we don't deal with them as such in this chapter. The various registration, permit and license requirements—including their associated fees—are dealt with in Chapter 6, "Federal, State and Local Start-Up Requirements."

2. Understanding Deductions

Maximizing profits while keeping taxes as low as possible is the name of the game in any business. The main way to do this is by claiming business deductions, which means subtracting certain expenses from your taxable income—which means you'll have less income to report and pay taxes on. Of course you can't deduct just any old expense you want. To stay out of trouble with the IRS, your state tax agency and your local tax collector, you need to understand which deductions are allowed and which ones are not.

a. What Expenses Are Deductible?

Allowable deductions are outlined in great length (to put it mildly) in the Internal Revenue Code—we'll summarize the basic guidelines below. You'll need to follow these rules when filling out your federal tax return, which reports your business income and deductions. When you file your state income tax return, you'll generally fill out a form that uses the information from your federal return, making a few adjustments to reflect your state's different rules on the deductibility of business expenses. As far as local taxes go, they may simply be based on gross income (also called "gross receipts") not allowing for any deductions. In short, the main rules for deductibility of business expenses that you need to worry about are the federal ones.

The Internal Revenue Code (IRC) says that any "ordinary and necessary" expenses for your business can be subtracted from your business income for federal tax purposes (IRC § 162). For lots of expenses, it's a no-brainer whether they qualify. Product costs, office rent, equipment and machinery, office supplies, your business computer system, business insurance and office utility bills are just a few examples of costs that easily count as deductible expenses. As long as an expenditure is in fact made for business—not personal—purposes, the general rule is that you can deduct it from your business's gross income.

It gets a little more complicated when expenditures aren't clearly made for business reasons. The IRS has special rules for expenses that border on the personal side, such as travel, entertainment and vehicle expenses. These costs are deductible, but only according to special IRS rules.

Consult additional resources for the details on expenses. The rules on allowable travel and entertainment expenses are fully explained in Nolo's *Tax Savvy for Small Business,* by tax attorney Fred Daily, and in the IRS's Publication 535, *Business Expenses,* available online at http://www.irs.treas. gov/forms_pubs/pubs/index.htm.

b. How Are Expenses Deducted?

In addition to determining whether an expense is deductible, you need to understand a number of special rules that govern how particular expenses may be deducted. First, you need to know there's a major distinction between current and capital expenses. Current expenses can best be described as your everyday costs of doing business, such as rent, supplies, utility bills and the like. These expenses are fully deductible in the year they occur. Capital expenses, on the other hand, are not fully deductible in the year you incur them. You incur a capital expense when you purchase an item with a useful life of at least one year—called a "business asset." Business assets include items such as vehicles, furniture, heavy equipment (like a forklift or printing press) and real estate. Rather than fully deducting a capital expense in the year it was made, you must spread out the deduction over a number of years. This process is variously called "depreciation," "amortization" or "capitalization." Different types of assets have different depreciation rules, and the number of years over which the cost of an item must be depreciated varies. Depreciation rules are explained in IRS Publication 534, *Depreciation*, as well as in other IRS publications that cover specific types of assets.

 There's a big exception to the rule that all capital expenses must be depreciated over time. The IRS allows every business to treat a certain amount of capital expenditures as current expenses, and fully deduct them in the year they were made. This major exception is known as a "179 deduction," because it's established in Internal Revenue Code Section 179. In the year 2000, businesses can write off up to $20,000 in expenditures that would normally qualify as capital expenses. The limit goes up to $24,000 in 2001 and 2002, and up to $25,000 in 2003. Whether and how much you should take advantage of a 179 deduction depends on your circumstances. Good general advice is to take a 179 deduction only when your taxable income is high enough that you'll get a decent tax benefit right away. Businesses with low

incomes might want to depreciate assets instead (take their deductions slowly), so that they'll have more deductions available in future years when their income might be higher. For more detailed information on the pros and cons of 179 deductions, see *Tax Savvy for Small Business,* by tax attorney Frederick W. Daily (Nolo).

Another important rule is that start-up expenses must be depreciated over time—you can't deduct their full cost in the year you incur them. For lots of businesses, this rule isn't too much of a big deal because their profits in the first year of operation are small (or, as is often the case, nonexistent)—meaning that a big tax deduction wouldn't result in a lot of savings anyway.

The introduction to tax deductions we've given you in this section is only the tiniest scratch on the surface of a huge and complex body of information. The book *Tax Savvy for Small Business,* by tax attorney Frederick W. Daily (Nolo), does an excellent job of leading you through the maze. Especially as your business grows and its finances become more complicated, you may well want to hire a tax advisor to help you use the tax rules to your best advantage. (See Chapter 12 on hiring and working with tax professionals.)

Where to Get Tax Forms and Schedules

Although we do provide several tax forms in Appendix C and on CD-ROM (a list is included at the beginning of Appendix C), we've left out many federal and state tax forms because they change from year to year and are readily available from other sources. Besides the flood of tax forms that are available at post offices and libraries as April 15 comes near, you can always obtain the most current forms, schedules and publications by ordering them over the phone or downloading them off the Web.

- Order federal tax forms and other publications from the IRS by calling 800-829-3676. Or download them from the Web at http://www.irs.ustreas.gov/prod/forms_pubs/index.html.
- For state tax forms, contact your state tax agency. We've included contact information in Appendix A for tax agencies in each state. Also, most states have tax forms and information available online. On the CD-ROM that comes with this book, we've included a list of links to business- and tax-related websites for each state. You can use this file with your Web browser to link directly to these sites (see Appendix B for instructions on how to use this list with your browser).
- Local tax forms and instructions are often automatically sent to businesses once they've registered with their city or county. Otherwise, contact the agency in charge of business taxes in your city or county (depending on where your business is located) for more information on how to obtain local tax forms. To find your local tax agency, look in the city government section of your white pages under "Tax Collector," "Business Tax Division" or sometimes "City Clerk."

3. Hobby Businesses: A Possible Source of Tax Deductions

For many small business owners, their "business" is more a labor of love than a reliable source of income. This is most often the case when an owner has other means of financial support—such as a regular job or a spouse who brings home wages or other income—allowing his microbusiness to continue even though it makes little or no money. These types of tiny businesses are usually operated from the home (renting an office would be too expensive) and are often based on activities near and dear to the owner, which has earned them the nickname "hobby businesses."

There is no one type of hobby business, but examples might include a basement jewelry studio, a jazz band for hire, or an antique-refinishing business. The owners would probably keep on making jewelry, playing jazz or restoring antiques even if they never made a penny, but are making a go of turning their hobby into a profitable business.

Often, profits fail to materialize. For most regular businesses, anything more than a year or so of losing money is a cue to close up shop. But if you love doing whatever you're doing, it might make sense for you to stick with your losing business rather than fold it up. Why? Because if you have another source of income (as many owners of hobby businesses do), the losses from your hobby business can be used to offset that income. Deducting business losses—including everyday expenses and depreciation on assets such as computer equipment—can not only lower the amount of income upon which taxes are calculated, but also may drop you into a lower tax bracket. This is what is commonly referred to as a tax shelter: an unprofitable business whose losses offset the owner's taxable income from other sources.

Of course, most entrepreneurs would much rather earn a healthy profit than lose money with their business. And the savings made possible by a tax shelter do not always justify continuing a marginal or losing business. But they definitely can make a difference in deciding whether it's worth it to keep your unprofitable—but enjoyable!—business going.

> **EXAMPLE:** Kay and Reza are married and file joint tax returns. Reza earns a salary as a chef in a local restaurant, and Kay is a magazine editor. Kay has a passion for plants, and decides to try to make a business of selling some of the hundreds of plants she grows and propagates in her backyard greenhouse. After she's spent thousands of dollars on exotic plants and better lighting equipment, the greenhouse heater goes on the fritz and over 300 of Kay's expensive, exotic plants die. Her expenses for the year total nearly $10,000, and she has not yet sold any plants. The silver lining for Kay and Reza comes at tax time, when they deduct the $10,000 loss from their joint taxable income of $105,000. This not only reduces their taxable income, but—depending on their income level and any other deductions they take—might drop them into a lower tax bracket as well.

On the down side, if you consistently use your unprofitable business as a tax shelter, deducting your losses from your other income year after year, you'll likely catch the attention of the IRS. An issue that often arises with hobby businesses is whether the venture is really a business at all. An important thing to understand about tax shelters is that in order to deduct expenses from your taxable income, those expenses must have been incurred by a legitimate profit-motivated business—not merely a personal hobby. As you might expect, not every hobby counts as a hobby business. If you claim expenses from your hobby business as tax deductions and you're audited, you'll have to prove to the IRS that your hobby is in fact a legitimate business.

a. Proving Your Hobby Is a Business

Before you start claiming deductions for the costs of your favorite art projects or toy car collections, make sure your venture will pass IRS scrutiny and qualify as a real business. Thankfully, the IRS's definition is fairly broad. Basically, any activity that you engage in to make a profit counts as a business. In other words, you need only prove to the IRS that you're trying—not necessarily succeeding—to make a profit with your venture. The IRS uses a few different criteria for deciding whether your business truly has a profit motive.

The main test for profit motive is called the "3-of-5" test. If your business makes a profit in three out of five consecutive years, it is legally presumed to have a profit motive. You may be surprised—and relieved—to know that the amount of the profit is irrelevant; even if you just barely break even and earn only $1 profit in your business year, you've officially had a profitable year.

While the IRS gives a lot of weight to the 3-of-5 test, it is not conclusive. In other words, if you flunk the 3-of-5 test, you still may be able to prove that your business is motivated by profit. You can use virtually any kind of evidence to prove this. Business cards, a well-maintained set of books, a separate business bank account, current business licenses and permits, and proof of advertising will all help to persuade an IRS auditor that your activity is in fact a business.

b. Watch Out for Local Tax Rules

When planning out your hobby business, don't forget that local requirements and taxes will increase your costs of doing business, both in time and money. Lots of small business people are surprised to find out that state and local tax regulations for small businesses can be more of a bear than IRS rules. For one, if you sell tangible products, you may be subject to state sales taxes. Plus, many cities impose taxes or fees on small businesses and require them to go through some sort of registration process, and counties often have similar requirements for businesses in rural areas. Generally speaking, these rules technically apply to any money-making activity within the locality—even if the hobby business doesn't intend to claim any federal or state tax deductions. (Local taxes and fees are discussed later in this chapter, in Section F, as well as in Chapter 6, Section D.)

In practice, many tiny hobby businesses—so tiny that the word "business" even seems excessive—might be able to get away unnoticed, assuming you don't deduct business losses on your tax return. Even so, you should be aware that depending on your local rules, you may be penalized if you're caught doing business without having gotten the permits or licenses required by your state or local government. These penalties may include fines and any back taxes that apply.

John Tilles, co-founder of Portland River Company, a river rafting outfit in Portland, Oregon:

The real can of worms for us was in dealing with taxes. As a new and undercapitalized business, a professional accountant was out of the question. This left me to figure it out as I went which was pretty straightforward in the early days, but as the years went on and things became more complicated I finally had to use a professional C.P.A.

B. Income Taxes for Sole Proprietors

As mentioned throughout this book, a sole proprietorship is one and the same as its owner (the sole proprietor) for most legal and tax purposes. It follows that the sole proprietor must report and pay federal and state income taxes on all business profits, including any profits the sole proprietor leaves in the business for expansion. In other words, the business itself does not file tax returns or pay income taxes.

1. Federal Income Taxes

You're probably already familiar with the process of filing IRS Form 1040, based on income you earned at a job. Good—this means much of the process of filing federal income taxes as a sole proprietor will already be familiar to you. That's because income from your business will be treated as personal income, which you report on Form 1040 much as you report wages or returns on investments. But there are two additional steps: you'll use a separate sheet (called Schedule C) to report your business profit, and you'll also have to pay self-employment taxes based on your income (and file Schedule SE).

a. Income Tax

As mentioned, you report business profits or losses on Schedule C (*Profit or Loss from Business*), which is submitted once a year with your 1040 return, usually by April 15. (See "Defining Your Business Year" in Section E2 for information on using a business year other than the calendar year for tax-reporting purposes.) If a sole proprietor owns more than one business, a separate Schedule C is used for each business. (See "Where to Get Tax Forms and Schedules" in Section A2, above, for information on obtaining the most current forms.)

You're not required to file Schedule C if your sole proprietorship doesn't make at least $400 profit in the business year, though it's a good idea to file one anyway. One big reason is that if your business loses money in any year, filing Schedule C allows the loss to be deducted from any other income you make for that year, reducing your total taxable income. Or you can carry over the loss into a future profitable year to offset those profits and thereby reduce your taxes. Another reason to report losses or profits under $400 on Schedule C is that doing so triggers the beginning of the time window during which the IRS can audit you (otherwise, the IRS can audit you virtually forever).

Simplified Tax Schedule for Super-Small Sole Proprietorships

Extra-small sole proprietorships may be able to use a simplified schedule to report their income, Schedule C-EZ. (This schedule may only be used by sole proprietors.) To use this simplified form, which works just like Schedule C, as discussed in the text, the following criteria must be met:

- You claim less than $2,500 in business expenses.
- You had no inventory during the year.
- You had no employees during the year.
- You use the cash method of accounting. (See Chapter 10, Section B, for an explanation of the difference between the cash and accrual methods of accounting.)
- You owned and operated only one sole proprietorship during the year.
- You do not deduct expenses for business use of your home.
- You don't report a net business loss.

If you depreciate assets or have unallowed passive activity losses from previous years, you may not be able to use this schedule. See the IRS instructions for details on who may use Schedule C-EZ.

Though it's easier to fill out than Schedule C, you won't save enough time or trouble to warrant trying to squeeze a too-large business into Schedule C-EZ. Don't, for example, neglect to claim over $2,500 in business expenses or to claim depreciation expenses just so you qualify to use the schedule. The marginal convenience of the simplified schedule just isn't worth it.

Besides using Schedule C, there's an important procedural difference between reporting and paying taxes on income from a job and income from a sole proprietorship: Regular employees are subject to tax withholding by their employer, but sole proprietors must usually estimate their tax for the year and pay it in quarterly installments. The IRS is a stickler when it comes to making these quarterly payments and won't hesitate to fine you for doing it incorrectly or late, and especially for not doing it at all. Even if you pay your taxes in full by April 15 (or whenever your business year ends), failure to make quarterly payments means you'll be charged a steep penalty (8%–9% in 2000). Be sure to read Section E, below, on who needs to make estimated quarterly tax payments and how to do it.

b. Self-Employment Taxes

Sole proprietors must also make contributions to the Social Security and Medicare systems, together called "self-employment taxes." Regular employees make contributions to these two programs through deductions from their paychecks. Sole proprietors must make their contributions when paying their other income taxes. However, an important difference between employees and sole proprietors is that employees only have to pay half as much into these programs because their contributions are matched by their employers. Sole proprietors must pay the entire amount themselves.

For the year 2000, self-employment taxes include:

- Social Security tax of 12.4% on profits up to $76,200, and
- Medicare tax of 2.9% on all profits.

In other words, profits of $76,200 and less will be taxed at 15.3% (both Social Security and Medicare), and profits above that will be taxed at 2.9% (Medicare only). (In comparison, regular employees only pay a 7.65% tax on wages of $76,200 or less, and a 1.45% tax on wages above that.)

Fortunately, there is a small silver lining to this dark tax cloud; half of the total self-employment tax you'll pay can be deducted from your taxable income at year-end. And if your sole proprietorship makes less than $400 profit in the business year, no self-employment taxes need to be paid.

Reporting and Paying Are Not the Same

As we discuss the often complex rules of taxes, keep in mind that a requirement that you must report income is not the same as an obligation to pay. Sometimes, a tax agency like the IRS or your state tax office requires you to submit a tax return even if you don't owe any taxes. Generally, a "filing" or "reporting" requirement means simply that you need to provide income and expense information, which may or may not add up to an actual tax obligation.

Self-employment taxes are reported on Schedule SE, which, like Schedule C (*Profit or Loss from a Business*), is submitted yearly with your 1040 income tax return. (See "Where to Get Tax Forms and Schedules" in Section A2, above, for information on obtaining the latest forms.) Once you determine the amount of self-employment taxes you owe on Schedule SE, the result is entered on your 1040 form in the "Other Taxes" section and is added to your personal income tax obligation. Remember, however, that most sole proprietors must estimate their total taxes for the year and pay them in quarterly installments. Read Section E, below, for details on estimated tax payments, which must be paid by most businesses owners.

2. State Income Taxes

For the most part, state income taxes are filed and paid in much the same way as federal income taxes. Any profit generated by a sole proprietorship is generally treated as personal income of the sole proprietor and reported on her individual state tax return. In most states the sole proprietor will need to attach a separate schedule, similar to the federal Schedule C, to report her business income. Unlike the federal rule, some states require this schedule to be filed even if your business loses money or

makes less than $400 profit. In these states you won't owe any taxes unless you've made a profit, but you must file the form in any case. Check with your state for its rule.

Like federal taxes, many states require businesses to estimate and pay their income taxes in quarterly installments. Again, estimating your taxes and making quarterly payments is covered in Section E, below.

State tax rules vary considerably from state to state so it's important that you check with your state tax agency for its requirements. In the Appendix we've included contact information for state tax agencies, and on the CD-ROM that comes with this book we've included a list of links to state tax websites. See Appendix B for information on how to use this file with your Web browser.

C. Income Taxes for Partnerships

When it comes to federal and state income taxes for partnerships, the main thing to remember is that while a partnership itself does not pay taxes (its owners do), it does need to submit an annual informational return to the IRS and usually the state to report its income. As is true for sole proprietorships, taxes are paid only by the partners (business owners), not the business itself, and the partners have to pay taxes on all business profits, whether or not they take any money out of the business. This section will explain what partnerships need to do to comply with the IRS and state rules.

1. Federal Income Taxes

As discussed elsewhere in this book, partnerships are called "pass-through tax entities," which means that profits pass right through the business to the owners, who report them on their individual income tax returns. The partnership itself is not taxed, though it must report its income and losses each year. (Although few do, a partnership can also elect to be taxed as a corporation, by submitting Form 8832 and electing corporate tax status.) Besides income taxes, partners must also file and pay self-employment taxes.

a. Income Tax

Even though the partnership itself does not pay taxes on profits, it must report profits and losses using an informational return, Form 1065, *U.S. Partnership Return of Income.* No tax is due with this return, which is generally due by April 15. (See "Defining Your Business Year" in Section E2 for information on using a business year other than the calendar year.)

Along with Form 1065, the partnership must also submit a Schedule K-1, *Partner's Share of Income, Credit and Deductions,* for each partner, reporting each partner's share of profits or losses. The K-1 schedule is used to inform the IRS of the partners' chosen profit division. (Often, partners own equal shares of the business, which normally means they will choose to share profits and pay taxes equally—such as four partners each getting ¼ of a business's profits and paying ¼ of its taxes. But if they so choose, partners can divide profits and losses in another way. See Chapter 2, Section B, for more on partnerships.) A copy of the completed K-1 must also be given to each partner on or before the date that the partnership return is due to the IRS. (Section A2, above, includes information on obtaining current tax forms.)

As we mentioned above, profits earned by a partnership are taxed as personal income of the individual partners. Each partner reports her allocated share of business income or losses on her individual federal income tax return (Form 1040) using Schedule E (*Supplemental Income and Loss*). Schedule E repeats the information reported about that partner's income on Schedule K-1 (which each partner should have received from the partnership). Since the partnership already filed Schedule K-1

with the IRS, partners do not need to submit this schedule with their individual tax returns.

Partners who earn income from a profitable partnership often must estimate their taxes and pay the total in quarterly installments. Section E, below, covers estimated tax payments, an important aspect of taxes for all small businesses.

b. Self-Employment Taxes

Partners and other self-employed individuals who earn more than $400 profit during the business year must contribute to Social Security and Medicare through federal self-employment taxes. In 2000, self-employment taxes include:

- Social Security tax of 12.4% on profits up to $76,200, and
- Medicare tax of 2.9% on all profits.

Put another way, profits of $76,200 and less will be taxed at 15.3% (both Social Security and Medicare), and profits above that will be taxed at 2.9% (Medicare only).

On a brighter note, half of the total self-employment tax you'll pay can be deducted from your taxable income at year-end. And if your partnership makes less than $400 profit in the business year, no self-employment taxes need be filed or paid. (See "Reporting and Paying Are Not the Same" in Section B1, above, if you're confused about the difference between filing taxes and paying them.)

Self-employment taxes are reported on Schedule SE, which, like Schedule E (*Supplemental Income and Loss*), is submitted yearly with a partner's 1040 return. Once you determine your self-employment tax with Schedule SE, the result is entered on your 1040 form in the "Other Taxes" section, which is added to your personal income tax obligation. But don't forget about estimating and paying taxes quarterly—most partners of profitable businesses must do so, or face the IRS's penalties. Ouch. (See Section E, below, for how to estimate and pay your taxes.)

2. State Income Taxes

Like the federal government, most states require partnerships to file informational returns reporting business income and losses. Fortunately, many of these state forms are almost identical to the federal Form 1065. Partnerships may also be required to file a schedule analogous to the federal Schedule K-1 for each partner, indicating the partner's share of the business profit or loss, and to give each partner a copy. Typically the state schedules are similar to the federal version, but account for differences between state and federal tax laws. Generally, no tax is due with the partnership return or schedules.

Any partnership profit is taxed as personal income of the partners, who report their share on their individual state income tax return. Partnership income is usually recorded on a schedule similar to the federal Schedule E and included with the state tax form. Keep in mind that some states require partners to file this schedule even if the partnership loses money and no taxes are due.

Finally, like federal taxes, state income taxes must often be paid in quarterly installments. Estimating your taxes and making quarterly payments are covered in Section E, below.

D. Income Taxes for LLCs

The limited liability company (LLC), which is explained in greater detail in Chapter 2, Section C, is a relatively new business ownership structure. LLCs combine several key attributes that distinguish the traditional partnership and corporation, allowing LLC owners (usually called "members") to enjoy the protection from personal liability that a corporation offers, yet avoid the complicated and often expensive corporate tax system—LLC profits are taxed to the owners as individuals (like a sole proprietor or owners of a partnership). Although LLC members (owners) can instead choose to be taxed like a corporation, this choice is somewhat

unusual (but see Chapter 2, Section C, for why some LLCs may want to be taxed like a corporation). In this section we will assume your LLC will stick with pass-through tax status.

1. Federal Income Taxes

Like owners of partnerships, most LLC owners will report business profits on their individual federal income tax returns. Although this means the LLC itself is not taxed, if it has two or more members it must still report its income and losses to the IRS each year. Besides regular income taxes, members may be obligated to pay self-employment taxes, which are also based on business income.

a. Income Tax

LLCs with only one member are treated as sole proprietorships for tax purposes, so that business profits and losses are reported on Schedule C, to be submitted with the member's regular individual income tax return. If (like many LLCs) the LLC has two or more members, it must file an annual informational return with the IRS, similar to the requirement faced by partnerships. Since the IRS hasn't yet come up with tax forms specifically for LLCs, LLC profits and losses are reported on Form 1065, *U.S. Partnership Return of Income*. No tax is paid with this return, which is generally due by April 15. (See "Defining Your Business Year" in Section E2 for information on using a business year other than the calendar year.)

Along with Form 1065, an LLC must also submit a Schedule K-1 (again, the same schedule used by partnerships) to the IRS for each member reporting each member's share of profits or losses. The K-1 schedule is used to inform the IRS of the members' chosen profit division. (Often, members own equal shares of the business, which normally means they will choose to share profits and pay taxes equally—such as four members each getting ¼ of a business's profits and paying ¼ of its taxes. But if they so choose, LLC members can divide profits and losses in another way. See Chapter 2, Section C, for more on LLCs and profit allocations.) A copy of the completed K-1 must also be given to each member on or before the date that the LLC return is due to the IRS.

Profits earned by an LLC are taxed as personal income of the individual members. The information from Schedule K-1 is used by members to report business income or losses on their individual federal income tax returns (Form 1040) using Schedule E (*Supplemental Income and Loss*). Since the LLC already filed Schedule K-1s with the IRS, members do not need to submit this form with their returns. (See "Where to Get Tax Forms and Schedules" in Section A2, above, for information on obtaining the latest forms.)

Like sole proprietors and partners, LLC members will have to estimate their taxes for the year and pay them in quarterly installments. Read Section E, below, on estimated tax payments.

b. Self-Employment Taxes

The current rule is that LLC members who are actively involved in the business must pay self-employment taxes, which include payments into the Social Security and Medicare systems. If an LLC member is non-active and merely an investor in the company, she may be exempt from the self-employment tax obligation.

The rules on self-employment taxes for LLCs are far from settled. Due to the somewhat contradictory nature of LLCs—partnership-like in some respects, corporation-esque in others—it's not clear to what extent LLC owners are subject to self-employment tax. If the issue affects you, it may be wise to do some research or consult a business attorney to find out the latest word on how these taxes apply to LLC members. Chapter 12 gives information on legal resources beyond this book.

For tax year 2000, self-employment taxes include:

- Social Security tax of 12.4% on profits up to $76,200, and
- Medicare tax of 2.9% on all profits.

This translates into a 15.3% tax on profits up to $76,200 (both Social Security and Medicare), and a 2.9% tax on profits above that amount (Medicare only). (In comparison, regular employees only pay a 7.65% tax on wages of $76,200 or less, and a 1.45% tax on wages above that.)

Fortunately, if self-employment taxes are due, half of the total self-employment taxes you pay can be deducted from your taxable income at year-end. And if your LLC made less than $400 profit in the business year or lost money, you're totally exempt from having to pay self-employment taxes. (See "Reporting and Paying Are Not the Same" in Section B1, above, on the distinction between filing taxes and paying them.)

Self-employment taxes are reported on Schedule SE, which, like Schedule E (*Supplemental Income and Loss*), is submitted yearly with an LLC member's 1040 return. Once you determine the self-employment taxes you owe on Schedule SE, the result is entered on your 1040 form in the "Other Taxes" section, which is added to your individual income tax obligation. If the LLC member is required to pay advance quarterly tax installments, however, any self-employment taxes will be included in those payments. See Section E, below, for information on estimating taxes and paying them quarterly. This is a requirement all businesses need to understand.

2. State Taxes

While the federal government treats LLCs with pass-through tax status almost exactly like partnerships, the tax treatment LLCs receive in their states of formation may vary somewhat. Most states follow the IRS's lead and treat LLCs as pass-through entities unless the members have elected corporate tax treatment for the LLC. However, some states also impose special taxes on LLCs themselves, despite treating them as pass-through tax entities in most other respects.

First, most states collect income tax from LLC members on their share of business profits. Essentially, most states simply follow the IRS classification scheme for LLCs, which translates into treatment either as a partnership or a sole proprietorship. In states that allow one-person LLCs (every state except Massachusetts and D.C.), an LLC with a single owner is usually treated as a sole proprietorship, and business profits will be taxed on the sole member's individual state income tax return. LLCs with two or more owners will typically be treated as partnerships, and must file the same tax returns as owners of partnerships in that state.

Where some states diverge from the IRS's treatment is in levying certain special taxes upon LLCs themselves. States including California, Delaware, Florida, Massachusetts, Wyoming and others impose various charges upon LLCs alternately called "franchise taxes," "annual fees," "surcharge taxes" or other similar names. Depending on the state these additional costs can range from $10 to thousands of dollars, so be sure to understand your state's rules well in advance of tax time. In Appendix A, we offer contact information for state tax agencies, which can tell you how your state treats LLCs tax-wise. You'll also find information on where to get the latest forms for your state.

Like federal taxes, state income taxes for members must often be paid in quarterly installments. Estimating your taxes and making quarterly payments is covered in Section E, just below.

E. Estimating and Paying Your Taxes Quarterly

An important federal (and often state) tax rule for anyone who earns income from a business is that income taxes must generally be paid in quarterly installments over the course of the business year. (Some businesspeople who expect a very low level of taxation are exempt from these estimated payment requirements. See Section 1, below.) At year-

end, if you've paid more than what you owe, you'll get a refund. If, on the other hand, you didn't pay enough in your quarterly installments, you will owe more.

While it might not seem so at first, this system isn't all that different from the way taxes on employment wages are handled. From each paycheck, the federal (and often state) governments require an employer to withhold income taxes from each employee's wages based on her expected annual salary or hourly pay. At year-end the employee calculates and reports her tax obligation based on how much money she actually earned during the year. Depending on the dollar amount of her tax obligation, she'll either owe more money (if her employer didn't withhold enough) or be due a refund (if her employer withheld too much).

The IRS and state tax agencies require taxes to be withheld or tax payments to be estimated and paid in advance for a simple, practical reason: they know that a sudden multi-thousand dollar bill on April 15 can be difficult for anyone. Spreading out payments by wage withholding or estimated payments is the tax agencies' way of making your life a little easier—and to make sure they get their money. (Plus, it means the government can spend your money sooner.)

Unfortunately, it's much easier for an employer to figure out an employee's estimated tax burden knowing his yearly salary or hourly wage than it is for a small business owner to estimate taxes based on future income from a new and unproven business. If you're wondering, "How can I estimate taxes on business income that hasn't come in yet?" you're not alone. Projecting future income in order to estimate your tax obligation can be a dicey task, especially for brand-new business owners whose income hasn't yet evened out into any predictable rhythm. To make matters worse, you'll be socked with a penalty if your estimates are off and you don't pay enough each quarter.

But here's the good news: you don't need to start making estimated tax payments until you earn enough income to subject you to a threshold quarterly payment requirement. Usually this gives you enough time to get a pretty good feel for how much and how quickly money—and, by extension, taxable profits—are coming into your business. And even if you do underestimate your taxes and face a penalty of a few hundred dollars, you can at least take heart that you owe extra only because your business has become profitable sooner than you anticipated.

Besides the IRS, many state tax agencies also require profitable businesses to make estimated tax payments. For the most part, these states' rules are similar to the federal one, but they use slightly different formulas. The rest of this section will address just the federal requirement; check with your state tax agency to find out its formula for estimating taxes. We've included contact information for each state's tax agency in Appendix A.

1. Who Must Pay Estimated Taxes?

In a nutshell, business owners have to pay federal estimated taxes if they expect to owe at least $1,000 in federal taxes for any particular year (including income taxes and self-employment taxes). We'll go into the details later, but generally, this means you'll have to make estimated payments if your adjusted gross income (taxable net profits minus tax exemptions, deductions and credits) will be from about $3,000 to $6,000, depending on your tax bracket. The point here is, if your business is at all profitable, count on estimating and paying your taxes quarterly. On the other hand, if you're operating at a net business loss or making next to nothing, you may not have to make estimated payments.

> **EXAMPLE:** On December 31, 2000, as part of a New Year's resolution Jason quits his job as computer salesman and opens a river-rafting outfit called the Rapids Transit Company. For the first few months of 2001, every dollar he takes in pays for equipment, insurance and marketing. At the rate he's going, he doesn't

know if he'll make a profit at all that year, so he doesn't worry about estimated taxes. However, starting in June with the heavy tourist season, he starts clearing about $1,300 per month, after all deductions. He thinks he may have at least four more months like that before winter slows business down. If so, his annual profit will be about $6,500 ($1,300 x five months). Depending on his tax status, he'll probably owe between $1,000 and $2,000 in taxes at the end of the year. He realizes he'd better start making estimated quarterly payments to be safe, or risk a penalty.

Your Day Job May Help You Avoid Estimated Taxes

If, in addition to the business you own, you have a job where taxes are withheld from your income, you may be less likely to have to pay estimated taxes if your income from your business is not a significant part of your total income Why? In essence, the taxes withheld from your job may cover you for any estimated taxes owed on your business income. In other words, the IRS wants to make sure that a certain portion of the total taxes you'll owe are paid in installments over the year, and it's possible that the taxes withheld from your paycheck will be enough to meet this requirement. On the other hand, if your business is bringing in significant income, chances are that your wage withholding won't be enough.

Now for the nitty-gritty details. The IRS has a relatively straightforward formula (okay, we may be stretching this just a bit) for determining whether you need to estimate and pay your taxes in installments. You'll have to pay estimated taxes if:

1. you expect to owe at least $1,000 in federal taxes (including income taxes and self-employment taxes) for the year 2000, after subtracting any withheld taxes, and

2. you expect your withheld taxes to be less than the smaller of:
- 100% of your total tax owed for 1999, or
- 90% of your total tax obligation for 2000.

This formula sounds complicated, but it's not. First, it requires you to make estimated payments only if you expect to owe at least $1,000 to the IRS at year-end, above and beyond any taxes withheld from wages. This translates to about $3,000 to $6,000 in adjusted gross income from your business, depending on your tax bracket. So if your business is barely breaking even, you probably won't have to make estimated payments.

Second, if you do expect to make at least that amount from your business, you may not have to pay estimated taxes on your business income if you're having enough taxes withheld from a paycheck (assuming you receive one). If the taxes that are withheld from your paycheck in 2000 will come out to be more than 90% of what you'll owe in taxes for that year, you won't have to make estimated payments. Or, if that's not true, there's one more way you can escape paying estimated tax payments. If the taxes withheld in 2000 will come out to more than what your entire tax bill was the previous year, you're free of the estimated tax requirement.

> **EXAMPLE:** Nels works as a manager of an auto parts store, which pays him a salary and deducts federal and state taxes from each paycheck. He starts a sole proprietorship called Falcon's Auto Tow. In the first few months of his auto-towing business, Nels operates at a loss. Since his only taxable income during those months is his paychecks, from which taxes are being withheld, he doesn't have to worry about estimated payments. In the fifth month he starts to turn a profit, at which point Nels starts to pay attention to whether he must pay estimated taxes. If he thinks his wage withholding will account for at least 90% of his total tax bill at the end of the year, he doesn't need to file and pay estimated taxes. In other words, if he thinks that taxes on his small

business income will account for less than 10% of his total tax bill, he'll just file his taxes at year-end like most people whose income is all subject to wage withholding.

If you're not sure whether you have to pay federal estimated taxes, help is available. IRS Form 1040-ES contains a worksheet to use to calculate your estimated taxes, and Publication 505, *Tax Withholding and Estimated Tax,* explains in detail whether you have to pay estimated taxes. You can obtain these by calling 800-829-3676, or at http://www.irs.ustreas.gov/prod/forms_pubs/index.html. Or, even better, if you have a computerized accounting program, it can help you with the calculations.

2. When to Make Estimated Tax Payments

As just discussed, you become subject to the federal estimated tax payment requirement when you expect to earn enough profit during a business year to trigger the payment requirement. Once you expect to earn that much income, you need to do your best to estimate your income for the year and pay a quarterly installment based on the taxes due. (See Section 3, below, for how to do this.) Each quarterly payment must be filed a half-month after the end of the quarter. For federal estimated taxes, the quarterly due dates are as follows:

Income made during:	Tax installment due:
Jan. 1 through Mar. 31	April 15
Apr. 1 through May 31	June 15
June 1 through Aug. 31	September 15
Sept. 1 through Dec. 31	January 15 of the next year

If your business uses a fiscal rather than a calendar year, your payments will be due on the 15th day of the 4th, 6th and 9th months of your fiscal year and the 1st month of the following fiscal year.

Defining Your Business Year

Except for C corporations, a business must use the calendar year as its business year unless it gets permission from the IRS to choose a different starting and ending point. A bit of tax jargon is important here. Any one-year period other than the calendar year (ending on December 31) that a business uses for tax purposes, is called a "fiscal year," a "tax year" or an "accounting period." The IRS allows sole proprietorships, partnerships, LLCs and S corporations to use a fiscal year only if there is a valid business reason for it, such as significant seasonal fluctuations in business. Fiscal years must begin on the first day of a month and end on the last day of the previous month one year later. An unincorporated business that wants to use a fiscal year must submit Form 8716, *Election To Have a Tax Year Other Than a Required Tax Year,* to the IRS and have it approved. This form is included in Appendix C and on the CD-ROM.

3. Calculating and Paying Your Estimated Taxes

There are three ways to estimate your taxes properly. You can:

- base it on how much tax you owed last year.
- estimate your current year's income and deductions, and calculate the taxes you'd owe for those figures, or
- calculate your tax liability after each quarter (called the "annualized income installment method"), prorating your deductions and personal exemptions (you must also file Form 2210 if you use this method).

With the exception of the first method, you'll need help making these calculations. Instructions and worksheets that can help you calculate your estimated tax payments are included with the federal Form 1040-ES (the form you'll send to the IRS). This form also includes vouchers to submit with each periodic payment. Both the Appendix and the CD-ROM that accompanies this book offer information on getting the latest forms. For more information on federal estimated tax payments, refer to IRS Publication 505, *Tax Withholding and Estimated Tax.*

⚠️ **Don't overlook your self-employment taxes.** Self-employment taxes (see Section B1b, C1b or D1b, above), like income taxes, are subject to the estimated tax payment requirement. Be sure to include them when figuring your estimated tax burden for the year.

F. City and County Taxes

Unlike the federal or state governments, many cities and counties impose taxes directly on your business, even if your business is a pass-through entity such as a sole proprietorship, partnership or limited liability company. Of course, you, as the owner of the business, are personally liable for these financial obligations, but the difference is that your business itself—not merely the profits that flow through to you and any other owners—incurs taxes by local governments. Often, these taxes can be more of a burden than federal or state ones because many of them are based on your business income before you deduct business costs and expenses. Some areas, for instance, impose a gross receipts tax, which calculates the tax based simply on how much total income your business brings in, without regard for your expenses.

Local taxes vary a lot from one area to the next, but basically your business can expect to face some sort of "business taxes" from your city or county, which may include property taxes.

1. Business Taxes

This vague term simply refers to the money your local government imposes on all businesses within the city or county limits. Businesses in rural areas will probably only deal with their county tax authority. Whether the tax is imposed by a city or a county tax authority, the information about business taxes discussed in this section generally applies.

Unlike the IRS or most state tax agencies, which simply collect taxes after they're incurred, most local tax collectors require you to go through a tax registration process before you start your business. (Information on how the registration process generally works is provided in Chapter 6, Section D.) Once you've registered, you'll obtain what's commonly called a "tax registration certificate" (or sometimes a "business license"). Registration gives notice to your local tax authority that your business exists and allows them to charge taxes upon it, based on whatever method your locality has adopted for your type of business.

In many cities and counties, you actually start paying your local taxes when you purchase your business license or registration certificate. Often, a locality will base its registration fee on your

expected local tax for the year. In some localities, your registration fee is like a prepaid tax that can be applied toward your total year-end tax. In other places, the registration cost is purely an administrative fee and cannot be applied to your tax bill. And in still other areas, part of the registration cost is a prepaid tax that can be credited towards your tax bill, and part is an administrative fee.

The schemes used to tax your business in various cities and counties are usually based on certain attributes of your business. Most localities divide businesses into a number of different categories or types, such as retail sales, wholesale sales, hotels/apartments and service businesses. Each category uses a certain criterion to calculate taxes on, usually called a "tax base." The most common tax base, for example, is "gross receipts" (total income, before expenses). Each category has a certain tax rate for each tax base.

For example, in San Francisco, for retail sales businesses (category 08) the tax rate is $1.50 per $1,000 of gross receipts (the tax base). Contractors (category 02) in San Francisco also have gross receipts as their tax base, but the tax rate is $3.00 per $1,000. Other criteria used as tax bases include total payroll, number of employees or number of company vehicles. Other tax bases exist as well. Certain professionals such as accountants, attorneys and podiatrists may be taxed based on the number of years they have been licensed in the state. The moral of the story here is that local tax systems have about just as many ways of taxing your business as there are types of businesses.

Since rules vary widely from city to city and county to county, you'll need to check with your local tax agency for information on how it will tax your business. When looking up the appropriate tax agency, look in the government section of your white pages under City Government (or County Government if you live in an unincorporated area) for names such as "Tax Collector," "Business Licenses and Permits" or "Business Tax Division." And since local taxation of businesses is usually closely tied to start-up registration requirements, most businesses will automatically receive tax-filing information either when they register or soon thereafter by mail. (For more information on start-up registration requirements, see Chapter 6.)

2. Property Taxes

Many localities impose taxes on certain kinds of business property such as real estate, business equipment, furniture and vehicles. Property tax reporting procedures vary considerably from area to area, but a common requirement is for businesses to provide their local tax authority with an itemized list of business property subject to tax. Since local rules vary so widely you'll have to check in your area to determine what (if any) property taxes apply to your business and how to go about paying them.

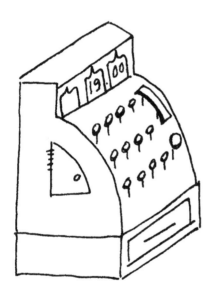

G. Sales Taxes

⚠️ **Sales tax rules are closely related to seller's permit requirements.** Recall from Chapter 6, Section E, that most businesses that engage in retail sales must apply for a seller's permit. This can be true even if the business ultimately makes no taxable sales (for instance, if all sales fall into a tax-exempt category, like groceries). Refer to

Chapter 6, Section E, to help you figure out whether your business needs a seller's permit.

In many states, retail sales are subject to state, county and local district sales taxes. We often just refer to them as state sales taxes, since they're often filed and paid to one state sales tax agency with just one return. In states that use this system, it's up to the state sales tax agency to distribute the collected taxes to the counties and districts across the state.

1. Taxable vs. Non-Taxable Sales

In most states that impose sales taxes, the general rule for whether a transaction is taxable is that the sale must:

- involve the sale of a tangible item, and
- be made to the final user of the item.

First, a final user is a consumer—either an individual or a business—rather than a reseller (a wholesaler or distributor). Sales that are made directly to end users (consumers), rather than resellers, are retail sales (taxable), rather than wholesale sales (nontaxable). This means that if you operate as a wholesaler and sell tangible goods to resellers, who will in turn sell them to consumers, your sales are likely exempt from sales tax. See Section 4, below, for rules on sales to resellers.

Second, generally speaking, tangible items are things you can touch, such as books, toys or furniture. Non-tangible items might include services, downloadable books, software, or intellectual property items such as patents or copyrights.

Keep in mind, however, that this rule is by no means uniform from state to state. For instance, while some states may consider sales of software to be taxable sales of tangible items, others will not. A common source of confusion is the fact that states often have unique (to put it delicately) definitions of the terms "tangible item," "final user" or whatever other terms apply within the state. For example, more than a few graphic artists in California were surprised to learn that the state did not consider their transactions to be services (which are not taxable in California), but instead to be taxable sales of tangible items, merely because the artists' work was given to the client on a physical piece of paper. The moral here is not to rely on common definitions, but to find out specifically how your state tax agency interprets sales tax terminology.

Besides the fact that many states use broad definitions in deciding what is taxable, a few states diverge from the general rule described above. Unlike the majority of states, Hawaii, New Mexico, South Dakota and West Virginia impose sales taxes on all services. Still other states charge sales taxes upon certain services, and others tax services when they're performed along with a taxable sale of a tangible item, such as charges for delivering a taxable item. Again, the state rules regarding these sales tax situations are complex and fraught with exceptions, so it's crucial that you check with your state agency to find out the details that apply to your business. Appendix A contains contact information for state sales tax agencies, including Web addresses and phone numbers. Be sure to get in contact with your state agency if you think sales taxes might apply to your business.

Sales Tax Exemptions

Part of the reason that the rules on sales taxes can be so convoluted is that the "rules" are clouded by swarms of exceptions and exemptions. Here are several examples of common exemptions from sales tax:

- most groceries (but not restaurant or take-out food)
- sales to out-of-state customers
- sales to the U.S. government, and
- some sales related to the entertainment industry.

Rules vary from state to state, so be sure to check with your state sales tax agency about which sales are exempt from sales tax.

⚠ **A seller's permit is usually required in order to sell tangible goods.** As we mentioned earlier, businesses that sell tangible goods must typically obtain a seller's permit from the state before sales begin, even if the sales aren't taxable (such as wholesale sales, discussed below). Selling tangible goods without a seller's permit is a misdemeanor crime in some states, but typically the state sales tax agency will give you the opportunity to comply (get a permit) before it files any criminal charges. But keep in mind that if you made any sales that were taxable before you got your seller's permit, you may be required not only to get a permit, but to pay all back taxes that are due.

2. The Nexus Requirement

Besides the criteria described above, for a sale to be taxable it must be made to a customer who is a resident of the state in which you're doing business. In other words, sales to out-of-state customers (such as by mail order) are not subject to sales tax.

The general rule—established by the U.S. Supreme Court in *Quill v. North Dakota,* 504 U.S. 298 (1992)—is that your business needs to collect sales taxes only on sales conducted within the state where your business is physically located. In legal terms, this is known as having a "nexus," which essentially means a physical presence. For instance, if your business has a store in California and warehouses in Texas and Illinois, then your business would have a nexus in those states and would need to collect sales taxes from customers there. Orders shipped to customers in Wisconsin, on the other hand, where your business has no physical presence, would not be taxed. This explains why mail-order forms often contain language such as "California residents add 8.5% sales tax." When you see such language, you can infer that the business is located in California and must collect sales tax from customers in the state, but not from residents of other states.

Your business is likely to be deemed to have a nexus in a state if any of the following are true:

- You operate a retail store in the state.
- Your company's salespeople conduct business within the state.
- You own or lease a warehouse or office in the state, even if it's not open to the public.

Generally speaking, simply shipping a product or a catalog to a customer in a certain state isn't enough to establish a nexus in that state (assuming that you use a third-party shipper such as UPS or the U.S. Post Office).

Once a nexus exists in a given state, your business will be subject to all of that state's sales tax laws, including any seller's permit and sales tax collecting and reporting requirements. For this reason, many businesses limit their physical presence to one or a small number of states and conduct nationwide business by mail-order or e-commerce. This approach is sound in theory, but the explosion of e-commerce has created a number of wrinkles you should know about. We discuss how sales taxes apply to the online world in the next section.

3. Sales Taxes Online

While the Web can be great for leaping geographical boundaries and bringing the world into your living room, it also makes a quagmire out of state and local laws that are supposed to apply to specific areas of the map. Sales tax laws have had a particularly hard time adapting to the new world of e-commerce. As more and more companies have started selling products online, there's been an increasing amount of confusion over which of these sales are subject to sales tax and which state's rules apply. Online businesses charge sales tax in a seemingly random manner, causing many lawmakers and businesspeople to call for the reform of sales tax laws. In particular, brick-and-mortar businesses are bitter that many online businesses unfairly escape paying sales taxes, giving them a competitive advantage over the real-world stores. Before we go into any details, simply keep in mind that online sales tax rules are still emerging and highly controversial. Expect a good deal of development and change over the next few years.

Currently, the rules that apply to businesses that sell products online are technically no different than those applying to non-Web retailers. Businesses that sell products over the Web are subject to the sales tax laws in the states where the business has a physical presence. An important part of this is that, even for online businesses, only a traditional physical presence counts with regard to sales taxes—the fact that customers can access your website from a particular state currently isn't considered to create a nexus in that state. In other words, online retailers don't need to pay sales taxes upon transactions in all states where the website appears (which, of course, is everywhere). E-tailers only need to pay sales taxes on sales in states where the business has an office, salespeople or other type of physical presence. Of course, if the business has a nexus in a state that doesn't charge sales taxes, then transactions there are tax-free.

EXAMPLE: Killer Computers sells computers and related accessories from its website, killercomputers.com. Killer Computers has a main office and a phone bank in Nebraska and warehouses in Oregon, Texas and New Hampshire. Because of its physical presence in these four states, Killer Computers will need to comply with those states' sales tax laws. This means that when killercomputers.com sells computers to customers in Nebraska, Oregon, Texas and New Hampshire, the sales tax laws of those respective states will apply to those transactions. Since Oregon and New Hampshire don't charge sales taxes, Killer Computers doesn't have to worry about paying sales taxes when it sells computers to customers in those two states. Nebraska and Texas, on the other hand, do charge sales taxes on retail sales, so when killercomputers.com sells to Nebraska or Texas residents, those sales will be subject to Nebraska or Texas sales taxes.

If you think that the rules for online retailers sounds pretty much the same as for other businesses, you're right. Things get a little kooky, however, when it comes to certain e-tailers like barnesandnoble.com. Major chains such as Barnes & Noble and WalMart have found a way to sell their goods online free of sales tax, even to customers who live in states teeming with Barnes & Noble and WalMart retail stores. How can they get away without paying sales tax on their online sales, even in states where they have a physical presence? By doing what big corporations do best: being crafty. The website called barnesandnoble.com is a different legal entity from the Barnes & Noble company, so the fact that Barnes & Noble has a physical presence in virtually every state doesn't matter. The barnesandnoble.com website only needs to charge sales taxes upon sales to residents in the state where the website is headquartered or has some other physical presence. The strategy is to make sure the website has a nexus only in states that don't charge sales tax (Alaska, Delaware, Montana, New Hampshire or Oregon).

It's tough to say what the future holds. Not only is the questionable practice of creating legally separate, tax-free websites under attack, but the e-business boom in general is being blamed for states losing billions of dollars each year from lost sales tax revenues. State revenue departments as well as brick-and-mortar companies are lobbying heavily for sales tax reform to make the system fairer for everyone.

However, it appears that it may be a while before any significant reform will take place. In 1998, Congress passed the Internet Tax Freedom Act (ITFA), which established a three-year moratorium on any new taxes on e-commerce. This means that states won't be able to apply any new taxes to Internet purchases, even if the state is losing billions of dollars of sales tax revenue. A bill to extend the moratorium until 2006 is currently pending (as of November, 2000) and has a good chance of being passed. Information on the status of this bill, H.R. 3709, is available online at http://thomas. loc.gov/bss/d106query.html. In the mean-time, note that the traditional sales tax laws still apply—the Internet Tax Freedom Act only creates a moratorium on new Internet and e-commerce taxes.

4. Sales to Final Users vs. Sales to Resellers

As mentioned above, a common condition for a sale to be taxable is that it is made to the final user. The fact that a sale is made directly to an end user (a consumer), rather than a reseller or wholesaler, is generally what differentiates retail sales (taxable) from wholesale sales (nontaxable). This means that if you operate as a wholesaler and sell tangible goods to a reseller, who will in turn sell them to a consumer, you are likely exempt from collecting and paying sales tax on any of the products you sell. The idea behind this rule is to make sure that items are taxed only once. Rather than taxing the sale of a lamp, for instance, each time it is sold—from its manufacturer, to the wholesaler, to the final customer—it is taxed only when it is sold to the final consumer. (Some transactions that are exempt from sales tax, however, may be subject to a nearly identical tax, a "use tax." See Section 6, below.)

How can you be sure that a customer is a final user? Customers that intend to resell your product should present you with a "resale certificate," which states that the product is being purchased for resale. Depending on your state's law, the certificate must usually contain certain information, including:

- the purchaser's name and address
- the number of the purchaser's seller's permit
- a description of the property to be purchased
- a statement that the property is being used for resale, in terms such as "will be resold" or "for resale" (language such as "nontaxable" or "exempt" is not enough)
- the date of the sale, and
- the signature of the purchaser or her authorized agent.

If you are not presented with such a certificate, you should assume the customer is the final user and treat the sale as taxable. If you sell to the same customer repeatedly, you'll usually need only to collect one resale certificate, which should be kept on file at your office. From then on, whenever you sell items to that company, you shouldn't have to collect another resale certificate.

5. Using Resale Certificates

Just as your customers can escape paying sales taxes to you by presenting a resale certificate, you can use one to purchase goods and supplies free of sales tax, as long as the goods and supplies are for legitimate resale. This applies whether you'll resell purchased goods as is, or whether you'll incorporate purchased supplies into your products (but see the discussion of "use tax" in Section 6, below). If you buy regularly from the same supplier, you should only have to present one resale certificate.

This exception to paying sales taxes doesn't apply to goods and supplies that you don't plan to resell or use in manufacturing products. You must pay sales taxes on all items that you'll use in your business and not pass on to a customer. In other words, when you are actually the final user, you have to pay sales tax like anyone else. This includes paying sales tax on goods and supplies you use to perform services or operate your business. For example, a hairdresser must pay sales tax on the shampoo he uses to wash people's hair. Or if you purchase a computer to keep track of your sales, you should pay the sales tax on that purchase (don't be tempted to give the company that sells it to you a resale certificate). When purchasing a combination of goods, only some of which you intend to resell, you should clearly indicate which items are for resale and pay sales taxes on the rest.

6. Use Taxes

To a certain degree, the numerous exceptions to sales taxes are a myth. That's because of a little-understood tax called the "use tax." While it's true that some sales of tangible goods are exempt from sales tax, many of these transactions are actually subject to a use tax. In keeping with its name, a use tax is due when you use a tangible good on which you didn't pay sales tax.

Use taxes commonly apply to purchases of tangible goods from outside your state. For instance, if you order 20 computers, 20 chairs and 20 desks for your office from an out-of-state mail order catalog, you probably didn't pay sales taxes on those items, because most states don't require businesses to collect sales tax from out-of-state purchasers. But under use tax laws in many states, your state can collect use taxes from you, the buyer, thus making up for the revenue it would have gotten if you had bought the equipment within the state.

Other transactions subject to use tax include purchases of items you originally intended to resell (and bought tax-free because you used your resale certificate), but used for another purpose. Also, items that you buy to incorporate into a new product to sell, as well as items you lease, are subject to the use tax (assuming you bought them sales tax-free with a resale certificate). Inventory that you store for future resale is not subject to use tax.

To pay use taxes, you typically fill out a use tax return, which is often the same as or related to the one that your business will use for paying sales taxes to the state. Essentially, you'll enter information into the form about the purchases you made that are subject to use tax, and follow the form's instructions for calculating your tax. There's not much more to it than sending it off to the state sales tax office, along with a check (assuming you owe money).

Keep in mind that there's a high blow-off factor when it comes to use taxes. Use taxes have largely been ignored by individuals and businesses, and the inherent difficulty of enforcing this tax allows virtually everyone to get away with it. It's true, however, that some states that have traditionally been lax in enforcing and collecting use taxes are now stepping up their efforts to collect them.

Particularly in today's environment of thriving e-commerce, the issue of sales taxes on out-of-state purchases is becoming a hot one. Keep an eye out for developments in this area, and don't get caught with your use taxes down.

Who Actually Owes Sales Taxes?

Despite the fact that most of us consumers pay sales taxes on a daily basis, there's a lot of misunderstanding out there over who really owes sales taxes—purchasers or sellers. Here's the deal: In most states, consumers are technically responsible for paying sales taxes. In these states, the retailer is essentially merely a collector for the sales tax owed by the consumer. In some states, however, the actual responsibility for sales taxes falls upon the retailer. This sort of tax is sometimes called a "privilege tax," since businesses are taxed for the privilege of conducting retail sales.

Keep in mind that these are often technical distinctions without a whole lot of practical effect. For example, if consumers are legally responsible for paying sales taxes in a certain state, that doesn't mean that businesses can escape paying state sales taxes. Usually, all it means is that the business must state the selling price and the sales tax separately on receipts and invoices. That way, consumers see that they are in fact being charged sales tax.

---

7. Keeping Track of Your Sales

When you obtain a seller's permit in most states, you obligate yourself to file a sales (and use) tax return, meaning that you'll need to keep careful records of both your sales and purchases. Most state sales tax agencies require that you keep:

- books or computer files recording your sales and purchases

- bills, receipts, invoices, contracts or other documents (called "documents of original entry"), that support your books and
- schedules and working papers used in preparing your tax returns.

In addition, if you conduct business in more than one county, city or other local tax district, you may need to keep separate records of sales made in each area.

Finally, your records should show all sales your business makes, even sales that aren't taxable.

8. Calculating, Paying and Filing Sales Taxes

Sales taxes in many states are actually a combination of state, county and city sales taxes. For example, an 8% sales tax may actually break down into a 5% state tax, a 2% county tax and a 1% city tax. The sales taxes that apply to your business will often depend on where your taxable sales are being conducted. If you conduct taxable sales in more than one tax district, you may end up paying several different rates. Conveniently, many states allow businesses to file just one state tax return that includes all taxes for all applicable districts. The return will usually ask you to identify where your sales were made so that the state can allocate the fair share of taxes to each tax district.

Businesses that have been issued a seller's permit will often receive their state sales tax return package automatically, along with an account number, due date and filing instructions. Depending on your sales volume, you'll need to submit your sales tax return yearly, quarterly or monthly. Contact your state agency for details.

Filling out the sales tax return is generally fairly straightforward, and will vary only slightly in format depending on the form used by your state. Basically, you'll enter sales information for each tax district in your state where you conducted taxable sales, and identify the tax rates that apply to each of these sales. The return will typically walk you though the calculations, and will tell you how much sales tax you owe (if any). In most states you can get telephone assistance if you're having trouble filling out your return. Contact your state sales tax agency (contact information is included in Appendix A) for detailed instructions on filing your sales tax return.

If you have a seller's permit, you may be required to file a sales tax return. If you applied for and received a seller's permit because you anticipated selling goods but never made a sale, you may need to submit your sales tax return anyway. If you didn't make any taxable sales, you shouldn't owe any taxes, but you may still need to submit the form. If you don't, you may risk losing your seller's permit, which could mean you couldn't legally make any sales at all. Check with your state agency (listed in Appendix A) for its requirements.

☑ Chapter 8 Checklist

☐ Familiarize yourself with the general scheme of taxes faced by small businesses.

☐ Remember that you may have to pay estimated taxes in quarterly installments. Other taxes may also have to be paid more often than once a year, such as your state sales taxes. Make a calendar of important tax dates so you don't miss them and incur penalties.

☐ Keep careful track of your expenses so that you may deduct them.

☐ Consult a tax professional at least once a year to help you organize your books and minimize your taxes.

☐ File and pay your annual taxes each year, and other taxes as they become due.

■

Entering Into Contracts and Agreements

A. Contract Basics 9/2

   1. Elements of a Valid Contract 9/2

   2. Oral vs. Written Contracts 9/6

B. Using Standard Contracts 9/7

C. How to Draft a Contract 9/8

   1. What to Include in a Basic Contract 9/9

   2. Putting Your Contract Together 9/13

D. Reading and Revising a Contract 9/14

E. Special Issues for Electronic Contracts 9/14

   1. What Is an Electronic Contract? 9/14

   2. Taking Traditional Contract Principles Online 9/15

   3. Tips for Creating Contracts Online 9/17

As a business owner, you'll often have to enter into agreements (legal contracts) with other businesses and people: suppliers, customers, creditors and the landlord, for example. While a few of these transactions will be so simple and short-term that it's enough to complete them with a handshake, most will be sufficiently complicated, long-term, or financially important that a written contract is essential. Thankfully—and contrary to what many people believe—a contract is often a fairly simple legal creature that sets forth mutual promises to do whatever specific acts are listed in the contract: "A promises to pay B $1,000 if B delivers 50,000 twist-ties to A's warehouse on or before March 1, 1999." A written contract will usually include the main terms of the agreement: the price of goods, important dates and the time and place of delivery. For most contractual agreements, standard forms are readily available. Except in the relatively few instances where lots of money or cutting legal issues are involved, lawyers won't normally be needed.

Simple as some types of contracts may be, the important thing to remember about them is that they are legally enforceable. If you fail to keep your end of the bargain, you can be sued and forced to pay monetary damages to the other party or, in some circumstances, to do the things you promised in the contract.

This chapter will explain the basics behind binding, legal contracts, such as what makes a contract enforceable and which contracts are legally required to be in writing.

Kimberly Torgerson, owner of Your Word's Worth, a freelance editing and writing service in Berkeley, California:

Several years ago, I took on a short-term project managing the last-minute editing for a medical software program. The timeline was extremely tight, and I needed to locate and manage about ten additional freelance editors, who got paid directly from the company who hired me. Because I had not worked with the company before, or many of the editors I had located, I
drafted an agreement that spelled out delivery, completion and payment terms for everyone involved. To draft this agreement, I looked at my previous professional service agreements and a Nolo book, and ran it by a friend who is a lawyer. A seat-of-the-pants approach, but it worked.

A. Contract Basics

Although lots of contracts are filled with mind-bending legal gibberish, there's no reason why this has to be true. For most contracts, legalese is not essential or even helpful. On the contrary, the agreements you'll want to put into a written contract are best expressed in simple, everyday English.

Don't be afraid to redraft contract language. When reading a contract that has been presented to you, your first task is to be sure you understand all of its terms. It is just plain foolish to sign a contract if you're unclear on the meaning of any of its language. If a clause is poorly written, hard to understand or doesn't accomplish your key goals, rewrite it in clearer language. By refusing to sign at the "X" unless your goals are clearly met, you'll be less likely to find yourself in a breach-of-contract lawsuit later on. (A breach of contract occurs when one party fails to live up to the terms or promises of the contract.) For more on changing contract language, see Section D, below, on reading and revising a contract.

1. Elements of a Valid Contract

A contract will be valid if the following elements are present:
- all parties are in agreement (after an offer has been made by one party and accepted by the other)
- something of value has been exchanged, such as cash, services or goods, for some-

thing else of value (or there is a promise to exchange an item for something else of value), and

- in a few situations, such as the sale of real estate, to be valid the agreement must be put into writing (see Section 2, below). (Of course, because oral contracts can be difficult or impossible to prove, it is wise to write out most agreements.)

Now let's look at each of these elements in more detail.

a.   Agreement Between Parties, a.k.a. Offer and Acceptance

Although it may seem like stating the obvious, an essential element of a valid contract is that all parties really do agree on all major issues. In real life there are plenty of situations that blur the line between a full agreement and a preliminary discussion about the possibility of making an agreement. To help clarify these borderline cases, the law has developed some rules defining when an agreement legally exists.

The most basic rule of contract law is that a legal contract exists when one party makes an offer and the other party accepts it. For most types of contracts, this can be done either orally or in writing. (For a few, discussed in Section 2, below, the offer and acceptance must be made in writing.)

Let's say, for instance, you're shopping around for a print shop to produce brochures for your business. One printer says (or faxes) that he'll print 5,000 two-color flyers for $200. This constitutes his offer. If you tell him to go ahead with the job, you've accepted his offer. In the eyes of the law, when you tell the printer to go ahead, you create a contract, which means you're liable for your side of the bargain (in this case, payment of $200). But if you tell the printer you're not sure and want to continue shopping around (or don't even respond, for that matter), you clearly haven't accepted his offer and no agreement has been reached. Or if you say his offer sounds great, except that you

want the printer to use three colors instead of two, no contract has been made, since you have not accepted all of the important terms of the offer—you've changed one term of the offer. (Depending on your wording, you may have made a "counter-offer," which is discussed below.)

Advertisements As Offers

Generally speaking, an advertisement to the public does not count as an offer in the legal sense. In other words, if you advertised your catering services in your local weekly newspaper, and included a price quote of $300 for your standard menu serving 20 people, you would not be legally bound to live up to that service if someone called you and said, "I accept!" If, for instance, you were too busy with other catering jobs and unable to do the job for the eager caller, you could decline. Since your ad wasn't, legally speaking, an offer, the caller couldn't claim that he "accepted" it to create a binding contract.

That being said, you do need to watch what you say in your advertisements. Some states require retailers to stock enough of an advertised item to meet reasonably expected demand, or else your ad must state that stock is limited.

Of course, false or misleading advertising is always a bad idea. Federal laws regulating trade and state consumer protection laws prohibit deceptive advertising, even if no one was in fact misled. And check your ad's facts—false advertising is illegal, even if you believed the ad to be truthful.

Sure enough, in real, day-to-day business the seemingly simple steps of offer and acceptance can become quite convoluted. For instance, sometimes when you make an offer, it isn't quickly and unequivocally accepted; the other party may want to think about it for a while or try to get a better deal for himself. And before he accepts your offer, you might change your mind and want to withdraw or amend your offer. Delaying acceptance of an offer, revoking an offer and making a counteroffer are common situations in business transactions that often lead to confusion and conflict. To minimize the potential for dispute, here are some general issues you should understand and rules you should follow.

- **How long an offer stays open.** Unless an offer includes a stated expiration date, it remains open for a "reasonable" period of time. (But an open offer can always be "revoked." An offer that can't be revoked for a certain amount of time is known as an "option," which we discuss below.) What's reasonable, of course, is open to interpretation and will vary depending on the type of business and the particular situation. Because the law in this area is so vague, if you want to accept someone else's offer, the best approach is to do it as soon as possible, while there's little doubt that the offer is still open. Keep in mind that until you accept, the person or company who made the offer—called the offeror—may revoke it.

  If you are the offeror, it's best to be very clear about how long your offer will remain open. The best way to do this is to include an expiration date in the offer. But to leave yourself room to revoke the offer, avoid wording such as, "This offer will remain open until December 31, 2000." Instead use language such as, "This offer will expire on December 31, 2000."

 Include an expiration date clause in all bids. In many types of businesses, from replacing roofs to redesigning websites, it is common to bid (in other words, to make an offer to create a contract) on lots more jobs than you really need or want. But sometimes this strategy can backfire. With lots of offers floating around, there is always the possibility that too many will be accepted, raising the embarrassing specter of your not being able to deliver on all the work. One easy way to minimize this problem is to print right on your bid or offer form that all offers are good for only ten days (or some other relatively short period) unless extended in writing.

- **Revoking an offer.** Whoever makes an offer can revoke it as long as it hasn't yet been accepted. This means if you make an offer and the other party says she needs some time to think it through, you can revoke your original offer. If she accepts while your offer is still open, however, you'll have a binding agreement. In other words, revocation must happen before acceptance.

  An exception to this rule occurs if the offeror promises that an offer will remain open for a stated period of time—and that he cannot and will not revoke the offer during that time. This type of agreement is called an option, and options don't usually come for free. Say someone offers to sell you a forklift for $10,000, and you want to

think the offer over free of the worry that the seller will revoke the offer or sell to someone else. You and the seller could agree that the offer will stay open for a certain period of time, say 30 days. Often, however, the offeror will ask you to pay for this 30-day option—which is understandable, since during the 30-day option period he can't sell to anyone else. But payment or no payment, when an option agreement exists, the offeror cannot revoke the offer until the time period ends.

- **Counteroffers.** Often when an offer is made, the other party's response will not be to accept the terms of the offer right off, but to start bargaining. Of course, haggling over price is the most common type of negotiating that occurs in business situations. When one party responds to an offer by proposing something different, this proposal is called a "counteroffer." When a counteroffer is made, the legal responsibility to accept or decline the offer or make another counteroffer shifts to the original offeror. For instance, if your printer (here, the original offeror) offers to print 5,000 brochures for you for $300, and you respond by saying you'll pay $250 for the job, you have not accepted his offer (no contract has been formed), but instead have made a counteroffer. It is then up to your printer to accept, decline or counteroffer. If your printer decides to agree to do the job exactly as you have specified for $250, he's accepted your counteroffer and a legal agreement has been reached (a contract has been formed).

⚠ **Inconsequential differences between an offer and the actual execution of the contract don't nix a contract.** While it is true that a contract is only formed if the accepting party agrees to all substantial terms of an offer, this doesn't mean you can rely on inconsequential differences to void a contract later. For example, if you offer to buy 100 chicken sandwiches on one-inch-thick sourdough bread, and the other party replies he will provide 100 emu filets on rye bread, there is no contract. But if the other party agrees to provide the 100 chicken sandwiches on one-inch-thick sourdough bread, a valid contract exists, and you can't later refuse to pay if the bread turns out to be a hair thicker or thinner than one inch.

b. Exchange of Things of Value

In addition to both parties' agreeing to the terms, a contract isn't valid unless both parties exchange something of value in anticipation of the completion of the contract. The "thing of value" being exchanged—which every law student who ever lived has been taught to call "consideration"—is most often a promise to do something of value in the future, such as a promise to perform a certain job or a promise to pay a fee for that job. For instance, let's return to the example of the print job. Once you and the printer agree on terms, there is an exchange of things of value (consideration): the printer has promised to print the 5,000 brochures and you have promised to pay $250 for them.

Contract law requires things of value to be exchanged for a valid contract to exist to differentiate a contract from generous statements and one-sided promises that are not enforceable by law. If a friend offers you a favor, for instance, such as offering to stop by and help you move a pile of rocks without asking anything in return, that arrangement wouldn't count as a contract because you didn't give or promise him anything of value. If the other party never followed through with his favor, you would not be able to force him to keep his promise. However, if in exchange for helping you move rocks on Saturday, you promise your friend you'll help him weed his vegetable garden on Sunday, a contract exists.

Although the exchange-of-value requirement is met in most business transactions by an exchange of promises ("I'll promise to pay money if you promise to paint my building next month"), actually doing the work or paying the money can also satisfy the rule. If, for instance, you leave your printer a voice-mail message that you'll pay an extra $100 if your brochures are cut and stapled when you pick them up, the printer can create a binding contract by actually doing the cutting and stapling. And once he does so, you can't weasel out of the deal by claiming you changed your mind.

2. Oral vs. Written Contracts

Before answering the question "Does a contract have to be in writing to be legally enforceable?" here's some advice: Put your contracts in writing. For compelling practical reasons, all contracts of more than a trivial nature should be written out and signed by both parties. Here is why:

- Writing down terms tends to make both parties review them more carefully, eliminating fatal flaws that oral contracts often have from the start.
- An oral agreement—no matter how honestly made—is hard to remember accurately.
- Oral agreements are subject to willful misinterpretation by a not-so-innocent party who wants to get out of the deal.
- Oral contracts are often difficult, and commonly impossible, to prove, making them hard to enforce in court.

That's our good advice; now here's what the law says: All states have laws that require certain contracts to be in writing. These laws often go by the name "Statute of Frauds" and are quite similar from state to state. They typically require the following types of contracts to be in writing:

- An agreement that by its terms can't be completed in a year or less. For example, a contract for a bakery to provide fresh bread to a restaurant for two years must be in

writing. On the other hand, if the contract might take longer than a year to complete but could be completed within a year, it doesn't need to be in writing. For example, a contract for a gardener to landscape five big properties would not need to be written, because it is quite possible that the landscaper would finish the work within one year. Similarly, a contract for a bakery to bake bread for a restaurant with no time period stated would not need to be in writing.

- A lease whose term is longer than one year, or an agreement authorizing an agent to execute such a lease on your behalf.
- Any sale of real estate (or of an interest in real estate), or an agreement authorizing an agent to purchase or sell real estate or (an interest in real estate) on your behalf.
- An agreement that by its terms will not be completed during the lifetime of one of the parties.
- A promise to pay someone else's debt, such as a business partner's promising to pay your car payments, or an agreement that the person who prints your brochure will also pay the cost of photographic work done at another shop.

In addition to the Statute of Frauds laws, each state has a special body of law on commercial issues called the Uniform Commercial Code (UCC). (While Louisiana has not fully adopted the UCC, it has implemented some of its more important provisions.) Under the UCC, a sale of goods for $500 or more requires at least a brief written note or memo indicating the agreement on the sale of the goods. The note can be much less detailed than a normal contract; it needs only to show an agreement between the parties and the quantity of goods being sold. Other terms that are typically covered in contracts, such as the price of goods or the time and place of delivery, don't need to be included to satisfy the UCC rule. This written memo usually needs to be signed, although if one party doesn't object to the memo within ten days of receiving it then her signature isn't required.

Special State Requirements for Contracts

Various state laws impose additional requirements for contracts involving particular businesses or certain kinds of transactions. In California, for instance, contracts for weight-loss services and dating services must be in writing. Plus, the law requires some contracts to include special language. For example, California dating service contracts must include the following language in at least 10-point boldface type:

"You, the buyer, may cancel this agreement, without any penalty or obligation, at any time prior to midnight of the original contract seller's third business day following the date of this contract, excluding Sundays and holidays. To cancel this agreement, mail or deliver a signed and dated notice, or send a telegram which states that you, the buyer, are canceling this agreement, or words of similar effect." (California Civil Code § 1694.2.)

Unfortunately, there's no centralized place where a business owner can learn if any special contract laws apply to his type of business. One way to is to read over your state's statutes for mentions of your type of business.

If doing legal research to find any required contract language is too time-consuming or overwhelming for you, a good alternative is to use the limited help of a lawyer who's generally familiar with small business issues and, if possible, already works with businesses in your field (other plant nurseries, website designers or restaurants, for example). Many small business lawyers are now more flexible in offering just as much or as little help as clients need, and offer coaching services to those who want to handle their simple legal affairs themselves. Using a legal coach is especially useful for small businesspeople who often need simple legal questions answered, rather than full-blown attorney services. Chapter 12 discusses working with lawyers and finding one that's willing to coach you through simple legal matters.

Now that you have an idea of which contracts must by law be in writing, it bears mentioning again that in practice, written contracts are almost always preferable over oral ones. As an illustration of how the process of putting a contract in writing can produce a better result, consider the following example.

EXAMPLE: Kay opens a plant shop called The Green Scene, and is in the process of installing all the necessary equipment in her storefront space. Because she needs specialized grow-lights for her extensive line of tropical plants, she checks with several contractors familiar with installing lighting systems. One company, Got a Light, says they will install a system for $3,000, which would include the lights themselves and installation. Their quote is the lowest among the companies Kay has checked, so she tells them she'll accept their offer but only with a written contract.

When they send her a contract detailing the job, she notices that nothing in the contract addresses rewiring her shop. She calls Got a Light and talks with Dan, who tells her that, indeed, she needs to have an electrician add several new circuits and provide six specialized outlets before Got a Light can install the lighting system. Based on this discovery, Kay and Dan discuss exactly what needs to be done before Got a Light's work begins and include this new agreement in an additional contract clause. Dan recommends an electrician, whom Kay hires to do the rewiring. She also manages to negotiate a lower price with Got a Light, based on the fact that the rewiring will be done according to Got a Light's specifications, making their installation much easier.

B. Using Standard Contracts

By now you should understand that your contracts should be written, but you may still be clueless about how to write the ones you'll need. Luckily for you and most other businesspeople, virtually every type of business transaction is covered by a readily available standard contract. Service contracts, rental agreements, independent contractor agreements, contracts for sales of goods and licensing agreements are just a few examples of blank-form contracts you should easily be able to find.

Anyone who has ever picked up a fill-in-the-blank lease or promissory note from an office supply store, torn one out of a self-help law book or downloaded one from a website is familiar with how this works. Blank rental agreements, for example, are widely available at office supply stores, through landlords' associations, at most public libraries, in Nolo's LeaseWriter software and from many other sources. Once you find the blank-form contract you need, you simply fill it in and, if necessary, modify it before signing.

If you can't easily find a blank-form contract that meets your needs, try these sources:

- Trade associations are excellent resources for fill-in-the-blank contracts.
- Your competitors might be less than willing to share their contracts with you, but similar businesses in faraway locations (which you won't be competing with) might be willing to show you theirs.

- The Web has oceans of information for small businesses, including sample contracts. Try searching for terms particular to your type of business to find specific contracts you need.
- Nolo.com's website offers many interactive forms such as promissory notes, bills of sale, contracts for services and more. You can see a list at http://www.nolo.com/product/forms_home.html. And on Nolo's contracts home page, you'll be able to read more information about contracts for specific situations and browse our many products that include contracts. Go to http://www.nolo.com/keyword/contracts_home.html.
- Nolo books offer many different blank-form agreements. For general business contracts, a great resource is the *Legal Guide for Starting and Running a Small Business, Volume 2: Legal Forms,* by attorney Fred S. Steingold.

Once you've found a contract that generally fits your needs, you can amend it for your particular situation. It's entirely appropriate and often necessary to change clauses of a fill-in-the-blank contract to suit your needs. Of course, it's crucial that you understand what you're doing. Don't just strike a clause because you don't understand what it means, or add a clause without fully knowing the consequences of including it. To help you educate yourself about typical contract language, the next section explains which clauses commonly appear in contracts and what they mean.

C. How to Draft a Contract

If you can't find a form agreement or if you find one that needs a load of revisions, you may need to draft a clause or two—or possibly even the whole contract—from scratch. Don't be intimidated. Either way, your goal is simple: to state clearly what each party is agreeing to do and the specifics of how they'll do it (usually called the terms of the contract). Put another way, your written contract should be the most accurate reflection possible of the understanding you have with the other party.

Good Ideas to Keep Your Contracts Crystal Clear

- Avoid the use of "he," "she," "they" or other pronouns in your contracts to prevent confusion over what parties you're talking about. Use either the actual names of the parties or their roles, such as Landlord and Tenant. It might seem repetitive or clumsy to write this way, but your goal is to be clear— not to write beautiful prose.
- Stay away from legalistic words like wherefore, herewith or hereinafter. Far from making your contract sound more impressive, this type of language is simply unnecessary and outdated. Stick to modern, clear English. Likewise, don't include legal expressions you think you may have heard elsewhere. Legal-sounding jargon will not make your contract more binding—and if you get it wrong, you may be bound to terms you didn't want, or your contract may be void.
- Make at least a couple drafts of your contract. After the first draft, let it rest a day or so and then reread it. Does it leave any questions in your mind? If it does, you need to fill in the gaps with more information.

This section explains the important things to include in most contracts and alerts you to the situations that might require more specialized provisions. The information we provide will help you in editing or drafting amendments to a standard contract, or in drafting a contract from scratch if necessary. We'll present examples of how to state certain terms—although, as mentioned above, clear English is really all that's usually necessary.

Don't paralyze your contract with too many specifics. Although a good contract covers all the important aspects of a deal, there is no need to be too anal when it comes to specifying every minute detail. For instance, if you hire a cleaning service to scrub your floors, you probably don't need to specify what type of brushes they'll use. Better to put your energy into picking the right person or company to do the job and to leave some of the specifics of the actual work up to them. How do you know when enough detail is enough? You'll simply have to judge for yourself which nit-picky details are so important that they should be covered in your contract and which ones you can safely ignore. For example, if you need fresh salmon for a party at 6 p.m., the time of delivery and quality of the fish are extremely important points, but the exact weight of each fish or the method of delivery may be a lot less so.

1. What to Include in a Basic Contract

So you've reached an agreement with another party and are ready to put your agreement into writing. Before you start editing a form contract or writing one on your own, step back a moment to consider the goals of all contracts:

- to clearly outline what each party is agreeing to do (including timelines and payment arrangements),
- to anticipate areas of confusion or points of potential conflict, and
- to provide for recourse (remedy) in case the agreement is not followed through to completion.

Also remember that the more you have at stake, the more carefully you'll have to approach the task of putting together your contract. For example, if you're entering into a contract to buy a truckload of bicycle tires for $1,000, you won't need your agreement to be outlined nearly as meticulously as you would in a contract for the construction of a building. For high-stakes, complex agreements, don't leave any of your bases uncovered. In fact, if the stakes are high enough, you might want to hire an attorney or other expert to help with some or all of the contract-writing process or at least to check your draft and make suggestions (see "For complex agreements, you may need an attorney," just below).

For complex agreements, you may need an attorney. More complex contracts—especially those in areas unfamiliar to you—are often best handled with the help of a lawyer. Certainly if a transaction is so huge or elaborate it makes your head spin, you shouldn't go it alone. First, decide how much help you need. Rather than having an attorney draft your contract from start to finish, you could simply have her look over a contract that you or the other party has written. Ideally, you should hire a lawyer with some experience with small business, preferably your type of business. Even better would be an attorney with whom you have a long-term working relationship so that she knows the ins and outs of your business. See Chapter 12 on getting legal assistance.

Let's look at the information most contracts include to fulfill these three goals and how that info is presented. Except where noted, no special wording is required in a contract.

- **Title.** Generally a contract will have a simple, to-the-point title like "Contract for Printing Services" or "Agreement for Sale of Ball Bearings."
- **The names and addresses of all the parties.** It should be clear what role each party has in the contract, such as seller or buyer; landlord or tenant; client or service person.

  EXAMPLE: Christopher Johnson ("Client") desires to enter into a contract with Virgil's Printing ("Printer") for printing services for Client's newspaper.

  The addresses of the parties generally appear at the end of a contract in the section with the signatures.

- **A brief description of the background of the agreement (called "recitals").** While not always included, this type of information is often necessary to frame the contents of the agreement. Typically this section includes a brief description of what kinds of businesses the parties run and the nature of the transaction being entered into in the contract.

  EXAMPLE: Client prints and distributes a free, weekly, 24-page newspaper called *El Norte* with a circulation of 40,000. Printer operates a full-service print shop with three printing presses. The subject of this contract is an agreement that Printer shall print Client's newspaper each week in exchange for payment.

- **A full description of what each party is promising to do as part of the agreement.** This section is sometimes called the "specifications," or just "specs," which describes the terms of the deal. If a product is being sold, describe the product and then state when it will be delivered. If a service is being performed, describe the job and then state when it will be completed, including any intermediate deadlines that must be met before the final completion date. Indicate whether strict compliance with deadlines is necessary by throwing in the phrase, "Time is of the essence." This phrase is a standard one used in contracts that simply indicates that deadlines will be enforced strictly.

  EXAMPLE: Client promises to deliver materials ("boards") for printing to Printer's shop no later than 10:00 a.m. each Wednesday morning. Printer promises to print, fold and bundle 40,000 copies of Client's newspaper and have them ready for Client to pick up from Printer's shop by 8:00 p.m. that same Wednesday. Time is of the essence regarding this contract. If, however, Client fails to deliver boards to Printer by 10:00 a.m. Wednesday morning, Printer may take extra time to complete the job. The amount of extra time will depend on how late Client is in delivering the boards and on Printer's schedule of other jobs, but in no case shall be longer than 24 hours after delivery of the boards.

If specifications are complicated (for example, intricate performance details for a software contract), they should normally be set out in attachments to the contract, which may include scale drawings, formulas or other detailed information about the transaction.

- **The price of the product or service.** This section states how much one party will pay for the other party's goods or services. If the price may vary (say, based on the time or quality of performance) or if it will be established later, a description of how it will be calculated should be included.

    EXAMPLE: Client will pay Printer $1,000 for every 10,000 24-page newspapers printed, up to 50,000 newspapers. The price will be renegotiated if Client orders more than 50,000 newspapers, or if the number of pages per newspaper changes.

- **Payment arrangements.** This section should explain when payment is due, whether it will be paid all at once or in installments, whether interest will be charged if payments are late, plus any other special requirements, such as whether payment must be by certified or cashier's check (otherwise a garden-variety check will normally suffice). Again, if strict compliance with payment deadlines is necessary, use the phrase "Time is of the essence."

    EXAMPLE: Client will pay Printer the full amount of each week's printing cost within three days of picking up the completed newspapers.

- **A statement of any warranties made by either party regarding the product or service being provided.** A warranty is essentially a guarantee made by one party to another that a product or service will meet certain standards. If a warranty is provided by either party, the contract should state what will happen if the guarantee isn't satisfied—for instance, if certain standards aren't met, the party who got the raw end of the deal will be given a refund or may give the other party another chance to do the job right.

Automatic Warranties

Under the Uniform Commercial Code, which is adopted in some form in all 50 states, all sales of products are automatically covered by some warranties whether or not the seller promised anything to the buyer. These warranties are called "implied warranties," and include two guarantees: that the product is fit for its ordinary use and that it is fit for any special purpose that the seller knows the buyer wants to use it for. For example, the sale of a kitchen knife comes with an implied warranty that the knife will work in ordinary kitchen uses. If the buyer asked the retailer to help her pick out a knife that would cut through heavy beef bones, then whatever knife the retailer sold her would come with a warranty that it would work for cutting heavy beef bones. This is true regardless of whether or not the knife came with an express, written warranty that it could be used for heavy butcher work.

Be aware of the existence of implied warranties when drafting your contracts. Even if you don't make specific promises in your contracts, you will still be legally bound by the two kinds of implied warranties described above: fitness for ordinary use, and fitness for a particular purpose. The law regarding warranties can be complex, and you may want to consult an attorney for more detailed information about your obligations as a seller.

EXAMPLE: Printer warrants that the completed newspapers shall be free from printing defects or errors attributable to the printer. In case such errors do occur, Printer and Client may negotiate a discount not to exceed actual damages suffered by Client.

- **A statement whether either party may transfer the contract to an outside party.** Transferring contract rights is also called assigning. If you have chosen a company to provide products or services because of particular characteristics, such as good personal service or artistic detail, you may not want that company to be able to hand off the job to someone else, who may not do as good a job.

    EXAMPLE: Neither Printer nor Client may assign this contract or any part of it to another party.

- **The contract term.** This section, usually only one sentence, establishes how long the contract will be in effect.

    EXAMPLE: This contract will remain in effect for a period of one year, or until it is terminated by one of the parties, whichever is first.

- **A description of any conditions under which either party may terminate the agreement.** For some types of contracts (for example, contracts to provide an ongoing service), a termination clause often states that either party must give a written termination notice in order to end the contract, often 30 or 60 days in advance.

    EXAMPLE: Upon written notice of at least 30 days to the other party, either Printer or Client may terminate this agreement.

But you may not want either party to be able to terminate the contract, even with advance notice, just any old time they feel like it. In this case, you can specify a limited number of certain events that might allow a party to end a contract. For instance, say you want to be able to rely on using your website hosting service for at least a year, so you include a clause in your contract with them that neither party can terminate the contract for the next 12 months except if either party goes bankrupt, in which case either party would have the right to terminate the contract.

On the other hand, there may be situations in which you want to be able to terminate a contract yourself. For instance, say you own a rock shop that sells lots of agate, so you contract with a supplier to sell you a half-ton of agate each month for a year. To protect yourself, you could include a clause in your contract stating that if you resell less than a quarter-ton of agate in any calendar month, you may terminate the agreement.

- **An outline of how you will deal with a breach-of-contract situation.** Though signing a contract may not head off a subsequent dispute, it may be able to channel the dispute in ways that will lead to its being resolved as quickly and cheaply as possible. There are a number of different approaches you can take.

You can pre-set the amount of damages (financial compensation) to be paid by a breaching party in order to avoid the often lengthy and contentious process of calculating a party's damages after the other party breaches the contract. When damages are pre-set in a contract, they are called liquidated damages. In order for a liquidated damages clause to be valid, the dollar amount of damages that you set must be a reasonable estimate of what actual damages would be, not merely a pre-set penalty for breaking the contract.

Another option is for both parties to agree in the contract to try mediation and, if that fails, arbitration to settle a dispute as an alternative to going to court.

> EXAMPLE: If any dispute arises under the terms of this agreement, the parties agree to select a mutually agreeable, neutral third party to help them mediate it. The costs of mediation will be shared equally. If the dispute is not resolved after 30 days in mediation, the parties agree to choose a mutually agreeable arbitrator who will arbitrate the dispute. The costs of arbitration will be assigned to the parties by the arbitrator. The results of any arbitration will be binding and final.

Or, if for some reason one or both of you prefers going to court, you can provide in the contract that the losing party in a dispute must pay the other party's legal fees, or you can establish that each party is responsible for their own legal fees regardless of who prevails. Note that, for some commercial transactions, neither party in a lawsuit can collect attorney's fees from the other unless it is provided for in a written contract.

- **For contracts with out-of-state entities, a statement of which state's laws apply to the transaction.** Although contract law in all states is very similar, using the law in your state will generally be the simplest for you, since you'll have more resources at your disposal, including law libraries and people knowledgeable in your state's law.

> EXAMPLE: This contract shall be governed by and interpreted in accordance with the laws of New Mexico.

- **Signatures and Dates.** Your signature section should always include room for the date the contract was signed, as well as the addresses of the parties.

Jennifer F. Mahoney, owner of an illustration service in Northern California:

My creativity is exercised just as much by drawing up a good agreement with a client as it is by the way I create art for that client.

2. Putting Your Contract Together

Besides making sure your contract includes all the necessary information, you'll need to present it in an easy-to-follow, professional format. Generally, contract clauses are organized in a series of numbered paragraphs for easy reference to specific terms.

If your agreement includes any hard-to-articulate details, such as the specifications of a software product, the drawing of a company logo or architectural blueprints, you can include them as attachments to the main contract. If you do include an attachment, be sure to label it and refer to it in the main contract. To officially make it a part of the contract, state somewhere in the main contract that you "include the Attachment in the contract," or that you "incorporate the Attachment into the contract."

> EXAMPLE 1: Company agrees to pay artist $100 for use of logo. Logo is attached to this contract as Attachment A and is hereby included in this contract.

> EXAMPLE 2: Contractor agrees to complete remodeling within one year. The final plans are attached to this contract as Exhibit B and are hereby incorporated into this contract.

D. Reading and Revising a Contract

If you don't like certain terms of a contract that's presented to you, you can propose changes to the contract. By doing this, you are technically making a counteroffer. Contracts are commonly negotiated back and forth (offer and counteroffer) this way until all the terms are accepted by both parties. (Remember, if the parties aren't in agreement, there's no contract—oral or otherwise. See Section A, above, on offers and counteroffers.)

Changes to a contract—whether to a form contract or one drafted from scratch—can be made in a number of ways. One is by simply crossing out language and filling in new language directly on the contract itself. Each party should initial any such changes to show that each approves of them, and should then sign the contract as a whole.

In today's world, however, it's more than likely that there will be an electronic copy of the contract either on your computer, your lawyer's or the other party's. If so, it makes much more sense to make the necessary changes on the computer and then print out a clean copy for both parties to sign. In some industries, such as the real estate industry, on the other hand, it's common to use a separate document when making a counteroffer that states the desired changes and refers back to the original offer. In that case, both the original offer and the counteroffer form the contract.

A contract can also be amended at a later date with a separate document called an addendum. The addendum should state that its terms prevail over the terms of the original contract, especially if the terms are in direct conflict, as would be the case if the price or completion time for a job is changed. Both parties should sign the addendum.

E. Special Issues for Electronic Contracts

So far, the rules we've gone through cover the basic legal principles underlying how contracts are formed and what makes a contract legally valid.

Understanding these fundamentals is important when you're figuring out how to create a contract or evaluating whether an agreement you're about to make with someone will be enforced by a court. While these basics generally apply to any contract regardless of form—whether the contract is printed in a formal document, scratched on a cocktail napkin or just spoken and sealed with a handshake—there are new and emerging rules that apply specifically to contracts created online. Before we give you a very general overview of the special issues involved in electronic contracts, keep in mind that law in this area is rapidly evolving—scrambling, in fact—to catch up with fast-evolving technology.

1. What Is an Electronic Contract?

When we say "electronic contract," we essentially mean any agreement that is created and executed in electronic form—in other words, no paper or other hard copies are used. Typically, electronic agreements are created either via email or on interactive Web pages. For instance, many companies use interactive forms at their websites that users must complete in order to purchase goods or software, join a membership organization, participate in a mail listserver or do whatever else the company is offering. Besides asking the user to enter various items of personal information, these forms will typically display the terms of the contract between the company and the user, and ask the user to agree to the terms by clicking on a button such as "I Accept."

Here's another example of an electronic contract: a business associate of yours emails you a request to purchase a specified number of items you sell, at a named price, for immediate delivery. If you email back to the associate that you agree to all the proposed terms, you've probably just entered into a legally enforceable electronic contract. Why the "probably"? Because there is no way for you to sign the contract with pen and ink, and states vary in how they treat digital signatures (read on).

2. Taking Traditional Contract Principles Online

As mentioned above, contract law is only beginning to grapple with the details of this paperless way of entering into agreements. When electronic contracts have been challenged, courts have had a difficult time determining whether an actual binding contract existed, since it can be unclear whether all the traditional elements of contract formation were met.

Shortcut Contracts for e-Commerce

When it comes to small transactions where you pay for goods by credit card, most sites get around the issue of whether a valid contract has been formed by saying that if you are dissatisfied for any reason, they will give you your money back. This is another way of saying that if you don't want a contract to exist, it doesn't. Or put another way, the online site has conceded in advance that they won't try to enforce the contract. This trust-the-customer approach does work well for small transactions, but has obvious limitations when it comes to major purchases (a car, for example) or significant business-to-business transactions. In these situations, a real signature on an enforceable contract is needed.

---

a. Clickwrap Agreements

Businesses have traditionally used standard contracts that aren't open to negotiation; customers are often faced with either accepting the contract as is or not completing the transaction. Examples might include a car purchase contract or an agreement to rent a moving truck, where the consumer would not be allowed to buy the car or rent the truck if she insisted on changing any of the terms of the company's standard contract. Over the years, these types of contracts have been challenged on the grounds that they are not fair to the consumer, since they are typically presented in a take-it-or-leave-it manner, leaving the consumer little or no power to amend a contract that is often highly favorable to the seller. Whether or not these types of contracts (sometimes called contracts of adhesion, because consumers are forced to "adhere" to the contract) are valid has long been a contentious area of contract law. Generally speaking, adhesion contracts are held to be valid, as long as the terms are clear to the consumer and not grossly unreasonable.

Today, Internet click-to-agree contracts (often called clickwrap agreements)—as well as other non-negotiated agreements, such as the software licenses included with packaged software (called shrinkwrap agreements)—are facing similar challenges. While these types of agreements have generally been held to be valid, courts have refused to enforce certain terms that are deemed too burdensome or unfair to the consumer. For example, in one case a customer sued Gateway computers, claiming that certain terms of the agreement included in his computer package were unfair and invalid—particularly the clause that tried to force the customer to use arbitration in case of a dispute. While the court upheld the validity of the shrinkwrap agreement as a whole, it struck out terms that would have forced the customer to use specific arbitration procedures instead of being able to pursue legal claims in a more evenhanded arena. *(Brower v. Gateway 2000, Inc.,* 676 N.Y.S. 2d 569 (New York Supreme Ct. App. Div. [Aug.] 1998).)

Over the past few years there have been a number of legislative efforts to deal with the issues and problems raised by clickwrap agreements. Problem is, the state laws governing electronic contracts that have been developed are not consistent, which has actually done more harm than good. And the state courts that have heard and ruled upon electronic contract cases have come up with different decisions, with the result that checking an "I accept" box may create a contract in one state, but not in another. No question, this lack of uniformity has been a real thorn in the side of e-commerce, which of course recognizes no state boundaries.

In response, the National Conference of Commissioners on Uniform State Laws (NCCUSL) decided to tackle the problem by drafting model legislation for adoption by the states. One of these proposed laws, the Uniform Computer Information Transactions Act (UCITA), addresses the issue of clickwrap and shrinkwrap agreements, essentially making these types of contracts valid and binding. As of mid-2000, only a handful of states had adopted the UCITA.

The UCITA has raised a fair amount of controversy. Many consumer advocates, as well as over 25 state attorneys general, argue that the UCITA is biased in favor of software vendors and information services providers, leaving consumers with significantly less protection than under current law. The Computer Professionals for Social Responsibility offers a UCITA Fact Sheet at http://www.cpsr.org/program/UCITA/ucita-fact.html.

b. Electronic and Digital Signatures

One of the stickier issues involving electronic contracts has to do with whether agreements executed in a purely online environment have been "signed" (outside of clickwrap agreements, discussed separately above). For many centuries, the traditional way to indicate your acceptance of a contract (and most other binding documents) has been to sign it with your unique signature. But electronic contracts can't be signed this same way. Instead, people and businesses use other means to indicate they accept the terms of a contract, such as simply typing their name into the signature area of the document. But increasingly, better technological approaches to the problem of signing contracts online are being developed, such as fingerprint or iris scanning, or

a cryptographic technology known as Public Key Infrastructure (PKI). These methods are collectively known as electronic signatures. The term "digital signature" refers specifically to cryptographic signature methods such as the Public Key Infrastructure (PKI) (see "What Is PKI?," below).

What Is PKI?

Security experts currently favor the cryptographic signature method known as Public Key Infrastructure (PKI) as the most secure and reliable method of signing contracts online. Without going too deep into the technical details, PKI involves using an algorithm to encrypt the document so that only the parties will be able to modify it or "sign" it. The process of encrypting the document is what's known as creating a digital signature. Each party will have a "key" allowing it to read and sign the document, thus ensuring that no one else will be able to sign it fraudulently. PKI standards are still evolving, but the technology is already widely accepted as the best electronic signature method currently available. A good (though slightly tech-heavy) source for more information on PKI technology is the Center for Information Technology Standards— Public Key Infrastructure (PKI) Standardization Home Page—at http://www-pki.itsi.disa.mil.

Until recently, most states didn't have any laws stating which of these ways to "sign" an electronic document was legally acceptable. In response, the NCCUSL drafted another model law, the Uniform Electronic Transactions Act (UETA), which specifically addresses electronic signatures. In a nutshell, the UETA provides that electronic signatures (in all their forms) and contracts are just as valid and legally binding as their paper counterparts. As of mid-2000, about a dozen states had enacted the UETA.

c. Federal Law on Electronic Signatures

Fortunately, as the states were mulling over whether to adopt the UETA and/or the UCITA, the U.S. Congress forged ahead and passed federal legislation establishing the validity of electronic signatures nationwide. This bill, known as the Electronic Signatures in Global and National Commerce Act, was signed into law in June 2000 and became effective on October 1, 2000. The law applies to all states that had not already adopted the UETA or a similar electronic signature law by mid-2000. In this way, the law finally gives some much-needed consistency to the way states treat electronic signatures in online transactions.

This bill is similar to the model UETA in that it makes electronic signatures and contracts (including clickwrap agreements) just as valid as paper ones. While certain transactions are exempted from this bill and must still be completed on paper (wills, cancellation of utility services, court orders and other official court documents, among others), the bill will allow an enormous range of business and consumer transactions to be completed totally online. In essence, it throws the door wide open for all types of e-commerce, allowing businesses and consumers to create (in theory at least) reliable, binding contracts online, without the inconvenience of shuttling paper documents back and forth.

 For more information on electronic contracts, see *Doing Business Online* in the Internet Law Area of Nolo's Legal Encyclopedia, at http://www.nolo.com/encyclopedia/ilaw_ency.html#Subtopic197.

3. Tips for Creating Contracts Online

While the new federal e-signature law, along with the UETA, creates a solid legal framework for online contracts, electronic signature technology is still evolving, which means the reality of online contracts still falls somewhat short of its promise. Like the UETA, the new e-signature law does not specify any particular technology for electronic signatures, leaving that up to software companies and the free market to establish. As mentioned above, Public Key Infrastructure (PKI) technology is currently favored by security experts, though its standards aren't completely nailed down or ready for common use. As developments in PKI and other electronic signature methods create solid, worldwide standards, e-commerce will only become more efficient and widespread.

While we wait for reliable standards to develop, it will be important to approach online contracts carefully. Of particular concern is the possibility for fraud in online contracts, especially since there is no set standard for what an electronic signature is. Until the technology is airtight, make sure that if you enter into an online contract you trust the other party and are comfortable with the type of electronic signature that you're using. If you're not comfortable with creating a contract online, you may want to stay lower-tech and stick with paper contracts, either faxed back and forth or sent by overnight mail.

The nonprofit Consumers Union, which publishes *Consumer Reports* magazine, has issued a set of tips to use when using electronic signatures and creating online contracts. These include:

- Don't consent to using an online contract if you are uncomfortable using a computer or do not understand how to use email.
- Don't agree to use an online contract or to receive electronic documents until you are sure that your computer's software and hardware will be able to read and use the documents provided by the company.
- Remember that the electronic signatures law allows you to opt to receive documents on paper instead of electronically if you prefer.
- Keep back-up paper copies of the electronic documents you receive, and keep a list of the businesses with which you agree to receive electronic documents.
- Notify the businesses of any changes that may affect your ability to receive and read email and attachments, such as changing

your email address, your hardware or your software.

- Close any unused email accounts.
- Don't give out your email address to any business if you don't want to receive email notices from that business.
- Notify the business right away if you have any problems receiving its emails or opening its documents.

You can find these tips and other information about online contracts at the Consumers Union website at www.consumersunion.org.

Never open attachments to email if you aren't expecting the email or don't know who it's from. Nasty viruses are often spread through email attachments, so it's good policy to just throw away suspicious mail as soon as you see it. Even when you know the sender of the email, you need to be cautious because some viruses use a computer user's email address book to replicate themselves, by sending themselves out to everyone in the book. This means that if you get an email with an attachment from your friend Steve Smith, there's a chance that Steve Smith didn't actually send the email. For this reason, don't open attachments unless you're expecting them. And remember, contrary to popular rumor, viruses do not spread themselves through the email messages themselves, only through the attachments.

More information on digital signatures. The American Bar Association has published a helpful tutorial on digital signature guidelines. You can read it online at http://www.abanet.org/scitech/ec/isc/dsg-tutorial.html.

☑ Chapter 9 Checklist

☐ Familiarize yourself with the legal basics of contracts.

☐ Put all your contracts into writing whenever possible. (Contracts created online or by email are considered to be "in writing.")

☐ Try to respond to offers promptly, and when making an offer, include an expiration date.

☐ When you need to draft a contract from scratch, try using standard form contracts to get you started.

☐ Be thorough in your contracts. Make sure that any points of potential conflict are clearly spelled out.

☐ Use caution when entering into electronic contracts (also sometimes called online contracts or digital contracts). If you're uncomfortable with creating a contract online or by email, don't do it—opt for a paper contract.

Bookkeeping, Accounting and Financial Management

A. Accounting Basics 10/4

B. Cash vs. Accrual Accounting 10/5

   1. How Each Method Works 10/5

   2. Accounting Methods and Taxes 10/6

   3. Which Method to Use 10/6

C. Step One: Keeping Your Receipts 10/7

   1. Receipts of Income 10/7

   2. Expenditure Receipts 10/9

D. Step Two: Setting Up and Posting to Ledgers 10/10

   1. Income Ledger 10/10

   2. Expenditure Ledger 10/12

   3. Designing a Ledger System for Your Business 10/15

E. Step Three: Creating Basic Financial Reports 10/15

   1. Profit and Loss Statement 10/15

   2. Cash Flow Projection 10/17

Perhaps the hardest part of accounting is getting over the psychological hang-up that most people seem to have about it. Many of us are loath to balance our checkbooks on any regular basis, much less keep detailed accounts of how our money comes and goes. The good news is that you don't need to be a financial wizard to start a small business; you just need a comfortable working knowledge of the basics.

If you read Chapter 5, "Drafting an Effective Business Plan," some of this material may be a review. In that chapter, we explained how to generate financial projections using sales and expense estimates to see if your business was likely to turn a profit. The financial tools used in business planning—particularly profit/loss analysis and cash flow projection—are the same tools used in accounting, just employed slightly differently. In this chapter, we'll focus on how to use these and other tools to keep track of current financial data (as opposed to projections) for your business.

This chapter will give you an idea of what records your business should keep and will describe simple ways to keep them. We'll also explain how to use the information in your financial records to calculate how much profit your business is making and to ensure that enough cash is regularly flowing through your business to pay your important bills on time.

Fortunately for today's entrepreneurs, inexpensive, powerful and easy-to-use software is available that will help simplify the accounting process. Programs such as Quickbooks, Quicken, and MYOB Accounting make this once unsavory task much more palatable. Once your income and expenses are entered into the system, you're only a few mouse clicks away from sophisticated financial reports that would have taken many hours and considerable skill to generate just a decade ago. In fact, these programs are so affordable (typically under $200) and user-friendly it makes little sense not to use one of them.

Don't expect your accounting software to do your accounting for you. You shouldn't simply rely on numbers that your software program spits out if you don't fully understand them. The accounting concepts and processes described in this chapter are the same whether done manually or by computer—and you should take the time to learn them. While accounting software makes it much easier to manipulate the numbers you've entered and to generate informative financial reports, you still need an understanding of what all the numbers mean in order to make them work for your business.

It often pays to get help with bookkeeping and accounting tasks. The basic information provided in this chapter will be valuable for all business owners who are unfamiliar with accounting basics. But depending on the size and type of your business, you may eventually want to do additional reading or hire experienced help. Our approach here is to provide enough information to get a new businessperson sensibly started. But even so, the owner of a small, relatively simple business can almost always benefit from an hour or two with an experienced small-business accountant who can often offer creative strategies for keeping records, selecting and configuring your computerized accounting system and managing your money.

Accounting Glossary

A big part of understanding the financial side of your business consists of nothing more than learning the language of accounting. Once you're familiar with basic terms, you'll be well prepared to make sense of basic written reports and better able to communicate with others about important financial information. And you'll also be well positioned to cope with a common business problem: Many people use key financial terms imprecisely or even incorrectly, thus needlessly confusing themselves and others.

- **Accounting** is a general term that refers to the overall process of tracking your business's income and expenses, and then using these numbers in various calculations and formulas to answer specific questions about the financial and tax status of the business.

- **Bookkeeping** refers to the task of recording the amount, date and source of all business revenues and expenses. Bookkeeping is essentially the starting point of the accounting process. Only with accurate bookkeeping can meaningful accounting be done.

- An **invoice** is a written record of a transaction, often submitted to a customer or client when requesting payment. Invoices are sometimes called **bills** or **statements**, though the latter term has its own technical meaning (see below).

- A **statement** is a formal written summary of an account. Unlike an invoice, a statement is not generally used as a formal request for payment, but is more of a reminder to a customer or client that payment is due.

- A **ledger** is a physical collection of related financial information, such as revenues, expenditures, accounts receivable and accounts payable. Ledgers used to be kept in books preprinted with lined ledger paper (which explains why a business's financial info is often referred to as the "books"), but are now commonly computer files that can be printed out.

- An **account** is a collection of financial information grouped according to customer or purpose. For example, if you have a regular customer, the collection of information regarding that customer's purchases, payments and debts would be called his "account." A written record of an account is called a **statement**.

- A **receipt** is a written record of a transaction. A buyer receives a receipt to show that he paid for an item. The seller keeps a copy of the receipt to show she received payment for the item. Receipts are sometimes called sales slips.

- **Accounts payable** are amounts that your business owes. For example, unpaid utility bills and purchases your business makes on credit are included in your accounts payable.

- **Accounts receivable** are amounts owed to your business that you expect to receive. Accounts receivable includes sales your business makes on credit.

A. Accounting Basics

Accounting has two basic goals:

- to keep track of your income and expenses, thereby improving your chances of making a profit, and
- to collect the necessary financial information about your business to file your various tax returns and local tax registration papers.

Sounds pretty simple, doesn't it? And it can be, especially if you remind yourself of these two goals whenever you feel overwhelmed by the details of keeping your financial records. Hopefully you will also be reassured to know that there is no requirement that your records be kept in any specific organizational system. (There is a requirement, however, that some businesses use a certain method of crediting their accounts. See Section B, below, on cash vs. accrual accounting.) In other words, there's no official system or format to organize your books—as long as your records accurately reflect your business's income and expenses, the IRS will find them acceptable.

Organization is everything. One thing that all good bookkeeping systems have in common is organization. A well-organized system with accessible, reasonably neat files will not only be a godsend in the event of an audit, but it will help you keep track of your business as well.

The actual process of accounting is easy to understand when broken down into three steps.

1. Keep receipts or other acceptable records of every payment to, and every expenditure from, your business.
2. Summarize your income and expenditure records on some periodic basis (generally daily, weekly or monthly).
3. Use these summaries to create financial reports that will tell you specific information about your business, such as how much monthly profit you're making or how much your business is worth at a specific point in time.

And, of course, whether you do your accounting by hand on ledger sheets or with accounting software, these principles are exactly the same.

Are you to beginning believe that you don't need to be afraid of accounting? Good, because it's something you absolutely need to embrace as part of running any business. Failing to keep track of income and expenses is one of the surest ways to run any business off a cliff. Here are a few more ways that a simple set of books will help your business.

- **You'll be able to price your goods and services more competitively.** Only by staying on top of your business's income and expenses will you know how much money you'll need to bring in each week, month or year to make a profit. And, of course, this knowledge is essential to allow you to price your goods and services appropriately. For instance, if you don't know your break-even point, you will only be able to guess at how much to charge your customers for products or services, with the likely result that you'll charge too low (and make an inadequate profit) or too high (and alienate customers).

- **You'll be able to pace your growth more effectively.** A good set of books will give you the information you need to decide when and how to expand your business. If your numbers tell you that sales and profits have been growing consistently for several months, that may be a signal that it's time to hire additional employees or enter into a new market—or both. Without meaningful financial numbers, making any decisions about growth can be a gamble. For example, just because your business has a lot of money in its checking account doesn't necessarily mean you're making good money (you might have received several big payments from past sales, while current sales are actually slowing down).

- **Your taxes can be minimized.** Knowing your company's finances inside and out will help you save money when tax time comes around. For example, if the end of the year is nearing and your up-to-date records clearly show the year to be profitable, you can purchase needed supplies or equipment before the end of the year and write off these expenses, thus reducing your taxable income. Also, keeping careful track of your expenses will prevent you from simply forgetting to claim them as deductions at year-end. Businesses that are sloppy about bookkeeping often miss opportunities for saving tax dollars. Don't be one of them.

- **You'll avoid tax penalties.** Besides being positioned to legally save tax dollars, responsible bookkeeping will help you avoid errors in your tax returns that can subject you to fines and other penalties. No question, if your business is audited, the IRS can be really nasty if it finds your books in bad shape—in extreme situations it may even refuse to recognize perfectly legitimate expenses. In short, neglecting your responsibility to maintain basic, accurate records is likely to result in the kind of trouble with the IRS that you might not even wish on your worst enemy.

B. Cash vs. Accrual Accounting

Before we discuss several simple systems for keeping your records, you need to understand the basics of the two principal methods of keeping track of a business's income and expenses: cash method and accrual method accounting (sometimes called cash basis and accrual basis accounting). In a nutshell, these methods differ only in the timing of when transactions—both sales and purchases—are credited or debited to your accounts.

1. How Each Method Works

If you use the cash method, income is counted when cash (or a check) is actually received, and

expenses are counted when actually paid. But under the more common accrual method, transactions are counted when they happen—regardless of when the money is actually received or paid. In other words, with the accrual method, income is counted when the sale occurs, and expenses are counted when you receive goods or services—you don't have to wait until you see the money, or until you actually pay money out of your checking account, to record the transaction.

Say you purchase a new laser printer on credit in May and pay $2,000 for it in July, two months later. Using cash-method accounting you would record a $2,000 payment for the month of July, the month when the money was actually paid. But under the accrual method, the $2,000 payment would be recorded in May, when you took the laser printer and became obligated to pay for it. Similarly, if your computer installation business finished a job on November 30, 2000, and didn't get paid until January 10, 2001, you'd record the payment in January 2001 if you used the cash method. Under the accrual method the income would be recorded in your books in November of 2000.

With some transactions, it may be tricky to identify exactly when the sale or purchase has occurred. Some sales aren't completed all at once, and if you use accrual accounting, you may sometimes wonder exactly when you can enter the transaction into your books. For instance, say someone buys two CDs from your record store but also makes a special order for another CD, and pays for all three at once. Or say your landscaping company finishes a large project, save for the last step of applying another lawn fertilizing treatment two weeks after laying the sod. The key date here is the job completion date. Not until you deliver all of the goods, finish all parts of a service, or otherwise meet all terms of a contract can you put the income down in your books. If a job is mostly completed but will take another few days to add the finishing touches, technically it doesn't go on your books until the job is completely done.

The cash and accrual methods can produce the same results. As you can readily see, the results produced by the cash and accrual accounting methods will only be different if you do some transactions on credit. If all your transactions are paid in cash as soon as completed, including your sales and your purchases, then your ledgers will look the same, regardless of what method you use.

2. Accounting Methods and Taxes

The most significant way your business is affected by the accounting method you choose involves the tax year in which income and expense items will be counted. (See "Tax Years and Accounting Periods," below.) For instance, if you use the cash method, and you incur expenses in the 2000 tax year but don't pay them until the 2001 tax year, you won't be able to claim them on your 2000 tax return. But you would be able to claim them if you use the accrual method, since the very essence of that system is to record transactions when they occur, not when money actually changes hands.

EXAMPLE 1: Zara runs a small flower shop called ZuZu's Petals. On December 22, 2000, Zara buys a number of office supplies for her shop for which she will be billed $400. She takes the supplies that day, but according to the terms of the purchase, doesn't pay for them for 30 days. Under her accrual system of accounting, she counts the $400 expense during the December 2000 accounting period, even though she didn't actually write the check until January of the next year. This means that Zara can deduct the $400 from her taxable income of 2000.

EXAMPLE 2: Scott and Lisa operate A Stitch in Hide, a leather repair shop. They're hired to repair an antique leather couch, and they finish their job on December 15, 2000. They bill the customer $750, which they receive on January 20, 2001. Since they use the accrual method of accounting, Scott and Lisa count the $750 income in December 2000, because that's when they earned the money by finishing the job. This income must be reported in their 2000 tax return even though they don't receive the money that year.

Tax Years and Accounting Periods

Income and expenses must be reported to the IRS for a specific period of time, alternately called your "tax year," your "accounting period" or your "fiscal year." Unless there is a valid business reason to use a different period, or unless your business is a corporation, you'll have to use the calendar year, beginning on January 1 and ending on December 31. Most business owners do use the calendar year for their tax year, simply because they find it easy and natural to use. But if you want to use a different period, you must request permission from the IRS by filing Form 8716, *Election to Have a Tax Year Other Than a Required Tax Year*. Also, your fiscal year can't begin and end on just any day of the month; it must begin on the first day of a month and end on the last day of the previous month one year later.

3. Which Method to Use

Most businesses that have sales of less than $5 million per year are free to adopt either accounting method, with one big exception: If your business stocks an inventory of items that you will sell to the public, the IRS requires that you use the accrual accounting method. Inventory includes any merchandise you sell as well as supplies you will incorporate into products you intend to sell.

Whichever method you use, it's important to realize that either one only gives you a partial picture of the financial status of your business. While the accrual method shows the ebb and flow of business income and debts more accurately, it may leave you in the dark as to what cash reserves are actually available—and not knowing this information could result in a serious cash flow problem. For instance, your income ledger may show thousands of dollars in sales, while in reality your bank account is empty because your customers haven't paid you yet.

And though the cash method will give you a truer idea of how much actual cash your business has, it may offer a misleading picture of longer-term profitability. Under the cash method, for instance, your books may show one month to be spectacularly profitable, when actually sales have been slow and, by coincidence, a lot of credit customers paid their bills in that month. To have a firm and true understanding of your business's finances, you need more than just a collection of monthly totals; you need to understand what your numbers mean and how to use them to answer specific financial questions, as discussed in the rest of this chapter.

C. Step One: Keeping Your Receipts

Comprehensive summaries of your business's income and expenses are the heart of the accounting process. But unless you want to flirt with tax fraud, you can't just make up the information in your books. Each of your business's sales and expenditures must be backed up by some type of record containing the amount, the date and other relevant information about that transaction. This is true whether your accounting is done by computer or on hand-posted ledgers.

From a legal point of view, your method of keeping receipts can range from slips kept in a cigar box to a sophisticated cash register hooked into a computer system. Practically, you'll want to choose a system that fits your business needs. For example, a small service business that handles only relatively few jobs may get by with a bare-bones approach. But the more sales and expenditures your business makes, the better your receipt filing system needs to be. This section discusses common ways of keeping your receipts. The bottom line is to choose or adapt one to suit your needs.

1. Receipts of Income

Every time your business brings in money, you need a record of that income. Most of your revenue will come from sales of your products or services. How you keep track of sales will vary a great deal depending on what type of business you run and how many sales you make. Businesses like grocery stores that make hundreds or even thousands of sales a day will likely need a cash register to produce a record of each sale. Other businesses with slower sales, such as hair salons or auto shops, can get by simply writing out a receipt for each sale from a receipt book. Hand-written receipts should include the date and a brief description of the goods or services sold. If some of your sales are made on credit, your receipts should indicate whether the customer paid, and if not, when payment is due.

Whether you use a cash register tape or hand-written receipts, make sure that you and your employees know the system and use it consistently. If your income records aren't accurate, neither will be the ledgers or financial statements you make from them.

Receipts are more important for you than for your customers. While it's good business practice to give receipts to customers who purchase goods or services, it's a legal requirement that you keep a copy for yourself. Therefore, if you write out your own receipts, you'll need to make two copies—one for you, and one for the customer. Cash registers and most receipt books make each record in duplicate.

One huge distinction your income records need to reflect is whether a sale is taxable or not for state sales-tax purposes—to compute and file your state sales taxes, you'll need to keep taxable sales separate from nontaxable sales. (See "Taxable Sales vs. Taxable Income," below.) If you use a cash register, this distinction can be made by the push of a button at the time of each sale. If you write out a receipt of each sale by hand, be sure to show any sales tax separately, not just as part of a total, and if the sale is nontaxable make that clear by writing "no tax," "nontaxable" or the like.

Assuming you follow our advice to keep your receipts of taxable sales separate from receipts of nontaxable sales, posting them to your accounting system (discussed in Section D) should be easy. If you plan to post daily, a simple method involves keeping your receipts for the day in two envelopes or two sections of an accordion folder (one for taxable sales, one for nontaxable) and adding them up at the end of the day. If you use a cash register, the process is simplified because you can simply run totals at the end of the day for taxable sales and nontaxable sales. Depending on your machine, you may also be able to print out totals for other periods of time, such as one week or a specified number of days.

Taxable Sales vs. Taxable Income

As discussed above (and in more detail in Chapter 8, Section G), many sales of goods are subject to sales tax, which retailers must pay to the state. But other large categories of sales are often exempt from sales tax, such as sales of services, sales to out-of-state residents or sales to resellers. So some sales income is taxable and some is not.

It is crucial to understand that whether a sale is taxable or not for sales-tax purposes is a different issue from whether income is taxable or not for income-tax purposes. Generally, taxable income—that is, money you take in that is subject to income taxes at the end of the year—includes any money earned by your business, minus certain deductions, and must be reported on your year-end income-tax return. This includes all income your business brings in, whether or not it is subject to state sales tax. Be sure you keep these two different issues straight.

Jennifer F. Mahoney, owner of an illustration service in Northern California:

It's helpful to learn about the accounts payable process for each client and to understand who in the company releases checks. It's often an entirely different person or department from the one who calls you to offer work. You don't necessarily want to strain your relationship with the person who calls offering you work just because a different department of their business doesn't pay on time. Pave the way for timely payments as much as possible by getting to know the correct procedure, and when it's time to press for payment, you'll know the right person to call.

You should also document any income your business receives from sources other than sales and keep these receipts separate from your sales receipts. If you get a loan or contribute your own personal money to the business, record this fact with some sort of a receipt or a promissory note. The key here is to be sure your written records adequately describe the source of income so you'll know whether to count it as taxable income or not. Most sales income, for example, will be taxed at the end of the year, while income that you personally contribute to the business will not.

2. Expenditure Receipts

Ever hear the business wisdom that the key to small-business success is to keep your costs down? While this isn't the only thing a successful business owner needs to do, watching those pennies is always a good idea. The first step in keeping costs down is keeping accurate track of what they are. Just as you keep a record of each individual sale, you need to keep a record of each time you spend money for your business. Business expenditures include paychecks to employees, money spent on supplies and payments on loans, as well as all other costs associated with your business. Legally and practically, each and every one of these expenses must be recorded.

First of all, be sure to get a written receipt for every transaction in which you spend money for the business. Not only is keeping and tallying these receipts an easy way to keep track of your expenses, but receipts also come in handy if there's a problem with any of the goods or services you purchased or a dispute over whether you paid a particular bill.

Many businesspeople like to use their checkbook registers to keep track of expenses. This is fine, but there are two thorns to watch out for. Since many of your expenditures will be paid for by check, for these transactions you may have two records of the same transaction: the notation in your checkbook and the receipt from the seller. Make sure you don't count that transaction twice! And don't forget to record cash purchases—they won't show up in your checkbook register. There

are several easy ways to avoid counting some expenses twice and forgetting others. One is to use your receipts as the sole record of expenditures, and not to count the amounts in your checkbook. Since most businesspeople don't want to sort through a pile of odd-sized bits of paper, another way is to rely solely on your checkbook for expenditure records, instead of on receipts. Fine, as long as you make sure to include the receipts of cash transactions in your checkbook register.

 Don't let multiple receipts screw up your bookkeeping. Sometimes you'll receive a number of sales slips for just one purchase: a credit card slip, a register receipt and an itemized statement, for example. If you throw all three receipts into your files to be posted later, you run the risk of counting all three separately. You might think that you'll remember the transaction, or that it will be obvious to you as you're posting your ledger that the three receipts correspond to a single transaction, but when dealing with dozens of receipts at the end of a long day it's all too easy for mistakes to creep into your paperwork. To avoid counting transactions more than once, either discard multiple copies of receipts immediately after the transaction or staple them all together.

Each record of an expenditure should include the date, the amount, the method of payment, who was paid and—most important—a description of what type of expense it was, such as rent, supplies or utilities. The description is important because later, when you post (enter) your expenses to your ledgers, you'll need to assign them into categories such as rent, advertising, supplies, utilities and taxes. These categories are important for tax purposes because different types of expenses have different rules for deductibility. So to make your bookkeeping job easier, make sure your expense receipts contain enough information for you to be able to assign the expense to the appropriate category when you post it in your ledger. Also, it's best to keep your expense receipts separated by category during the month prior to posting them.

In other words, keep all of your utilities receipts in one box or envelope, your supplies receipts in another, and so on. (We discuss the various expense categories in Section D2, below.)

D. Step Two: Setting Up and Posting to Ledgers

A completed ledger is really nothing more than a summary of revenues and expenditures, as well as whatever else you're keeping track of, entered from your receipts according to category and date. Later, you'll use these summaries to answer specific financial questions about your business—such as whether you're making a profit, and if so, how much.

You'll start with a blank ledger page (a sheet with lines) or, more often these days, a computer file of empty rows and columns. On some regular basis—like every day, once a week or at least once a month—you should transfer the amounts from your receipts for sales and expenditures into your ledger. Called "posting," how often you do this depends on how many sales and expenditures your business makes and how detailed you want your books to be.

Generally speaking, the more sales you make, the more often you should post to your ledger. A retail store, for instance, that does hundreds of sales amounting to thousands or tens of thousands of dollars every day should probably post daily. With that volume of sales, it's important to see what's happening every day and not to fall behind with the paperwork. To do this, the busy retailer should use a cash register that totals and posts the day's sales to a computerized bookkeeping system at the push of a button. A slower business, however, or one with just a few large transactions per month, such as a small website design shop, a dog-sitting service or a swimming-pool repair company, would probably be fine if it posted weekly or even monthly.

To get started on a hand-entry system, get ledger pads from any office supply store. Or, as is more practical these days, you should purchase an accounting software program that will generate its own ledgers as you enter your information. All but the tiniest new businesses are well advised to use an accounting software package to help keep their books (micro-businesses can often get by with personal finance software such as Quicken). That's because once you've entered your daily, weekly or monthly numbers, accounting software makes preparing monthly and yearly financial reports incredibly easy.

Learn bookkeeping by hand to prevent computer-induced ignorance. Even though a computerized accounting system allows you to generate sophisticated financial reports with a few mouse clicks, you should still take the time to understand how the numbers fit together and what they mean. A good way to do this is to learn how financial reports are done by hand, as we explain below, even if you plan to use a computer to generate them. The more you know about your numbers and the relationships between various figures, the more power you'll have to make positive and profitable business decisions.

Every business should have both an income ledger and an expenditure ledger to post its transactions to. We'll walk you through each of these ledgers below, and offer samples of each type. In Section 3, below, we'll also introduce you to some other types of ledgers that you may want to use, depending on your business.

1. Income Ledger

Despite its name, an income ledger should include only money earned in the course of business— your sales income—not income from every source. For example, income such as a loan or transfer of personal money into the business should not be included with sales income on this ledger.

Check out the following example.

Income for May 2000

| 1 | 2 | 3 | 4 Nontaxable Sales | | | 5 | 6 |
Date	Sales Period	Taxable Sales	Sales Tax	Sales to Retailers	Nontaxable Services	Other	Total Sales
1		$452.58	$38.47	$96.50	$75.00	$45.00	$707.55
2	closed						
3							
4	(May 3-4)	$765.50	$65.07	$143.50	$125.00	$65.75	$1,164.82
5...		$407.88	$34.67	$76.25	$60.00	$45.00	$623.80
...31		$502.45	$42.71	$105.00	$90.00	$53.50	$793.66
Totals		$9,456.82	$803.83	$1,845.50	$1,365.50	$854.00	$14,325.65

Most income ledgers—whether on paper or part of your accounting software—are set up like the above sample, covering a one-month period and allowing space for daily entries. Your income should be divided into taxable sales, sales tax and nontaxable sales. Also, your state may require your nontaxable sales to be broken down into certain categories such as wholesale sales, services, sales to out-of-state customers or freight charges, for example. Check with your state sales tax agency to find out which, if any, nontaxable subcategories you must use in your recordkeeping.

When you're ready to post your sales income, however often you decide to do it, go through your receipts for that period and enter the totals into the appropriate columns. Mark each receipt or cash-register tape "posted" (stamping is often easiest) once you've recorded it in your ledger. If you post daily, you'll have entries on each line except for days your business is closed, in which case you should enter "closed" in the Sales Period column. If you don't post daily, indicate in the Sales Period column which days are included for the totals you're entering (for example, "June 3 to June 6").

At the end of each month, total the entries in each column. Voila! You now have an income ledger for one month of business. As you can see,

even without the help of a computer, creating one is easy. When you've finished a ledger for one month, start a new income ledger for the next month.

After an income ledger has been completed each month for a year, it's easy to add the monthly totals to arrive at your yearly sales income, broken down into taxable and nontaxable sales and sales tax amounts. Simply use a separate ledger sheet or computer file to post your monthly totals into a year-end income ledger. It will look very similar to your monthly income ledgers.

Remember, however, that businesses using the cash method of accounting can only count transactions actually paid during the year. If your business uses the cash method and did any sales on credit, you may need to do a year-end adjustment. If you never recorded unpaid sales in your monthly ledgers, then you're all set—no adjustment is necessary. If, however, you included your total sales figures in your monthly ledgers, including unpaid credit sales, then you'll need to account for these in your year-end totals. Simply add an Accounts Receivable row at the bottom of the year-end ledger, with the totals of any unpaid sales, and subtract them from your yearly totals.

Here's a sample year-end ledger.

Income for 2000						
1	**2**		**4**		**5**	**6**
			Nontaxable Sales			
Month	**Taxable Sales**	**Sales Tax**	**Sales to Retailers**	**Nontaxable Services**	**Other**	**Monthly Total**
January	$7,873.46	$669.24	$1,595.75	$1,310.75	$749.50	$12,198.70
February	8,567.45	728.23	1,787.25	1,280.75	683.00	$13,046.68
March	8,349.05	709.67	1,640.50	1,150.50	745.50	$12,595.22
April	8,995.65	764.63	1,788.00	1,335.75	823.70	$13,707.73
December	10,483.88	891.13	1,825.25	1,458.50	880.50	$15,539.26
Total for Year	100,468.48	9,108.72	20,364.50	14,076.25	9,539.90	$153,557.85
Accounts Receivable	10,345.15	724.16	1,565.45	986.90	450.55	$14,072.21
Adjusted Year-End Totals	$90,123.33	$8,384.56	$18,799.05	$13,089.35	$9,089.35	$139,485.64

Keep your completed ledgers in a safe place—whether they're hard copies or computer files. For hard copies, keep them in a well-organized file, preferably in a fireproof file cabinet. For computer files, be sure to make regular printouts and back-ups. Your ledgers will be essential to create financial reports that will give you a picture of your business's financial health (explained in Section E below), and to complete your local, state and federal taxes. Losing your ledgers can be an expensive disaster—dealing with an IRS audit without your records is just one nightmare scenario—so be sure to treat them as the important business documents that they are.

2. Expenditure Ledger

The process of creating an expenditure ledger is quite similar to the income ledger process, but there are some key differences. Most importantly, the categories you'll divide your expenses into are different. Here you won't use the "taxable sales," "sales tax" and "nontaxable sales" categories; instead, you'll divide your expenses into categories such as rent, utilities, computer equipment, employee wages, legal fees, postage or travel, to name a few. Categorizing your expenses is important because different types of expenses have different rules for deductibility for tax purposes. Some expenditures can be deducted right away in full, others may be deducted only over several years (referred to as "depreciating expenses"), while other costs may not be deductible at all.

The IRS has oceans of rules on deductible expenses. For more information on different types of business expenses and their deductibility, read *Tax Savvy for Small Business,* by tax attorney Frederick Daily (Nolo). Reading the rules issued by the IRS isn't a bad idea, either. IRS Publication 334, *Tax Guide for Small Businesses,* is a good place to start.

Another reason for categorizing your expenses is so you'll be able to separate them into fixed costs vs. variable costs when you use your ledger information to generate financial reports. Variable costs, you may remember from Chapter 5, are the ones tied to your products or services, while fixed costs (overhead) are the ones that more or less stay the same regardless of your production and sales volume. Since the distinction between variable and fixed costs will be important when generating your profit and loss forecast, be sure to keep track of them separately in your expenditure ledger. For instance, if you run a Web development business and give your work to clients on a Zip disk, make sure to keep track of Zip disks for clients (a variable cost) separately from the Zip disks you use within your office (a fixed cost). One way to do this is to create a Zip disk category for client disks, and to simply count your office Zip disks in a general "office supplies" category.

The sample expenditure ledger below is a very simplified one, showing just a few common expense categories. Your business will almost certainly have several more categories of expenses. In defining your categories, keep in mind the distinction between variable and fixed expenses, and do your best to keep your categories tightly defined—but not so narrow that you end up with dozens of tiny groups. As a general reference, here's a list of common expense categories:

    advertising
    automobile
    bank charges
    copying
    dues & fees
    education (classes, workshops, etc.)
    equipment/furniture/computers
    equipment rental
    delivery/freight/shipping
    employee wages
    insurance
    interest on business debt
    legal & professional fees
    meals (business-related)
    office expenses/supplies
    office rent
    online services
    postage
    publications (books, magazines, etc.)
    software
    tax preparation fees
    taxes
    telephone
    travel
    utilities (gas, electric).

 Consider a quick consultation with an accountant to help you set up your ledgers. It's a good idea for every small business to use at least a minimal amount of help from an accountant, particularly in the early days when you're figuring out your accounting system. An accountant may be of particular help in figuring out which expense categories your business should use. For example, a carpenter will undoubtedly want to use different categories (such as a category for wood and another for hardware like nails and screws) than a Web designer (who might have a category for printing costs and another for storage media like Zip disks). An accountant, particularly one who's familiar with your type of business, has the expertise to know which expenses are important to group together.

Just as with your income receipts, you must periodically transfer (post) the information from your expenditure receipts to your expense ledger. Ideally you should do this reasonably promptly after you incur the expense. In the Payment Method/Check # column, enter "cash" if you paid in cash; the name of the credit card if you paid with plastic; or the check number if you paid by check. (Remember, if you use the cash method of accounting, you will only record expenditures when they are paid—not when you incur them—so for credit card purchases, you'll only record them when you pay your bill. See Section B above for a review of cash vs. accrual accounting.) In the Transaction column, enter a brief description of the purchase, and in the Payee column, enter whom you paid. Then enter the amount of the purchase in the appropriate category column.

Expenditures for February 2000

1	2	3	4	5	6	7	8	9
Date	Payment Method	Transaction	Payee	Office Supplies	Rent	Utilities	Misc.	Monthly Totals
2-1	ck. 1204	Rent	landlord		1,000.00			
2-5	Visa	Stationery	Office Depot	78.00				
2-13	cash	Business lunch	Monte Vista café				32.00	
2-22	ck. 1206	Electric bill	electric co.			65.00		
Feb. Totals				$78.00	$1,000.00	$ 65.00	$ 32.00	$1,175.00

Unlike your income ledgers, a new expenditure ledger isn't started each month—you'll have one running expense ledger. At the end of the month, simply add up the expenses for that month in each category, and enter each category's total in the next empty row. Then add up all the totals for each category and enter the result in the Monthly Totals column. Draw a double line under the monthly totals, and then continue entering expenses for the next month on the same sheet. Use a new sheet when you run out of room.

At year-end, you'll summarize your monthly expenditure totals on a separate ledger in much the same way that you summarized your monthly income totals. Remember that if you use the accrual accounting method, you'll need to include all expenses for the year, even if you haven't paid them yet. For those using accrual accounting,

Year-end Expenditure Summary

1	2	3	4	5	6
Month	Rent	Office Supplies	Utilities	Misc.	Totals
January	$1,100	$120	$254	$154	$1,628
February	1,100	75	236	209	$1,620
March	1,100	56	244	130	$1,530
April	1,100	90	197	104	$1,491
December	1,100	62	230	185	$1,577
Year Totals	13,200	1,082	2,164	1,845	$18,366
Accounts Payable	0	210	62	347	$619
Adjusted Year-End Totals		$1,292	$2,226	$2,192	$18,985

you'll be all caught up if, every month, you posted all expenses into your expenditure ledger as they became due, even if you didn't pay them. But if you only posted the expenses that you actually paid (as is common for ease of posting), then you'll need to account for your unpaid bills. Do this by including the totals of any unpaid bills in an Accounts Payable row, categorized like your other expenses, and added to your yearly total.

3. Designing a Ledger System for Your Business

The two ledgers just described help you keep track of your most basic business functions—earning and spending money. Depending on how you conduct your business, you may also need to use one or more additional ledgers. If you sell products or services on credit, you'll want to keep track of these sales (the amount you are owed) using an accounts receivable ledger. Similarly, if you make purchases on credit, you can keep track of what you owe with an accounts payable ledger. And if your business has assets such as machinery, computers or vehicles, you'll need to keep track of their depreciation with an equipment ledger. (Depreciation is explained in Chapter 8, Section A.) You'll find prototypes of various types of ledgers at office supply stores, or as a component of any accounting software product.

E. Step Three: Creating Basic Financial Reports

Financial reports are important because they bring together several key pieces of financial information about your business in one place. Think of it this way—while your income ledger may tell you that your business brought in a lot of money during the year, you have no way of knowing whether you turned a profit without measuring your income against your expenses. And even comparing your monthly totals of income and expenses won't tell

you whether your credit customers are paying fast enough to keep adequate cash flowing through your business to pay your bills on time. That's why you need financial reports: to combine data from your ledgers and sculpt it into a shape that shows you the big picture of your business.

The financial reports we talk about in this section are nothing to freak out about—they're really just the income and expense numbers from your ledgers, tweaked a bit in order to help you answer questions about how your business is doing. For instance, the mysterious-sounding "profit and loss statement" consists of nothing more than your company income and expense numbers coupled with one another so that you know how much profit (or loss) you're making over a specified period of time. As long as you've been consistent and thorough in keeping your ledgers, you'll be able to generate this and other reports easily and quickly.

1. Profit and Loss Statement

If the typical owner of a small business start-up got a nickel for every time she asked herself, "Will my business make a profit?" she'd probably be rich enough to retire before the doors were even open. A profit and loss statement (also called a P & L, or an income statement) is designed to answer this very question. In Chapter 5, "Drafting an Effective Business Plan," we discussed creating a profit and loss statement with projected numbers. Here we explain how to do it after you've opened your doors and have actual numbers to work with.

A P & L is made by totaling your revenues and then subtracting your expenses from that total for a specific period of time, usually each month. If you use accounting software, it will generate a P & L automatically with the data you enter from your sales and expense records. For each month you'll be able to see whether your revenues are higher or lower than your expenses and by how much. At year-end you can total the monthly results to obtain your annual profit or loss.

To create a profit and loss statement, you'll need to subtract your "fixed costs" and your "variable costs" from your sales revenue, but first you'll need to understand the difference between the two. Fixed costs (also called overhead) are the costs associated with running your business in general, not with individual products or services themselves. Variable costs (also called costs of sale, or product or labor costs) are the expenses that are directly tied to the product or service that you're selling. For example, say your business produces and sells greeting cards. Your variable costs would include the cost of the paper and printing of the cards and the labor cost for the workers that make, package and distribute the cards. As the name implies, these costs will vary depending on the amount and type of product you make and sell or service you perform. For example, if you produce more or less of a particular greeting card or if you emboss or use a heavier grade of card stock, your variable expenses will be affected.

Labor costs are sometimes considered variable, sometimes fixed. If you ask a group of accountants whether the labor costs associated with making a product are fixed or variable, you're likely to get conflicting answers. Some argue that as long as the workers will get paid regardless of whether they're working on that product, their salaries should be considered fixed, like rent or utilities. Others say that to have accurate financial records you need to reflect the cost of the labor that goes into a product. You or your accountant can decide how your business will categorize labor costs for making a product. Labor costs for providing services, on the other hand, are almost always treated as variable costs.

But other costs—your fixed costs—will not go up or down depending on the products you make or the services you perform. These costs, such as your rent, your office utility bills and the insurance you purchase for your company vehicles will be more or less the same, regardless of the amount or type of greeting cards you make. This is exactly why age-old business wisdom says to keep your overhead costs as low as you can. In times of slow sales you want to be saddled with as few fixed costs as possible.

Now that you know the distinction between variable and fixed costs, you need to understand how they're each subtracted from your revenue on a typical profit and loss statement (hang in there—we're almost done).

- A profit and loss statement starts with your total sales revenues (remember, you enter that information on your income ledger), and then subtracts your variable costs (recorded in one or more columns of your expenditure ledger). The result is called your gross profit—how much money you've earned from sales of your products or services above their cost to you.

- Next you subtract your fixed costs (again, from your expediter ledger) from your gross profit. Any money you're left with is your real profit—also called net income, net profit or pre-tax profit. Other than the various taxes you'll need to pay on this income, this is your (and any other business owners') money.

To sum up, the formula used in a profit and loss statement is basically as follows:

sales revenue
– variable costs (a.k.a. costs of sale)
= gross profit (a.k.a. gross margin)
– fixed costs
= net profit

Here's a typical P & L:

2000 Profit/Loss Statement							
	January	February	March	April	May	December	Year Total
Sales Revenues	$ 1,900	$1,950	$2,000	$1,850	$2,000	$2,100	$23,550
Variable Costs	300	310	350	300	325	350	$3,840
Gross Profit	**1,600**	**1,640**	**1,650**	**1,550**	**1,675**	**1,750**	**$19,180**
Fixed Expenses							
Rent	700	700	700	700	700	700	$8,400
Supplies	150	100	75	90	125	100	$1,220
Utilities	200	200	200	200	200	200	$2,400
Advertising	150	150	150	150	150	150	$1,800
Misc.	75	80	65	70	75	85	$830
Total Fixed Expenses	**1,275**	**1,230**	**1,190**	**1,210**	**1,250**	**1,235**	**$14,650**
Net Income (Loss)	**$ 325**	**$410**	**$460**	**$340**	**$425**	**$515**	**$4,530**

The P & L will not only tell you whether you're making or losing money, but is also an absolutely crucial tool to help you identify which aspects of your business need tinkering with in order to boost profits. Often, a profitability problem can be found in your expenses. Being able to see the totals of each of your various expense categories over the course of several months all on one sheet can help you pinpoint areas where you're spending too much money (and hopefully help give you the courage to do something about it). And, of course, accurately tracking income totals month by month will help you quickly spot a downturn in revenue and prompt you to take action to boost sales.

2. Cash Flow Projection

We discussed cash flow projections in Chapter 5, "Drafting an Effective Business Plan," as a way to find out if your business would be able to pay its bills once it got started. A cash flow projection is also a crucial tool to use in your ongoing business. It's essential for your business to have enough cash available at any given time to pay for its costs of operation. Having lots of customers and thriving sales isn't enough, especially if you sell on credit. If your customers pay you in 90 days, but you must pay your expenses in 30 days, or even immediately, you may face a situation where, even though your financial statement says you are making a profit, you can't pay your rent, utilities, delivery services or other key bills. Unless you make some changes, you may have to take out a line of credit or even close up shop.

Understanding why you may not be able to pay your bills despite being profitable—and how to take steps to avoid this—is where a cash flow projection comes in. A cash flow projection focuses on the actual cash payments made to and by your business. We call these payments cash-ins and cash-outs (or inflows and outflows) to differentiate them from sales and expenses, which may not be paid right away. Estimating your cash-ins and cash-outs for upcoming months can help you predict when you might run short, allowing you to take action early by tightening up on your credit terms, raising more capital, getting a loan or line of credit, or putting more effort into collecting accounts receivable. Without a prediction of when a cash shortage might happen, by the time it does it may be too late to do anything about it other than lock your doors.

Your cash flow projection will use most of the same numbers as your profit and loss statement, along with a few new ones. The big difference is that your cash flow projection will include all of your sources of income—not just sales income—and only income that's paid in cash (not credit). In other words, while your profit and loss statement is concerned with how much revenue your business is earning through sales of its products or services, your cash flow projection is designed to show you how much cash you will have on hand from all sources, including paid sales, loans, interest from investments, transfers from your personal accounts, lottery winnings, whatever. That's because when it comes to paying bills, the bottom line is whether you have enough money, period. Similarly, your cash flow projection will include all money you pay out of the business, whether for supplies, taxes (including any estimated taxes you owe; see Chapter 8, Section E), loan repayments or any other expenditure.

The basic formula for cash flow analysis is:

cash in bank at beginning of month
+ cash receipts for the month
– cash disbursements for the month
= cash in bank at end of month

In a cash flow projection, each month starts with the amount of money you have in the bank. (This will generally be the same amount that's left over from the previous month.) Next, you'll add any cash that came in during the month in all relevant categories, such as sales income, loans, interest earned and any personal money you put into the business—your total cash-ins for the month. Next, subtract the money you spent during the month, your cash-outs. The result is the cash left at the end of the month. Enter that figure into the beginning of the next month's column, and do the same process for the next month. If you use accounting software, a cash flow spreadsheet can be generated automatically once you've entered figures for income and expenses.

Now that you see the basic formula behind cash flow analysis, you need to understand that the real power of this tool is not in tracking actual cash-ins and cash-outs, but in predicting future cash flows. Periodically, say once a month or every couple months, you should use your actual figures to help you make estimates for upcoming months and complete a cash flow projection for the future, generally up to one year. Hopefully you'll see that you will have enough cash to cover your expenses each month. If not, don't panic. First, pat yourself on the back for doing a cash flow analysis and figuring out ahead of time that you won't be able to cover all your expenses. Then come up with a plan—either put off some expenses that can wait, get more money (perhaps through collecting accounts receivable or getting a short-term loan or line of credit), or sell, sell, sell more product.

Especially when you're in the early stages of a business and don't have much of a business history, predicting cash-ins and cash-outs for future months isn't easy. (Though cash-outs are often easier to predict than cash-ins because you have more control over them and many costs recur each month.) You'll need to make estimates of how much income will come in and what expenses must be covered—a task that may seem only slightly easier than reading tea leaves. The key is to do your best—with an emphasis on "do." Accept the fact that your estimates won't be close to 100% accurate, but make them anyway. As the months tick by and the flow of cash into and out from your business settles into daily, weekly and monthly patterns, making estimates will inevitably become easier and you'll find them increasingly more accurate.

An example of a cash flow projection you can do on a simple spreadsheet is shown below.

As you can see, arranging income and expense information into a cash flow projection reveals a lot about the financial workings of a business. For example, our sample cash flow forecast shows that cash is tight each and every month (look at the "Cash at End of Month" row), so the business owner might consider ways to cut costs or to tighten credit terms. Of more pressing importance is the projected cash shortfall starting in June. Knowing a few months in advance that a shortage is likely will help the business owner figure out what to do while there's still time to take action. She could contribute some personal money to the business (note that the cash flow didn't include any loans or personal transfers to the business), or she could try to cut some nonessential expenses, at least until later in the year when there will be a bit (but only a small bit) more cash available.

Credit lines provide flexibility and cash flow. One good strategy for a small business owner who expects seasonal fluctuations in her cash flow is to apply for a revolving line of credit from her bank. A line of credit works on the same principle as a credit card. The business can borrow funds up to the credit line limit on an as-needed basis and only has to pay interest on the outstanding balance (not the entire credit line). The business can choose to pay funds back and reborrow them as necessary during the time the credit line is open—credit lines can be open for a specified period, such as five or ten years, or can be open-ended (like a credit card).

Compare your projection to reality. Each month, replace your projections with actual results from your accounting system. It's a great way to see how good a job of projecting you're doing.

Who Needs to Do a Cash Flow Analysis?

David Rothenberg, a CPA who also happens to be Chief Financial Officer at Nolo, gives the following advice: "If your business is wildly profitable, you have little or no debt, you are not planning on expanding your business anytime soon and you don't grant your customers a long time to pay, you probably don't need to do a cash flow analysis—you already know you'll have plenty of cash to meet your needs. But if this doesn't sound like your business, then you probably will benefit from keeping a close eye on your cash flow. Remember, the cash flow statement isn't for the IRS and it isn't for the bank; it's for you! That's right, YOU! You're the one who won't sleep at night if your bank account is empty. So what are you waiting for? Get out there and start projecting!"

☑ Chapter 10 Checklist

☐ Decide whether to use the cash or accrual system of accounting.

☐ Keep records of all payments to and from your business. Create an organized system for keeping your receipts.

☐ Summarize your income and expense records into ledgers on a regular basis. Businesses with high volumes of sales or expenses should do this frequently, like daily or weekly.

☐ Use your income and expense ledgers to create financial reports such as a profit/loss statement and a cash flow analysis.

☐ Consult with an accountant or tax professional at least once a year to keep your system on track.

Cash Flow Projection, Completed April, 2000

	Jan	Feb	Mar	April	May
Cash at Beginning of Month	$ 2,000	$1,250	$600	$700	$350
Cash-ins					
Sales Paid	15,000	14,750	15,500	14,750	15,500
Loans and Transfers	0	0	0	0	0
Total Cash-ins	**15,000**	**14,750**	**15,500**	**14,750**	**15,500**
Cash-outs					
Variable Costs	3,000	3,100	3,500	3,000	3,250
Rent	7,000	7,000	7,000	7,000	7,000
Supplies	1,500	1,000	750	900	1,250
Utilities	2,000	2,000	2,000	2,000	2,000
Loan Payments	1,500	1,500	1,500	1,500	1,500
Misc.	750	800	650	700	750
Total Cash-outs	**15,750**	**15,400**	**15,400**	**15,100**	**15,750**
Cash at End of Month	**$1,250**	**$600**	**$700**	**$350**	**$100**

June	July	Aug	Sept	Oct	Nov	Dec	Year Total
$100	($300)	$150	$0	$0	($550)	$300	$ 2,000
15,000	16,100	16,250	15,500	15,250	16,750	16,900	$187,250
0	0	0	0	0	0	0	0
15,000	**16,100**	**16,250**	**15,500**	**15,250**	**16,750**	**16,900**	**$187,250**
3,150	3,450	3,500	3,250	3,300	3,400	3,550	$39,450
7,000	7,000	7,000	7,000	7,000	7,000	7,000	$84,000
900	1,100	850	1,000	1,100	950	900	$12,200
2,000	2,000	2,000	2,000	2,000	2,000	2,000	$24,000
1,500	1,500	1,500	1,500	1,500	1,500	1,500	$18,000
850	600	1,550	750	900	1,050	850	$10,200
15,400	**15,650**	**16,400**	**15,500**	**15,800**	**15,900**	**15,800**	**$187,850**
(300)	**150**	**0**	**0**	**(550)**	**300**	**1,400**	**$1,400**

Growing Your Business and Hiring Workers

A. Employees vs. Independent Contractors 11/2

    1. The Agencies That Matter 11/2

    2. IRS Criteria 11/3

B. Special Hurdles for Employers 11/5

If all your careful planning, hard work and good karma pays off, you may soon find yourself needing one or more people to help you handle your thriving business (if you haven't already). While part of you will surely be happy that your business is taking off, another, more practical side of you may worry about what's involved in hiring help. This chapter offers a broad overview of the many legal requirements that apply to businesses that have one or more employees. If you're thinking about hiring an employee but aren't sure, the information we give here should help you understand what you're getting into—and help you figure out if there's a better way to go.

Besides the practical and financial concerns involved in hiring one or more people to work for your business, you need to be aware of several legal rules that apply to businesses with workers (who are not the business owners). First of all, you'll need to understand the difference between the two types of hired help: employees and independent contractors. This distinction is a crucial one, because different rules will apply to your business depending on what kind of workers you hire. If the government considers your workers to be employees, you'll be subject to a number of state and federal laws that must be strictly observed

and taxes that must be paid. If, on the other hand, your workers can be characterized as independent contractors, you'll be spared many—but not all—of these requirements and taxes.

A. Employees vs. Independent Contractors

As just mentioned, whenever someone works for your business, that person is either an employee or an independent contractor (assuming they're not an owner). In a nutshell, an employee is someone who works for you, on your site, with your tools and equipment and according to your rules and procedures. Independent contractors, on the other hand, are in business for themselves; they work on their own time and with their own tools, and perform services for a number of different clients.

We'll cover this distinction more fully below and introduce the legal rules that go with each type of worker, but for now ingrain it in your mind that it's a distinction not to be taken lightly. The main reason it's a big deal is that businesspeople who hire employees owe a number of employment taxes, such as payroll tax and unemployment tax, while those who hire only independent contractors do not owe these taxes. If you treat an employee as an independent contractor and fail to pay employment taxes, you risk subjecting yourself a huge back-tax bill, plus interest and other state and federal penalties. More than a few businesses have been torpedoed and sunk into bankruptcy after making this mistake.

With that warning in mind, here's the lowdown on classifying your workers.

1. The Agencies That Matter

Since paying taxes is the main fallout of classifying workers as employees, it shouldn't surprise you to learn that the IRS takes a great interest in whether your workers are classified properly. At the federal level, the IRS will take swift and severe action if it finds out that you're treating a worker as an independent contractor, when he really meets the criteria of an employee. At the state level, there are rules for classifying workers that may be stricter or otherwise different from the IRS rules. Since the penalties at the state level can be at least as harsh as the IRS's, be sure you understand the rules in your state. The state agency in charge of worker status rules and enforcement is generally an employment agency, tax department, unemployment office or other employment-related bureau. A list of the state agencies in charge of worker classification—the unemployment compensations agencies—is included in Appendix A.

2. IRS Criteria

Strangely enough, the IRS has not issued any hard or fast rules as to when workers should be treated as employees and when they can be considered independent contractors. The IRS does, however, have internal guidelines for its auditors that are generally accepted in the business world as the rules to use when deciding what legal status to give to your workers.

A worker should normally be considered an employee, not an independent contractor, when he:
- works only for you and not for any other business
- works on your premises
- uses your tools and equipment
- follows work hours set by you
- follows your instructions on how to complete a job
- receives reimbursement for expenses incurred in doing a job
- supervises any of your other workers, or
- receives any employee benefits, such as holiday pay, vacation time or health insurance.

On the flip side, a worker should probably be considered an independent contractor if he:
- works for a number of different businesses or clients

- has his own office, studio, garage or other permanent place to work
- uses his own equipment and tools
- sets his own hours
- uses his own judgment as to how best to complete a job
- doesn't get reimbursed for expenses incurred in doing a job, or
- advertises his services to the public.

Of course, lots of times a worker you hire might display some characteristics of both categories, which makes it harder to say for sure how that worker should be classified. Ultimately, you'll need to consider these factors all together and weigh them against each other to decide whether a worker should be classified as an employee or as an independent contractor.

EXAMPLE 1: Bob does a lot of freelance proofreading for a publisher of books on alternative health, Wholeness Press. He often works for Wholeness Press (about ten projects per year), but he also does four or five jobs per year for other publishers. He always works at home, receives minimal instructions as to how to do his work, and does his proofreading whenever he feels like it. Bob can probably be categorized as an independent contractor.

EXAMPLE 2: Susan programs almost exclusively for one software developer, Fizz Games, but she also does approximately one outside project per year. She sometimes works from home, but often uses a computer at Fizz Games' office. She works closely with the software development team at Fizz Games, following instructions from some of the developers while training some of the newer workers in programming techniques. The government is likely to see Susan as a true employee. It would be risky to try to treat her as an independent contractor.

In borderline situations, it's of course safer to treat a worker as an employee than risk the penalties that may result if the IRS or your state decides you've misclassified an employee as an independent contractor. Keep in mind that the IRS and most states tend to disfavor independent contractor status—they'd much rather see borderline workers treated as employees, so that they can collect taxes on them.

If you can't decide how one of your workers should be classified, there are a few ways you can proceed. One is to consult a lawyer or an accountant who understands business tax laws. Another option is to go straight to the horse's mouth and ask the IRS or your state agency to tell you how they would classify a certain worker. To ask the IRS, you can file Form SS-8, *Determination of Employee Work Status*, to request a formal ruling on a worker's status. You can get this form from an IRS office or from their website at www.irs.ustreas.gov. Don't be surprised if the IRS says they're an employee!

Classifying Workers: Don't Make the Same Mistake Microsoft Did

"Microsoft." Who would think that lowly temporary workers would be able to beat one of the world's mightiest economic juggernauts? But they did just that, which should be a lesson to all businesses that hire independent contractors. Like many software companies, Microsoft added to its regular core of permanent employees a pool of workers whom it classified as independent "freelancers," paying them cash compensation (sometimes more than its employees), but none of the fringe benefits. Microsoft had the workers sign agreements providing that they were independent contractors, which meant Microsoft wouldn't give them fringe benefits or withhold or pay any taxes for them.

The problem with Microsoft's designation of these workers as ICs was that it failed to treat them like ICs—that is, people running their own independent businesses. Instead, Microsoft integrated the workers into its workforce: they often worked on teams along with regular employees, sharing the same supervisors, performing identical functions, and working the same core hours. And because Microsoft required that they work on site, they received admittance card keys, office equipment and supplies from the company. Microsoft's treatment of the workers clearly spelled out "employee," not independent contractor.

When the IRS audited the company's payroll tax accounts in 1989 and 1990, it determined that since Microsoft treated the workers as employees—not independent contractors who control the manner and means of how their services are performed—they had to be treated as employees for purposes of FICA, FUTA and withholding taxes. Microsoft agreed with the IRS and admitted that the workers should have been classified as employees for tax purposes. The company paid back-payroll taxes and overtime for the workers and moved some of them to permanent employee status.

Upon learning of the IRS's payroll tax determination, eight of the formerly misclassified workers sued Microsoft for full employee benefits for the time they worked as independent contractors. The workers finally won their lawsuit, and Microsoft had to pay a small fortune to its misclassified workers. (*Vizcaino v. Microsoft Corp.*, 120 F.3d 1006 (9th Cir. 1997).)

This case once again shows that merely having a worker sign an agreement that he or she is an IC will not make him or her one in the eyes of the law. Rather, the worker must be treated like an IC on the job. Since the penalties for misclassification can be severe, you must make sure that everyone who deals with ICs in your company understands that they can't be supervised or otherwise controlled in the same way as employees.

For a state determination, contact your state employment or other agency that governs worker classification and find out what procedure it uses. (See Appendix A for contact information for the agency that classifies workers in your state.) Like the IRS, it's common for states to classify workers as employees rather than independent contractors. You'll have to decide for yourself whether it makes sense to leave the determination up to these agencies, or whether you feel confident enough to classify your workers on your own. If you decide that all of your workers will be independent contractors, the rest of the rules in this chapter won't apply to you. You may still want to read on, however, if you'd like to get an overview of the regulations that apply to businesses with employees.

⚠️ Hiring independent contractors triggers some requirements. For instance, if you pay any independent contractor over $600 in a year, you need to report those payments on Form 1099, which gets sent to the worker and to the IRS. For in-depth information about hiring independent contractors, see *Hiring Independent Contractors: The Employer's Legal Guide,* by Stephen Fishman (Nolo).

B. Special Hurdles for Employers

As soon as you hire your first employee, you unleash a swarm of legal requirements that apply specifically to employers. Not only will you have to pay a number of employment taxes, but you'll need to register with certain government agencies, pay for certain types of insurance and comply with various laws, such as those requiring you to keep a smoke-free workplace and to post certain notices at your business premises.

While the many laws that apply to employers are beyond the scope of this book, here's an overview of the major requirements that apply to businesses with employees. If your needs can't be met by hiring an independent contractor and you

must hire an employee, you'll need to consult additional resources to make sure you comply with the many state and federal laws governing employers. (We list some additional resources at the end of this chapter.)

In general, owners of businesses with one or more employees are required to do the following:

- Report all new hires for your state's employment department within at least 20 days of the employee's first day of work.
- Obtain workers' compensation insurance and follow rules on notifying employees of their rights to workers' compensation benefits. You may purchase this insurance from a state fund or from a private insurance company.
- Comply with state and federal job safety laws, administered by the federal Occupational Safety and Health Administration (OSHA) and the agency in your state that governs workplace safety. This includes filing an illness and injury prevention plan, reporting work-related injuries and illnesses that result in lost work-time and keeping a log of all work-related injuries and illnesses. For more information about OSHA regulations, visit the OSHA website at www.osha.gov, or contact OSHA at U.S. Department of Labor, Occupational Safety & Health Administration, Office of Public Affairs, Room N3647, 200 Constitution Avenue, Washington, DC 20210, 202-693-1999.
- Withhold federal income taxes and FICA taxes (which basically consist of Social Security and Medicare taxes) from employees' paychecks and periodically report and send these withheld taxes to the IRS.
- Report wages and withholding to each employee and to the IRS with Form W-2.
- Pay the employer's portion of Social Security and Medicare tax for each employee, based on the employee's wages. The employer's portion is the same amount as the employee's share: 7.65% of the employee's wages up to $76,200, and 1.45% of wages in excess of that amount.

- Withhold state income taxes from employees' paychecks and periodically deposit them with your state income tax agency.

- Pay federal unemployment taxes. It's the sole responsibility of the employer to pay the Federal Unemployment Tax (FUTA) directly to the IRS; it may not be deducted from employees' paychecks. For the year 2000, the general rule is that you must pay FUTA taxes if you paid a total of $1,500 in wages or more in any calendar quarter or if you had one or more employees for at least some part of a day in each of 20 or more calendar weeks (not necessarily consecutive) during the year. If you have to pay FUTA taxes, you must pay a 6.2% tax (for the year 2000) on the first $7,000 of wages that you pay each employee during the year. The FUTA tax is reported annually on IRS Form 940, *Employer's Annual Federal Unemployment Tax Return.*

- Pay state unemployment taxes (not all states). Most states require employers to pay unemployment taxes, which go towards a state unemployment insurance fund. Generally, you can take a credit of up to 5.4% against your FUTA tax for amounts you paid into state unemployment funds. A list of state unemployment tax agencies is available in IRS Publication 926, *Household Employer's Tax Guide,* available from the IRS's website at www.irs.treas.gov.

Thinking twice about becoming an employer? There's no way around it: adding employees to your business will greatly complicate your life. (And we haven't even discussed providing optional benefits, such as health insurance and 401(k) plans.) If there's a way to meet your needs with independent contractors rather than employees, it may be a much more practical road to take. At the very least, you shouldn't jump into hiring employees without having a clear reason to do so.

 Consult additional resources for information on being an employer. Nolo's *The Employer's Legal Handbook,* by attorney Fred S. Steingold, is an indispensable, comprehensive reference for employers that covers the legal rules on hiring, firing, taxes, workplace safety and much more. Or, if you're strapped for time, but want a quick guide to steering clear of legal problems with your employees, check out *Avoid Employee Lawsuits,* by attorney Barbara Kate Repa, also published by Nolo. For information on hiring independent contractors, be sure to read *Hiring Independent Contractors: The Employer's Legal Guide,* by Stephen Fishman (Nolo).

☑ **Chapter 11 Checklist**

☐ Familiarize yourself with the legal differences between employees and independent contractors.

☐ Before hiring help, determine whether you need to hire employees or whether you could hire independent contractors instead.

☐ Don't avoid the obligations of having employees by misclassifying your workers as independent contractors. If the IRS decides your workers are really employees, you can face serious penalties including payment of back payroll taxes.

☐ Make sure you're ready to take care of all the legal, bureaucratic and tax requirements that apply to businesses with employees before hiring your first employee.

Getting Professional Help

A. Working With Lawyers 12/2

    1. What to Look for in a Lawyer.. 12/2

    2. How to Find a Lawyer 12/3

    3. Using a Lawyer as a Coach 12/3

    4. Dealing With Bills and Payments 12/4

B. Working With Accountants and Other Professionals 12/5

    1. Different Professionals for Different Needs 12/6

    2. Finding Good Professional Help 12/6

C. Internet Legal Research 12/7

Most business owners, especially sole proprietors and partners in general partnerships, won't need to rely on professional help for the vast majority of their day-to-day business affairs. As the chapters in this book have shown, the legal tasks involved in starting a business, as well as many of those involved in its ongoing operation, involve nothing more than complying with simple bureaucratic requirements, filling out standard forms and paying fees.

But life's not always so simple, of course, and from time to time you may find yourself feeling like you're in over your head. Maybe you're struggling to decide whether it's a good time, financially speaking, to expand your business. Or perhaps there's a dispute brewing between you and a business partner. These situations are just a couple of examples of the types of situations where an expert can come in handy.

Even when things are running smoothly, virtually every business should at least occasionally consult an accountant or other tax expert for help in preparing tax returns. A tax professional can also be extremely helpful in figuring out how to manage your business's finances in order to minimize your taxes. Making contact with a lawyer and a tax person early in your business life is often a sensible step. As your business grows, you'll be able to consult these pros for help with ongoing questions.

Once you decide you want to hire a professional, your next question very likely will be, "How do I find someone I can trust?" This chapter will offer strategies that will help you find and hire a professional such as a lawyer or an accountant who's competent and aboveboard. We'll also talk about an increasingly popular type of service called "legal coaching," which is starting to replace traditional lawyering in many cases.

A. Working With Lawyers

Despite the fact that the attorney section of the Yellow Pages is often the biggest section of the phone book, a good lawyer can be hard to find. This section discusses how to find a lawyer who meets your needs and how to make sure you're getting the most for your hard-earned money.

1. What to Look for in a Lawyer

There are a number of different qualities that are important for your lawyer to have. For one, you want to make sure to find an attorney who has some experience with small business issues, preferably for your type of small business. Plus, you want someone who's intelligent and competent—two qualities that don't necessarily go hand in hand with having a law degree. And, of course, you want a lawyer whom you can trust.

In today's world of ever-increasing specialization, lawyers often focus their areas of expertise rather narrowly. For example, an expert negotiator may not be an effective courtroom lawyer, and vice versa. Make sure that your lawyer can handle the particular type of problem you're facing, both in terms of its subject matter and the type of work involved.

In addition to finding a lawyer with the skills and experience relevant to your situation, it's important that you and the lawyer get along on a personal level. If an otherwise perfect lawyer—smart, experienced and trustworthy—is condescending or rude, you might as well keep looking for someone with better personal skills. This general rule is especially true for small business owners who will ideally develop a long-term relationship with a lawyer. The better an attorney knows you and your business, the more she will be able to provide the best advice and assistance for your specific situation.

Finally, you may want to make a special effort to find a lawyer who is willing to work with you collaboratively on certain matters that you can handle at least partially on your own. Some routine legal issues, such as amending your partnership agreement or executing a contract for services, may be well within your abilities to handle, though you may be more comfortable having a lawyer review your work or give you limited advice. While lawyers traditionally offered their services on an all-or-none basis (and charged fees accordingly), a trend has recently emerged where lawyers act as coaches for their clients, giving only as much service as the client wants. If you'd like to be more involved with your business's legal matters and minimize the attorney's fees you'll owe, be sure to ask the lawyer directly whether she is willing to have this kind of working relationship with you. Legal coaching is discussed in more detail in Section 3 below.

2. How to Find a Lawyer

Unfortunately, the easiest and quickest ways to find a lawyer are usually the least effective. Sure, you'll find hundreds of lawyers' names in the Yellow Pages, but how will you choose among them? You'll have the same problem if you look in legal newspapers for attorney ads. By the way, flashy, aggressive advertising is definitely not a good indicator of quality legal services. Also, watch out for commercial referral services that collect fees from lawyers who are in their referral database. To filter out the lawyers who are wrong for you, you'll need to do more research.

The best way to find a good lawyer is to get a personal referral, preferably from someone who runs a small business. Even better is a referral from an owner of a business that's similar to yours. Book publishers, for instance, face different types of legal issues than do auto repair shops, and would be best served by a lawyer familiar with legal areas such as copyright and the First Amendment. Ask other businesspeople for lawyer recommendations.

If you just can't find anyone who can give you a personal referral, try investigating which lawyers work in your industry. One good way to do this is to keep your eyes and ears open for names of attorneys who have worked on cases in your field. For example, a trade magazine might have an article about a current lawsuit involving a business

similar to yours that mentions the names of the attorneys working on it. You can also contact organizations and visit websites that focus on your type of business. They can often direct you to lawyers who have worked in your industry. Once you get some names, try calling these lawyers and asking if they're available. If not, there's a good chance they know someone else who might be able to help you.

 When you call a prospective lawyer, speak with the lawyer personally, not just the receptionist. You can probably get a good idea of how the attorney operates by paying close attention to the way your call is handled. Is the lawyer available right away, and if not, is your call promptly returned? Is the lawyer willing to spend at least a few minutes talking to you to determine if she really is the best person for the job? Do you get a good personal feeling from your conversation? The way you're treated during your initial call can be a good indicator of how the lawyer treats clients in general.

3. Using a Lawyer As a Coach

In a traditional attorney/client relationship, a client hires an attorney to take care of a legal problem and then hands over all responsibility for—and control of—the matter to the lawyer. While some clients like it this way, many would rather be more involved in their cases, both to maintain some control and to save money on legal fees. But until recently, limited legal help from a lawyer wasn't much of an option. Most lawyers wouldn't take cases unless they could handle them fully on their own.

But a new model of legal services is finally emerging. In this approach, sometimes called "legal coaching" or "unbundled legal services," a lawyer provides only the services that a client wants, and nothing more. For example, a client who wants legal help in drafting a contract can arrange a short consulting session with a lawyer to get answers to general questions, go home and draft the contract herself, and then fax it to the lawyer, who will review it and suggest changes. Or a client who wants to represent himself in small claims court can use a lawyer to help him draft motions and prepare for hearings but otherwise pursue the case on his own.

For a small business owner, using a lawyer as a coach can be especially useful. More often than not, the legal issues that arise in the course of business are relatively simple, and—with a bit of good legal advice—are within the capabilities of most people to handle. Many times, a business owner needs nothing more than some guidance through the bureaucratic maze that small businesses need to navigate. For instance, a business person facing a zoning conflict may be perfectly served by a five-minute explanation from a legal coach on the process of appealing a planning commission's decision. Rather than hiring an attorney for upwards of $1,000 to deal with the problem, using a coach might cost $50 and enable the business owner to proceed on her own.

Getting limited legal help from a lawyer has become an increasingly popular approach to legal problems in recent years, though it still can take some effort to find a lawyer who is willing to be just a coach. To find a legal coach, use the same strategies discussed above (personal referrals, for

example) but take the extra step of asking the lawyer directly whether he or she is willing to help you in your efforts to solve your own legal problems. If you don't find one right away, be persistent. In today's increasingly competitive legal marketplace, it's becoming easier to find lawyers who are willing to be flexible in the services they offer.

4. Dealing With Bills and Payments

One area of expertise in which most lawyers are well practiced is billing for their services. Before you hire any lawyer, be sure you fully understand how your fees will be calculated. All too often, clients are unpleasantly surprised by their bills because they didn't pay enough attention to the billing terms when they hired the lawyer. For instance, make sure you understand who's responsible for items like court fees, copy fees, transcription costs and phone bills. These costs aren't trivial, and can quickly send your otherwise affordable bill into the keep-you-awake-at-night range.

Lawyers generally use one of the following methods of calculating fees for their services.

- **Hourly fees.** This arrangement works just like it sounds: you pay the attorney's hourly rate for the number of hours she works on your case. Simple as this system is, there are some details to consider. One is to find out what hourly increments the lawyer uses for billing. For instance, if an attorney bills in half-hour increments, then you'll be charged a full half-hour even if you talk for just five minutes. That can easily total $100 or more for a five-minute phone call—a rate that would make even AT&T blush. You'd be better off if your lawyer uses ten- or 15-minute periods, though not all attorneys break down their time into such small increments.

    Another issue to ask about is whether all time spent on the case—even if the attorney isn't doing the work—is billed at the attorney's regular rate. For example, it's reasonable to expect a discounted rate for time spent by the attorney's administrative staff on making copies or organizing paperwork. Make sure that the hourly fee for the attorney applies only to the work of the actual attorney.

Hourly fees for attorneys range from $100 or so to over $400 per hour. High rates may reflect a lawyer's extensive experience—or they might simply reflect a need to pay for a swank office. Don't pay the highest rates unless you feel the lawyer's expertise—not his Armani suit—is worth it.

- **Flat fees.** For some types of cases, attorneys will charge a flat fee for a specific task, such as negotiating a contract or filing articles of incorporation for you. As long as the job goes as expected, you'll pay only the price you and the lawyer agreed to, regardless of how many hours she spent on the job. If the lawyer hits a snag, however, or if the case becomes convoluted for some reason, it's possible for the price to go up. Be sure you and the lawyer are on the same page regarding the situations that may result in a higher fee. Also, find out if any charges such as court costs or copy fees are charged in addition to the flat fee.

- **Contingency fees.** In a contingency fee arrangement, you pay an attorney's fee only if the lawyer wins money for you through a court judgment or a negotiated settlement. In that case, the fee you'd pay would be a percentage of the monetary award, usually one-third to one-half. In contingency fee arrangements, you need to be especially careful of costs such as travel expenses, transcription fees and phone bills. If you lose your case, you won't owe attorneys' fees because your lawyer didn't recover any money, but you will often be responsible for the lawyer's out-of-pocket expenses while he was working on your case.

Small business matters don't typically require contingency fee arrangements. This payment method is usually used in personal injury cases and others in which a plaintiff sues someone in hopes of winning a large money award.

- **Retainers.** Sometimes you can hire a lawyer to be more or less "on-call" by paying her a regular fee (usually monthly) called a retainer. This type of arrangement is useful when you have regular, ongoing legal needs such as contract review or negotiation, or a big lawsuit looming in your future. Based upon your expected needs, you and the lawyer settle on a mutually acceptable monthly fee. Then, you simply have the lawyer take care of any routine legal matters that arise. If you run into a sudden, complex legal dispute, or if your problems escalate greatly, you'll likely have to make additional payments. Obviously, for this type of arrangement to work it's important that you and the lawyer have a clear understanding of the routine services that you expect. Unless your legal needs are regular and predictable, a retainer arrangement is probably not your best option.

State laws may require a fee agreement to be in writing in some cases, such as if your lawyer estimates the total cost of legal services to be more than $1,000, or if you have a contingency fee arrangement. Even if it's not legally required, it's always a good idea to get your fee agreement in writing. A written agreement will help prevent disputes over billing, and is the best way to avoid getting gouged.

B. Working With Accountants and Other Professionals

Many, and perhaps most, of the issues that small businesspeople face can be solved by professionals other than lawyers. In particular, tax professionals are often indispensable in helping you deal with tax laws, which have a huge impact on your business both financially and legally. In fact, tax advice is so essential to a successful small business that we recommend that every small business owner consult with a tax expert at least occasionally, say once a year.

Obviously, you want to manage your business and the money flowing through it so as to minimize your tax bill. But you also need to be extremely careful not to violate any tax laws—which are insanely complex—and to avoid making simple mistakes that can result in costly penalties. While complicated tax troubles may indeed call for a tax attorney, many other more common questions can usually be answered by an accountant.

1. Different Professionals for Different Needs

For routine maintenance of your books, you probably don't need the experience—or expense—of an accountant (certified or otherwise). An experienced bookkeeper will be able to implement an effective system of tracking your income and expenses and stay on top of your important bills, including the various taxes your business will owe. Depending on the complexity of your business, you may even decide to do your own bookkeeping—a job that's undoubtedly easier these days with the availability of accounting software. As your business grows, however, the investment in an experienced bookkeeper will likely become worthwhile.

If you find yourself seeking specific tax advice or encountering a tricky financial problem, you may need to go up a step on the professional ladder and hire an accountant who's intimate with tax laws. The top dogs of accountants are called certified public accountants (CPAs), who are licensed and regulated by the state. Uncertified accountants, called public accountants, also may be licensed by your state. Since the licensing requirements for CPAs are more stringent, they are considered to be the most experienced and knowledgeable type of accountants, and accordingly will be the most expensive.

In addition to bookkeepers and accountants, there are other professionals out there who

specialize in tax preparation. The main thing to keep in mind is that some are licensed and some are not. An enrolled agent (EA) is a tax professional licensed by the IRS who can answer tax questions and help you prepare your returns. Others who simply use the title "tax preparer" or "tax return preparer" may not be licensed at all. If a tax professional doesn't have a license as an enrolled agent or as a public or certified public accountant, it may mean that the "professional" has no official qualifications whatsoever.

The bottom line is to use a professional who is best suited for your needs at hand. Obviously, you shouldn't pay a CPA to do simple bookkeeping, nor should you use a bookkeeper for preparing complex tax returns. You'll need to decide for yourself what kind of professional is appropriate for your needs.

2. Finding Good Professional Help

Finding a tax professional is a lot like finding a lawyer: your goal is to find someone both competent and trustworthy. The strategies we discussed above for finding a lawyer are equally useful in finding other professionals. Getting a personal referral is the best way to find someone you can trust. Referrals from businesspeople in your field are particularly valuable. Since virtually every business has consulted a tax pro at one point or another, it shouldn't be too hard to get a decent list of names.

As with attorneys, choose your tax professional carefully, with an eye to developing a long-term relationship. Don't be shy to ask lots of questions. Find out about the person's experience with small businesses similar to yours, and about his or her knowledge of bookkeeping methods, the tax code, the IRS or anything else that's relevant to the work you want the professional to do for you.

Also be sure you understand the professional's fee structure up front, before you have her do any work. Most charge hourly fees, which vary a great deal depending on what kind of qualifications the professional has. Like your attorney fee agreement, your fee agreement with a tax professional should be in writing—written fee agreements minimize the possibility of disputes over the bill.

C. Internet Legal Research

Some of the legal questions you may run into won't warrant an expensive consultation with an attorney, but may be beyond the scope of a self-help book. For instance, you may need to look up specific consumer-protection regulations on warranties and advertising, or find out what your state's rules are on hiring and firing practices. If you don't want to call your lawyer every time you have a question, you might consider doing a little legal research yourself.

Finding basic small business law is usually not difficult—much of the information you'll need can be found on the Internet. Start by visiting Nolo's Small Business Law Center at www.nolo.com/category/sb_home.html to see if your question has already been answered, or to get some background information in the area of the law you're interested in. If you still need to go to the horse's mouth for the answer, you can try looking up the text of the actual law by going to Nolo's Legal Research Center at www.nolo.com/research/index.html. From there you can access the statutes of all 50 states, where you'll be able to find corporation and LLC statutes, laws on contracts and products liability, regulations on health and safety and much more. You can also easily research federal law at Nolo's Legal Research Center, including laws on copyrights, environmental regulations, bankruptcy and IRS rules, to mention a few areas that might be of interest to small business owners.

Here are some other websites that offer helpful information on small business and tax law:

- National Federation of Independent Business at www.nfibonline.com. Here you can find small business news and practical information.

- Internal Revenue Service at www.irs.treas.gov. You can download forms and instructions as well as a wide range of publications that do a fairly good job of explaining the tax laws.
- U.S. Small Business Administration at www.sbaonline.sba.gov. This site has a lot of good information on starting and financing your own business. The SBA also offers links to state websites related to business issues.
- SCORE (Service Corps of Retired Executives) at www.score.org. SCORE's association of retired executives and business owners offers email counseling and mentoring and an excellent directory of small business resources on the Web.
- The Thomas Legislative Information site at thomas.loc.gov. Here you can read small business bills pending in Congress as well as laws that have recently been adopted.

 If, during your legal meandering, you come across strange phrases like "blue sky," "naked option," or "commercial frustration," and you just know there's got to be a legal meaning behind them, try looking them up in Nolo's online Legal Dictionary at http://www.nolo.com/dictionary/wordindex.cfm.

In addition to Nolo.com and other business-oriented sites, you should familiarize yourself with the official website of your state. These sites often offer valuable information for small businesses such as start-up registration requirements, state tax rules, laws on corporations and LLCs, and much more. Keep in mind that there's a lot of variation from state to state in how much info you'll find at their site, but in general the states have been rapidly improving their online information systems and making their sites more useful and accessible for citizens. On the CD-ROM that comes with this book, you'll find computer files that contain links to state websites, including business-related sites and tax sites. These files are simple to use with your Web browser; Appendix B explains how to use them.

Recommended reading on legal research.
We've given you a few helpful hints on getting answers to your small business questions, but there may be times when you'll need more guidance. An excellent resource that teaches you how to find answers to your legal questions is Nolo's book *Legal Research: How to Find and Understand the Law,* by attorneys Stephen Elias and Susan Levinkind. Learning how to use legal resources online or at the law library will empower you to take care of a wide range of simple, everyday matters rather than paying someone else to do them.

☑ Chapter 12 Checklist

☐ Ask business associates and friends for recommendations for lawyers as well as accountants or other tax professionals. Also check trade magazines and other industry sources.

☐ Try to find a lawyer who will work as a legal coach.

☐ Get your fee agreements in writing.

☐ Familiarize yourself with online sources of legal information such as Nolo.com, the IRS website and your official state website.

APPENDIX

A

State Contact Information

Small Business Start-Up Issues A/3

State Tax Agencies A/8

State Sales Tax/Seller's Permit Agencies A/13

LLC Offices A/18

State Unemployment Compensation Agencies A/24

Patent and Trademark Depository Libraries by State A/29

This appendix offers contact information for various business- and tax-related agencies for each state. While we've done our very best to direct you to the most appropriate agency or office for each topic, please keep in mind that governmental agencies often overlap and may not be organized in any logical structure. One state agency may have several offices or programs under its umbrella, and it may be under the administration of yet another office. Often, a governmental agency may provide information (at its website, for instance) that's actually administered by a different agency. And of course, addresses, phone numbers and websites are never permanent and are subject to change. In other words, when it comes to state government offices, it's a jungle out there.

Our goal with these appendixes is to direct you to the office that not only provides the best information on the subject, but that also has some actual authority over the matter. For example, our preference would be to provide contact information to an official state licensing office rather than the

state's chamber of commerce, because even if the chamber offered helpful business licensing information, it wouldn't have authority over licensing matters. We've also done our best to direct you to specific divisions within larger agencies, such as the sales tax division within a state's tax and revenue agency. Sometimes divisions don't offer their own contact info, in which case we simply direct you to the larger office.

A couple other things to keep in mind: As much as possible, we've provided walk-in addresses for the agencies in each appendix, though sometimes only a mailing address was available. Be sure to call before going to the office in person to make sure that office has a service center open to the public. Also, while many state offices offer toll-free phone numbers, some of them are only for calls within the state.

Feedback and information from our readers is always appreciated. If you find information in any of these appendixes, or anywhere else in this book, that is out-of-date or incorrect, please bring it to our attention at cs@nolo.com.

Small Business Start-Up Issues

Alabama

Department of Revenue
Sales, Use & Business Tax Division, Severance
  & License Section
3103 Gordon Persons Building
50 Ripley Street
Montgomery, AL 36132
334-353-7827
http://www.ador.state.al.us/licenses/index.html

Alaska

Department of Community and Economic
  Development
Division of Occupational Licensing
333 Willoughby Ave., 9th Floor, State Office
  Bldg.,
Juneau, AK 99801
907-465-2534
http://www.dced.state.ak.us/occ/home.htm

Arizona

Department of Commerce
Business Connection
3800 N. Central Avenue, Bldg. D
Phoenix, AZ 85012
602-542-4576
http://www.azcommerce.com/smallbus.htm

Arkansas

Department of Economic Development
One Capitol Mall
Little Rock, AR 72201
800-ARKANSAS
501-682-1060
http://www.aedc.state.ar.us/home.html

California

Office of Small Business
801 K Street, Suite 1700
Sacramento, CA 95814
800-303-6600
916-322-5790
http://www.commerce.ca.gov/business/small/

Colorado

Small Business Development Center
Business Assistance Center
1625 Broadway, Suite 805
Denver, CO 80202
303-592-5920
800-333-7798
http://www.state.co.us/gov_dir/oed/bac.html

Connecticut

Connecticut Economic Resource Center, Inc.
805 Brook Street, Building #4
Rocky Hill, CT 06067-3405
860-571-7136
800-392-2122
http://www.cerc.com

Delaware

Division of Revenue
820 North French Street
P.O. Box 2340
Wilmington, DE 19899-2340
302-577-5800
http://www.state.de.us/coop/basics.htm

District of Columbia

Department of Consumer and Regulatory Affairs
941 North Capitol Street, NE
Washington, DC 20002
202-442-4515
http://www.dcra.org

Florida

Enterprise Florida, Inc. (EFI)
390 North Orange Avenue
Suite 1300
Orlando, FL 32801
407-316-4600
http://www.floridabusiness.com/default.html

Georgia

Secretary of State
First Stop Business Information Center
Suite 315, West Tower
2 Martin Luther King, Jr. Drive
Atlanta, GA 30334
404-656-7061
800-656-4558
http://www.sos.state.ga.us/FirstStop/default.htm

Hawaii

Department of Commerce and Consumer Affairs
Business Registration Division
1010 Richards Street
Honolulu, HI 96813
808-586-2744
http://www.businessregistrations.com/

Idaho

Department of Commerce
700 West State Street
P.O. Box 83720
Boise, ID 83720-0093
208-334-2470
http://www.idoc.state.id.us

Illinois

Department of Commerce and Community
  Affairs
100 West Randolph St., Suite 3-400
Chicago, IL 60601
312-814-7179
http://www.commerce.state.il.us/doingbusiness/
  First_Stop/Permits.htm

Indiana

Department of Commerce
One North Capitol, Suite 700
Indianapolis, IN 46204
317-232-8800
http://www.ai.org/doc/doingbiz/index.html

Iowa

Department of Economic Development
Small Business Resource Office
200 East Grand
Des Moines, IA 50309
515-242-4750
800-532-1216
http://www.state.ia.us/ided/index.html

Kansas

Department of Commerce and Housing
Business Development Division
700 SW Harrison St., Suite 1300
Topeka, KS 66603-3712
785-296-5298
http://www.kansascommerce.com

Kentucky

Cabinet for Economic Development
Business Information Clearinghouse
Capital Plaza Tower
Frankfort, KY 40601
502-564-4252 ext. 4317
800-626-2250
http://www.edc.state.ky.us/kyedc/
  ebpermits.html

Louisiana

Secretary of State
First Stop Shop Division
P.O. Box 94125
Baton Rouge, LA 70804-9125
225-922-2675
800-259-0001
http://www.sec.state.la.us/comm/fss-index.htm

Maine

Department of Economic and Community
  Development
Office of Business Development
59 State House Station
Augusta, ME 04333
207-287-3153
http://www.econdevmaine.com/

Maryland

Department of Business and Economic
Development
217 East Redwood St.
Baltimore, MD 21202-3316
410-767-6300
http://www.blis.state.md.us/

Massachusetts

Office of Business Development
1 Ashburton Place, Room 2101
Boston, MA 02108
617-727-3206
800-5-CAPITAL
http://www.state.ma.us/mobd/toc.htm

Michigan

Economic Development Corporation
201 N. Washington Square, 4th Floor
Lansing, MI 48913
517-373-9808
http://medc.michigan.org/glocation/
starting_index.htm

Minnesota

Department of Trade and Economic
Development
Small Business Assistance Office
500 Metro Square
121 7th Place East
St. Paul, MN 55101
651-282-2103
800-657-3858
http://www.dted.state.mn.us/01x03x02.asp

Mississippi

Department of Economic and Community
Development
P.O. Box 849
Jackson, MS 39205
601-359-3593
http://www.mississippi.org/decd/existing/
exist_howto.htm

Missouri

Department of Economic Development
Business Assistance Center
301 West High Street, Room 720
P.O. Box 118
Jefferson City, MO 65102-0118
888-751-2863
http://www.ecodev.state.mo.us/mbac

Montana

Department of Commerce
Small Business Development Center
1424 Ninth Ave.
Helena, MT 59620
406-444-4109
800-221-8015
http://commerce.state.mt.us/EconDev/SBDC/
SBDC.htm

Nebraska

Department of Economic Development
301 Centennial Mall South
Lincoln, NE 68509-4666
402-471-3111
800-426-6505
http://assist.neded.org/index.html

Nevada

Department of Business and Industry
788 Fairview Ave.
Suite 100
Carson City, NV 89701-5491
775-687-4250
http://www.state.nv.us/binn/

New Hampshire

Small Business Development Center
1000 Elm Street, 12th floor
Manchester, NH 03101
603-624-2000
http://www.nhsbdc.org/

New Jersey

Division of Revenue
Business Gateway Services
225 West State Street,
Trenton, NJ 08608-1001
609-292-9292
http://www.state.nj.us/njbgs/index.html

New Mexico

Economic Development Department
1100 St. Francis Dr.
Santa Fe, NM 87503
505-827-0300
http://www.edd.state.nm.us/SERVICES/
   index.html

New York

Governor's Office of Regulatory Reform
Governor Alfred E. Smith Office Building
P.O. Box 7027, 17th Floor
Albany, NY 12225
518-474-8275
800-342-3464
http://www.gorr.state.ny.us/gorr/startbus.html

North Carolina

Department of the Secretary of State
Business License Information
111 Hillsborough Street (1st floor)
Raleigh, NC 27601
919-807-2166
800-228-8443
http://www.secretary.state.nc.us/blio/default.asp

North Dakota

Business Information Center
700 E. Main, 2nd Floor
P.O. Box 5509
Bismarck, ND 58506
701-328-5850
http://www.state.nd.us/businessreg/

Ohio

Greater Columbus Chamber of Commerce
37 North High Street
Columbus, OH 43215-3065
614-225-6910
http://www.ohiosbdc.org/main.shtml

Oklahoma

Tax Commission
2501 North Lincoln Boulevard
Oklahoma City, OK 73194
Connors Building, Capitol Complex
405-521-4321
http://www.oktax.state.ok.us/oktax/busreg.html

Oregon

Business Information Center
Public Service Building, Suite 151
255 Capitol Street NE
Salem, OR 97310-1327
503-986-2200
http://www.sos.state.or.us/corporation/bic/
   bizguide/contents.htm

Pennsylvania

Entrepreneurial Assistance Office
357 Forum Building
Harrisburg, PA 17120
717-783-8950
http://www.dced.state.pa.us/PA_Exec/DCED/
   business/starting.htm

Rhode Island

Economic Development Corp.
One West Exchange Street
Providence, RI 02903
401-222-2601
http://www.riedc.com/sab/sabframe.htm

South Carolina

Small Business Development Center
1710 College Street
Columbia, SC 29208
803-777-5118
http://sbdcweb.badm.sc.edu

South Dakota

Governor's Office of Economic Development
711 E. Wells Avenue
Pierre, SD 57501-3369
800-872-6190
605-773-5032
http://www.state.sd.us/oed/start-up/doingbus.htm

Tennessee

Department of Economic and Community
  Development
Business Services
11th Floor, William R. Snodgrass TN Tower
312 8th Avenue North
Nashville, TN 37243-0405
615-741-2626
http://www.state.tn.us/ecd/bus_start.htm

Texas

Department of Economic Development
1700 North Congress, SFA Building
Austin, TX 78711
512-936-0100
http://www.tded.state.tx.us/guide/

Utah

Department of Community and Economic
  Development
324 South State Street, Suite 500
Salt Lake City, UT 84111
801-538-8700
http://www.dced.state.ut.us/nav/library/
  bizutah/title.htm

Vermont

Department of Economic Development
National Life Bldg., Drawer 20
Montpelier, VT 05620-0501
800-VERMONT
802-828-3080
http://www.thinkvermont.com/business/
  starting/guide/index.shtml

Virginia

Economic Development Partnership
Post Office Box 798
Richmond, VA 23218-0798
804-371-8106
http://www.yesvirginia.org/lib.html

Washington

Department of Licensing
Master License Service (MLS)
405 Black Lake Blvd., Building 2
P.O. Box 9034
Olympia, WA 98507-9034
360-664-1400
http://www.wa.gov/dol/bpd/buslic.htm

West Virginia

Secretary of State
Bldg. 1, Suite 157-K
1900 Kanawha Blvd. East
Charleston, WV 25305-0770
304-558-8000
http://www.state.wv.us/sos/corp/startup.htm

Wisconsin

Department of Commerce
201 W. Washington Ave.
P.O. Box 7970
Madison, WI 53707
800-HELPBUS
608-266-1018
http://www.commerce.state.wi.us/MT/MT-COM-
  2600.html

Wyoming

Small Business Development Center
P.O. Box 3922
Laramie, WY 82071-3922
307-766-3505
800-348-5194
http://www.uwyo.edu/sbdc/starting.html   ■

State Tax Agencies

Alabama

Department of Revenue
Gordon Persons Building
50 N. Ripley Street
Montgomery, AL 36132
334-242-1170
http://www.ador.state.al.us/

Alaska

Department of Revenue—Tax Division
Income and Excise Audit Division
P.O. Box 110420
Juneau, AK 99811-0420
907-465-2320
http://www.revenue.state.ak.us/iea/

Arizona

Department of Revenue
1600 W. Monroe
Phoenix, AZ 85007
602-255-3381
800-352-4090
http://www.revenue.state.az.us/

Arkansas

Department of Finance and Administration
1509 W. 7th
Little Rock, AR 72201
501-682-2242
http://www.state.ar.us/dfa/taxes/new_bus.html

California

Franchise Tax Board
P.O. Box 942840
Sacramento, CA 94240-0040
800-852-5711
http://www.ftb.ca.gov/

Colorado

Department of Revenue
1375 Sherman St., Room 204
Denver, CO 80261
303-232-2416
http://www.revenue.state.co.us/

Connecticut

Department of Revenue Services
Taxpayer Services Division
25 Sigourney Street
Hartford, CT 06106-5032
800-382-9463
860-297-5962
http://www.drs.state.ct.us

Delaware

Department of Finance—Division of Revenue
Carvel State Office Building
820 N. French St.
Wilmington, DE 19801
302-577-8205
http://www.state.de.us/revenue/obt/obtmain.htm

District of Columbia

Office of Tax and Revenue
Customer Service Administration
941 N. Capitol St. NE
Washington, DC 20002
202-727-4829
http://www.dccfo.com/services/tax/customer/
   index.shtm

Florida

Department of Revenue, Tax Information
   Services
1379 Blountstown Highway
Tallahassee, FL 32304-2716
800-352-3671
850-488-6800
http://sun6.dms.state.fl.us/dor/taxes/

Georgia

Department of Revenue
507 Trinity-Washington Building
Atlanta, GA 30334
404-656-4095
http://www2.state.ga.us/departments/dor/

Hawaii

Department of Taxation
Taxpayer Services
830 Punchbowl Street
Honolulu, HI 96813-5045
808-587-4242
808-587-6515 (Jan.- Apr. 20)
800-222-3229
http://www.state.hi.us/tax/tax.html

Idaho

State Tax Commission
800 Park Blvd., Plaza IV
Boise, ID 83722
208-334-7660
800-972-7660
http://www2.state.id.us/tax/home.htm

Illinois

Department of Revenue
James R. Thompson Center
Concourse Level
100 West Randolph Street
Chicago, IL 60601-3274
312-814-5232
http://www.revenue.state.il.us/

Indiana

Department of Revenue
100 North Senate Ave.
202 State Office Bldg.
Indianapolis, IN 46204
317-233-4018
http://www.ai.org/dor/

Iowa

Department of Revenue and Finance
Taxpayer Services
P.O. Box 10457
Des Moines, IA 50306-0457
515-281-3114
800-367-3388
http://www.state.ia.us/government/drf/
   business/business.html

Kansas

Department of Revenue
Taxpayer Assistance Center
Docking State Office Building
915 SW Harrison St.
Topeka, KS 66612
785-368-8222
http://www.ink.org/public/kdor

Kentucky

Revenue Cabinet
Taxpayer Assistance Office
200 Fair Oaks Lane
Frankfort, KY 40602
502-564-4581
http://www.state.ky.us/agencies/revenue/
   revhome.htm

Louisiana

Department of Revenue
8490 Picardy Ave., Building 600
Baton Rouge, LA 70809-3684
225-763-5700
http://www.rev.state.la.us/

Maine

Revenue Services
24 State House Station
Augusta, ME 04333-0024
207-287-2076
http://janus.state.me.us/revenue/

Maryland

State Comptroller
Taxpayer Registration Assistance Center
Room 206
301 West Preston Street
Baltimore, MD 21201
410-767-1313
800-492-1751
http://www.comp.state.md.us/business/
    default.asp

Massachusetts

Department of Revenue
Customer Service Bureau
100 Cambridge Street
Boston, MA 02202
617-887-6367
800-392-6089
http://www.magnet.state.ma.us/dor/

Michigan

Department of Treasury
State of Michigan Plaza Building
1200 Fr. Kern (6th St)
Detroit, MI 48226
810-256-2202
http://www.treas.state.mi.us/

Minnesota

Department of Revenue
600 Robert Street North
St. Paul, MN 55146
651-296-3781
800-652-9094
http://www.taxes.state.mn.us/bus.html

Mississippi

State Tax Commission
1577 Springridge Rd.
Raymond, MS 39154-9602
601-923-7000
http://www.mstc.state.ms.us/regist.htm

Missouri

Department of Revenue
2018 William St.
Jefferson City, MO 65109
573-751-7191
http://dor.state.mo.us/tax/

Montana

Department of Revenue
Attn: Business Tax
P.O. Box 5805
Helena, MT 59604
406-444-6900
http://www.state.mt.us/revenue/index.htm

Nebraska

Department of Revenue
301 Centennial Mall South
P.O. Box 94818
Lincoln, NE 68509-4818
800-742-7474
http://www.nol.org/home/NDR/

Nevada

Department of Taxation
1550 E. College Parkway, Suite 100
Carson City, NV 89706
 775-687-4892
http://www.state.nv.us/taxation/bustax.htm

New Hampshire

Department of Revenue Administration
45 Chenell Drive, P.O. Box 457
Concord, NH 03302-0457
603-271-2191
http://www.state.nh.us/revenue/

New Jersey

Division of Taxation
P.O. Box 240
Trenton, NJ 08695-0240
609-292-6400
http://www.state.nj.us/treasury/taxation/

New Mexico

Taxation & Revenue Department

1100 S. St. Francis Dr.

P.O. Box 630

Santa Fe, NM 87504-0630

505-827-0700

http://www.state.nm.us/tax/

New York

Department of Taxation & Finance

W. Averill Harriman Campus

Albany, NY 12227

800-972-1233

http://www.tax.state.ny.us/sbc/default.htm

North Carolina

Department of Revenue

501 North Wilmington Street

Raleigh, NC 27604

919-733-3991

http://www.dor.state.nc.us/

North Dakota

Office of State Tax Commissioner

State Capitol

600 E. Boulevard Avenue

Bismarck, ND 58505-0599

701-328-2770

http://www.state.nd.us/taxdpt/index.html

Ohio

Department of Taxation

Taxpayer Services Division

830 Freeway Drive North

Columbus, OH 43229

888-405-4039

http://www.state.oh.us/tax/index.htm

Oklahoma

Tax Commission

2501 North Lincoln Boulevard

Connors Building, Capitol Complex

Oklahoma City, OK 73194

405-521-4321

http://www.oktax.state.ok.us/oktax/busreg.html

Oregon

Department of Revenue

955 Center Street NE

Salem, OR 97310

503-378-4988

800-356-4222

http://www.dor.state.or.us/taxInfo/newbus.html

Pennsylvania

Department of Revenue

Strawberry Square

Fourth and Walnut Streets Lobby

Harrisburg, PA 17128-0101

717-783-1405

http://www.revenue.state.pa.us/index.htm

Rhode Island

Division of Taxation

One Capitol Hill

Providence, RI 02908

401-222-3050

800-481-3700

http://www.tax.state.ri.us/

South Carolina

Department of Revenue

800 Dutch Square Blvd.

Dutch Plaza

Suite 211

P.O. Box 21588

Columbia, SC 29210

803-896-5700

http://www.sctax.org

South Dakota

Department of Revenue

445 E. Capitol Avenue

Pierre, SD 57501

800-829-9188

http://www.state.sd.us/revenue/bustax.htm

Tennessee

Department of Revenue
500 Deaderick St.
Nashville, TN 37242
800-342-1003
615-253-0600
http://www.state.tn.us/revenue/

Texas

Comptroller of Public Accounts
111 West Sixth Street
Austin, TX 78768-4843
512-463-4600
800-252-5555
http://www.cpa.state.tx.us/

Utah

State Tax Commission
210 N. 1950 West
Salt Lake City, UT 84134
801-297-2200
800-662-4335
http://www.tax.ex.state.ut.us/

Vermont

Department of Taxes
Taxpayer Services Division
109 State Street
Pavilion Office Building
Montpelier, VT 05609-1401
802-828-2551
http://www.state.vt.us/tax/index.htm

Virginia

Department of Taxation
3610 West Broad
Richmond, VA 23230
804-367-8037
http://www.tax.state.va.us/

Washington

Department of Revenue
Target Place Complex
2735 Harrison Ave. Northwest
Suite 440
P.O. Box 12900
Olympia, WA 98508-2900
360-753-3181
800-647-7706
http://dor.wa.gov/

West Virginia

State Tax Department
Rm 417-WW Capitol Building,
or 1001 Lee Street, E.
Charleston, WV 25301
304-558-3333
800-982-8297
http://www.state.wv.us/taxdiv/

Wisconsin

Department of Revenue
4638 University Ave.
Madison, WI 53702
608-266-2772
http://www.dor.state.wi.us/

Wyoming

Department of Revenue
Herschler Bldg., 2nd Floor West
122 West 25th Street
Cheyenne, WY 82002-0110
307-777-7961
http://revenue.state.wy.us/

State Sales Tax/Seller's Permit Agencies

Alabama

Department of Revenue
Sales, Use and Business Tax Section
Taxpayer Service Center
1021 Madison Avenue
Montgomery, AL 36104
334-242-2677
http://www.ador.state.al.us/salestax/index.html

Alaska

no state sales tax

Arizona

Department of Revenue
Transaction Privilege (Sales) and Use Tax
P.O. Box 29010
Phoenix, AZ, 85038-9010
602-255-2060
800-843-7196
http://www.revenue.state.az.us/

Arkansas

Sales and Use Tax
Department of Finance and Administration
Ledbetter Revenue Building
7th & Wolfe, Room 205
P.O. Box 1272
Little Rock, AR 72201
501-682-7104
http://www.state.ar.us/dfa/taxes/salestax/
   index.html

California

Board of Equalization
3321 Power Inn Road, Suite 210
Sacramento, CA 95826-3889
916-227-6700
800-400-7115
http://boe.dgs.ca.gov/btlg.html

Colorado

Department of Revenue
1375 Sherman St., Room 204
Denver, CO 80261
303-232-2416
http://www.state.co.us/gov_dir/revenue_dir/
   TPS_dir/sales_tax_lic_rev.html

Connecticut

Department of Revenue Services
Taxpayer Services Division
25 Sigourney Street
Hartford, CT 06106-5032
800-382-9463
860-297-5962
http://www.drs.state.ct.us

Delaware

(no state sales tax, but state gross receipts tax)
Department of Finance—Division of Revenue
820 N. French St.
Wilmington, DE 19801
302-577-8780
http://www.state.de.us/revenue/obt/lic_gr.htm

District of Columbia

Office of Tax and Revenue
Customer Service Administration
941 N. Capitol St. NE
Washington, DC 20002
202-727-4829
http://www.dccfo.com

Florida

Department of Revenue
Registration Information
5050 W. Tennessee St.
Tallahassee, FL 32399-0100
850-488-9750
800-352-3671
http://sun6.dms.state.fl.us/dor/taxes/
   sales_tax.html

Georgia

Department of Revenue
Sales and Use Tax Division
310 Trinity-Washington Building
Atlanta, GA 30334
404-656-4065
http://www2.state.ga.us/departments/dor/
salestax/index.shtml

Hawaii

Taxpayer Services Branch
830 Punchbowl Street
Honolulu, HI 96813-5045
808-587-4242
800-222-3229
http://www.state.hi.us/tax/tax.html

Idaho

State Tax Commission
800 Park Blvd., Plaza IV
Boise, ID 83722
208-334-7660
800-972-7660
http://www2.state.id.us/tax/home.htm

Illinois

Department of Revenue
James R. Thompson Center
Concourse Level
100 West Randolph Street
Chicago, IL 60601-3274
312-814-5232
http://www.revenue.state.il.us/resources/faq/
rotfaq.html

Indiana

Department of Revenue
100 North Senate Ave.
202 State Office Bldg.
Indianapolis, IN 46204
317-233-4018
http://www.ai.org/dor/

Iowa

Department of Revenue and Finance
Taxpayer Services
P.O. Box 10457
Des Moines, IA 50306-0457
515-281-3114
800-367-3388
http://www.state.ia.us/government/drf/educate/
78539.html

Kansas

Department of Revenue
Taxpayer Assistance Center
Docking State Office Building
915 SW Harrison St.
Topeka, KS 66612
785-368-8222
www.ink.org/public/kdor

Kentucky

Revenue Cabinet
Taxpayer Assistance Office
200 Fair Oaks Lane
Frankfort, KY 40602
502-564-4581
http://www.state.ky.us/agencies/revenue/
revhome.htm

Louisiana

Department of Revenue
8490 Picardy Ave., Building 600
Baton Rouge, LA 70809-3684
Sales Tax Division Taxpayer
Assistance Section:
225-925-7356
http://www.rev.state.la.us/

Maine

Revenue Services
Sales and Use Tax Division
P.O. Box 1065
Augusta, ME 04332-1065
207-287-2336
http://janus.state.me.us/revenue/bulletins/
homepage.htm

Maryland

State Comptroller
Taxpayer Registration Assistance Center
Room 206
State Office Building
301 West Preston Street,
Baltimore, MD 21201
410-767-1313
800-492-1751
http://www.comp.state.md.us/business/
default.asp

Massachusetts

Department of Revenue, Customer Service
Bureau
P.O. Box 7010
Boston, MA 02204
617-887-MDOR
800-392-6089
http://www.dor.state.ma.us/help/Guides/
STG.htm

Michigan

Department of Treasury
Sales, Use, and Withholding Taxes Division
Technical Section
Treasury Building
Lansing, MI 48922
517-373-3190
http://www.treas.state.mi.us/mitax/suw/
suwindex.htm

Minnesota

Department of Revenue
Mail Station 6330
St. Paul, MN 55146-6330
651-296-6181
800-657-3777
http://www.taxes.state.mn.us/salestax/factshts/
salestax.html

Mississippi

State Tax Commission
P.O. Box 1033
Jackson, MS 39215
601-923-7300
http://www.mstc.state.ms.us/taxareas/sales/
main.htm

Missouri

Department of Revenue
Sales/Use Tax
P.O. Box 840
Jefferson City, MO 65105-0840
573-751-2836
http://dor.state.mo.us/tax/salesfrm.htm

Montana

no general sales tax

Nebraska

Department of Revenue
301 Centennial Mall South
P.O. Box 94818
Lincoln, NE 68509-4818
800-742-7474
http://www.nol.org/revenue/salestax.htm

Nevada

Department of Taxation
1550 E. College Parkway, Suite 100
Carson City, NV 89706
775-687-4892
http://www.state.nv.us/taxation/taxmap.htm

New Hampshire

no state sales tax

New Jersey

Division of Taxation
P.O. Box 240
Trenton, NJ 08695-0240
609-292-6400
http://www.state.nj.us/treasury/taxation/
freqqsub.htm

New Mexico

Taxation & Revenue Department

1100 S. St. Francis Dr.

P.O. Box 630

Santa Fe, NM 87504-0630

505-827-0700

http://www.state.nm.us/tax/

New York

Department of Taxation & Finance

Sales Tax Registration

W. Averill Harriman Campus

Albany, NY 12227

800-462-8100

518-485-6800

http://www.tax.state.ny.us/nyshome/stidx.htm

North Carolina

Department of Revenue

Sales and Use Tax Division

501 N. Wilmington Street

Raleigh, NC 27634-0001

919-733-3661

http://www.dor.state.nc.us/downloads/
    salespub.html

North Dakota

Office of State Tax Commissioner

State Capitol

600 E. Boulevard Avenue

Bismarck, ND 58505-0599

701-328-3470

http://www.state.nd.us/taxdpt/forms/sales.html

Ohio

Department of Taxation

Sales and Use Tax Division

30 E. Broad Street, 20th Floor,

Columbus, OH 43215

888-405-4039

http://www.state.oh.us/tax/ASSIST/FAQs/FAQS-
    ST.HTM

Oklahoma

Tax Commission

2501 North Lincoln Boulevard

Connors Building, Capitol Complex

Oklahoma City, OK 73194

405-521-4321

http://www.oktax.state.ok.us/oktax/busreg.html

Oregon

no state sales tax

Pennsylvania

Department of Revenue

Strawberry Square

Fourth and Walnut Streets Lobby

Harrisburg, PA 17128-0101

717-787-1064

http://www.revenue.state.pa.us/caq/rev-585.htm

Rhode Island

Division of Taxation

One Capitol Hill

Providence, RI 02908

401-222-2950

http://www.tax.state.ri.us/info/synopsis/1.htm

South Carolina

Department of Revenue

P.O. Box 125

Columbia, SC 29214

803-898-5788

http://www.dor.state.sc.us/

South Dakota

Department of Revenue

445 E. Capitol Avenue

Pierre, SD 57501

800-829-9188

http://www.state.sd.us/revenue/bustax.htm

Tennessee

Department of Revenue
500 Deaderick St.
Nashville, TN 37242
800-342-1003
615-253-0600
http://www.state.tn.us/revenue/

Texas

Comptroller of Public Accounts
111 West Sixth Street
Austin, TX 78768-4843
512-463-3731
http://www.cpa.state.tx.us/taxinfo/salestax.html

Utah

State Tax Commission
210 N. 1950 West
Salt Lake City, UT 84134
801-297-2200
800-66-4335
http://www.tax.ex.state.ut.us/sales/
   SALESTAX.HTM

Vermont

Department of Taxes
Taxpayer Services Division
109 State Street
Pavilion Office Building
Montpelier, VT 05609-1401
802-828-2551
http://www.state.vt.us/tax/index.htm

Virginia

Department of Taxation
Sales and Use Tax Division
P.O. Box 1103
Richmond, VA 23208
804-367-8037
http://www.tax.state.va.us/bt_sutax.htm

Washington

Department of Revenue
Target Place Complex
2735 Harrison Ave. Northwest
Suite 440
P.O. Box 12900
Olympia, WA 98508-2900
360-753-3181
800-647-7706
http://dor.wa.gov/

West Virginia

State Tax Department
Rm 417-WW Capitol Building,
or 1001 Lee Street, E.
Charleston, WV 25301
304-558-3333
800-982-8297
http://www.state.wv.us/taxdiv/

Wisconsin

Compliance Bureau
P.O. Box 8902
Madison, WI 53708
608-266-2776
http://www.dor.state.wi.us/faqs/sales.html

Wyoming

Excise Tax Division
122 West 25th Street
Cheyenne, WY 82002
307-777-5220
http://159.238.111.110/excise/salesuse.htm

■

LLC Offices

Alabama

Secretary of State
Corporate Section
Box 5616
Montgomery, AL 36103
334-242-5324
http://www.sos.state.al.us/business/
corporat.htm

Alaska

Department of Community & Economic
Development
Division of Banking, Securities & Corporations
Corporations Section
Box 110808
Juneau, AK 99811-0808
907-465-2530
http://www.dced.state.ak.us/bsc/corps.htm

Arizona

Arizona Corporation Commission
Corporation Filing Section
1300 West Washington
Phoenix, AZ 85007-2996
800-345-5819 (in AZ only)
602-542-3135
Tucson Branch Office: 520-628-6560 (accepts
LLC filings)
http://www.cc.state.az.us/corp/index.htm

Arkansas

Arkansas Secretary of State
Corporations Division
State Capitol
Little Rock, AR 72201-1094
501-682-5151
http://www.sosweb.state.ar.us/corp_forms.html

California

California Secretary of State
Limited Liability Company Unit
P.O. Box 944228
Sacramento, CA 94244-2280
916-653-3795
http://www.ss.ca.gov/business/business.htm

Branch offices of the Secretary of State are
located in Fresno, Los Angeles, San Francisco
and San Diego. Currently, branch offices
provide LLC forms over-the-counter only, and
do not mail out forms or accept LLC filings.

Colorado

Secretary of State
1560 Broadway, Suite 200
Denver, CO 80202
303-894-2200
http://www.sos.state.co.us/pubs.html

Connecticut

Connecticut Secretary of State
30 Trinity Street
P.O. Box 150470
Hartford, CT 06115-0470
860-509-6002
http://www.sots.state.ct.us/

Delaware

Department of State
Division of Corporations
P.O. Box 898
Dover, DE 19903
302-739-3073
http://www.state.de.us/corp/index.htm

District of Columbia

Department of Consumer & Regulatory Affairs
Business Regulation Administration
Corporations Division
941 North Capitol Street, NE
Washington, DC 20002
202-442-8947
http://www.dcra.org/

Florida

Florida Department of State
Registration Section
Division of Corporations
P.O. Box 6327
Tallahassee, FL 32314
850-487-6051
http://www.dos.state.fl.us/doc/index.html

Georgia

Secretary of State
Corporations Division
Suite 315, West Tower
2 Martin Luther King Jr. Drive
Atlanta, GA 30334
404-656-2817
http://www.sos.state.ga.us/corporations/

Hawaii

Department of Commerce and Consumer Affairs
Business Registration Division
P.O. Box 40
Honolulu, HI 96810
808-586-2727
http://www.businessregistrations.com/

Idaho

Idaho Secretary of State
Corporations Division
700 West Jefferson
P.O. Box 83720
Boise, ID 83720-0080
208-334-2301
http://www.idsos.state.id.us/corp/corindex.htm

Illinois

Illinois Secretary of State
Department of Business Services
Limited Liability Company Division
Room 359, Howlett Building
Springfield, IL 62756
217-524-8008
http://www.sos.state.il.us/depts/bus_serv/
   feature.html

Branch Office: 17 North State Street, Suite 1137,
Chicago, IL 60602 (for questions and info only;
not LLC filing).

Indiana

Indiana Secretary of State
Corporations Division
302 W. Washington, Room E018
Indianapolis, IN 46204
317-232-6576
http://www.state.in.us/sos/bus_service

Iowa

Iowa Secretary of State
Corporations Division
Hoover Building, 2nd Floor
Des Moines, IA 50319
515-281-5204
http://www.sos.state.ia.us/business/services.html

Kansas

Kansas Secretary of State
Corporation Division
First Floor, Memorial Hall
120 SW 10th Ave.
Topeka, KS 66612-1594
913-296-4564
http://www.kssos.org

Kentucky

Kentucky Secretary of State
Business Filings
P.O. Box 718
Frankfort, KY 40602
502-564-2848
http://www.sos.state.ky.us/

Louisiana

Louisiana Secretary of State
Corporations Division
P.O. Box 94125
Baton Rouge, LA 70804-9125
504-925-4704
http://www.sec.state.la.us/comm/corp-index.htm

Maine

Secretary of State
Bureau of Corporations, Elections &
 Commissions
101 State House Station
Augusta, ME 04333-0101
ATTN: Corporate Examining Section
207-287-3676
http://www.state.me.us/sos/cec/cec.htm

Maryland

Maryland Department of Assessments & Taxation
Corporate Charter Division
Room 809
301 West Preston Street
Baltimore, MD 21201-2392
410-767-1184
http://www.dat.state.md.us/sdatweb/charter.html

Massachusetts

Commonwealth of Massachusetts
Corporations Division
One Ashburton Place, 17th Floor
Boston, MA 02108
617-727-9640
http://www.state.ma.us/sec/cor

Michigan

Michigan Department of Consumer and Industry
 Services
Corporation and Land Development Bureau
Corporation Division
7150 Harris Drive
P.O. Box 30054
Lansing, MI 48909
517-241-6400
http://www.cis.state.mi.us/corp/

Minnesota

Minnesota Secretary of State
Business Services Division
180 State Office Building
100 Constitution Avenue
St. Paul, MN 55155-1299
612-297-1455
http://www.sos.state.mn.us/business/index.html

Mississippi

Mississippi Secretary of State
Corporate Division
P.O. Box 136
Jackson, MS 39205-0136
601-359-1333
http://www.sos.state.ms.us

Missouri

Secretary of State
Corporation Division
P.O. Box 778
Jefferson City, MO 65102
573-751-4153
http://mosl.sos.state.mo.us/bus-ser/soscor.html

Montana

Montana Secretary of State
Corporation Bureau
P.O. Box 202801
Helena, MT 59620-2801
406-444-3665
http://www.state.mt.us/sos/Business_Services/
 business_services.html

Nebraska

Nebraska Secretary of State
Corporate Division
P.O. Box 94608
Lincoln, NE 68509-4608
402-471-4079
http://www.nol.org/home/SOS/corps/
 corpform.htm

Nevada

Secretary of State
New Filings Section
101 N. Carson Street, Suite 3
Carson City, NV 89701-4786
775-684-5708
http://sos.state.nv.us/comm_rec/index.htm

Filings may also be made at the Secretary of
State Satellite Office in Las Vegas (702-486-2880)

New Hampshire

New Hampshire Secretary of State
State House, Room 204
107 North Main Street
Concord, NH 03301-4989
603-271-3246
http://www.state.nh.us/sos/corporate/index.htm

New Jersey

New Jersey Department of Treasury
Division of Revenue
Corporate Filings
P.O. Box 308
Trenton, NJ 08625-0308
609-530-6400
http://www.state.nj.us/business.htm

New Mexico

State Corporation Commission
Corporation Department
Chartered Documents Bureau
P.O. Drawer 1269
Santa Fe, NM 87504-1269
505-827-4511
http://www.nmprc.state.nm.us

New York

Department of State
Division of Corporations
State Records and Uniform Commercial Code
41 State Street
Albany, NY 12231
518-473-2492
http://www.dos.state.ny.us/corp/corpspub.html

North Carolina

North Carolina Department of the Secretary of
State
Corporations Division
300 North Salisbury Street
Raleigh, NC 27603-5909
919-733-4201
(toll free 888-246-7636)
http://www.secretary.state.nc.us/corporations/

North Dakota

North Dakota Secretary of State
Corporations Division
600 East Boulevard Avenue
Bismarck, ND 58505-0500
701-328-4284
http://www.state.nd.us/sec/Business/
businessinforegmnu.htm

Ohio

Ohio Secretary of State
Business Services Division
P.O. Box 1329
Columbus, OH 43216
614-466-3910
Toll Free: 877-SOS-FILE (877-767-3453)
http://www.state.oh.us/sos/

Oklahoma

Oklahoma Secretary of State
2300 N. Lincoln Blvd.
Room 101
State Capitol Building
Oklahoma City, OK 73105-4897
405-522-4560
http://www.sos.state.ok.us/business/
business%20information.htm

Oregon

Oregon Secretary of State
Corporation Division
255 Capitol Street, NE, Suite 151
Salem, OR 97310-1327
503-986-2200
http://www.sos.state.or.us/corporation/bizreg/
  bizreg.htm

Pennsylvania

Commonwealth of Pennsylvania
Department of State
Corporation Bureau
P.O. Box 8722
Harrisburg, PA 17105-8722
717-787-1057
http://www.dos.state.pa.us/corp/index.htm

Rhode Island

Rhode Island Secretary of State
Corporations Division
100 North Main Street
Providence, RI 02903-1335
401-222-3040
http://www.state.ri.us/corporations/

South Carolina

South Carolina Secretary of State
Corporations Department
P.O. Box 11350
Columbia, SC 29211
803-734-2158
http://www.scsos.com/Corporations.htm

South Dakota

South Dakota Secretary of State
State Capitol
500 East Capitol Ave.
Pierre, SD 57501-5070
605-773-4845
http://www.state.sd.us/state/executive/sos/
  Corpadmn.htm

Tennessee

Tennessee Department of State
Division of Business Services
Suite 1800, James K. Polk Building
Nashville, TN 37243-0306
615-741-2286
http://www.state.tn.us/sos/
  service.htm#corporations

Texas

Texas Secretary of State
Statutory Filings Division
Corporations Section
P.O. Box 13697
Austin, TX 78711-3697
512-463-5586
http://www.sos.state.tx.us/function/forms/
  index.html

Utah

Utah Division of Corporations & Commercial
  Code
160 East 300 South, 2nd Floor
Box 146705
Salt Lake City, UT 84114-6705
801-530-4849
http://www.commerce.state.ut.us/corporat/
  corpcoc.htm

Vermont

Vermont Secretary of State
81 River Street, Drawer 09
Montpelier, VT 05609-1104
802-828-2386
http://www.sec.state.vt.us/corps/corpindex.htm

Virginia

Clerk of the State Corporation Commission
P.O. Box 1197
First Floor
Richmond, VA 23218-1197
804-371-9733
http://www.state.va.us/scc/division/clk/
  corp.htm

Washington

Washington Secretary of State
Corporations Division
P.O. Box 40234
Olympia, WA 98504-0234
360-753-7115
http://www.secstate.wa.gov/corps/default.htm

West Virginia

West Virginia Secretary of State
Corporations Division
Bldg. 1, Suite 157-K
1900 Kanawha Blvd. East
Charleston, WV 25305-0770
304-558-8000
http://www.state.wv.us/sos/corp/startup.htm

Wisconsin

Department of Financial Institutions
P.O. Box 7846
Madison, WI 53707-7846
608-261-7577
http://www.wdfi.org/corporations/default.htm

Wyoming

Secretary of State's Office
Corporations Division
The Capitol
Cheyenne, WY 82002-0020
307-777-7311
http://soswy.state.wy.us/corporat/corporat.htm

State Unemployment Compensation Agencies

Alabama

Department of Industrial Relations
649 Monroe Street
Montgomery, AL 36131
334-242-8467
http://www.dir.state.al.us

Alaska

Department of Labor
P.O. Box 25509
Juneau, AK 99802-5509
800-448-3527
http://www.labor.state.ak.us

Arizona

Department of Economic Security
3225 N. Central Avenue
Suite 1400
Phoenix, AZ 85012
602-248-9396
http://www.de.state.az.us

Arkansas

Employment Security Department
P.O. Box 2981
Little Rock, AR 72203
501-682-3253
http://www.state.ar.us/esd

California

Employment Development Department
3321 Power Inn Road, Suite 220
Sacramento, CA 95826-6110
916-464-3502
http://www.edd.cahwnet.gov

Colorado

Department of Labor and Employment
1515 Arapahoe Street
Tower 2, Suite 400
Denver, CO 80202-2117
303-603-8231
http://unemploytax.cdle.state.co.us

Connecticut

Department of Labor
200 Folly Brook Blvd.
Wethersfield, CT 06109-1114
860-263-6550
http://www.ctdol.state.ct.us

Delaware

Department of Labor
4425 North Market Street
Wilmington, DE 19802
302-761-8446
http://www.delawareworks.com

District of Columbia

Department of Employment Services
500 C Street, NW, Room 501
Washington, DC 20001
202-724-7461
http://does.ci.washington.dc.us

Florida

Department of Labor and Employment Security
107 East Madison Street
Tallahassee, FL 32399-0211
850-921-5000
http://www.fdles.state.fl.us

Georgia

Department of Labor
148 International Blvd.
Suite 800
Atlanta, GA 30303
404-656-5590
http://www.dol.state.ga.us

Hawaii

Department of Labor and Industrial Relations
830 Punchbowl Street
Room 437
Honolulu, HI 96813
808-586-8913
http://www.state.hi.us/dlir

Idaho

Department of Labor
317 Main Street
Boise, ID 83735-0760
208-334-6385
http://www.doe.state.id.us

Illinois

Department of Employment Security
401 South State Street
Chicago, IL 60605
312-793-1918
http://www.ides.state.il.us

Indiana

Department of Workforce Development
10 North Senate Avenue
Indianapolis, IN 46204
317-232-7436
http://www.dwd.state.in.us

Iowa

Workforce Development
1000 East Grand Avenue
Des Moines, IA 50319
515-281-8200
http://www.state.ia.us/government/des

Kansas

Department of Human Resources
401 SW Topeka Blvd.
Topeka, KS 66603
785-296-5025
http://www.hr.state.ks.us

Kentucky

Division of Unemployment Insurance
P.O. Box 948
Frankfort, KY 40602
502-564-6838
http://www.des.state.ky.us

Louisiana

Department of Labor
P.O. Box 98146
Baton Rouge, LA 70804
225-342-2992
http://www.ldol.state.la.us

Maine

Department of Labor
P.O. Box 259
Augusta, ME 04332-0259
207-287-3176
http://janus.state.me.us/labor

Maryland

Office of Unemployment Insurance
1100 North Eutaw Street, Room 411
Baltimore, MD 21201
410-767-2414
http://www.dllr.state.md.us/employment

Massachusetts

Division of Employment and Training
19 Staniford Street
Boston, MA 02114
617-626-5050
http://www.detma.org

Michigan

Employment Security Division
7310 Woodward Avenue
Detroit, MI 48202
313-876-5131
http://www.cis.state.mi.us/ua

Minnesota

Department of Economic Security
390 North Robert Street
St. Paul, MN 55101
651-296-3736
http://www.des.state.mn.us

Mississippi

Employment Security Commission
P.O. Box 22781
Jackson, MS 39225-2781
601-961-7755
http://www.mesc.state.ms.us/tax

Missouri

Division of Employment Security
P.O. Box 59
Jefferson City, MO 65104
573-751-3328
http://www.dolir.state.mo.us/es

Montana

Department of Labor and Industry
P.O. Box 1728
Helena, MT 59624
406-444-2747
http://dli.state.mt.us

Nebraska

Department of Labor
Box 94600
State House Station
Lincoln, NE 68509
402-471-9839
http://www.dol.state.ne.us/uihome.htm

Nevada

Department of Employment Training and
  Rehabilitation
500 East Third Street
Carson City, NV 89713
775-687-4599
http://www.state.nv.us/detr

New Hampshire

Department of Employment Security
32 South Main Street
Concord, NH 03301
603-228-4045
http://www.nhworks.state.nh.us

New Jersey

Department of Labor
P.O. Box 947
Trenton, NJ 08625-0947
609-292-2811
http://www.state.nj.us/labor

New Mexico

Department of Labor
P.O. Box 2281
Albuquerque, NM 87103
505-841-8568
http://www3.state.nm.us/dol

New York

Department of Labor
State Campus, Building 12, Room 542
Albany, NY 12240
518-457-4120
http://www.labor.state.ny.us

North Carolina

Employment Security Commission
P.O. Box 26504
Raleigh, NC 27611
919-733-7395
http://www.esc.state.nc.us

North Dakota

Job Service of North Dakota
P.O. Box 5507
Bismarck, ND 58506-5507
701-328-2791
http://www.state.nd.us/jsnd

Ohio

Bureau of Employment Services
P.O. Box 923
Columbus, OH 43216
614-466-2319
http://www.state.oh.us/obes

Oklahoma

Employment Security Commission
Will Rogers Memorial Office Building
2401 North Lincoln
Oklahoma City, OK 73105
405-557-7226
http://www.oesc.state.ok.us

Oregon

Employment Department
875 Union Street NE
Salem, OR 97311
503-947-1696
http://www.emp.state.or.us

Pennsylvania

Department of Labor and Industry
7th and Forster Street
Harrisburg, PA 17121
717-787-7679
http://www.dli.state.pa.us

Rhode Island

Division of Taxation
One Capitol Hill
Providence, RI 02908-5829
401-222-3696
http://www.det.state.ri.us

South Carolina

Employment Security Commission
P.O. Box 995
Columbia, SC 29202
803-737-3070
http://www.sces.org/ui

South Dakota

Department of Employment Security
P.O. Box 4730
Aberdeen, SD 57402
605-626-2312
http://www.state.sd.us/dol

Tennessee

Department of Employment Security
500 James Robertson Parkway
8th Floor, Davy Crocket Tower
Nashville, TN 37245-3500
615-741-2486
http://www.state.tn.us/labor-wfd

Texas

Workforce Commission
101 East 15th Street
Austin, TX 78778
512-463-2699
http://www.twc.state.tx.us

Utah

Department of Employment Security
P.O. Box 45288
Salt Lake City, UT 84145
801-526-9400
http://www.dws.state.ut.us

Vermont

Department of Employment Security
P.O. Box 488
Montpelier, VT 05602
877-214-3331
http://www.det.state.vt.us

Virginia

Employment Commission
P.O. Box 1358
Richmond, VA 23211
804-371-6325
http://www.vec.state.va.us

Washington

Employment Security Department
P.O. Box 9046
Olympia, WA 98507-9046
360-902-9554
http://www.wa.gov/esd

West Virginia

Bureau of Employment Programs
112 California Avenue
Charleston, WV 25305-0112
304-558-2675
http://www.state.wv.us/bep

Wisconsin

Department of Workforce Development
P.O. Box 7942, GEF 1
Madison, WI 53702
608-266-3177
http://www.dwd.state.wi.us

Wyoming

Department of Employment
P.O. Box 2760
Casper, WY 82602
307-235-3201
http://wydoe.state.wy.us/erd

■

Patent and Trademark Depository Libraries by State

Alabama

Auburn

Ralph Brown Draughon Library, Auburn
University
334-844-1747
http://www.lib.auburn.edu/scitech/faq/
patent.html

Birmingham

Birmingham Public Library
205-226-3620
http://www.bham.lib.al.us/GovDocs/
govdocs.html

Alaska

Anchorage

Z. J. Loussac Public Library, Anchorage
Municipal Libraries
907-562-7323
http://www.ci.anchorage.ak.us/Services/
Departments/Culture/Library/collect.html

Arizona

Tempe

Noble Science and Engineering Library, Arizona
State University
480-965-7010
http://www.asu.edu/lib/noble/ptdl/ptdl.htm

Arkansas

Little Rock

Arkansas State Library
501-682-2053
http://www.asl.lib.ar.us/patents/index.html

California

Los Angeles

Los Angeles Public Library
213-228-7220
http://www.lapl.org/central/science.html

Sacramento

California State Library, Library—Courts
Building
916-654-0069
http://www.library.ca.gov/index.html

San Diego

San Diego Public Library
619-236-5813
http://www.ci.san-diego.ca.us/public-library/
index.shtml

San Francisco

San Francisco Public Library
415-557-4500
http://206.14.7.53/gic/ptdl.htm

Sunnyvale

Sunnyvale Center for Innovation, Invention &
Ideas
408-730-7290
http://www.sci3.com

Colorado

Denver

Denver Public Library
303-640-6220
http://www.denver.lib.co.us/dpl/govpubs/
govpub.html

Connecticut

Hartford

Hartford Public Library
860-543-8628
http://www.hartfordpl.lib.ct.us

New Haven

New Haven Free Public Library
203-946-8130
http://www.nhfpl.lib.ct.us

Delaware

Newark
University of Delaware Library
302-831-2965
http://www.lib.udel.edu/

District of Columbia

Washington
Founders Library, Howard University
202-806-7252
http://www.founders.howard.edu/

Florida

Fort Lauderdale
Broward County Main Library
954-357-7444
http://www.co.broward.fl.us/lii05700.htm

Miami
Miami-Dade Public Library
305-375-2665
http://www.mdpls.org/

Orlando
University of Central Florida Libraries
407-823-2562
http://library.ucf.edu/GovDocs/PAT_TRAD.htm

Tampa
Tampa Campus Library, University of South
Florida
813-974-2726
http://www.lib.usf.edu/virtual/govdocs/

Georgia

Atlanta
Library and Information Center, Georgia
Institute of Technology
404-894-4508
http://gtel.gatech.edu/patents

Hawaii

Honolulu
Hawaii State Library
808-586-3477
http://www.hcc.hawaii.edu/hspls/fd/
fdmore.html

Idaho

Moscow
University of Idaho Library
208-885-6235
http://www.lib.uidaho.edu/

Illinois

Chicago
Chicago Public Library
312-747-4450
http://www.chipublib.org/008subject/
009scitech/patents.html

Springfield
Illinois State Library
217-782-5659
http://www.library.sos.state.il.us/isl/collect.html

Indiana

Indianapolis
Indianapolis-Marion County Public Library
317-269-1741
http://www.imcpl.lib.in.us/bst_patents.htm

West Lafayette
Siegesmund Engineering Library, Purdue
University
765-494-2872
http://www.lib.purdue.edu/index.html

Iowa

Des Moines
State Library of Iowa
515-242-6541
http://www.silo.lib.ia.us

Kansas

Wichita
Ablah Library, Wichita State University
316-978-3155
http://www.twsu.edu/library/govdoc/
patents.html

Kentucky

Louisville

Louisville Free Public Library

502-574-1611

http://lfpl.org/

Louisiana

Baton Rouge

Troy H. Middleton Library, Louisiana State
University

225-388-8875

http://www.lib.lsu.edu/sci/eng/int-prop.html

Maine

Orono

Raymond H. Fogler Library, University of Maine

207-581-1678

http://libraries.maine.edu/oroptdl/

Maryland

College Park

Engineering and Physical Sciences Library,
University of Maryland

301-405-9157

http://www.lib.umd.edu/UMCP/ENGIN/
engin.html

Massachusetts

Amherst

Physical Sciences and Engineering Library,
University of Massachusetts

413-545-1370

http://www.library.umass.edu/physci.html

Boston

Boston Public Library

617-536-5400, Ext. 265

http://www.bpl.org/WWW/science/
patent_trademark.html

Michigan

Ann Arbor

Media Union Library, The University of Michigan

734-647-5735

http://www.lib.umich.edu/ummu/
nwpatentstmstds.html

Big Rapids

Abigail S. Timme Library, Ferris State University

231-591-3602

http://www.ferris.edu/library/

Detroit

Great Lakes Patent and Trademark Center,
Detroit Public Library

313-833-3379

http://www.detroit.lib.mi.us/glptc/

Minnesota

Minneapolis

Minneapolis Public Library

612-630-6120

http://www.mpls.lib.mn.us/central.asp

Mississippi

Jackson

Mississippi Library Commission

601-961-4111

http://www.mlc.lib.ms.us/patent_trademark.htm

Missouri

Kansas City

Linda Hall Library

816-363-4600

http://www.lindahall.org

St. Louis

St. Louis Public Library

314-241-2288, Ext. 390

http://www.slpl.lib.mo.us/library.htm

Montana

Butte

Montana Tech Library of the University of
Montana

406-496-4281

http://www.mtech.edu/library/

Nebraska

Lincoln

Engineering Library, Nebraska Hall, 2nd Floor West, University of Nebraska-Lincoln

402-472-3411

http://www.unl.edu/libr/libs/engr/engr.html

Nevada

Las Vegas

Clark County Library, Las Vegas—Clark County Library District

Not yet operational

http://www.lvccld.lib.nv.us/ccl/ccl.shtml

Reno

University Library

775-784-6500, Ext. 257

http://www.library.unr.edu/depts/bgic/

New Hampshire

Concord

New Hampshire State Library

603-271-2239

http://www.state.nh.us/nhsl/patents/index.html

New Jersey

Newark

Newark Public Library

973-733-7779

http://www.npl.org/Pages/Collections/bst.html

Piscataway

Library of Science and Medicine, Rutgers University

732-445-2895

http://www.libraries.rutgers.edu/rul/

New Mexico

Albuquerque

Centennial Science and Engineering Library, The University of New Mexico

505-277-4412

http://eLibrary.unm.edu/csel/patents/

New York

Albany

New York State Library, Cultural Education Center

518-474-5355

http://www.nysl.nysed.gov/patents.htm

Buffalo

Buffalo and Erie County Public Library

716-858-7101

http://www.buffalolib.org/

New York

Science, Industry and Business Library, New York Public Library

212-592-7000

http://www.nypl.org/research/sibl/pattrade/pattrade.htm

Rochester

Central Library of Rochester and Monroe County

716-428-8110

http://www.rochester.lib.ny.us/central/

Stony Brook

Melville Library, Room 1101, SUNY at Stony Brook

516-632-7148

http://www.sunysb.edu/sciencelib/patents.htm

North Carolina

Raleigh

D. H. Hill Library, North Carolina State University

919-515-2935

http://www.lib.ncsu.edu/risd/patent/

North Dakota

Grand Forks

Chester Fritz Library, University of North Dakota

701-777-4888

http://www.und.nodak.edu/dept/library/

Ohio

Akron

Akron-Summit County Public Library

330-643-9075

http://ascpl.lib.oh.us/pat-tm.html

Cincinnati

The Public Library of Cincinnati and
Hamilton County

513-369-6971

http://plch.lib.oh.us/main/pd/

Cleveland

Cleveland Public Library

216-623-2870

http://www.cpl.org/

Columbus

Ohio State University

614-292-3022

http://www.lib.ohio-state.edu/OSU_profile/
phyweb

Toledo

Toledo/Lucas County Public Library

419-259-5212

http://www.library.toledo.oh.us/

Oklahoma

Stillwater

Oklahoma State University

405-744-7086

http://www.library.okstate.edu/dept/patents/

Oregon

Portland

Lewis & Clark College

503-768-6786

http://www.lclark.edu/~lawlib/#Special

Pennsylvania

Philadelphia

The Free Library of Philadelphia

215-686-5331

http://www.library.phila.gov/index.htm

Pittsburgh

The Carnegie Library of Pittsburgh

412-622-3138

http://www.clpgh.org/clp/Scitech/

University Park

Business Library, Paterno Library

814-865-6369

http://www.libraries.psu.edu/crsweb/business/
patents/

Rhode Island

Providence

Providence Public Library

401-455-8027

http://www.provlib.org

South Carolina

Clemson

R. M. Cooper Library, Clemson University

864-656-3024

http://www.lib.clemson.govdos/patents/
newpat.htm

South Dakota

Rapid City

Devereaux Library, South Dakota School of
Mines and Technology

605-394-1275

http://www.sdsmt.edu/services/library/
library.html

Tennessee

Memphis

Memphis & Shelby County Public Library &
Information Center

901-725-8877

http://www.memphislibrary.lib.tn.us/ftsbc/
pttr.htm

Nashville

Stevenson Science and Engineering Library,
Vanderbilt University

615-322-2717

http://www.library.vanderbilt.edu/science/
science.html

Texas

Austin
McKinney Engineering Library, ECJ 1.300
The University of Texas at Austin
512-495-4500
http://www.lib.utexas.edu/Libs/ENG/engin.html

College Station
Texas A&M University
409-845-5745
http://library.tamu.edu/govdocs/intprop.html

Dallas
Dallas Public Library
214-670-1468
http://www.lib.ci.dallas.tx.us/cgi/cgi.htm

Houston
Fondren Library—MS 225, Rice University
713-348-5483
http://www.rice.edu/Fondren/PTDL/

Lubbock
Texas Tech University Library
806-742-2282
http://www.lib.ttu.edu/gov_docs/index.htm

San Antonio
San Antonio Public Library
Not yet operational
http://www.sat.lib.tx.us

Utah

Salt Lake City
University of Utah Marriott Library
801-581-8394
http://www.lib.utah.edu/govdoc/

Vermont

Burlington
Bailey/Howe Library, University of Vermont
802-656-2542
http://bailey.uvm.edu/govdocs/vptdl.html

Virginia

Richmond
James Branch Cabell Library, Virginia
Commonwealth University
804-828-1104
http://www.library.vcu.edu/jbc/govdocs/
govhome.html

Washington

Seattle
Engineering Library, University of Washington
206-543-0740
http://www.lib.washington.edu/Engineering/

West Virginia

Morgantown
Evansdale Library, West Virginia University
304-293-4695, Ext.5113
http://www.libraries.wvu.edu/evansdale/
index.htm

Wisconsin

Madison
Kurt F. Wendt Library, University of Wisconsin-
Madison
608-262-6845
http://www.wisc.edu/wendt/patent/patent.html

Milwaukee
Milwaukee Public Library
414-286-3051
http://www.mpl.org/

Wyoming

Casper
Natrona County Public Library
307-237-4935
http://www-wsl.state.wy.us/natrona/ptdl.htm

How to Use the Forms CD-ROM

A. Installing the Form Files Onto Your Computer B/2

    1. Windows 95, 98 and 2000 Users B/2

    2. Macintosh Users B/2

B. Using the Word Processing Files B/3

C. Using IRS Form Files B/4

D. Using the Charts B/6

E. List of Files Included on the Forms CD-ROM B/6

The charts in Appendix A and the tear-out forms in Appendix C are included on a CD-ROM disk in the back of the book. This CD-ROM, which can be used with Windows computers, installs files that can be opened, printed and edited using a word processor or other software. It is NOT a stand-alone software program. Please read this Appendix and the README.TXT file included on the CD-ROM for instructions on using the forms CD.

Note to Mac users: This CD-ROM and its files should also work on a Macintosh and other operating systems. Please note, however, that Nolo cannot provide technical support for non-Windows users.

How to View the README File

If you do not know how to view the file README.TXT, insert the forms disk into your computer's CD-ROM drive and follow these instructions:

- Windows 95, 98 and 2000: (1) On your PC's desktop, double-click the My Computer icon; (2) double-click the icon for the CD-ROM drive into which the forms disk was inserted; (3) double-click the file README.TXT.
- Macintosh: (1) On your Mac desktop, double-click the icon for the CD-ROM that you inserted; (2) double-click on the file README.TXT.

While the README file is open, print it out by using the Print command in the File menu.

Three different kinds of files are contained on the CD-ROM:

- Word processing forms that you can open, complete, print and save with your word processing program (see Section B, below), and
- Forms from the IRS that can be viewed only with Adobe Acrobat Reader 3.0 or higher.

You can install Acrobat Reader from the forms CD (see Section C below). Some of these forms have fill-in text fields. Once you complete a form, you will not be able to save a copy of the filled-in form to disk. You can, however, print out a completed version.

- Charts from Appendix A that can be viewed only with Adobe Acrobat Reader 3.0 or higher. These charts contain contact information as well as linked URLs for various states' agencies.

See Section E for a list of files and file formats.

A. Installing the Form Files Onto Your Computer

Before you can do anything with the files on the CD-ROM, you need to install them onto your hard disk. In accordance with U.S. copyright laws, remember that copies of the disk and its files are for your personal use only.

Insert the forms CD and do the following:

1. Windows 95, 98 and 2000 Users

Follow the instructions that appear on the screen. (If nothing happens when you insert the forms CD-ROM, then (1) double-click the My Computer icon; (2) double-click the icon for the CD-ROM drive into which the forms disk was inserted; and (3) double click the file SETUP.HLP.)

By default, all the files are installed to the \Small Business Start-Up Forms folder in the \Program Files folder of your computer. A folder called "Small Business Start-Up Forms" is added to the "Programs" folder of the Start menu.

2. Macintosh Users

Step 1: If the "Small Business Start-Up CD" window is not open, open it by double-clicking the "Small Business Start-Up CD" icon.

Step 2: Select the "Small Business Start-Up Forms" folder icon.

Step 3: Drag and drop the folder icon onto the icon of your hard disk.

B. Using the Word Processing Files

This section concerns the partnership agreement form that can be opened and edited with your word processing program. (Other files in PDF format are discussed in Sections C and D, below.)

A Partnership Agreement can be created using the file PARTAGRE.RTF. RTF files can be read by most recent word processing programs including all versions of MS Word for Windows and Macintosh, WordPad for Windows 95, 98 and 2000, and recent versions of WordPerfect for Windows and Macintosh.

To use an RTF file to create your documents, you must: (1) open a file in your word processor or text editor; (2) edit the form by filling in the required information; (3) print it out; (4) rename and save your revised file.

The following are general instructions on how to do this. However, each word processor uses different commands to open, format, save and print documents. Please read your word processor's manual for specific instructions on performing these tasks.

DO NOT CALL NOLO'S TECHNICAL SUPPORT IF YOU HAVE QUESTIONS ON HOW TO USE YOUR WORD PROCESSOR.

Step 1: Opening a File

There are three ways to open the word processing files included on the CD-ROM after you have installed them onto your computer.

- Windows users can open a file by selecting its "shortcut" as follows: (1) Click the Windows "Start" button; (2) open the "Programs" folder; (3) open the "Small Business Start-Up Forms" subfolder; and (4) click on the shortcut to the form you want to work with.

- Both Windows and Macintosh users can open a file directly by double-clicking on it. Use My Computer or Windows Explorer (Windows 95, 98 and 2000) or the Finder (Macintosh) to go to the folder you installed or copied the disk's files to. Then, double-click on the specific file you want to open.

Where Are the Files Installed?

Windows Users

- RTF files are installed by default to a folder named \Small Business Start-Up Forms\ in the \Program Files folder of your computer.

Macintosh Users

- RTF files are located in the the "Small Business Start-Up Forms" folder.

- You can also open a file from within your word processor. To do this, you must first start your word processor. Then, go to the File menu and choose the Open command. This opens a dialog box where you will tell the program (1) the type of file you want to open (*.RTF); and (2) the location and name of the file (you will need to navigate through the directory tree to get to the folder on your hard disk where the CD's files have been installed). If these directions are unclear you will need to look through the manual for your word processing program—Nolo's technical support department will NOT be able to help you with the use of your word processing program.

Step 2: Editing Your Document

Fill in the appropriate information according to the instructions and sample agreements in the book. Underlines are used to indicate where you need to enter your information, frequently followed by instructions in brackets. *Be sure to delete the underlines and instructions from your edited document.* If you do not know how to use your word processor to edit a document, you will need to look through the manual for your word processing program—Nolo's technical support department will NOT be able to help you with the use of your word processing program.

Editing Forms That Have Optional or Alternative Text

Some of the forms have check boxes before text. The check boxes indicate:

- Optional text, which you choose whether to include or exclude
- Alternative text, where you select one alternative to include and exclude the other alternatives.

If you are using the tear-out forms in Appendix C, you simply mark the appropriate box to make your choice.

If you are using the forms CD, however, we recommend that instead of marking the check boxes, you do the following:

Optional text

If you **don't want** to include optional text, just delete it from your document.

If you **do want** to include optional text, just leave it in your document.

In either case, delete the check box itself as well as the italicized instructions that the text is optional.

Alternative text

First delete all the alternatives that you do not want to include.

Then delete the remaining check boxes, as well as the italicized instructions that you need to select one of the alternatives provided.

Step 3: Printing Out the Document

Use your word processor's or text editor's "Print" command to print out your document. If you do not know how to use your word processor to print a document, you will need to look through the manual for your word processing program—Nolo's technical support department will NOT be able to help you with the use of your word processing program.

Step 4: Saving Your Document

After filling in the form, use the "Save As" command to save and rename the file. Because all the files are "read-only" you will not be able to use the "Save" command. This is for your protection. IF YOU SAVE THE FILE WITHOUT RENAMING IT, THE UNDERLINES THAT INDICATE WHERE YOU NEED TO ENTER YOUR INFORMATION WILL BE LOST AND YOU WILL NOT BE ABLE TO CREATE A NEW DOCUMENT WITH THIS FILE WITHOUT RECOPYING THE ORIGINAL FILE FROM THE CD-ROM.

If you do not know how to use your word processor to save a document, you will need to look through the manual for your word processing program—Nolo's technical support department will NOT be able to help you with the use of your word processing program.

C. Using IRS Form Files

Electronic copies of useful forms from the IRS are included on the CD-ROM disk in Adobe Acrobat PDF format. You must have the Adobe Acrobat Reader installed on your computer (see below) to use these forms. All forms, their file names and file formats are listed in Section E, below.

These files were created by the IRS, not by Nolo.

These forms were created with fill-in text fields. To create your document using these files, you must: (1) open a file; (2) fill-in the text fields using either your mouse or the tab key on your keyboard to navigate from field to field; and (3) print it out;

NOTE: While you can print out your completed form, you will NOT be able to save your completed form to disk.

Installing Acrobat Reader

To install the Adobe Acrobat Reader, insert the CD into your computer's CD-ROM drive and follow these instructions:

- Windows 95, 98 and 2000: Follow the instructions that appear on screen. (If nothing happens when you insert the forms CD-ROM, then (1) double-click the My Computer icon; (2) double-click the icon for the CD-ROM drive into which the forms disk was inserted; and (3) double click the file SETUP.HLP)
- Macintosh: (1) If the "Small Business Start-Up CD" window is not open, open it by double-clicking the "Small Business Start-Up CD" icon; and (2) double-click on the "Reader Installer" icon.

If you do not know how to use Adobe Acrobat to view and print the files, you will need to consult the online documentation that comes with the Acrobat Reader program.

Do NOT call Nolo technical support if you have questions on how to use Acrobat Reader.

Step 1: Opening IRS Files

PDF files, like the word processing files, can be opened one of three ways.

- Windows users can open a file by selecting its "shortcut" as follows: (1) Click the Windows "Start" button; (2) open the "Programs" folder; (3) open the "Small Business Start-Up Forms" subfolder; and (4) click on the shortcut to the form you want to work with.

- Both Windows and Macintosh users can open a file directly by double-clicking on it. Use My Computer or Windows Explorer (Windows 95, 98 and 2000) or the Finder (Macintosh) to go to the folder you created and copied the disk's files to. Then, double-click on the specific file you want to open.
- You can also open a PDF file from within Acrobat Reader. To do this, you must first start Reader. Then, go to the File menu and choose the Open command. This opens a dialog box where you will tell the program the location and name of the file (you will need to navigate through the directory tree to get to the folder on your hard disk where the CD's files have been installed). If these directions are unclear you will need to look through the manual for your word processing program—Nolo's technical support department will NOT be able to help you with the use of your word processing program.

Step 2: Filling in IRS Files

The IRS files included on this disc were created with fill-in form fields. Use your mouse or the Tab key on your keyboard to navigate from field to field within these forms. Be sure to have all the information you will need to complete a form on hand, because you will not be able to save a copy of the filled-in form to disk. You can, however, print out a completed version.

Where Are the PDF Files Installed?

- Windows Users: PDF files are installed by default to a folder named \Small Business Start-Up Forms in the \Program Files folder of your computer.
- Macintosh Users: PDF files are located in the "Small Business Start-Up Forms" folder.

Step 3: Printing IRS Files

Choose Print from the Acrobat Reader File menu. This will open the Print dialog box. In the "Print Range" section of the Print dialog box, select the appropriate print range, then click OK.

D. Using the Charts

Electronic copies of the charts in Appendix A are included on the CD-ROM disk in Adobe Acrobat PDF format. You must have the Adobe Acrobat Reader installed on your computer to use these forms.

For your convenience, these these charts have been included on the CD with "hot" URLs. If you want to go to a website listed on one of the charts in Appendix A, you can open the appropriate file (following the instructions in Section C, Step 1, above) and simply click on the URL. Clicking on the link will launch your Web browser and take you to the indicated website. Linked URLs will be green.

NOTE: The URL links have been provided for your convenience. However, things change rapidly and without warning on the Internet, so we can't guarantee that all the URLs will remain live.

For instructions on how to view these files, please follow the instructions in Section C, Step 1, above.

E. List of Files Included on the Forms CD-ROM

The following forms are included on the CD-ROM:

File Name	Chart Name
PARTAGRE.rtf	Partnership Agreement
F8716.pdf	Election to Have a Tax Year Other Than a Required Tax Year
F8832.pdf	Entity Classification Election
FSS4.pdf	Application for Employer Identification Number
FSS8.pdf	Determination of Employee Work Status for Purposes of Federal Employment Taxes and Income Tax Withholding

The following charts (from Appendix A) are also included on the CD-ROM:

File Name	Chart Name
ISSUES.pdf	Contact Information for Small Business Start-Up Issues
TAXAGENC.pdf	Contact Info for State Tax Agencies
SALES.pdf	Contact Info for State Sales Tax/ Seller's Permit Agencies
LLCOFFIC.pdf	Contact Info for LLC Offices
UNEMPLOY.pdf	Contact Info for State Unemployment Compensation Agencies
PATTRADE.pdf	Patent and Trademark Depository Libraries by State

■

Tear-Out Forms

Partnership Agreement

Application for Employer Identification Number (Form SS-4)

Determination of Employee Work Status for Purposes of Federal Employment Taxes and Income Tax Withholding (Form SS-8)

Election To Have a Tax Year Other Than a Required Tax Year (Form 8716)

Entity Classification Election (Form 8832)

Partnership Agreement

1. Partners

_____ (Partners)

make the following Partnership Agreement.

2. Creation of Partnership

As of _____, the Partners agree to enter into a Partnership for

the purpose of operating a business known as: _____

_____ (Partnership Business).

The name of the Partnership (if different from name of Partnership Business) shall be: _____

_____ (Partnership Name).

3. Nature of Partnership Business

The Partnership Business will consist of the following business activities: _____

_____ .

4. Contributions to the Partnership

The Partners will make the following contributions to the Partnership:

Name:_____ Cash: $_____

Property Description:_____ Property Value: $_____

Total: $_____

Name:_____ Cash: $_____

Property Description:_____ Property Value: $_____

Total: $_____

Name:_____ Cash: $_____

Property Description:_____ Property Value: $_____

Total: $_____

Name:_____ Cash: $_____

Property Description:_____ Property Value: $_____

Total: $_____

5. Profit and Loss Allocation

The Partners will share business profits and losses as follows:

□ in the same proportions as their contributions to the business.

□ as follows:_____ .

6. Management of Partnership Business

The Partners will have the following management powers and responsibilities:

□ The Partners will have equal management powers and responsibilities.

□ The Partners will share management powers and responsibilities as follows: _____ .

7. Addition of a Partner

A new partner may be added to the Partnership under the following conditions:

☐ unanimous vote of all Partners

☐ majority vote of Partners

☐ other conditions: _____.

8. Departure of a Partner

If any Partner leaves the Partnership for any reason, including voluntary withdrawal, expulsion or death, the Partnership shall ☐ survive ☐ dissolve.

If Partnership survives, the remaining Partner(s) shall pay the departing Partner, or the deceased Partner's estate, the fair market value of the departing Partner's share of the business as of the date of his or her departure. The Partnership's accountant shall determine the fair market value of the departing Partner's share of the business according to the following method:_____

_____.

9. Dispute Resolution

If a dispute arises under this Agreement, the Partners agree to first try to resolve the dispute with the help of a mutually agreed-upon mediator. Any costs and fees other than attorney fees shall be shared equally by the Partners. If it proves impossible to arrive at a mutually satisfactory solution, the Partners agree to submit the dispute to binding arbitration in the same city or region, conducted on a confidential basis pursuant to the Commercial Arbitration Rules of the American Arbitration Association.

10. Amendment of Agreement

This agreement may not be amended without the written consent of all Partners.

11. Partner Signatures

Name: _____ Date:_____

Address: _____

Signature:_____ SSN: _____

Name: _____ Date:_____

Address: _____

Signature:_____ SSN: _____

Name: _____ Date:_____

Address: _____

Signature:_____ SSN: _____

Name: _____ Date:_____

Address: _____

Signature:_____ SSN: _____

Form **SS-4**

(Rev. April 2000)

Department of the Treasury
Internal Revenue Service

Application for Employer Identification Number

(For use by employers, corporations, partnerships, trusts, estates, churches, government agencies, certain individuals, and others. See instructions.)

▶ Keep a copy for your records.

EIN

OMB No. 1545-0003

Please type or print clearly.

1 Name of applicant (legal name) (see instructions)

2 Trade name of business (if different from name on line 1)

3 Executor, trustee, "care of" name

4a Mailing address (street address) (room, apt., or suite no.)

5a Business address (if different from address on lines 4a and 4b)

4b City, state, and ZIP code

5b City, state, and ZIP code

6 County and state where principal business is located

7 Name of principal officer, general partner, grantor, owner, or trustor—SSN or ITIN may be required (see instructions) ▶

8a Type of entity (Check only one box.) (see instructions)

Caution: *If applicant is a limited liability company, see the instructions for line 8a.*

☐ Sole proprietor (SSN) _____
☐ Partnership
☐ REMIC
☐ State/local government
☐ Church or church-controlled organization
☐ Other nonprofit organization (specify) ▶ _____
☐ Other (specify) ▶

☐ Personal service corp.
☐ National Guard
☐ Farmers' cooperative

☐ Estate (SSN of decedent) _____
☐ Plan administrator (SSN) _____
☐ Other corporation (specify) ▶ _____
☐ Trust
☐ Federal government/military
(enter GEN if applicable) _____

8b If a corporation, name the state or foreign country (if applicable) where incorporated

State

Foreign country

9 Reason for applying (Check only one box.) (see instructions)
☐ Started new business (specify type) ▶_____
_____
☐ Hired employees (Check the box and see line 12.)
☐ Created a pension plan (specify type) ▶

☐ Banking purpose (specify purpose) ▶ _____
☐ Changed type of organization (specify new type) ▶ _____
☐ Purchased going business
☐ Created a trust (specify type) ▶ _____
☐ Other (specify) ▶

10 Date business started or acquired (month, day, year) (see instructions)

11 Closing month of accounting year (see instructions)

12 First date wages or annuities were paid or will be paid (month, day, year). **Note:** *If applicant is a withholding agent, enter date income will first be paid to nonresident alien. (month, day, year)* . . . . ▶

13 Highest number of employees expected in the next 12 months. **Note:** *If the applicant does not expect to have any employees during the period, enter -0-. (see instructions)* . . . . ▶

Nonagricultural	Agricultural	Household

14 Principal activity (see instructions) ▶

15 Is the principal business activity manufacturing? . . . . ☐ Yes ☐ No
If "Yes," principal product and raw material used ▶

16 To whom are most of the products or services sold? Please check one box. ☐ Business (wholesale)
☐ Public (retail) ☐ Other (specify) ▶ ☐ N/A

17a Has the applicant ever applied for an employer identification number for this or any other business? . . . . ☐ Yes ☐ No
Note: *If "Yes," please complete lines 17b and 17c.*

17b If you checked "Yes" on line 17a, give applicant's legal name and trade name shown on prior application, if different from line 1 or 2 above.
Legal name ▶   Trade name ▶

17c Approximate date when and city and state where the application was filed. Enter previous employer identification number if known.

Approximate date when filed (mo., day, year)	City and state where filed	Previous EIN

Under penalties of perjury, I declare that I have examined this application, and to the best of my knowledge and belief, it is true, correct, and complete.

Business telephone number (include area code)
( )

Fax telephone number (include area code)
( )

Name and title (Please type or print clearly.) ▶

Signature ▶   Date ▶

Note: *Do not write below this line. For official use only.*

Please leave blank ▶

Geo.	Ind.	Class	Size	Reason for applying

For Privacy Act and Paperwork Reduction Act Notice, see page 4.

Cat. No. 16055N

Form **SS-4** (Rev. 4-2000)

General Instructions

Section references are to the Internal Revenue Code unless otherwise noted.

Purpose of Form

Use Form SS-4 to apply for an employer identification number (EIN). An EIN is a nine-digit number (for example, 12-3456789) assigned to sole proprietors, corporations, partnerships, estates, trusts, and other entities for tax filing and reporting purposes. The information you provide on this form will establish your business tax account.

Caution: *An EIN is for use in connection with your business activities only. Do **not** use your EIN in place of your social security number (SSN).*

Who Must File

You must file this form if you have not been assigned an EIN before and:

• You pay wages to one or more employees including household employees.

• You are required to have an EIN to use on any return, statement, or other document, even if you are not an employer.

• You are a withholding agent required to withhold taxes on income, other than wages, paid to a nonresident alien (individual, corporation, partnership, etc.). A withholding agent may be an agent, broker, fiduciary, manager, tenant, or spouse, and is required to file **Form 1042,** Annual Withholding Tax Return for U.S. Source Income of Foreign Persons.

• You file **Schedule C,** Profit or Loss From Business, **Schedule C-EZ,** Net Profit From Business, or **Schedule F,** Profit or Loss From Farming, of **Form 1040,** U.S. Individual Income Tax Return, **and** have a Keogh plan or are required to file excise, employment, or alcohol, tobacco, or firearms returns.

The following must use EINs even if they do not have any employees:

• State and local agencies who serve as tax reporting agents for public assistance recipients, under Rev. Proc. 80-4, 1980-1 C.B. 581, should obtain a separate EIN for this reporting. See **Household employer** on page 3.

• Trusts, except the following:

  1. Certain grantor-owned trusts. (See the **Instructions for Form 1041,** U.S. Income Tax Return for Estates and Trusts.)

  2. Individual retirement arrangement (IRA) trusts, unless the trust has to file **Form 990-T,** Exempt Organization Business Income Tax Return. (See the **Instructions for Form 990-T.**)

• Estates

• Partnerships

• REMICs (real estate mortgage investment conduits) (See the **Instructions for Form 1066,** U.S. Real Estate Mortgage Investment Conduit (REMIC) Income Tax Return.)

• Corporations

• Nonprofit organizations (churches, clubs, etc.)

• Farmers' cooperatives

• Plan administrators (A plan administrator is the person or group of persons specified as the administrator by the instrument under which the plan is operated.)

When To Apply for a New EIN

New Business. If you become the new owner of an existing business, **do not** use the EIN of the former owner. **If you already have an EIN, use that number.** If you do not have an EIN, apply for one on this form. If you become the "owner" of a corporation by acquiring its stock, use the corporation's EIN.

Changes in Organization or Ownership. If you already have an EIN, you may need to get a new one if either the organization or ownership of your business changes. If you incorporate a sole proprietorship or form a partnership, you must get a new EIN. However, **do not** apply for a new EIN if:

• You change only the name of your business,

• You elected on **Form 8832,** Entity Classification Election, to change the way the entity is taxed, or

• A partnership terminates because at least 50% of the total interests in partnership capital and profits were sold or exchanged within a 12-month period. (See Regulations section 301.6109-1(d)(2)(iii).) The EIN for the terminated partnership should continue to be used.

Note: *If you are electing to be an "S corporation," be sure you file* **Form 2553,** *Election by a Small Business Corporation.*

File Only One Form SS-4. File only one Form SS-4, regardless of the number of businesses operated or trade names under which a business operates. However, each corporation in an affiliated group must file a separate application.

EIN Applied for, But Not Received. If you do not have an EIN by the time a return is due, write "Applied for" and the date you applied in the space shown for the number. **Do not** show your social security number (SSN) as an EIN on returns.

If you do not have an EIN by the time a tax deposit is due, send your payment to the Internal Revenue Service Center for your filing area. (See **Where To Apply** below.) Make your check or money order payable to "United States Treasury" and show your name (as shown on Form SS-4), address, type of tax, period covered, and date you applied for an EIN. Send an explanation with the deposit.

For more information about EINs, see **Pub. 583,** Starting a Business and Keeping Records, and **Pub. 1635,** Understanding Your EIN.

How To Apply

You can apply for an EIN either by mail or by telephone. You can get an EIN immediately by calling the Tele-TIN number for the service center for your state, or you can send the completed Form SS-4 directly to the service center to receive your EIN by mail.

Application by Tele-TIN. Under the Tele-TIN program, you can receive your EIN by telephone and use it immediately to file a return or make a payment. To receive an EIN by telephone, complete Form SS-4, then call the Tele-TIN number listed for your state under **Where To Apply.** The person making the call must be authorized to sign the form. (See **Signature** on page 4.)

An IRS representative will use the information from the Form SS-4 to establish your account and assign you an EIN. Write the number you are given on the upper right corner of the form and sign and date it.

Mail or fax (facsimile) the signed Form SS-4 **within 24 hours** to the Tele-TIN Unit at the service center address for your state. The IRS representative will give you the fax number. The fax numbers are also listed in Pub. 1635.

Taxpayer representatives can receive their client's EIN by telephone if they first send a fax of a completed **Form 2848,** Power of Attorney and Declaration of Representative, or **Form 8821,** Tax Information Authorization, to the Tele-TIN unit. The Form 2848 or Form 8821 will be used solely to release the EIN to the representative authorized on the form.

Application by Mail. Complete Form SS-4 at least 4 to 5 weeks before you will need an EIN. Sign and date the application and mail it to the service center address for your state. You will receive your EIN in the mail in approximately 4 weeks.

Where To Apply

The Tele-TIN numbers listed below will involve a long-distance charge to callers outside of the local calling area and can be used only to apply for an EIN. **The numbers may change without notice.** Call 1-800-829-1040 to verify a number or to ask about the status of an application by mail.

If your principal business, office or agency, or legal residence in the case of an individual, is located in:	Call the Tele-TIN number shown or file with the Internal Revenue Service Center at:
Florida, Georgia, South Carolina	Attn: Entity Control Atlanta, GA 39901 770-455-2360
New Jersey, New York (New York City and counties of Nassau, Rockland, Suffolk, and Westchester)	Attn: Entity Control Holtsville, NY 00501 516-447-4955
New York (all other counties), Connecticut, Maine, Massachusetts, New Hampshire, Rhode Island, Vermont	Attn: Entity Control Andover, MA 05501 978-474-9717
Illinois, Iowa, Minnesota, Missouri, Wisconsin	Attn: Entity Control Stop 6800 2306 E. Bannister Rd. Kansas City, MO 64999 816-926-5999
Delaware, District of Columbia, Maryland, Pennsylvania, Virginia	Attn: Entity Control Philadelphia, PA 19255 215-516-6999
Indiana, Kentucky, Michigan, Ohio, West Virginia	Attn: Entity Control Cincinnati, OH 45999 859-292-5467

Kansas, New Mexico, Oklahoma, Texas	Attn: Entity Control Austin, TX 73301 512-460-7843
Alaska, Arizona, California (counties of Alpine, Amador, Butte, Calaveras, Colusa, Contra Costa, Del Norte, El Dorado, Glenn, Humboldt, Lake, Lassen, Marin, Mendocino, Modoc, Napa, Nevada, Placer, Plumas, Sacramento, San Joaquin, Shasta, Sierra, Siskiyou, Solano, Sonoma, Sutter, Tehama, Trinity, Yolo, and Yuba), Colorado, Idaho, Montana, Nebraska, Nevada, North Dakota, Oregon, South Dakota, Utah, Washington, Wyoming	Attn: Entity Control Mail Stop 6271 P.O. Box 9941 Ogden, UT 84201 801-620-7645
California (all other counties), Hawaii	Attn: Entity Control Fresno, CA 93888 559-452-4010
Alabama, Arkansas, Louisiana, Mississippi, North Carolina, Tennessee	Attn: Entity Control Memphis, TN 37501 901-546-3920
If you have no legal residence, principal place of business, or principal office or agency in any state	Attn: Entity Control Philadelphia, PA 19255 215-516-6999

Specific Instructions

The instructions that follow are for those items that are not self-explanatory. Enter N/A (nonapplicable) on the lines that do not apply.

Line 1. Enter the legal name of the entity applying for the EIN exactly as it appears on the social security card, charter, or other applicable legal document.

Individuals. Enter your first name, middle initial, and last name. If you are a sole proprietor, enter your individual name, not your business name. Enter your business name on line 2. Do not use abbreviations or nicknames on line 1.

Trusts. Enter the name of the trust.

Estate of a decedent. Enter the name of the estate.

Partnerships. Enter the legal name of the partnership as it appears in the partnership agreement. **Do not** list the names of the partners on line 1. See the specific instructions for line 7.

Corporations. Enter the corporate name as it appears in the corporation charter or other legal document creating it.

Plan administrators. Enter the name of the plan administrator. A plan administrator who already has an EIN should use that number.

Line 2. Enter the trade name of the business if different from the legal name. The trade name is the "doing business as" name.

Note: *Use the full legal name on line 1 on all tax returns filed for the entity. However, if you enter a trade name on line 2 and choose to use the trade name instead of the legal name, enter the trade name on all returns you file. To prevent processing delays and errors, **always** use either the legal name only or the trade name only on all tax returns.*

Line 3. Trusts enter the name of the trustee. Estates enter the name of the executor, administrator, or other fiduciary. If the entity applying has a designated person to receive tax information, enter that person's name as the "care of" person. Print or type the first name, middle initial, and last name.

Line 7. Enter the first name, middle initial, last name, and SSN of a principal officer if the business is a corporation; of a general partner if a partnership; of the owner of a single member entity that is disregarded as an entity separate from its owner; or of a grantor, owner, or trustor if a trust. If the person in question is an alien individual with a previously assigned individual taxpayer identification number (ITIN), enter the ITIN in the space provided, instead of an SSN. You are not required to enter an SSN or ITIN if the reason you are applying for an EIN is to make an entity classification election (see Regulations section 301.7701-1 through 301.7701-3), and you are a nonresident alien with no effectively connected income from sources within the United States.

Line 8a. Check the box that best describes the type of entity applying for the EIN. If you are an alien individual with an ITIN previously assigned to you, enter the ITIN in place of a requested SSN.

Caution: *This is not an election for a tax classification of an entity. See "Limited liability company (LLC)" below.*

If not specifically mentioned, check the "Other" box, enter the type of entity and the type of return that will be filed (for example, common trust fund, Form 1065). Do not enter N/A. If you are an alien individual applying for an EIN, see the **Line 7** instructions above.

Sole proprietor. Check this box if you file Schedule C, C-EZ, or F (Form 1040) and have a qualified plan, or are required to file excise, employment, or alcohol, tobacco, or firearms returns, or are a payer of gambling winnings. Enter your SSN (or ITIN) in the space provided. If you are a nonresident alien with are a nonresident alien with no effectively

connected income from sources within the United States, you do not need to enter an SSN or ITIN.

REMIC. Check this box if the entity has elected to be treated as a real estate mortgage investment conduit (REMIC). See the Instructions for Form 1066 for more information.

Other nonprofit organization. Check this box if the nonprofit organization is other than a church or church-controlled organization and specify the type of nonprofit organization (for example, an educational organization).

If the organization also seeks tax-exempt status, you must file either **Package 1023,** Application for Recognition of Exemption, or **Package 1024,** Application for Recognition of Exemption Under Section 501(a). Get **Pub. 557,** Tax Exempt Status for Your Organization, for more information.

Group exemption number (GEN). If the organization is covered by a group exemption letter, enter the four-digit GEN. (Do not confuse the GEN with the nine-digit EIN.) If you do not know the GEN, contact the parent organization. Get Pub. 557 for more information about group exemption numbers.

Withholding agent. If you are a withholding agent required to file Form 1042, check the "Other" box and enter "Withholding agent."

Personal service corporation. Check this box if the entity is a personal service corporation. An entity is a personal service corporation for a tax year only if:

● The principal activity of the entity during the testing period (prior tax year) for the tax year is the performance of personal services substantially by employee-owners, and

● The employee-owners own at least 10% of the fair market value of the outstanding stock in the entity on the last day of the testing period.

Personal services include performance of services in such fields as health, law, accounting, or consulting. For more information about personal service corporations, see the **Instructions for Forms 1120 and 1120-A,** and **Pub. 542,** Corporations.

Limited liability company (LLC). See the definition of limited liability company in the **Instructions for Form 1065,** U.S. Partnership Return of Income. An LLC with two or more members can be a partnership or an association taxable as a corporation. An LLC with a single owner can be an association taxable as a corporation or an entity disregarded as an entity separate from its owner. See Form 8832 for more details.

Note: *A domestic LLC with at least two members that does not file Form 8832 is classified as a partnership for Federal income tax purposes.*

● If the entity is classified as a partnership for Federal income tax purposes, check the "partnership" box.

● If the entity is classified as a corporation for Federal income tax purposes, check the "Other corporation" box and write "limited liability co." in the space provided.

● If the entity is disregarded as an entity separate from its owner, check the "Other" box and write in "disregarded entity" in the space provided.

Plan administrator. If the plan administrator is an individual, enter the plan administrator's SSN in the space provided.

Other corporation. This box is for any corporation other than a personal service corporation. If you check this box, enter the type of corporation (such as insurance company) in the space provided.

Household employer. If you are an individual, check the "Other" box and enter "Household employer" and your SSN. If you are a state or local agency serving as a tax reporting agent for public assistance recipients who become household employers, check the "Other" box and enter "Household employer agent." If you are a trust that qualifies as a household employer, you do not need a separate EIN for reporting tax information relating to household employees; use the EIN of the trust.

QSub. For a qualified subchapter S subsidiary (QSub) check the "Other" box and specify "QSub."

Line 9. Check only **one** box. Do not enter N/A.

Started new business. Check this box if you are starting a new business that requires an EIN. If you check this box, enter the type of business being started. **Do not** apply if you already have an EIN and are only adding another place of business.

Hired employees. Check this box if the existing business is requesting an EIN because it has hired or is hiring employees and is therefore required to file employment tax returns. **Do not** apply if you already have an EIN and are only hiring employees. For information on the applicable employment taxes for family members, see **Circular E,** Employer's Tax Guide (Publication 15).

Created a pension plan. Check this box if you have created a pension plan and need an EIN for reporting purposes. Also, enter the type of plan.

Note: *Check this box if you are applying for a trust EIN when a new pension plan is established.*

Banking purpose. Check this box if you are requesting an EIN for banking purposes only, and enter the banking purpose (for example, a bowling league for depositing dues or an investment club for dividend and interest reporting).

Changed type of organization. Check this box if the business is changing its type of organization, for example, if the business was a sole proprietorship and has been incorporated or has become a partnership. If you check this box, specify in the space provided the type of change made, for example, "from sole proprietorship to partnership."

Purchased going business. Check this box if you purchased an existing business. **Do not** use the former owner's EIN. **Do not** apply for a new EIN if you already have one. Use your own EIN.

Created a trust. Check this box if you created a trust, and enter the type of trust created. For example, indicate if the trust is a nonexempt charitable trust or a split-interest trust.

Note: *Do not check this box if you are applying for a trust EIN when a new pension plan is established. Check "Created a pension plan."*

Exception. **Do not** file this form for certain grantor-type trusts. The trustee does not need an EIN for the trust if the trustee furnishes the name and TIN of the grantor/owner and the address of the trust to all payors. See the Instructions for Form 1041 for more information.

Other (specify). Check this box if you are requesting an EIN for any other reason, and enter the reason.

Line 10. If you are starting a new business, enter the starting date of the business. If the business you acquired is already operating, enter the date you acquired the business. Trusts should enter the date the trust was legally created. Estates should enter the date of death of the decedent whose name appears on line 1 or the date when the estate was legally funded.

Line 11. Enter the last month of your accounting year or tax year. An accounting or tax year is usually 12 consecutive months, either a calendar year or a fiscal year (including a period of 52 or 53 weeks). A calendar year is 12 consecutive months ending on December 31. A fiscal year is either 12 consecutive months ending on the last day of any month other than December or a 52-53 week year. For more information on accounting periods, see **Pub. 538,** Accounting Periods and Methods.

Individuals. Your tax year generally will be a calendar year.

Partnerships. Partnerships generally must adopt one of the following tax years:
* The tax year of the majority of its partners,
* The tax year common to all of its principal partners,
* The tax year that results in the least aggregate deferral of income, or
* In certain cases, some other tax year.

See the Instructions for Form 1065 for more information.

REMIC. REMICs must have a calendar year as their tax year.

Personal service corporations. A personal service corporation generally must adopt a calendar year unless:
* It can establish a business purpose for having a different tax year, or
* It elects under section 444 to have a tax year other than a calendar year.

Trusts. Generally, a trust must adopt a calendar year except for the following:
* Tax-exempt trusts,
* Charitable trusts, and
* Grantor-owned trusts.

Line 12. If the business has or will have employees, enter the date on which the business began or will begin to pay wages. If the business does not plan to have employees, enter N/A.

Withholding agent. Enter the date you began or will begin to pay income to a nonresident alien. This also applies to individuals who are required to file Form 1042 to report alimony paid to a nonresident alien.

Line 13. For a definition of agricultural labor (farmwork), see **Circular A,** Agricultural Employer's Tax Guide (Publication 51).

Line 14. Generally, enter the exact type of business being operated (for example, advertising agency, farm, food or beverage establishment, labor union, real estate agency, steam laundry, rental of coin-operated vending machine, or investment club). Also state if the business will involve the sale or distribution of alcoholic beverages.

Governmental. Enter the type of organization (state, county, school district, municipality, etc.).

Nonprofit organization (other than governmental). Enter whether organized for religious, educational, or humane purposes, and the principal activity (for example, religious organization—hospital, charitable).

Mining and quarrying. Specify the process and the principal product (for example, mining bituminous coal, contract drilling for oil, or quarrying dimension stone).

Contract construction. Specify whether general contracting or special trade contracting. Also, show the type of work normally performed (for example, general contractor for residential buildings or electrical subcontractor).

Food or beverage establishments. Specify the type of establishment and state whether you employ workers who receive tips (for example, lounge—yes).

Trade. Specify the type of sales and the principal line of goods sold (for example, wholesale dairy products, manufacturer's representative for mining machinery, or retail hardware).

Manufacturing. Specify the type of establishment operated (for example, sawmill or vegetable cannery).

Signature. The application must be signed by (a) the individual, if the applicant is an individual, (b) the president, vice president, or other principal officer, if the applicant is a corporation, (c) a responsible and duly authorized member or officer having knowledge of its affairs, if the applicant is a partnership or other unincorporated organization, or (d) the fiduciary, if the applicant is a trust or an estate.

How To Get Forms and Publications

Phone. You can order forms, instructions, and publications by phone 24 hours a day, 7 days a week. Just call 1-800-TAX-FORM (1-800-829-3676). You should receive your order or notification of its status within 10 workdays.

Personal computer. With your personal computer and modem, you can get the forms and information you need using IRS's Internet Web Site at **www.irs.gov** or File Transfer Protocol at **ftp.irs.gov.**

CD-ROM. For small businesses, return preparers, or others who may frequently need tax forms or publications, a CD-ROM containing over 2,000 tax products (including many prior year forms) can be purchased from the National Technical Information Service (NTIS).

To order **Pub. 1796,** Federal Tax Products on CD-ROM, call **1-877-CDFORMS** (1-877-233-6767) toll free or connect to **www.irs.gov/cdorders**

Privacy Act and Paperwork Reduction Act Notice. We ask for the information on this form to carry out the Internal Revenue laws of the United States. We need it to comply with section 6109 and the regulations thereunder which generally require the inclusion of an employer identification number (EIN) on certain returns, statements, or other documents filed with the Internal Revenue Service. Information on this form may be used to determine which Federal tax returns you are required to file and to provide you with related forms and publications. We disclose this form to the Social Security Administration for their use in determining compliance with applicable laws. We will be unable to issue an EIN to you unless you provide all of the requested information which applies to your entity.

You are not required to provide the information requested on a form that is subject to the Paperwork Reduction Act unless the form displays a valid OMB control number. Books or records relating to a form or its instructions must be retained as long as their contents may become material in the administration of any Internal Revenue law. Generally, tax returns/return information are confidential, as required by section 6103.

The time needed to complete and file this form will vary depending on individual circumstances. The estimated average time is:

Recordkeeping	7 min.
Learning about the law or the form	22 min.
Preparing the form	46 min.
Copying, assembling, and sending the form to the IRS . .	20 min.

If you have comments concerning the accuracy of these time estimates or suggestions for making this form simpler, we would be happy to hear from you. You can write to the Tax Forms Committee, Western Area Distribution Center, Rancho Cordova, CA 95743-0001. **Do not** send the form to this address. Instead, see **Where To Apply** on page 2.

Form **SS-8**

(Rev. June 1997)

Department of the Treasury
Internal Revenue Service

Determination of Employee Work Status
for Purposes of Federal Employment Taxes
and Income Tax Withholding

OMB No. 1545-0004

Paperwork Reduction Act Notice

We ask for the information on this form to carry out the Internal Revenue laws of the United States. You are required to give us the information. We need it to ensure that you are complying with these laws and to allow us to figure and collect the right amount of tax.

You are not required to provide the information requested on a form that is subject to the Paperwork Reduction Act unless the form displays a valid OMB control number. Books or records relating to a form or its instructions must be retained as long as their contents may become material in the administration of any Internal Revenue law. Generally, tax returns and return information are confidential, as required by Code section 6103.

The time needed to complete and file this form will vary depending on individual circumstances. The estimated average time is: **Recordkeeping,** 34 hr., 55 min.; **Learning about the law or the form,** 12 min.; and **Preparing and sending the form to the IRS,** 46 min. If you have comments concerning the accuracy of these time estimates or suggestions for making this form simpler, we would be happy to hear from you. You can write to the Tax Forms Committee, Western Area Distribution Center, Rancho Cordova, CA 95743-0001. **DO NOT** send the tax form to this address. Instead, see **General Information** for where to file.

Purpose

Employers and workers file Form SS-8 to get a determination as to whether a worker is an employee for purposes of Federal employment taxes and income tax withholding.

General Information

Complete this form carefully. If the firm is completing the form, complete it for **ONE** individual who is representative of the class of workers whose status is in question. If you want a written determination for more than one class of workers, complete a separate Form SS-8 for one worker

from each class whose status is typical of that class. A written determination for any worker will apply to other workers of the same class if the facts are not materially different from those of the worker whose status was ruled upon.

*Caution: Form SS-8 is **not** a claim for refund of social security and Medicare taxes or Federal income tax withholding. Also, a determination that an individual is an employee does not necessarily reduce any current or prior tax liability. A worker must file his or her income tax return even if a determination has not been made by the due date of the return.*

Where to file.—In the list below, find the state where your legal residence, principal place of business, office, or agency is located. Send Form SS-8 to the address listed for your location.

Location:	Send to:
Alaska, Arizona, Arkansas, California, Colorado, Hawaii, Idaho, Illinois, Iowa, Kansas, Minnesota, Missouri, Montana, Nebraska, Nevada, New Mexico, North Dakota, Oklahoma, Oregon, South Dakota, Texas, Utah, Washington, Wisconsin, Wyoming	Internal Revenue Service SS-8 Determinations P.O. Box 1231, Stop 4106 AUSC Austin, TX 78767
Alabama, Connecticut, Delaware, District of Columbia, Florida, Georgia, Indiana, Kentucky, Louisiana, Maine, Maryland, Massachusetts, Michigan, Mississippi, New Hampshire, New Jersey, New York, North Carolina, Ohio, Pennsylvania, Rhode Island, South Carolina, Tennessee, Vermont, Virginia, West Virginia, All other locations not listed	Internal Revenue Service SS-8 Determinations Two Lakemont Road Newport, VT 05855-1555
American Samoa, Guam, Puerto Rico, U.S. Virgin Islands	Internal Revenue Service Mercantile Plaza 2 Avenue Ponce de Leon San Juan, Puerto Rico 00918

Name of firm (or person) for whom the worker performed services	Name of worker	
Address of firm (include street address, apt. or suite no., city, state, and ZIP code)	Address of worker (include street address, apt. or suite no., city, state, and ZIP code)	
Trade name	Telephone number (include area code) ( )	Worker's social security number
Telephone number (include area code) ( )	Firm's employer identification number	

Check type of firm for which the work relationship is in question:

☐ **Individual**   ☐ **Partnership**   ☐ **Corporation**   ☐ **Other** (specify) ▶ ....

Important Information Needed To Process Your Request

This form is being completed by: ☐ Firm   ☐ Worker

If this form is being completed by the worker, the IRS **must** have your permission to disclose your name to the firm.

Do you object to disclosing your name and the information on this form to the firm? . . . .   ☐ Yes   ☐ No

If you answer "Yes," the IRS cannot act on your request. **Do not complete the rest of this form unless the IRS asks for it.**

Under section 6110 of the Internal Revenue Code, the information on this form and related file documents will be open to the public if any ruling or determination is made. However, names, addresses, and taxpayer identification numbers will be removed before the information is made public.

Is there any other information you want removed? . . . .   ☐ Yes   ☐ No

If you check "Yes," we cannot process your request unless you submit a copy of this form and copies of all supporting documents showing, in brackets, the information you want removed. Attach a separate statement showing which specific exemption of section 6110(c) applies to each bracketed part.

Form **SS-8** (Rev. 6-97)

This form is designed to cover many work activities, so some of the questions may not apply to you. **You must answer ALL items or mark them "Unknown" or "Does not apply."** *If you need more space, attach another sheet.*

Total number of workers in this class. (Attach names and addresses. If more than 10 workers, list only 10.) ▶ _____

This information is about services performed by the worker from _____ to _____
(month, day, year)   (month, day, year)

Is the worker still performing services for the firm? . . . . ☐ **Yes** ☐ **No**

- If "No," what was the date of termination? ▶ _____
  (month, day, year)

1a Describe the firm's business ....

  b Describe the work done by the worker ....

....

2a If the work is done under a written agreement between the firm and the worker, attach a copy.

  b If the agreement is not in writing, describe the terms and conditions of the work arrangement ....

....

....

  c If the actual working arrangement differs in any way from the agreement, explain the differences and why they occur ....

....

....

3a Is the worker given training by the firm? . . . . ☐ **Yes** ☐ **No**
    ● If "Yes," what kind? ....
    ● How often? ....

  b Is the worker given instructions in the way the work is to be done (exclusive of actual training in 3a)? . ☐ **Yes** ☐ **No**
    ● If "Yes," give specific examples ....

  c Attach samples of any written instructions or procedures.

  d Does the firm have the right to change the methods used by the worker or direct that person on how to
do the work? . . . . ☐ **Yes** ☐ **No**
    ● Explain your answer ....

....

  e Does the operation of the firm's business require that the worker be supervised or controlled in the
performance of the service? . . . . ☐ **Yes** ☐ **No**
    ● Explain your answer ....

....

4a The firm engages the worker:
    ☐ To perform and complete a particular job only
    ☐ To work at a job for an indefinite period of time
    ☐ Other (explain) ....

  b Is the worker required to follow a routine or a schedule established by the firm? . . . . ☐ **Yes** ☐ **No**
    ● If "Yes," what is the routine or schedule? ....

....

....

  c Does the worker report to the firm or its representative?. . . . . ☐ **Yes** ☐ **No**
    ● If "Yes," how often? ....
    ● For what purpose? ....
    ● In what manner (in person, in writing, by telephone, etc.)? ....
    ● Attach copies of any report forms used in reporting to the firm.

  d Does the worker furnish a time record to the firm? . . . . ☐ **Yes** ☐ **No**
    ● If "Yes," attach copies of time records.

5a State the kind and value of tools, equipment, supplies, and materials furnished by:
    ● The firm ....

....

    ● The worker ....

....

  b What expenses are incurred by the worker in the performance of services for the firm? ....

....

  c Does the firm reimburse the worker for any expenses? . . . . ☐ **Yes** ☐ **No**
    ● If "Yes," specify the reimbursed expenses ....

6a Will the worker perform the services personally? . . . . ☐ **Yes** ☐ **No**

  b Does the worker have helpers? . . . . ☐ **Yes** ☐ **No**
- If "Yes," who hires the helpers? ☐ Firm ☐ Worker
- If the helpers are hired by the worker, is the firm's approval necessary? . . . . ☐ **Yes** ☐ **No**
- Who pays the helpers? ☐ Firm ☐ Worker
- If the worker pays the helpers, does the firm repay the worker? . . . . ☐ **Yes** ☐ **No**
- Are social security and Medicare taxes and Federal income tax withheld from the helpers' pay? . . ☐ **Yes** ☐ **No**
- If "Yes," who reports and pays these taxes? ☐ Firm ☐ Worker
- Who reports the helpers' earnings to the Internal Revenue Service? ☐ Firm ☐ Worker
- What services do the helpers perform? --

7 At what location are the services performed? ☐ Firm's ☐ Worker's ☐ Other (specify) -----------------------

8a Type of pay worker receives:
  ☐ Salary   ☐ Commission ☐ Hourly wage   ☐ Piecework ☐ Lump sum   ☐ Other (specify) ----------------

  b Does the firm guarantee a minimum amount of pay to the worker? . . . . ☐ **Yes** ☐ **No**

  c Does the firm allow the worker a drawing account or advances against pay? . . . . ☐ **Yes** ☐ **No**
- If "Yes," is the worker paid such advances on a regular basis? . . . . ☐ **Yes** ☐ **No**

  d How does the worker repay such advances? --

9a Is the worker eligible for a pension, bonus, paid vacations, sick pay, etc.? . . . . ☐ **Yes** ☐ **No**
- If "Yes," specify --

  b Does the firm carry worker's compensation insurance on the worker? . . . . ☐ **Yes** ☐ **No**

  c Does the firm withhold social security and Medicare taxes from amounts paid the worker? . . . . . ☐ **Yes** ☐ **No**

  d Does the firm withhold Federal income tax from amounts paid the worker? . . . . ☐ **Yes** ☐ **No**

  e How does the firm report the worker's earnings to the Internal Revenue Service?
  ☐ Form W-2 ☐ Form 1099-MISC ☐ Does not report ☐ Other (specify) ----------------------------
- Attach a copy.

  f Does the firm bond the worker? . . . . ☐ **Yes** ☐ **No**

10a Approximately how many hours a day does the worker perform services for the firm? ---------------------

  b Does the firm set hours of work for the worker? . . . . ☐ **Yes** ☐ **No**
- If "Yes," what are the worker's set hours? _____ a.m./p.m. to _____ a.m./p.m. (Circle whether a.m. or p.m.)

  c Does the worker perform similar services for others? . . . . ☐ **Yes** ☐ **No** ☐ **Unknown**
- If "Yes," are these services performed on a daily basis for other firms? . . . . . ☐ **Yes** ☐ **No** ☐ **Unknown**
- Percentage of time spent in performing these services for:
  This firm .... % Other firms .... % ☐ **Unknown**
- Does the firm have priority on the worker's time? . . . . ☐ **Yes** ☐ **No**
- If "No," explain --

  d Is the worker prohibited from competing with the firm either while performing services or during any later period? . . . . ☐ **Yes** ☐ **No**

11a Can the firm discharge the worker at any time without incurring a liability? . . . . ☐ **Yes** ☐ **No**
- If "No," explain --

  b Can the worker terminate the services at any time without incurring a liability? . . . . ☐ **Yes** ☐ **No**
- If "No," explain --

12a Does the worker perform services for the firm under:
  ☐ The firm's business name   ☐ The worker's own business name   ☐ Other (specify) -----------------

  b Does the worker advertise or maintain a business listing in the telephone directory, a trade journal, etc.? . . . . ☐ **Yes** ☐ **No** ☐ **Unknown**
- If "Yes," specify --

  c Does the worker represent himself or herself to the public as being in business to perform the same or similar services? . . . . ☐ **Yes** ☐ **No** ☐ **Unknown**
- If "Yes," how? ---

  d Does the worker have his or her own shop or office? . . . . ☐ **Yes** ☐ **No** ☐ **Unknown**
- If "Yes," where? --

  e Does the firm represent the worker as an employee of the firm to its customers? . . . . ☐ **Yes** ☐ **No**
- If "No," how is the worker represented? --

  f How did the firm learn of the worker's services? --

13 Is a license necessary for the work? . . . . ☐ **Yes** ☐ **No** ☐ **Unknown**
- If "Yes," what kind of license is required? --
- Who issues the license? ---
- Who pays the license fee? ---

14 Does the worker have a financial investment in a business related to the services performed?. . . . . ☐ **Yes** ☐ **No** ☐ **Unknown**
- If "Yes," specify and give amount of the investment _____

15 Can the worker incur a loss in the performance of the service for the firm? . . . . ☐ **Yes** ☐ **No**
- If "Yes," how? _____

16a Has any other government agency ruled on the status of the firm's workers? . . . . ☐ **Yes** ☐ **No**
- If "Yes," attach a copy of the ruling.

b Is the same issue being considered by any IRS office in connection with the audit of the worker's tax return or the firm's tax return, or has it been considered recently? . . . . ☐ **Yes** ☐ **No**
- If "Yes," for which year(s)? _____

17 Does the worker assemble or process a product at home or away from the firm's place of business? ☐ **Yes** ☐ **No**
- If "Yes," who furnishes materials or goods used by the worker? ☐ Firm   ☐ Worker   ☐ Other
- Is the worker furnished a pattern or given instructions to follow in making the product? . . . . . ☐ **Yes** ☐ **No**
- Is the worker required to return the finished product to the firm or to someone designated by the firm? ☐ **Yes** ☐ **No**

18 Attach a detailed explanation of any other reason why you believe the worker is an employee or an independent contractor.

Answer items 19a through o only if the worker is a salesperson or provides a service directly to customers.

19a Are leads to prospective customers furnished by the firm?. . . . . ☐ **Yes** ☐ **No** ☐ **Does not apply**
b Is the worker required to pursue or report on leads? . . . . ☐ **Yes** ☐ **No** ☐ **Does not apply**
c Is the worker required to adhere to prices, terms, and conditions of sale established by the firm? . . ☐ **Yes** ☐ **No**
d Are orders submitted to and subject to approval by the firm? . . . . ☐ **Yes** ☐ **No**
e Is the worker expected to attend sales meetings?. . . . . ☐ **Yes** ☐ **No**
- If "Yes," is the worker subject to any kind of penalty for failing to attend?. . . . . ☐ **Yes** ☐ **No**
f Does the firm assign a specific territory to the worker? . . . . ☐ **Yes** ☐ **No**
g Whom does the customer pay?   ☐ Firm   ☐ Worker
- If worker, does the worker remit the total amount to the firm? . . . . ☐ **Yes** ☐ **No**
h Does the worker sell a consumer product in a home or establishment other than a permanent retail establishment? . . . . ☐ **Yes** ☐ **No**
i List the products and/or services distributed by the worker, such as meat, vegetables, fruit, bakery products, beverages (other than milk), or laundry or dry cleaning services. If more than one type of product and/or service is distributed, specify the principal one _____
j Did the firm or another person assign the route or territory and a list of customers to the worker? . . ☐ **Yes** ☐ **No**
- If "Yes," enter the name and job title of the person who made the assignment _____
k Did the worker pay the firm or person for the privilege of serving customers on the route or in the territory? ☐ **Yes** ☐ **No**
- If "Yes," how much did the worker pay (not including any amount paid for a truck or racks, etc.)? $ _____
- What factors were considered in determining the value of the route or territory? _____
l How are new customers obtained by the worker? Explain fully, showing whether the new customers called the firm for service, were solicited by the worker, or both _____
m Does the worker sell life insurance? . . . . ☐ **Yes** ☐ **No**
- If "Yes," is the selling of life insurance or annuity contracts for the firm the worker's entire business activity?. . . . . ☐ **Yes** ☐ **No**
- If "No," list the other business activities and the amount of time spent on them _____
n Does the worker sell other types of insurance for the firm? . . . . ☐ **Yes** ☐ **No**
- If "Yes," state the percentage of the worker's total working time spent in selling other types of insurance _____ %
- At the time the contract was entered into between the firm and the worker, was it their intention that the worker sell life insurance for the firm: ☐ on a full-time basis   ☐ on a part-time basis
- State the manner in which the intention was expressed _____
o Is the worker a traveling or city salesperson? . . . . ☐ **Yes** ☐ **No**
- If "Yes," from whom does the worker principally solicit orders for the firm? _____
- If the worker solicits orders from wholesalers, retailers, contractors, or operators of hotels, restaurants, or other similar establishments, specify the percentage of the worker's time spent in the solicitation _____ %
- Is the merchandise purchased by the customers for resale or for use in their business operations? If used by the customers in their business operations, describe the merchandise and state whether it is equipment installed on their premises or a consumable supply _____

Under penalties of perjury, I declare that I have examined this request, including accompanying documents, and to the best of my knowledge and belief, the facts presented are true, correct, and complete.

Signature ▶ _____   Title ▶ _____   Date ▶ _____

If the firm is completing this form, an officer or member of the firm must sign it. If the worker is completing this form, the worker must sign it. If the worker wants a written determination about services performed for two or more firms, a separate form must be completed and signed for each firm. Additional copies of this form may be obtained by calling 1-800-TAX-FORM (1-800-829-3676).

Form **8716**

(Rev. July 1997)

Department of the Treasury
Internal Revenue Service

Election To Have a Tax Year Other Than a Required Tax Year

OMB No. 1545-1036

Please Type or Print	Name	Employer identification number
	Number, street, and room or suite no. (or P.O. box number if mail is not delivered to street address)	
	City or town, state, and ZIP code	

1 Check applicable box to show type of entity:
- ☐ Partnership
- ☐ S corporation (or C corporation electing to be an S corporation)
- ☐ Personal service corporation (PSC)

2 Name and telephone number (including area code) of person who may be called for information:

3 Enter ending date of the tax year for the entity's last filed return. A new entity should enter the ending date of the tax year it is adopting. . . . .

Month	Day	Year

4 Enter ending date of required tax year determined under section 441(i), 706(b), or 1378 . . .

Month	Day

5 Section 444(a) Election.—Check the applicable box and enter the ending date of the first tax year for which the election will be effective that the entity is (see instructions):
- ☐ Adopting
- ☐ Retaining
- ☐ Changing to

Month	Day	Year

Under penalties of perjury, I declare that the entity named above has authorized me to make this election under section 444(a), and that the statements made are, to the best of my knowledge and belief, true, correct, and complete.

▶ _____
Signature and title (see instructions)

▶ _____
Date

General Instructions

Section references are to the Internal Revenue Code unless otherwise noted.

Purpose of Form

Form 8716 is filed by partnerships, S corporations, and personal service corporations (as defined in section 441(i)(2)) to elect under section 444 to have a tax year other than a required tax year.

Attach a copy of the Form 8716 you file to Form 1065 or a Form 1120 series form (1120, 1120-A, 1120S, etc.), whichever is applicable, for the first tax year for which the election is made.

When To File

Form 8716 must be filed by the earlier of:

1. The 15th day of the 5th month following the month that includes the 1st day of the tax year the election will be effective, or

2. The due date (not including extensions) of the income tax return for the tax year resulting from the section 444 election.

Items **1** and **2** relate to the tax year, or the return for the tax year, for which the ending date is entered on line 5 above.

Under Temporary Regulations section 301.9100-2T, the entity is automatically granted a 12-month extension to make an election on Form 8716. To obtain an

extension, type or legibly print "FILED PURSUANT TO SECTION 301.9100-2T" at the top of a properly prepared Form 8716, and file the form within 12 months of the original due date.

Where To File

File the election with the Internal Revenue Service Center where the entity will file its return. See the instructions for Form 1065 or a Form 1120 series form for service center addresses. For a foreign entity, file Form 8716 with the Internal Revenue Service Center, Philadelphia, PA 19255.

Effect of Section 444 Election

Partnerships and S corporations.—An electing partnership or S corporation must file **Form 8752,** Required Payment or Refund Under Section 7519, for each year the election is in effect. Form 8752 is used to figure and make the payment required under section 7519 or to obtain a refund of net prior year payments. Form 8752 must be filed by May 15 following the calendar year in which each applicable election year begins.

The section 444 election will end if the partnership or S corporation is penalized for willfully failing to make the required payments.

Personal service corporations.—An electing personal service corporation (PSC) should not file Form 8752. Instead, it must comply with the

minimum distribution requirements of section 280H for each year the election is in effect. If the PSC does not meet these requirements, the applicable amounts it may deduct for payments made to its employee-owners may be limited.

Use **Schedule H (Form 1120),** Section 280H Limitations for a Personal Service Corporation (PSC), to figure the required minimum distribution and the maximum deductible amount. Attach Schedule H to the income tax return of the PSC for each tax year the PSC does not meet the minimum distribution requirements.

The section 444 election will end if the PSC is penalized for willfully failing to comply with the requirements of section 280H.

Members of Certain Tiered Structures May Not Make Election

No election may be made under section 444(a) by an entity that is part of a tiered structure other than a tiered structure that consists entirely of partnerships and/or S corporations all of which have the same tax year. An election previously made will be terminated if an entity later becomes part of a tiered structure that is not allowed to make the election. See Temporary Regulations section 1.444-2T for other details.

Acceptance of Election

After your election is received and accepted by the service center, the center will stamp it "ACCEPTED" and return a copy to you. Be sure to keep a copy of the form marked "ACCEPTED" for your records.

End of Election

The election is made only once. It remains in effect until the entity changes its accounting period to its required tax year or some other permitted year or it is penalized for willfully failing to comply with the requirements of section 280H or 7519. If the election is terminated, the entity may not make another section 444 election.

Signature

Form 8716 is not a valid election unless it is signed. For partnerships, a general partner or limited liability company member must sign and date the election.

For corporations, the election must be signed and dated by the president, vice president, treasurer, assistant treasurer, chief accounting officer, or any other corporate officer (such as tax officer) authorized to sign its tax return.

If a receiver, trustee in bankruptcy, or assignee controls the entity's property or business, that person must sign the election.

Specific Instructions

Line 1

Check the applicable box to indicate whether the entity is classified for Federal income tax purposes as a partnership, an S corporation (or a C corporation electing to be an S corporation), or a personal service corporation.

A corporation electing to be an S corporation that wants to make a section 444 election is not required to attach a copy of Form 8716 to its **Form 2553**, Election by a Small Business Corporation. However, the corporation is required to state on Form 2553 its intention to make a section 444 election (or a backup section 444 election). If a corporation is making a backup section 444 election (provided for in item Q, Part II, of Form 2553), it must type or print the words "BACKUP ELECTION" at the top of the Form 8716 it files. See Temporary Regulations section 1.444-3T for more details.

Line 2

Enter the name and telephone number (including the area code) of a person that the IRS may call for information needed to complete the processing of the election.

Line 4

For a definition of a required tax year and other details, see the instructions for Form 1065 or a Form 1120 series form, whichever is applicable, and section 441(i), 706(b), or 1378.

Line 5

The following limitations and special rules apply in determining the tax year an entity may elect.

New entity adopting a tax year.—An entity adopting a tax year may elect a tax year under section 444 only if the deferral period of the tax year is not longer than 3 months. See below for the definition of deferral period.

Existing entity retaining a tax year.— In certain cases, an entity may elect to retain its tax year if the deferral period is no longer than 3 months. If the entity does not want to elect to retain its tax year, it may elect to change its tax year as explained below.

Existing entity changing a tax year.— An existing entity may elect to change its tax year if the deferral period of the elected tax year is no longer than the shorter of 3 months or the deferral period of the tax year being changed.

Example. ABC, a C corporation that historically used a tax year ending October 31, elects S status and wants to make a section 444 election for its tax year beginning 11-1-97. ABC's required tax year under section 1378 is a calendar tax year. In this case, the deferral period of the tax year being changed is 2 months. Thus, ABC may elect to retain its tax year beginning 11-1-97 and ending 10-31-98, or change it to a short tax year beginning 11-1-97 and ending 11-30-97. However, it may not elect a short tax year beginning 11-1-97 and ending 9-30-98 because the deferral period for that elected tax year is 3 months (9-30 to 12-31), which is longer than the 2-month deferral period of the tax year being changed. After filing the short year return (11-1-97 to 11-30-97), and as long as the section 444 election remains in effect, the corporation's tax year will begin 12-1 and end 11-30.

Deferral period.—The term "deferral period" means the number of months that occur between the last day of the elected tax year and the last day of the required tax year. For example, if you elected a tax year that ends on September 30 and your required tax year is the calendar year, the deferral period would be 3 months (the number of months between September 30 and December 31).

Paperwork Reduction Act Notice.—We ask for the information on this form to carry out the Internal Revenue laws of the United States. You are required to give us the information. We need it to ensure that you are complying with these laws and to allow us to figure and collect the right amount of tax.

You are not required to provide the information requested on a form that is subject to the Paperwork Reduction Act unless the form displays a valid OMB control number. Books or records relating to a form or its instructions must be retained as long as their contents may become material in the administration of any Internal Revenue law. Generally, tax returns and return information are confidential, as required by section 6103.

The time needed to complete and file this form will vary depending on individual circumstances. The estimated average time is:

Recordkeeping . . . . 2 hr., 38 min.

Learning about the law or the form . . . . 1 hr., 5 min.

Preparing and sending the form to the IRS. . . 1 hr., 11 min.

If you have comments concerning the accuracy of these time estimates or suggestions for making this form simpler, we would be happy to hear from you. You can write to the Tax Forms Committee, Western Area Distribution Center, Rancho Cordova, CA 95743-0001. **DO NOT** send the form to this address. Instead, see **Where To File** on page 1.

Form **8832**
(December 1996)
Department of the Treasury
Internal Revenue Service

Entity Classification Election

OMB No. 1545-1516

Please Type or Print	Name of entity	Employer identification number (EIN)
	Number, street, and room or suite no. If a P.O. box, see instructions.	
	City or town, state, and ZIP code. If a foreign address, enter city, province or state, postal code and country.	

1 **Type of election** (see instructions):

a ☐ Initial classification by a newly-formed entity (or change in current classification of an existing entity to take effect on January 1, 1997)

b ☐ Change in current classification (to take effect later than January 1, 1997)

2 **Form of entity** (see instructions):

a ☐ A domestic eligible entity electing to be classified as an association taxable as a corporation.

b ☐ A domestic eligible entity electing to be classified as a partnership.

c ☐ A domestic eligible entity with a single owner electing to be disregarded as a separate entity.

d ☐ A foreign eligible entity electing to be classified as an association taxable as a corporation.

e ☐ A foreign eligible entity electing to be classified as a partnership.

f ☐ A foreign eligible entity with a single owner electing to be disregarded as a separate entity.

3 Election is to be effective beginning (month, day, year) (see instructions) . . . . ▶ ___ / ___ / ___

4 Name and title of person whom the IRS may call for more information

5 That person's telephone number

Consent Statement and Signature(s) (see instructions)

Under penalties of perjury, I (we) declare that I (we) consent to the election of the above-named entity to be classified as indicated above, and that I (we) have examined this consent statement, and to the best of my (our) knowledge and belief, it is true, correct, and complete. If I am an officer, manager, or member signing for all members of the entity, I further declare that I am authorized to execute this consent statement on their behalf.

Signature(s)	Date	Title

For Paperwork Reduction Act Notice, see page 2.

Cat. No. 22598R

Form **8832** (12-96)

General Instructions

Section references are to the Internal Revenue Code unless otherwise noted.

Paperwork Reduction Act Notice

We ask for the information on this form to carry out the Internal Revenue laws of the United States. You are required to give us the information. We need it to ensure that you are complying with these laws and to allow us to figure and collect the right amount of tax.

You are not required to provide the information requested on a form that is subject to the Paperwork Reduction Act unless the form displays a valid OMB control number. Books or records relating to a form or its instructions must be retained as long as their contents may become material in the administration of any Internal Revenue law. Generally, tax returns and return information are confidential, as required by section 6103.

The time needed to complete and file this form will vary depending on individual circumstances. The estimated average time is:

Recordkeeping . . .1 hr., 20 min.
Learning about the law or the form . . .1 hr., 41 min.
Preparing and sending the form to the IRS . . . .17 min.

If you have comments concerning the accuracy of these time estimates or suggestions for making this form simpler, we would be happy to hear from you. You can write to the Tax Forms Committee, Western Area Distribution Center, Rancho Cordova, CA 95743-0001. **DO NOT** send the form to this address. Instead, see **Where To File** on page 3.

Purpose of Form

For Federal tax purposes, certain business entities automatically are classified as corporations. See items **1** and **3** through **8** under the definition of corporation on this page. Other business entities may choose how they are classified for Federal tax purposes. Except for a business entity automatically classified as a corporation, a business entity with at least two members can choose to be classified as either an association taxable as a corporation or a partnership, and a business entity with a single member can choose to be classified as either an association taxable as a corporation or disregarded as an entity separate from its owner.

Generally, an eligible entity that does not file this form will be classified under the default rules described below. An eligible entity that chooses not to be classified under the default rules or that wishes to change its current classification must file Form 8832 to elect a classification. The IRS will use the information entered on this form to establish the entity's filing and reporting requirements for Federal tax purposes.

Default Rules

Existing entity default rule.— Certain domestic and foreign entities that are already in existence before January 1, 1997, and have an established Federal tax classification, generally do not need to make an election to continue that classification. However, for an eligible entity with a single owner that claimed to be a partnership under the law in effect before January 1, 1997, that entity will now be disregarded as an entity separate from its owner. If an existing entity decides to change its classification, it may do so subject to the rules in Regulations section 301.7701-3(c)(1)(iv). A foreign eligible entity is treated as being in existence prior to the effective date of this section only if the entity's classification is relevant at any time during the 60 months prior to January 1, 1997.

Domestic default rule.—Unless an election is made on Form 8832, a domestic eligible entity is:

1. A partnership if it has two or more members.

2. Disregarded as an entity separate from its owner if it has a single owner.

Foreign default rule.—Unless an election is made on Form 8832, a foreign eligible entity is:

1. A partnership if it has two or more members and at least one member does not have limited liability.

2. An association if all members have limited liability.

3. Disregarded as an entity separate from its owner if it has a single owner that does not have limited liability.

Definitions

Business entity.—A business entity is any entity recognized for Federal tax purposes that is not properly classified as a trust under Regulations section 301.7701-4 or otherwise subject to special treatment under the Code. See Regulations section 301.7701-2(a).

Corporation.—For Federal tax purposes, a corporation is any of the following:

1. A business entity organized under a Federal or state statute, or under a statute of a federally recognized Indian tribe, if the statute describes or refers to the entity as incorporated or as a corporation, body corporate, or body politic.

2. An association (as determined under Regulations section 301.7701-3).

3. A business entity organized under a state statute, if the statute describes or refers to the entity as a joint-stock company or joint-stock association.

4. An insurance company.

5. A state-chartered business entity conducting banking activities, if any of its deposits are insured under the Federal Deposit Insurance Act, as amended, 12 U.S.C. 1811 et seq., or a similar Federal statute.

6. A business entity wholly owned by a state or any political subdivision thereof.

7. A business entity that is taxable as a corporation under a provision of the Code other than section 7701(a)(3).

8. A foreign business entity listed in Regulations section 301.7701-2(b)(8). However, a foreign business entity listed in those regulations generally will not be treated as a corporation if all of the following apply:

a. The entity was in existence on May 8, 1996.

b. The entity's classification was relevant (as defined below) on May 8, 1996.

c. No person (including the entity) for whom the entity's classification was relevant on May 8, 1996, treats the entity as a corporation for purposes of filing that person's Federal income tax returns, information returns, and withholding documents for the tax year including May 8, 1996.

d. Any change in the entity's claimed classification within the 60 months prior to May 8, 1996, was a result of a change in the organizational documents of the entity, and the entity and all members of the entity recognized the Federal tax consequences of any change in the entity's classification within the 60 months prior to May 8, 1996.

e. The entity had a reasonable basis (within the meaning of section 6662) for treating the entity as other than a corporation on May 8, 1996.

f. Neither the entity nor any member was notified in writing on or before May 8, 1996, that the classification of the entity was under examination (in which case the entity's classification will be determined in the examination).

Binding contract rule.—If a foreign business entity described in Regulations section 301.7701-2(b)(8)(i) is formed after May 8, 1996, under a written binding contract (including an accepted bid to develop a project) in effect on May 8, 1996, and all times thereafter, in which the parties agreed to engage (directly or indirectly) in an active and substantial business operation in the jurisdiction in which the entity is formed, **8** on page 2 is applied by substituting the date of the entity's formation for May 8, 1996.

Eligible entity.—An eligible entity is a business entity that is not included in items **1** or **3** through **8** under the definition of corporation on page 2.

Limited liability.—A member of a foreign eligible entity has limited liability if the member has no personal liability for any debts of or claims against the entity by reason of being a member. This determination is based solely on the statute or law under which the entity is organized (and, if relevant, the entity's organizational documents). A member has personal liability if the creditors of the entity may seek satisfaction of all or any part of the debts or claims against the entity from the member as such. A member has personal liability even if the member makes an agreement under which another person (whether or not a member of the entity) assumes that liability or agrees to indemnify that member for that liability.

Partnership.—A partnership is a business entity that has **at least** two members and is not a corporation as defined on page 2.

Relevant.—A foreign eligible entity's classification is relevant when its classification affects the liability of any person for Federal tax or information purposes. The date the classification of a foreign eligible entity is relevant is the date an event occurs that creates an obligation to file a Federal tax return, information return, or statement for which the classification of the entity must be determined.

Effect of Election

The resulting tax consequences of a change in classification remain the same no matter how a change in entity classification is achieved. For example, if an organization classified as an association elects to be classified as a partnership, the organization and its owners must recognize gain, if any, under the rules applicable to liquidations of corporations.

Who Must File

File this form for an **eligible entity** that is one of the following:

● A domestic entity electing to be classified as an association taxable as a corporation.

● A domestic entity electing to change its current classification (even if it is currently classified under the default rule).

● A foreign entity that has more than one owner, all owners have limited liability, and it elects to be classified as a partnership.

● A foreign entity that has at least one owner without limited liability, and it elects to be classified as an association taxable as a corporation.

● A foreign entity with a single owner having limited liability, and it elects to have the entity disregarded as an entity separate from its owner.

● A foreign entity electing to change its current classification (even if it is currently classified under the default rule).

Do not file this form for an eligible entity that is:

● Tax-exempt under section 501(a), or

● A real estate investment trust (REIT), as defined in section 856.

When To File

See the instructions for line 3.

Where To File

File Form 8832 with the Internal Revenue Service Center, Philadelphia, PA 19255. Also attach a copy of Form 8832 to the entity's Federal income tax or information return for the tax year of the election. If the entity is not required to file a return for that year, a copy of its Form 8832 must be attached to the Federal income tax or information returns of all direct or indirect owners of the entity for the tax year of the owner that includes the date on which the election took effect. Although failure to attach a copy will not invalidate an otherwise valid election, each member of the entity is required to file returns that are consistent with the entity's election. In addition, penalties may be assessed against persons who are required to, but who do not, attach Form 8832 to their returns. Other penalties may apply for filing Federal income tax or information returns inconsistent with the entity's election.

Specific Instructions

Employer Identification Number (EIN)

Show the correct EIN on Form 8832. If the entity does not have an EIN, it generally must apply for one on **Form SS-4,** Application for Employer Identification Number. If the filing of Form 8832 is the only reason the entity is applying for an EIN, check the "Other" box on line 9 of Form SS-4 and write "Form 8832" to the right of that box. If the entity has not received an EIN by the time Form 8832 is due, write "Applied for" in the space for the EIN. **Do not** apply for a new EIN for an existing entity that is changing its classification. If you are electing to disregard an entity as separate from its owner, enter the owner's EIN.

Address

Include the suite, room, or other unit number after the street address. If the Post Office does not deliver mail to the street address and the entity has a P.O. box, show the box number instead of the street address.

Line 1

Check box 1a if the entity is choosing a classification for the first time **and** the entity does not want to be classified under the applicable default classification. **Do not** file this form if the entity wants to be classified under the default rules.

Check box 1b if the entity is changing its current classification to take effect later than January 1, 1997, whether or not the entity's current classification is the default classification. However, once an eligible entity makes an election to change its classification (other than an election made by an existing entity to change its classification as of January 1, 1997), the entity cannot change its classification by election again during the 60 months after the effective date of the election. However, the IRS may permit (by private letter ruling) the entity to change its classification by election within the 60-month period if more than 50% of the ownership interests in the entity as of the effective date of the election are owned by persons that did not own any interests in the entity on the effective date of the entity's prior election.

Line 2

Check the appropriate box if you are changing a current classification (no matter how achieved), or are electing out of a default classification. **Do not** file this form if you fall within a default classification that is the desired classification for the new entity.

Line 3

Generally, the election will take effect on the date you enter on line 3 of this form or on the date filed if no date is entered on line 3. However, an election specifying an entity's classification for Federal tax purposes can take effect no more than 75 days prior to the date the election is filed, nor can it take effect later than 12 months after the date on which the election is filed. If line 3 shows a date more than 75 days prior to the date on which the election is filed, the election will take effect 75 days before the date it is filed. If line 3 shows an effective date more than 12 months from the filing date, the election will take effect 12 months after the date the election was filed.

Regardless of the date filed, an election will in no event take effect before January 1, 1997.

Consent Statement and Signatures

Form 8832 must be signed by:

1. Each member of the electing entity who is an owner at the time the election is filed; or

2. Any officer, manager, or member of the electing entity who is authorized (under local law or the organizational documents) to make the election and who represents to having such authorization under penalties of perjury.

If an election is to be effective for any period prior to the time it is filed, each person who was an owner between the date the election is to be effective and the date the election is filed, and who is not an owner at the time the election is filed, must also sign.

If you need a continuation sheet or use a separate consent statement, attach it to Form 8832. The separate consent statement must contain the same information as shown on Form 8832.

Index

A

Accountants, 10/2, 12/6–7
Accounting, 10/2–21
  accrual method, 10/5–7, 10/14–15
  basics, 10/4–5
  cash method, 10/5–7, 10/13
  defined, 10/3
  financial reports, 10/15–19
  income and expense recordkeeping, 10/7–10
  professional help, 10/2, 12/6–7
  terminology, 10/3
  using ledgers, 10/10–15
Accounting periods, 8/18, 10/6
Accounting software, 5/9–10, 10/2, 10/10
Accounts, defined, 10/3
Accounts payable, 10/3, 10/15
Accounts receivable, 10/3, 10/11
Accrual-method accounting, 10/5–7, 10/14–15
ADA (Americans with Disabilities Act), 4/10
Adhesion contracts, 9/15
Advertising, 5/7–8, 9/3
Agency authority
  LLC members, 2/11
  partners, 2/6
Agreements
  buy-sell, resource, 1/6
  nondisclosure, resource, 1/7
  shrinkwrap/clickwrap, 9/15–16
  See also Contracts
American Bar Association, digital signature guidelines, 9/18
Americans with Disabilities Act (ADA), 4/10
Amortization, 8/3, 8/6
Anti-Cybersquatting Consumer Protection Act, 3/14, 3/15

Arbitration clauses, 9/13, 9/15
Attachments, contracts, 9/13
Attorney fees clauses, 9/13
Attorneys. See Lawyers
Audits, IRS, 8/9, 10/5
Auto insurance, 7/2, 7/4

B

Bids, expiration dates, 9/4
Bonuses, shareholder employees, 2/18
Bookkeepers, 12/6
Bookkeeping, 10/3
  See also Accounting
Breach of contract, 9/2, 9/12
Break-even analysis, 5/9, 5/10–19
Break-even point, 5/10, 5/17–18
Business assets, 8/3, 8/5
Business expenses. See Deductible expenses; Expenses
Business interruption insurance, 7/4
Business licenses
  local tax registration, 2/3, 2/5, 4/7, 6/11–12, 6/15, 8/4, 8/19
  specialized licenses and permits, 6/11–12, 6/13–16, 8/4–5
Business losses. See Losses
Business names, 3/2–26
  basics, 3/2–4
  domain names, 1/7, 3/12–16, 3/21–23
  on FEIN application, 6/6, 6/8
  guidelines for choosing, 3/24–26
  local registration, 2/3, 2/5, 3/2, 6/8–11
  name searches, 3/16–20, 6/4, 6/9–10
  online trademark issues, 3/9, 3/11–16
  resources, 3/21

state registration, 3/2, 3/3, 6/4

terminology, 3/3–4

trademark law overview, 3/5–11

trademark registration, 3/5–6, 3/13, 3/23–24

and unfair competition laws, 3/7–8, 3/9

See also Fictitious business names

Business plans, 5/2–27

break-even analysis, 5/9, 5/10–19

business purpose and description, 5/3–8

cash flow projections, 5/9, 5/19, 5/23–26

financial projections, basics, 5/8–10

presentation, 5/3, 5/26

profit/loss forecast, 5/9, 5/19–22

resources, 1/6

software for, 5/10

start-up cost estimate, 5/9, 5/22–23

Business structure

choosing, 2/19–20

and personal liability, 2/2, 2/4–5, 2/6

See also Corporations; LLCs; Partnerships; Sole
proprietorships

Buy-sell agreements, resources, 1/6

C

Calendar year tax reporting, 8/18, 10/6

Capital expenses, 8/3, 8/5–6

Capital gains taxes, and home office depreciation
deductions, 4/15

Capitalization, 8/3, 8/6

Car insurance, 7/2, 7/4

Cash flow projections, 5/9, 5/19, 5/23–26, 10/17–19

samples, 5/24–25, 10/20–21

Cash-method accounting, 10/5–7, 10/13

C corporations, 2/16–18

See also Corporations

CD-ROM, how to use, Appendix B/2–6

Center for Information Technology Standards, 9/16

Certified public accountants (CPAs), 12/6

Clickwrap agreements, 9/15–16

Commercial leases, 4/7, 4/9–10, 7/2

Commercial rents, researching, 4/3

Computer Professionals for Social Responsibility,
9/16

Conditional use permits, 4/8, 4/9, 6/14

Condominiums, home business restrictions, 4/11

Confidentiality agreements, resource, 1/7

Consumers Union, electronic contract tips, 9/17–18

Contracts, 9/2–18

authority to bind business to, 2/6, 2/11

basics, 9/2–7

changing contract language, 9/2, 9/8, 9/14

drafting your own, 9/8–13

electronic, 9/14–18

oral vs. written, 9/6–7

resources, 9/8

standard forms, 9/7–8

state requirements, 9/6, 9/7

See also Agreements

Co-ops, home business restrictions, 4/11

Corporate tax rates, 2/17

Corporate tax status, for LLCs and partnerships,
2/12, 8/12, 8/13

Corporations, 2/14–19

accounting periods, 8/18

C corporations, 2/16–18

costs of running, 2/14

and FBN registration, 6/9

federal registration requirements, 6/5

forming and ruinning, 2/18–19

and liability for business debts, 2/2, 2/5, 2/11,
2/15–16

names, 3/2, 3/3

resources, 2/19, 6/5

S corporations, 2/13–14, 2/16, 2/18, 8/18

state registration requirements, 2/18, 6/3, 6/4

taxation, 2/12–13, 2/13–14, 2/16–18, 8/2, 8/4

Costs of goods, costs of sale. *See* Variable costs

Counteroffers, 9/5, 9/14

Court judgments, liability for, 2/5

CPAs (certified public accountants), 12/6

Credit insurance, 7/4

Credit lines, 10/19

Credit transactions, 5/26, 10/6, 10/13, 10/15

Current expenses, 8/3, 8/5

Cybersquatting, 3/14–15

D

DBA, 3/3

See also Fictitious business names

Deductible expenses, 2/17, 4/13, 8/3, 8/5–9

current vs. capital expenses, 8/3, 8/5–6

fringe benefits, 2/17

home-office deduction, 4/13–16

recordkeeping, 10/9–10

resources, 8/6, 10/12

start-up costs, 8/6

See also Expenses

Depreciation, 8/3, 8/6, 10/15

Depreciation deduction, home offices, 4/15

Digital signatures, 9/16–17, 9/18

Dilution, trademark law, 3/11, 3/14

Disability insurance

for business owners, 7/5

for employees, 7/2

Dispute resolution, contract clause, 9/13

Dividends, non-deductibility, 2/18

Domain names

checking availability, 3/16

choosing and registering, 3/21–23

conflicts over, 3/12–16

resources, 1/7, 3/23

as trademarks, 3/13, 3/17, 3/22

Double taxation, corporations, 2/18

Duty of care. *See* Fiduciary duty

E

EAs (enrolled agents), 12/6

E-commerce. *See* Online commerce

EIN (employer identification number). *See* FEIN

Electrical power, 4/5

Electronic contracts, 9/14–18

Electronic signatures, 9/16–17, 9/18

Electronic Signatures in Global and National
   Commerce Act, 9/17

Email attachments, 9/18

Email contracts. *See* Electronic contracts

Employees, 11/2–6

classification of spouses as, 2/3

and FEIN requirement, 6/5

vs. independent contractors, 11/2–5

legal overview, 11/5–6

non-owned auto insurance, 7/4

resources, 1/4, 1/7, 11/6

state employment departments, Appendix
   A/24–28

See also Payroll taxes

Employer ID number. *See* FEIN

Employers

insurance requirements, 7/2

resources, 1/7, 11/6

See also Employees

Employment taxes. *See* Payroll taxes; Self-
   employment taxes

Enrolled agents, 12/6

Estimated tax payments

federal, 8/10, 8/11, 8/12, 8/14, 8/15–18

resources, 8/17

state, 8/11, 8/13, 8/15, 8/16

Excise taxes, 8/4

Expenditure ledgers, 10/12–15

Expenses

categorizing, 10/9, 10/12–13

current vs. capital, 8/3, 8/5–6

fixed vs. variable costs, 5/11, 5/12, 8/3,
   10/12–13, 10/16

recordkeeping, 10/9–10, 10/12–15

See also Deductible expenses; Fixed costs;
   Variable costs

Expiration dates, bids, 9/4

F

False advertising, 9/3

FBNs. *See* Fictitious business names

Federal employer identification number. *See* FEIN

Federal income taxes, 8/4

estimated tax payments, 8/10, 8/11, 8/12, 8/14,
   8/15–18

LLCs, 8/13–14

partnerships, 8/11–12

sole proprietors, 8/9–11

Federal trademark database, 3/17, 3/18–19

Fees

attorney fees clauses in contracts, 9/13

lawyers, 12/4–5

LLC filing, 2/14

local business tax registration, 6/12, 8/19

vs. taxes, 8/4–5

tax professionals, 12/6–7

trademark searches, 3/19

FEIN (federal employer identification number), 6/5–8
  sample application form, 6/7
Fictitious business names (FBNs), 3/3, 6/3, 6/8
  abandonment, 6/11
  on FEIN application, 6/6
  publishing notice, 6/10–11
  registration, 2/3, 2/5, 3/2, 6/8–11
  searching, 3/18, 6/9–10
Fiduciary duty
  corporate officers, 2/16
  LLC owners, 2/12
  partners, 2/8
Financial management. *See* Accounting
Financial projections
  basics, 5/8–10
  break-even analysis, 5/9, 5/10–19
  cash flow projections, 5/9, 5/19, 5/23–26, 10/17–21
  profit/loss forecast, 5/9, 5/19–22
  start-up cost estimate, 5/9, 5/22–23
Financial reports, 10/15–19
  profit/loss statements, 10/15–17
  See also Cash flow projections
Financial terminology, 8/3
Fiscal year, 8/18, 10/6
Fixed costs, 5/11, 8/3, 10/13, 10/16
  in break-even analysis, 5/9, 5/10, 5/18
  estimating, 5/16–17
  labor costs, 5/12, 5/14, 10/16
Forms
  IRS. *See* IRS forms
  online, 9/8
  tear-out, Appendix C
Forms CD-ROM, how to use, Appendix B/2–6
Fringe benefits, deductibility, 2/17
FUTA taxes, 11/6

G

General partnerships, 2/5–6
  See also Partnerships
Gross, defined, 8/3
Gross profit, 5/9, 5/13–16, 8/3
Guarantees
  personal, for business debt, 2/11–12, 2/14, 2/15

  See also Warranties

H

Health department requirements, 4/6, 4/12
Hobby businesses, 1/5, 8/7–9
Home-based businesses, 4/2, 4/10–16
  insurance, 4/16, 7/3
  zoning compliance, 4/10, 4/11–13
Home occupation permits, 4/11, 4/12
Home-office tax deduction, 4/13–16
  resources, 4/16
Homeowners insurance, 4/16, 7/3
Home sales, and home-office depreciation deduction, 4/15
Husband-wife sole proprietorships, 2/3

I

ICANN (International Corporation for Assigned Names and Numbers), 3/15
Implied warranties, 9/11
Income
  recordkeeping, 10/7–12
  taxable, 10/8, 10/9
  See also Sales
Income ledgers, 10/10–12
Income splitting, 2/17–18
Income statements. *See* Profit/loss statements
Income taxes, 8/4, 8/9–18
  corporations, 2/12–13, 2/16–18
  employee withholding, 11/5, 11/6
  LLCs, 2/12, 8/13–15
  partnerships, 2/6, 8/11–13
  shareholder employees, 2/17, 2/18
  sole proprietorships, 2/4, 8/9–11
  See also Estimated tax payments
Independent contractors, 1/4, 5/12, 11/2–5
  IRS criteria, 11/3–4
  resources, 1/7, 11/5
Insurance, 2/16, 2/20, 7/2–5
  auto, 7/2, 7/4
  business interruption, 7/4
  choosing and purchasing, 7/5
  disability, 7/2, 7/5
  employers, 7/2
  home-based businesses, 4/16, 7/3

liability, 2/5, 2/7, 7/3–4

malpractice, 7/4

property insurance, 7/2–3

specialized coverages, 7/4–5

theft, 7/3, 7/4

workers' compensation, 7/2, 11/5

Intellectual property, nondisclosure agreements
resource, 1/7

Intellectual property insurance, 7/4–5

Intentional acts, personal liability for, 2/12, 2/15–16

International Corporation for Assigned Names and
Numbers. *See* ICANN

Internet

name searches, 3/17

online legal research, 12/7

trademark issues, 3/9, 3/11–12

Web-based advertising, 5/7

See also Domain names; Online commerce;
Websites

Internet Service Providers (ISPs), locating, 3/21

Internet Tax Freedom Act (ITFA), 8/23

Inventories, and accounting method, 10/6

Invoices, 10/3

IRS (Internal Revenue Service), 1/5, 8/4

employee/independent contractor classification,
11/2–5

and husband-wife sole proprietorships, 2/3

website, 12/7

IRS audits, 8/9, 10/5

IRS forms, 8/7

on CD-ROM, Appendix B/4–5

Form 940 (Employer's Annual Federal
Unemployment Tax Return), 11/6

Form 1040 (Individual Income Tax Return), 2/4,
2/6, 2/12, 8/4, 8/9, 8/12, 8/14

Form 1040-ES, 8/17, 8/18

Form 1065 (U.S. Partnership Return of Income),
2/6, 2/12, 8/4, 8/12, 8/13

Form 1099, 11/5

Form 2210, 8/18

Form 8716 (Election To Have a Tax Year Other
Than a Required Tax Year), 8/18, 10/6,
Appendix C

Form 8832 (Entity Classification Election), 8/12,
Appendix C

Form SS-4 (Application for Employer Identification
Number), 6/5–8, Appendix C

Form SS-8 (Determination of Employee Work
Status), 11/4, Appendix C

Form W-2, 11/5

Schedule C (Profit or Loss from Business), 2/4,
8/4, 8/9–10, 8/13

Schedule C-EZ, 8/10

Schedule E (Supplemental Income and Loss),
2/6, 2/12, 8/4, 8/12, 8/14

Schedule K-1 (Partner's Share of Income, Credit
and Deductions), 8/12, 8/13–14

Schedule SE, 8/11, 8/12, 8/14

IRS publications, 4/15, 8/6, 8/17, 10/12, 11/6

obtaining, 8/7

ISPs, locating, 3/21

ITFA (Internet Tax Freedom Act), 8/23

J

Job safety laws, 11/5

L

Labor costs, categorizing, 5/12, 5/14, 10/16

Lawsuits

cybersquatting, 3/14–15

trademark infringement, costs, 3/14

Lawyers, 9/7, 12/2–5

Leases, 4/7, 4/9–10

insurance requirements, 7/2

Ledgers, 10/3, 10/10–15

Legal coaching, 12/3–4

Legal names, 3/3, 3/4

on FEIN application, 6/6

Legal research, 12/7–8

Legal structure. *See* Business structure

Liability for business debts. *See* Limited liability;
Personal liability; *specific business structures*

Liability insurance, 2/5, 2/7, 7/3–4

Licenses

local tax registration, 2/3, 2/5, 4/7, 6/11–12,
6/15, 8/4, 8/19

specialized, 6/11–12, 6/13–16, 8/4–5

Limited liability, 1/3

and business structure, 2/2, 2/5

defined, 2/2

See also Personal liability

Limited liability companies. *See* LLCs

Limited liability partnerships (LLPs and RLLPs), 2/6

Limited partnerships, 2/6

    and FBN registration, 6/9

    names, 3/2, 3/3

    resources, 6/5

    state registration requirements, 6/3, 6/4

    taxation, 8/4

    See also Partnerships

Lines of credit, 10/19

Liquidated damages clauses, 9/12–13

LLCs (limited liability companies), 2/11–14

    accounting periods, 8/18

    costs, 2/14

    and FBN registration, 6/9

    federal registration requirements, 6/5

    and liability for business debts, 2/2, 2/5

    names, 3/2, 3/3

    one-person, 2/11

    resources, 1/6, 1/7, 2/14, 6/4–5

    vs. S corporations, 2/13–14

    self-employment taxes, 8/14

    state offices listed, Appendix A/18–23

    state registration requirements, 2/14, 6/3, 6/4

    taxes, 2/12–13, 8/4, 8/13–15

LLPs (limited liability partnerships), 2/6

Loans

    credit lines, 10/19

    in financial projections and reports, 5/19, 5/23,
      10/18

    personal guarantees, 2/11–12, 2/14, 2/15

Local business registration requirements, 2/3, 2/5,
    4/7, 6/11–12, 6/15, 8/4, 8/19

    home occupation permits, 4/11, 4/12

Local taxes

    business taxes, 8/4, 8/8–9, 8/18–20

    property taxes, 8/20

    See also Sales taxes

Location, choosing, 4/2–6

Losses

    allocation among owners, 2/8, 2/13, 8/12,
      8/13–14

    carryover, 8/9

    tax treatment, 2/4, 2/13–14, 8/7–8, 8/9

M

Malpractice, liability for, 2/6

Malpractice insurance, 7/4

Marketing, 5/7–8

    resources, 1/6, 5/7–8

Mediation, 9/13

Medicare taxes. *See* Payroll taxes; Self-employment
    taxes

Meta tags, Web pages, 3/15–16

Microsoft, worker misclassification case, 11/4

MYOB Accounting, 10/2

N

Names. *See* Business names

National Conference of Commissioners on Uniform
    State Laws (NCCUSL), 9/16

National Federation of Independent Business, 12/7

Negligence, personal liability for, 2/12, 2/15–16

Neighbors, and zoning compliance, 4/6–7, 4/12–13

Net, defined, 8/3

Net profit, 5/9, 5/18, 5/19, 8/3

Network Solutions (NSI), 3/16, 3/22

New hire reporting, 11/5

Nexus requirement, sales taxes, 8/21–22

Nolo website, 1/3, 9/8, 12/7

    contract resources, 9/8

      FAQs for LLCs and corporations, 2/14, 2/19

      Internet Law Center, 3/23

      trademark resources, 3/21

Nondisclosure agreements, resource, 1/7

NSI. *See* Network Solutions

O

Occupational Safety & Health Administration
    (OSHA), 11/5

Offer and acceptance, contract law, 9/3–5

One-person LLCs, 2/11

179 deduction, 8/6

Online commerce

    domain name conflicts, 3/12–15

    electronic contracts, 9/14–18

    resources, 9/17

    and sales taxes, 8/22–23

    tax moratorium, 8/23

    trademark issues, 3/9, 3/11–16

See also Domain names; Websites; World Wide Web

Options, 9/4–5

Oral contracts, 9/6, 9/7

Organizational documents, state filing, 6/4

OSHA (Occupational Safety & Health Administration), 11/5

Overhead. *See* Fixed costs

Ownership share, and profit/loss allocation, 2/13

P

P & Ls. *See* Profit/loss statements

Parking, 4/5, 4/6

Partners, classification of spouses as, 2/3

Partnership agreements, 2/7–8
    samples, 2/9, 2/10

Partnerships, 1/3, 2/5–8, 6/5
    and FBN registration, 6/9
    and FEINs, 6/5, 6/6
    general partnerships, 2/5–6
    and liability for business debts, 2/2, 2/5, 2/6–7, 2/8
    limited liability (LLPs and RLLPs), 2/6
    resources, 2/8
    taxes, 2/6, 2/12, 8/11–13
    See also Limited partnerships

Pass-through taxation
    LLCs, 2/12–13
    partnerships, 2/6, 8/11–12
    S corporations, 2/13, 2/16, 2/18
    sole proprietorships, 2/4

Patent and Trademark Depository Libraries (PTDLs), 3/19, Appendix A/29–34

Patent and Trademark Office (PTO), 3/19, 3/23–24

Payroll taxes, 2/12, 2/15, 8/4, 8/10, 11/2, 11/5–6

Permits
    conditional use permits, 4/8, 4/9, 6/14
    home occupation permits, 4/11, 4/12
    seller's permit, 2/5, 6/13, 8/21, 8/26
    specialized, 6/13–16

Personal guarantees, 2/11–12, 2/14, 2/15

Personal liability, 2/2
    corporations, 2/2, 2/5, 2/11, 2/15–16
    LLCs, 2/11–12
    partnerships, 2/5–6, 2/6–7, 2/8

sole proprietors, 2/2, 2/4–5
    See also Limited liability

Personal names, in trademarks, 3/7

"Piercing the corporate veil", 2/16

PKI (Public Key Infrastructure), 9/16, 9/17

Planned subdivisions, home business restrictions, 4/11

Planning department requirements, 4/6

Pre-tax profit. *See* Net profit

Product costs. *See* Variable costs

Product liability insurance, 7/4

Professional partnerships, 2/6

Profit/loss forecasts, 5/9, 5/19–22
    sample, 5/20–21

Profit/loss statements, 10/15–17
    sample, 10/17

Profit motivation, proving to IRS, 8/8

Profits
    allocation among owners, 2/8, 2/13, 8/12, 8/13–14
    gross profit, 5/9, 5/13–16, 8/3
    net profit, 5/9, 5/18, 5/19, 8/3

Property insurance, 7/2–3

Property taxes, local, 8/20

PTDLs (Patent and Trademark Depository Libraries), 3/19, Appendix A/29–34

PTO (U.S. Patent and Trademark Office), 3/19, 3/23–24

Public accountants, 12/6

Public Key Infrastructure (PKI), 9/16, 9/17

Q

Quickbooks, 5/9–10, 10/2

Quicken, 5/9–10, 10/2, 10/10

R

Receipts, 10/3

Recordkeeping, income and expenses, 10/7–10

Registration of trademarks
    federal, 3/5–6, 3/13, 3/18, 3/22, 3/23–24
    resources, 1/6, 3/21
    state, 3/23, 3/24

Registration requirements, 6/2–16
    corporations, 6/3, 6/4–5

federal employer identification numbers (FEINs), 6/5–8

federal licenses and permits, 6/15

fictitious business name registration, 2/3, 2/5, 3/2, 6/8–11

hobby businesses, 8/8–9

home businesses, 4/11, 4/12

limited partnerships, 6/3, 6/4

LLCs, 6/3, 6/4

local tax registration, 2/3, 2/5, 4/7, 6/11–12, 6/15, 8/4, 8/19

partnerships, 2/5

seller's permit, 2/5, 6/13, 8/21, 8/26

sole proprietorships, 2/5

specialized licenses and permits, 6/13–16, 8/4–5

state, 6/4, 6/13, 6/15

Renters, home business restrictions, 4/11

Rents, researching, 4/3

Resale certificates, 8/23–24

Revised Uniform Partnership Act (RUPA), 2/7

Risk analysis, 2/20

RLLPs, 2/6

RUPA. *See* Revised Uniform Partnership Act

S

Salaries

  categorizing, 5/12, 5/14, 10/16

  shareholder employees, 2/17–18

Sales

  estimating revenue, 5/12–13, 5/15

  taxable vs. non-taxable, 6/13, 8/20–21, 8/23, 10/8

  See also Income

Sales taxes, 6/13, 8/2, 8/4, 8/20–26

  calculating and paying, 8/25–26

  common exemptions, 6/13, 8/21, 10/8

  legal responsibility for, 8/25

  nexus requirement, 8/21–22

  obtaining a seller's permit, 6/13

  and online commerce, 8/22–23

  recordkeeping and, 10/8, 10/11

  resale certificates, 8/23–24

  state agencies listed, Appendix A/13–17

  taxable vs. non-taxable sales, 6/13, 8/20–21, 8/23, 10/8

SBA (Small Business Administration), 12/7

SCORE (Service Corps of Retired Executives), 12/7

S corporations, 2/13–14, 2/16, 2/18, 8/18

  See also Corporations

Secondary meaning, trademark law, 3/7, 3/13

Section 179 deduction, 8/6

Securities and Exchange Commission website, 2/19

Securities laws

  corporations and, 2/14–15, 2/18–19

  LLCs and, 2/14

Self-employment taxes, 8/4, 8/10–11, 8/12

  LLC members, 8/14

  spouses and, 2/3

  See also Estimated tax payments

Seller's permits, 2/5, 8/21, 8/26

  obtaining, 6/13

  state agencies, Appendix A/13–17

Selling your home, and home-office depreciation deduction, 4/15

Service businesses, and sales taxes, 6/13, 8/20–21

Service Corps of Retired Executives (SCORE), 12/7

Service marks, 3/3, 3/4, 3/6

  See also Trademarks

Shrinkwrap agreements, 9/15–16

Signatures, electronic/digital, 9/16–17, 9/18

Signs, 4/6

Small Business Administration (SBA), 12/7

Small business resources, 1/6–7, 12/7

  state agencies, Appendix A/3–7

Social Security taxes. *See* Payroll taxes; Self-employment taxes

Software

  accounting, 5/9–10, 10/2, 10/10

  business plan preparation, 5/10

Sole proprietorships, 1/3, 2/2–5

  accounting periods, 8/18

  and FBN registration, 6/8–9

  and FEINs, 6/5, 6/6

  husband-wife, 2/3

  and liability for business debts, 2/2, 2/4–5

  setting up, 2/5, 6/5

  taxes, 2/4, 8/9–11

Spouses, and business structure, 2/3

Start-up costs

  deductibility, 8/6

estimating, 5/9, 5/22–23
in financial projections, 5/19, 5/23
State agencies
    labor/unemployment compensation, Appendix A/24–28
    LLC offices, Appendix A/18–23
    sales taxes/seller's permits, Appendix A/13–17
    small business offices, Appendix A/3–7
    tax departments, Appendix A/8–12
State business name databases, 3/18
State disability insurance, 7/2
State government websites, 12/7
Statements, 10/3
State registration requirements, 6/4, 6/13, 6/15
State taxes, 8/4
    estimated tax payments, 8/11, 8/13, 8/15, 8/16
    income taxes, 8/4, 8/11, 8/13, 8/14–15
    LLCs, 8/14–15
    obtaining forms, 8/7
    state tax agencies listed, Appendix A/8–12
    See also Payroll taxes; Sales taxes
Statute of Frauds laws, 9/6
Stock
    sales to public, 2/14–15, 2/18
    S corporation ownership restrictions, 2/13

T

Taxable income, 10/8, 10/9
Tax deductions
    business losses, 2/4, 2/13–14, 8/7–8, 8/9
    See also Deductible expenses
Taxes, 8/2–26
    accounting and, 10/4–5
    audits, 8/9, 10/5
    basics, 8/2–7
    capital gains, and home office depreciation deductions, 4/15
    C corporations, 2/14, 2/16–18, 8/2
    deductibility of losses, 2/4, 2/13–14, 8/7–8, 8/9
    estimated quarterlies. *See* Estimated tax payments
    excise taxes, 8/4
    in financial projections, 5/19, 5/23
    hobby businesses, 8/7–9
    home-office deduction, 4/13–16

income. *See* Income taxes
    LLCs, 2/12–13, 2/14, 8/13–15
    local business taxes, 8/4, 8/18–20
    non-deductibility of dividends, 2/18
    partnerships, 2/6, 8/11–13
    payroll taxes, 2/12, 2/15, 8/4, 8/10, 11/2, 11/5–6
    personal liability for, 2/12, 2/15
    resources, 1/6, 2/4
    sales taxes. *See* Sales taxes
    S corporations, 2/13–14, 2/16, 2/18
    self-employment taxes, 2/3, 8/4, 8/10–11, 8/12, 8/14
    sole proprietorships, 2/4, 8/9–11
    unemployment taxes, 11/6
    use taxes, 8/24–25
    See also Deductible expenses; Tax deductions
Tax forms
    obtaining, 8/7
    See also IRS forms
Taxpayer identification number. *See* FEIN
Tax professionals, 12/5–7
Tax rates, corporate, 2/12–13, 2/17
Tax year, 8/18, 10/6
Telephone lines, 4/5
Temporary employees, 5/12
Tenant modifications to leased space, 4/9, 4/10
Termination clauses, 9/12
Theft insurance, 7/3, 7/4
Thomas Legislative Information website, 12/7
Thomas Register, 3/17
3-of-5 test, 8/8
TIN (taxpayer identification number). *See* FEIN
Trademarks, 3/3, 3/4
    defined, 3/3, 3/5–6
    domain names as, 3/13, 3/17, 3/22
    failure to defend, 3/14
    federal registration, 3/5–6, 3/13, 3/18, 3/22, 3/23–24
    infringement criteria, 3/6, 3/8–11, 3/14, 3/15–16
    legal overview, 3/2, 3/5–11
    online issues, 3/9, 3/11–16
    resources, 1/6, 3/21
    state registration, 3/23, 3/24
    strong vs. weak marks, 3/6–7, 3/8–9, 3/10

willful infringement, 3/17, 3/18

Trademark searches, 3/16–20

Trademark search services, 3/19

Trade names, 3/3, 3/4, 6/6, 6/8

    See also Fictitious business names

U

UCC (Uniform Commercial Code), 9/6, 9/11

UCITA (Uniform Computer Information Transactions Act), 9/16

UDRP (Uniform Domain Name Dispute Resolution Policy), 3/15

UETA (Uniform Electronic Transactions Act), 9/16, 9/17

Unemployment compensation, state agencies, Appendix A/24–28

Unemployment taxes/insurance, 7/2, 11/6

Unfair competition laws, 3/7–8, 3/9

Uniform Commercial Code (UCC), 9/6, 9/11

Uniform Computer Information Transactions Act (UCITA), 9/16

Uniform Domain Name Dispute Resolution Policy (UDRP), 3/15

Uniform Electronic Transactions Act (UETA), 9/16, 9/17

Uniform Partnership Act (UPA), 2/7

UPA. *See* Uniform Partnership Act

Use permits, conditional, 4/8, 4/9, 6/14

Use taxes, 8/24–25

U.S. Patent and Trademark Office (PTO)

    online registration, 3/23–24

    online trademark database, 3/19

V

Variable costs, 5/11, 8/3, 10/13, 10/16

    in break-even analysis, 5/9, 5/10, 5/18

    estimating, 5/14

    labor costs, 5/12, 5/14, 10/16

Variances, 4/7, 4/8, 6/14

Vehicle insurance, 7/2, 7/4

W

Wages, categorizing, 5/12, 5/14, 10/16

Warranties, 9/11–12

Websites

    meta tag conflicts, 3/15–16

    setting up, 3/21

    See also Domain names; Online commerce

Willful infringement of trademark, 3/17, 3/18

Wiring, 4/5

Withholding, employee income taxes, 11/5, 11/6

Worker classification, 11/2–5

    IRS criteria, 11/3–4

    state labor agencies, Appendix A/24–28

Workers' compensation insurance, 7/2, 11/5

Workplace safety requirements, 11/5

World Wide Web

    legal research online, 12/7

    name searches, 3/17

    trademark issues, 3/9, 3/11–12

    Web-based advertising, 5/7

    See also Domain names; Websites

Z

Zoning requirements, 4/6–9, 6/14

    home-based businesses, 4/10, 4/11–13

■

CATALOG

...more from Nolo

		PRICE	CODE

BUSINESS

	PRICE	CODE
Avoid Employee Lawsuits (Quick & Legal Series)	$24.95	AVEL
⊙ The CA Nonprofit Corporation Kit (Binder w/CD-ROM)	$49.95	CNP
▣ Consultant & Independent Contractor Agreements (Book w/Disk—PC)	$24.95	CICA
▣ The Corporate Minutes Book (Book w/Disk—PC)	$69.95	CORMI
The Employer's Legal Handbook	$39.95	EMPL
Firing Without Fear (Quick & Legal Series)	$29.95	FEAR
▣ Form Your Own Limited Liability Company (Book w/Disk—PC)	$44.95	LIAB
▣ Hiring Independent Contractors: The Employer's Legal Guide (Book w/Disk—PC)	$34.95	HICI
▣ How to Create a Buy-Sell Agreement & Control the Destiny of your Small Business (Book w/Disk—PC)	$49.95	BSAG
▣ How to Form a California Professional Corporation (Book w/Disk—PC)	$49.95	PROF
▣ How to Form a Nonprofit Corporation (Book w/Disk —PC)—National Edition	$44.95	NNP
⊙ How to Form a Nonprofit Corporation in California (Book w/CD-ROM)	$44.95	NON
▣ How to Form Your Own California Corporation (Binder w/Disk—PC)	$39.95	CACI
▣ How to Form Your Own California Corporation (Book w/Disk—PC)	$39.95	CCOR
▣ How to Form Your Own New York Corporation (Book w/Disk—PC)	$39.95	NYCO
⊙ How to Form Your Own Texas Corporation (Book w/CD-ROM)	$39.95	TCOR
How to Write a Business Plan	$29.95	SBS
The Independent Paralegal's Handbook	$29.95	PARA
Leasing Space for Your Small Business	$34.95	LESP
Legal Guide for Starting & Running a Small Business, Vol. 1	$29.95	RUNS
▣ Legal Guide for Starting & Running a Small Business, Vol. 2: Legal Forms (Book w/Disk—PC)	$29.95	RUNS2
Marketing Without Advertising	$22.00	MWAD
▣ Music Law (Book w/Disk—PC)	$29.95	ML
Nolo's California Quick Corp (Quick & Legal Series)	$19.95	QINC
Nolo's Guide to Social Security Disability	$29.95	QSS
Nolo's Quick LLC (Quick & Legal Series)	$24.95	LLCQ
⊙ Open Your California Business in 24 Hours (Book w/CD-ROM)	$24.95	OPEN
▣ The Partnership Book: How to Write a Partnership Agreement (Book w/Disk—PC)	$39.95	PART
Sexual Harassment on the Job	$24.95	HARS
Starting & Running a Successful Newsletter or Magazine	$29.95	MAG
Tax Savvy for Small Business	$34.95	SAVVY
Wage Slave No More: Law & Taxes for the Self-Employed	$24.95	WAGE
▣ Your Limited Liability Company: An Operating Manual (Book w/Disk—PC)	$49.95	LOP
Your Rights in the Workplace	$29.95	YRW

CONSUMER

	PRICE	CODE
Fed Up with the Legal System: What's Wrong & How to Fix It	$9.95	LEG
How to Win Your Personal Injury Claim	$29.95	PICL
Nolo's Everyday Law Book	$24.95	EVL
Nolo's Pocket Guide to California Law	$15.95	CLAW
Trouble-Free Travel...And What to Do When Things Go Wrong	$14.95	TRAV

ESTATE PLANNING & PROBATE

	PRICE	CODE
8 Ways to Avoid Probate (Quick & Legal Series)	$16.95	PRO8
9 Ways to Avoid Estate Taxes (Quick & Legal Series)	$24.95	ESTX
Estate Planning Basics (Quick & Legal Series)	$18.95	ESPN
How to Probate an Estate in California	$39.95	PAE
▣ Make Your Own Living Trust (Book w/Disk—PC)	$34.95	LITR

▣ Book with disk   ⊙ Book with CD-ROM

	PRICE	CODE
Nolo's Law Form Kit: Wills	$24.95	KWL
▣ Nolo's Will Book (Book w/Disk—PC)	$34.95	SWIL
Plan Your Estate	$39.95	NEST
Quick & Legal Will Book (Quick & Legal Series)	$21.95	QUIC

FAMILY MATTERS

	PRICE	CODE
Child Custody: Building Parenting Agreements That Work	$29.95	CUST
Child Support in California: Go to Court to Get More or Pay Less (Quick & Legal Series)	$24.95	CHLD
The Complete IEP Guide	$24.95	IEP
Divorce & Money: How to Make the Best Financial Decisions During Divorce	$34.95	DIMO
Do Your Own Divorce in Oregon	$29.95	ODIV
Get a Life: You Don't Need a Million to Retire Well	$24.95	LIFE
The Guardianship Book for California	$34.95	GB
⊙ How to Adopt Your Stepchild in California (Book w/CD-ROM)	$34.95	ADOP
A Legal Guide for Lesbian and Gay Couples	$25.95	LG
⊙ The Living Together Kit (Book w/CD-ROM)	$34.95	LTK
Nolo's Pocket Guide to Family Law	$14.95	FLD
Using Divorce Mediation: Save Your Money & Your Sanity	$21.95	UDMD

GOING TO COURT

	PRICE	CODE
Beat Your Ticket: Go To Court and Win! (National Edition)	$19.95	BEYT
The Criminal Law Handbook: Know Your Rights, Survive the System	$29.95	KYR
Everybody's Guide to Small Claims Court (National Edition)	$18.95	NSCC
Everybody's Guide to Small Claims Court in California	$24.95	CSCC
Fight Your Ticket ... and Win! (California Edition)	$24.95	FYT
How to Change Your Name in California	$34.95	NAME
How to Collect When You Win a Lawsuit (California Edition)	$29.95	JUDG
How to Mediate Your Dispute	$18.95	MEDI
How to Seal Your Juvenile & Criminal Records (California Edition)	$34.95	CRIM
Mad at Your Lawyer	$21.95	MAD
Nolo's Deposition Handbook	$29.95	DEP
Represent Yourself in Court: How to Prepare & Try a Winning Case	$29.95	RYC

HOMEOWNERS, LANDLORDS & TENANTS

	PRICE	CODE
California Tenants' Rights	$24.95	CTEN
▣ Contractors' and Homeowners' Guide to Mechanics' Liens (Book w/Disk—PC)—California Edition	$39.95	MIEN
The Deeds Book (California Edition)	$24.95	DEED
Dog Law	$14.95	DOG
⊙ Every Landlord's Legal Guide (National Edition, Book w/CD-ROM)	$44.95	ELLI
Every Tenant's Legal Guide	$26.95	EVTEN
For Sale by Owner in California	$29.95	FSBO
How to Buy a House in California	$29.95	BHCA
The Landlord's Law Book, Vol. 1: Rights & Responsibilities (California Edition)	$44.95	LBRT
⊙ The California Landlord's Law Book, Vol. 2: Evictions (Book w/CD-ROM)	$44.95	LBEV
Leases & Rental Agreements (Quick & Legal Series)	$24.95	LEAR
Neighbor Law: Fences, Trees, Boundaries & Noise	$24.95	NEI
⊙ The New York Landlord's Law Book (Book w/CD-ROM)	$39.95	NYLL
Renters' Rights (National Edition—Quick & Legal Series)	$19.95	RENT
Stop Foreclosure Now in California	$34.95	CLOS

HUMOR

	PRICE	CODE
29 Reasons Not to Go to Law School	$12.95	29R
Poetic Justice	$9.95	PJ

IMMIGRATION

	PRICE	CODE
How to Get a Green Card	$29.95	GRN
U.S. Immigration Made Easy	$44.95	IMEZ

▣ Book with disk   ⊙ Book with CD-ROM

		PRICE	CODE

MONEY MATTERS

	PRICE	CODE
▣ 101 Law Forms for Personal Use (Quick & Legal Series, Book w/Disk—PC)	$29.95	SPOT
Bankruptcy: Is It the Right Solution to Your Debt Problems? (Quick & Legal Series)	$19.95	BRS
Chapter 13 Bankruptcy: Repay Your Debts	$29.95	CH13
▣ Credit Repair (Quick & Legal Series, Book w/Disk—PC)	$18.95	CREP
▣ The Financial Power of Attorney Workbook (Book w/Disk—PC)	$29.95	FINPOA
How to File for Chapter 7 Bankruptcy	$29.95	HFB
IRAs, 401(k)s & Other Retirement Plans: Taking Your Money Out	$24.95	RET
Money Troubles: Legal Strategies to Cope With Your Debts	$24.95	MT
Nolo's Law Form Kit: Personal Bankruptcy	$16.95	KBNK
Stand Up to the IRS	$29.95	SIRS
Surviving an IRS Tax Audit (Quick & Legal Series)	$24.95	SAUD
Take Control of Your Student Loan Debt	$24.95	SLOAN

PATENTS AND COPYRIGHTS

	PRICE	CODE
◉ The Copyright Handbook: How to Protect and Use Written Works (Book w/CD-ROM)	$34.95	COHA
Copyright Your Software	$24.95	CYS
Domain Names	$24.95	DOM
▣ Getting Permission: How to License and Clear Copyrighted Materials Online and Off (Book w/Disk—PC)	$34.95	RIPER
How to Make Patent Drawings Yourself	$29.95	DRAW
The Inventor's Notebook	$34.95	INOT
Nolo's Patents for Beginners (Quick & Legal Series)	$29.95	QPAT
▣ License Your Invention (Book w/Disk—PC)	$39.95	LICE
Patent, Copyright & Trademark	$29.95	PCTM
Patent It Yourself	$49.95	PAT
Patent Searching Made Easy	$29.95	PATSE
The Public Domain	$34.95	PUBL
◉ Software Development: A Legal Guide (Book w/ CD-ROM)	$44.95	SFT
Trademark: Legal Care for Your Business and Product Name	$39.95	TRD
The Trademark Registration Kit (Quick & Legal Series)	$19.95	TREG

RESEARCH & REFERENCE

	PRICE	CODE
Legal Research: How to Find & Understand the Law	$34.95	LRES

SENIORS

	PRICE	CODE
Beat the Nursing Home Trap: A Consumer's Guide to Assisted Living and Long-Term Care	$21.95	ELD
The Conservatorship Book for California	$44.95	CNSV
Social Security, Medicare & Pensions	$24.95	SOA

SOFTWARE

Call or check our website at www.nolo.com for special discounts on Software!

	PRICE	CODE
◉ LeaseWriter CD—Windows/Macintosh	$129.95	LWD1
◉ Living Trust Maker CD—Windows/Macintosh	$89.95	LTD3
◉ LLC Maker—Windows	$89.95	LLPC
◉ Patent It Yourself CD—Windows	$229.95	PPC12
◉ Personal RecordKeeper 5.0 CD—Windows/Macintosh	$59.95	RKD5
◉ Small Business Pro 4 CD—Windows/Macintosh	$89.95	SBCD4
◉ WillMaker 8.0 CD—Windows	$69.95	WP8

Order Form

Name _____

Address _____

City _____

State, Zip _____

Daytime Phone _____

E-mail _____

Item Code	Quantity	Item	Unit Price	Total Price

Subtotal	
Add your local sales tax (California only)	
Shipping: RUSH $8, Basic $3.95 (See below)	
"I bought 3, ship it to me FREE!"(Ground shipping only)	
TOTAL	

Method of payment

☐ Check ☐ VISA ☐ MasterCard
☐ Discover Card ☐ American Express

Account Number _____

Expiration Date _____

Signature _____

Shipping and Handling

Rush Delivery—Only $8

We'll ship any order to any street address in the U.S. by UPS 2nd Day Air* for only $8!

* Order by noon Pacific Time and get your order in 2 business days. Orders placed after noon Pacific Time will arrive in 3 business days. P.O. boxes and S.F. Bay Area use basic shipping. Alaska and Hawaii use 2nd Day Air or Priority Mail.

Basic Shipping—$3.95

Use for P.O. Boxes, Northern California and Ground Service.

Allow 1-2 weeks for delivery. U.S. addresses only.

For faster service, use your credit card and our toll-free numbers

Order 24 hours a day

Online	www.nolo.com
Phone	1-800-992-6656
Fax	1-800-645-0895
Mail	Nolo.com
	950 Parker St.
	Berkeley, CA 94710

Visit us online at
www.nolo.com

Take 2 Minutes & Give Us Your 2 cents

Your comments make a big difference in the development and revision of Nolo books and software. Please take a few minutes and register your Nolo product—and your comments—with us. Not only will your input make a difference, you'll receive special offers available only to registered owners of Nolo products on our newest books and software. Register now by:

PHONE
1-800-992-6656

FAX
1-800-645-0895

EMAIL
cs@nolo.com

or **MAIL** us
this registration card

REMEMBER:
Little publishers have big ears. We really listen to you.

- - - - - - - - - - - - - - - fold here - - - - - - - - - - - - - - -

REGISTRATION CARD

NAME	DATE	
ADDRESS		
CITY	STATE	ZIP
PHONE	E-MAIL	

WHERE DID YOU HEAR ABOUT THIS PRODUCT?

WHERE DID YOU PURCHASE THIS PRODUCT?

DID YOU CONSULT A LAWYER? (PLEASE CIRCLE ONE)   YES   NO   NOT APPLICABLE

DID YOU FIND THIS BOOK HELPFUL?   (VERY)   5   4   3   2   1   (NOT AT ALL)

COMMENTS

WAS IT EASY TO USE?   (VERY EASY)   5   4   3   2   1   (VERY DIFFICULT)

DO YOU OWN A COMPUTER? IF SO, WHICH FORMAT? (PLEASE CIRCLE ONE)   WINDOWS   DOS   MAC

❏ If you do not wish to receive mailings from these companies, please check this box.
❏ You can quote me in future Nolo promotional materials. Daytime phone number _____.

SMBU 1.0

NOLO IN THE NEWS

"Nolo helps lay people perform legal tasks without the aid—or fees—of lawyers."

—USA TODAY

Nolo books are ..."written in plain language, free of legal mumbo jumbo, and spiced with witty personal observations."

—ASSOCIATED PRESS

"...Nolo publications...guide people simply through the how, when, where and why of law."

—WASHINGTON POST

"Increasingly, people who are not lawyers are performing tasks usually regarded as legal work... And consumers, using books like Nolo's, do routine legal work themselves."

—NEW YORK TIMES

"...All of [Nolo's] books are easy-to-understand, are updated regularly, provide pull-out forms...and are often quite moving in their sense of compassion for the struggles of the lay reader."

—SAN FRANCISCO CHRONICLE

fold here

- -

Place
stamp here

nolo
950 Parker Street
Berkeley, CA 94710-9867

Attn: SMBU 1.0